PRIESTS AND POLITICIANS

PAUL CRUNICAN

Priests and Politicians: Manitoba schools and the election of 1896

To Bob Trisco,
with my warmest
regards,
Paul Crunican

UNIVERSITY OF TORONTO PRESS

© University of Toronto Press 1974
Toronto and Buffalo
Printed in Canada

ISBN 0-8020-5265-7
LC 73-84437

Pour ma mère

Contents

viii Contents

Abbreviations

Preface

This book grew out of many sources, but all come down to three. First was a desire, rooted in my mother's French-Canadian background, to work on a topic involving the always narrowly won battle for 'survivance.' Second was the conviction that one of the neglected, yet most interesting, areas of Canadian history involved the relations between church and state. Finally, a pet peeve as historian, the ever-present tendency to lump persons together as easy images one of another; the Quebec clergy in particular seemed to me to have been easy targets for this exercise. As the work progressed, my conviction grew that, as elsewhere, virtue and weakness, perspicacity and obtuseness, prejudice and openness, were, like the evangelical rainfall, distributed with remarkable impartiality among cleric and layman, French and English, Catholic and Protestant alike.

All of this made it worthwhile doing, but much help was needed along the way. I wish to express appreciation to the Canada Council for the grant under which this study was begun. I must also thank, without hoping to be adequate, John Saywell and Ramsay Cook, who directed the thesis stage of the project; Donald Kerr, Blair Neatby and Lovell Clark, who made specific and helpful suggestions for revisions; and the many other colleagues who encouraged my pursuit of the subject. Finally, thanks are owing to the prelates and curators who made collections of documents available, the staff members of archives visited, the charming ladies who typed the various stages of the work, Archbishop Philip Pocock of Toronto and Monsignor L.A. Wemple of London for their encouragement to begin the study in Manitoba, and Bishop G.E. Carter of London for his support to complete it.

This book has been published with the help of a grant from the Social Science Research Council of Canada, using funds provided by the Canada Council, and a grant from the Andrew W. Mellon Foundation to the University of Toronto Press.

Paul Crunican
London, 1973

PRIESTS AND POLITICIANS

Introduction

'Is there no one who will free me from this turbulent priest?' So went the outburst of Henry II that sealed the fate of Thomas Becket. The consequences have usually been less drastic, but variations on the same question have been asked by kings and civil rulers at many crucial points in human history. Priests and politics have always made an explosive mixture.

The dilemma is not surprising; allegiance can be given for certain purposes to the state, for others to the church. In theory such areas of jurisdiction are readily distinguishable; in practice they cannot always be kept separate. As long as politics involves religious and moral issues, the official church, however conditioned by time and place, cannot remain serenely silent; church reticence in the Nazi era serves as an instructive and sobering reminder. And both churchmen and politicians repeatedly have found each other useful, or inescapable, or both.

Canada has had its share of church-state tension. For many reasons, not the least of which has been the deliberate avoidance of a wall between the two realms, the Canadian experience in this area has differed from the American.[1] Absence of constitutional boundaries between civil and ecclesiastical jurisdictions has not always meant greater Canadian harmony, as proved by the bitter controversy over the clergy reserves in both Upper

---

1 J.S. Moir provides an enlightening discussion of the particular character of the Canadian church-state atmosphere in his introduction to the documentary collection, *Church and State in Canada, 1627–1867*. Readers should note that the Bibliography supplements the author/short title entries in the footnotes.

and Lower Canada. The sharpest and most enduring clashes in Canada's church-state history, however, have involved the French 'fact' and the French-Canadian clergy. And, perhaps more than any other single issue, education has been the subject that has brought both religious and ethnic loyalties into action and has most deeply drawn the clergy into politics.

In the decade beginning with the hanging of Louis Riel in 1885, a series of racial and religious crises shook Canada in an unprecedented manner. The culmination of these crises was the Manitoba school question. By the time of the election of 1896, the focal point of the controversy was re-medialism, the attempt to have Roman Catholic school privileges in Manitoba restored by federal action against a provincial government that had removed these privileges by a school bill of 1890. The struggle over re-medialism involved nearly every main theme of Canada's internal history – Conservative-Liberal, federal-provincial, east-west, French-English, Catholic-Protestant, church-state. But, illustrating as it did the complexity and sensitivity of the ground where politics and religion meet, the 1896 electoral contest has remained particularly fascinating for the degree to which Roman Catholic church authorities, above all in Quebec, entered or attempted to enter the political process and were involved in the struggle to power of Wilfrid Laurier.

From their point of view. French-Canadian clerics had compelling reasons to be concerned. For good or ill, French survival in a North American, English-speaking sea had, before and after Canadian confederation, been closely identified with the Roman Catholic church. By the 1890s, confidence in the Canadian federal system as a bulwark of minority rights against a local majority had been rudely shaken. Primarily because of concern to protect English and Protestant rights in Quebec, section 93 of the British North America Act had provided that education, a subject normally under exclusive provincial jurisdiction, would be hedged about by emergency federal power. A quarter of a century later, however, economic, geographic, social, legal, and political factors had combined in such a way as to make federal response to provincial attack against minority privileges extremely problematic.[2] Ironically, it was not English rights in Quebec that were in jeopardy, but French and Catholic rights in Manitoba.

The Manitoba school question was thus an unmistakeably 'French'

2 For a stimulating analysis of the major steps in this decentralizing process, particularly of the New Brunswick school case in the early 1870s, see Morton, 'Confederation, 1870–1896: The End of the Macdonaldian Constitution and the Return to Duality.'

problem. But it was also a 'Catholic' problem, and the distinction between the cultural and religious factors was not always clear. Clifford Sifton seemed confident that the 'political power of the priesthood' and the 'educational policy of the Roman Catholic church' was the primary issue. To D'Alton McCarthy, the necessity of the domination of the English language and culture and the fear of French preponderance, was more fundamental.[3] At all events, French-Canadian churchmen were profoundly involved under both cultural and religious titles. Traditional party loyalties added their own complication; clerical support for the Conservative party was too much a fact of Quebec experience to be either ignored or easily overcome.

The school question and the struggle over remedialism thus presents a marvellous case study of many complex relations at a formative period in Canadian history. A number of works have already been written on various aspects of the Manitoba controversy.[4] A detailed investigation of the school question's impact on the national level, particularly of the church-state dimensions involved, has long been needed.

This study attempts to fill one of the major gaps. Its focus is the 'scene behind the scene,' seeking in particular to discover how Quebecers, civil and ecclesiastical, were reacting to a key problem of French and Catholic rights outside Quebec. There is thus a heavy emphasis on personal correspondence, rather than on formal statement or published opinion. Similarly, there is a fairly strict adherence to a chronological treatment, in an attempt to assess the impact on the central figures in the story of each major event as it developed. Many of the classic questions connected with the church-state theme are brought into focus. What, for example, happens when ecclesiastics bring pressure to bear on politicians? What if the reverse process takes place, if politicians take the initiative to involve clerics? And what kind of situation arises when both clerics and politicians are concerned with obtaining a piece of legislation, but for different reasons and looking to different long-range consequences? Finally, what can be considered legitimate or even viable action for clerics attempting to influence church members on a religious issue that cannot be separated from the political process and the rise and fall of parties? All these and other intriguing problems were involved in the Manitoba school crisis, and are

3 For Sifton, see the *Manitoba Free Press*, 8 March 1890. A sample of McCarthy's thinking can be found in his speech in the 1890 debate on the Northwest Territories, *Canada: House of Commons, Debates*, 22 January 1890.
4 See bibliographic note, p. 343.

raised in this story. Many other key questions are scarcely mentioned and clearly demand further study. In particular, the crucial, if largely hidden, economic and social implications of the rise of Laurier are only briefly touched. What has been attempted above all is an account of tactics and pressures brought to bear and through this a reflection on the preoccupations and temper of the times. It is a story often of fear, prejudice, and narrow outlook on all sides of the religious, racial, and political dividing lines. But it is also a story of strength and resiliency. Certainly it is uniquely Canadian. It tells something important of the shift from the Canada of John A. Macdonald to the Canada of Wilfrid Laurier.

I
Beginnings, 1889–95

THE ORIGIN OF THE QUESTION

The third session of the seventh Parliament of Manitoba opened on January 30, 1890. On February 12, Joseph Martin, attorney general in the Liberal government of Thomas Greenway, introduced two measures of particular interest: a 'Bill Respecting the Department of Education' (No 12), and a 'Bill Respecting Public Schools' (No. 13). Together they contained 227 clauses: 171 directly copied from similar legislation in Ontario, 31 from former school statutes of Manitoba, and 25 new ones.[1] In effect they abolished the existing separate-school system and the division of funds between the Protestant and Catholic sectors. Second reading was set for February 13, but debate did not actually begin until March 4. The Department of Education bill passed second reading rather quickly over one protesting amendment on March 5 by a vote of 26 to 10. Debate on the public schools bill was, however, much more protracted. Opponents to the measure were hopelessly out-numbered, yet they extended the debate for six days, with former minister J.E.P. Prendergast taking a leading part. The core argument of opposition, as seen in the proposed amendments, was that the legislation contravened the BNA and Manitoba acts and withdrew Roman Catholic school privileges granted by the Education Act of 1871. Most of all it was emphasized that no mandate from the people had been obtained for such a radical change. Protestant Conservatives moved for

---

1 *Manitoba Free Press*, February 13, 1890; also Taché, *Une Page de l'Histoire*, p.83.

delay until amendments to constitutional acts could be secured. French Catholics moved that the bill be postponed for six months in order to consult the electorate. Both amendments were downed by the government majority; opposition arguments met with the contention that the existing system was costly and divisive and that the government must have the power to rule its own house in education. At 1:45 AM on Thursday, March 13, the public schools bill passed second reading by the margin of 22 to 6.[2]

The bill then passed into committee, where twenty-seven sections were revised.[3] On March 18, along with the Department of Education bill, the public schools bill was returned for third reading. A further opposition amendment, this time to obtain the opinion of the Supreme Court of Canada on constitutionality, was rejected and early Wednesday morning, March 19, the bill passed third reading, 25 to 11.[4] The Department of Education bill passed on the following morning. Along with the brief bill establishing English as the sole official language, the school bill received royal assent in the form of the signature of Lieutenant Governor Schultz on March 31, 1890.[5]

Thus enacted into law, the public schools bill became the point of departure of the issue which was first to irritate and then to dominate the politics of both the province and the country for nearly seven years. The facts of the immediate genesis of the Manitoba action were fairly clear. On August 5, 1889, D'Alton McCarthy, most prominent of those who had pressed for federal disallowance of the Jesuits' Estates settlement, gave a strong anti-French, anti-Catholic speech at Portage la Prairie, Manitoba. Present and replying in the spirit of McCarthy's appeal was the attorney general of Manitoba, Joseph Martin. Martin promised the abolition of the official use of French and of the dual school system, in practice meaning the withdrawal of public tax support from the Catholic schools. Despite hesitations on the part of Premier Thomas Greenway and the resignation of the Roman Catholic member of the provincial cabinet, J.E.P. Prendergast, events moved inexorably to the passage of the public schools bill in March 1890.

The sources and motivation of the province's radical decision were far more complicated. The most detailed investigation of the genesis of the school question rejects emphatically the Manitoba government's claim that

---

2 Manitoba, *Journals of the Legislative Assembly of Manitoba*, 1890, pp. 70–92. Reports of the debates are found in the *Manitoba Free Press*, March 6–13, 1890.
3 Taché, *Une Page de L'Histoire*, p.85.
4 Manitoba, *Journals*, 1890, p.709.
5 *Ibid.*

the schools were abolished in response to a massive popular demand within the province, insisting that this argument and others 'followed rather than preceded the Government's attack on the separate school system.'[6] The issues of efficiency and pro-Catholic distribution of school funds were repeatedly emphasized in 1895 and 1896 by provincial spokesmen such as F.C. Wade and Clifford Sifton. In these presentations, the fact that the per-pupil grant had been roughly equal before 1890 was overlooked or ignored. Moreover, questionable arguments based on desperate post-1890 conditions within surviving Catholic schools were used to condemn the pre-1890 situation.[7] There is persuasive evidence, therefore, to conclude that the most immediate reason for stirring up the school issue was 'the political requirements of the moment ... an emergency policy adopted by the Greenway government in an effort to tide it over an evil hour.'[8]

6 Clague, 'Political Aspects of the Manitoba School Question,' p.61. Clague shows that the brief campaign against the school system of the late 1870s died out in the 1880s. Indeed, the man who led the earlier campaign, W.F. Luxton of the *Manitoba Free Press*, opposed Greenway in 1890.

7 Clague, 'Political Aspects of the Manitoba School Question,' p.162. The Manitoba education reports for 1889 showed 18,850 children in 557 Protestant schools (an average of slightly less than 34 per school); 4364 children in 73 Catholic schools (slightly less than 60 per school) (Manitoba, *Journals*, 1889, no.18, p.25). The total expenditure reported by the superintendent of Catholic schools for the year ending July 1889 was $22,131.08 (Manitoba, Legislative Assembly, *Sessional Papers*, 1890, no.18, p.53). The total expenses reported by the superintendent of Protestant schools for the year ending December 1889 was $98,362.19. Thus the expenses seem to have been about proportionate, slightly more than five dollars per child. (*Sessional Papers*, 1890, no.17, pp.36–49). These statistics, with some minor variations, were also quoted by the minister of public works, James Smart, during the 1890 school bill debate. Smart, however, emphasized only the fact that the Catholic schools received a higher per-school grant than did the Protestant.
W.L. Morton's summary of the debate on the conduct of the schools generally accepts Clague's findings, pointing out that 'not much was made ... of the charge, popular among anti-Catholic speakers and pamphleteers, that the Catholic schools were inefficient' (*Manitoba*, p.249). Martin himself was later quoted as praising the conduct of the pre-1890 Roman Catholic schools; the dual system as such, not the efficiency of its Catholic section, was his complaint (*Manitoba Free Press*, March 5, 1890). L.C. Clark's estimate is that 'in only four districts ... did the schools system impose duplicate school facilities which would not otherwise have been required' (*The Manitoba School Question*, p.3). For the most popular of the government pamphlets, see Wade, *The Manitoba School Question*. For the best summary of the Catholic argument, see Ewart, *The Manitoba School Question*, and *The Manitoba School Question: A Reply to Mr. Wade*. A sampling of Archbishop Taché's ideas can be found in MacGregor, *Some Letters from Archbishop Taché on the Manitoba School Question*.

8 Clague, 'Political Aspects of the Manitoba School Question,' p.292. Suspicious railway deals, specifically involving Joseph Martin and the Northern Pacific, were the main source of the 'evil hour.'

Every study of the background of the controversy, however, brings out the declining strength of the French and the Catholics in the Manitoba population and the rise, in the 1800s, of a 'new Ontario' in the first western province.[9] This raises the question of whether majority inevitably leads to tyranny,[10] but also emphasizes that Manitoba was not isolated. Along with strong men, strong prejudices came from the East. There can be no doubt that the atmosphere was prepared for a demagogue such as McCarthy.

Receptive conditions or not, it can be strongly argued – as it was by the famed editor of the *Winnipeg Free Press*, J.W. Dafoe – that the school question 'descended upon Manitoba out of a clear sky.'[11] At the very least, Ontario was transposing the most virulent of its opinions onto a relatively peaceful Manitoba scene. But Ontario was not alone to blame. The whole escalation of events that followed the execution of Riel was exacting a bitter price. Honoré Mercier had come to power in Quebec in the long shadow of Riel's hanging and had angered Orangemen and Protestants everywhere by his overly demonstrative Catholicism. His Jesuits' Estates Act of 1888, even though it had received Protestant support in the Quebec legislature, was the spark that ignited the anti-French, anti-Catholic 'Equal Rights Association' in Ontario. And D'Alton McCarthy had gained notoriety, probably at the cost of more substantial political power, by supporting the unsuccessful attempt of rural Ontario's 'noble thirteen' in the House of Commons to obtain federal disallowance of the Jesuit settlement. But too many prejudices and fears of 'French and Catholic pretensions' had been stirred to let the movement accept defeat without seeking another ground of battle. It is quite possible that the 'eastern fire' would have been transported to the prairie without McCarthy, and it is not certain who was the prime mover in his August visit. It was, nonetheless, McCarthy who gave Martin the catalyst he needed.[12]

9 Clague, 'Political Aspects of the Manitoba School Question,' pp. 33–48. The phrase 'new Ontario' is W.L. Morton's. From slightly over fifty per cent of a total of some 12,000 population in 1870, the Catholic proportion in Manitoba had declined by 1890 to approximately 20,000 in a total of 150,000. Of these 20,000 the non-French Catholics totalled perhaps one-quarter. The Catholic school population, however, was still about one-fifth of the total. (Estimates compiled from *Census of Canada*, 1891, pp.226–30 and p.333.)

10 Clark, *The Manitoba School Question*, p.4.

11 *Clifford Sifton in Relation to His Times*, p.36.

12 J.R. Miller's important study, 'The Impact of the Jesuits' Estates Act on Canadian Politics, 1888–91,' ascribes to McCarthy somewhat less initiative than has traditionally been accepted, both in the equal rights movement and the stirring up of the Manitoba question. Whatever his motivation, McCarthy's stature within the Conservative party and his subsequent involvement with the school issue in the courts and federal parliament make him a central figure in the story. See also O'Sullivan, 'Dalton McCarthy and the Conservative Party,' and Noble, 'D'Alton McCarthy and the Election of 1896.'

McCarthy's emotional drive thus coincided with the Greenway government's need. Martin's report to Greenway of the Portage incident revealed that important changes in the dual school system already had been discussed in caucus. The same letter, however, admitted that the attorney general had taken a 'root-and-branch' position on both language and school rights more quickly and more radically than the premier was prepared to accept.[13] A compromise arrangement similar to that in Ontario, less directly church controlled than the existing Manitoba system, might have been the outcome of the Greenway government's projected changes, had a calmer atmosphere prevailed. The actual situation made compromise on either side unlikely.

At all events, while Greenway gave the impression that McCarthy's torrent had carried Martin along with it, he did nothing effective to stem the tide. As one author has put it, Greenway was 'led from one position to another, from dependence on the French vote to independence of it, from the determination to amend the school laws to the abolition of the dual system in both language and schools, by the pressure of events and the fretful irascibility of Martin, until in the end he had betrayed colleagues whom he had not planned to betray and abolished constitutional rights he had not proposed to abolish.'[14] It may be concluded, therefore, that responsibility for the genesis of the Manitoba school bill and its profound attack on the terms of the composition of Canada, rested primarily with Joseph Martin, indirectly but ultimately with Thomas Greenway – with the tone of violence and bitterness vastly increased by D'Alton McCarthy.[15]

TWO DEFENDERS: TACHE AND LAFLECHE

At the outset of the school crisis, the central Roman Catholic figure was Archbishop Alexandre Taché of St Boniface.[16] As leader of the Roman

13 PAM, Greenway Papers, Martin to Greenway, August 6, 1889.
14 Morton, *Manitoba*, p.246.
15 That the Manitoba action in fact constituted such a 'profound attack' continues to be the subject of sharp controversy. D.G. Creighton is the most emphatic of those who hold that 1890 simply removed a burden unfairly imposed in 1870. A careful answer to Creighton's position may be found in Heintzman, 'The Spirit of Confederation: Professor Creighton, Biculturalism and the Use of History,' pp.245–75.
16 Born in Rivière-du-Loup in 1823, Taché went to Red River as a missionary in 1845. He was ordained in 1846, and at the age of twenty-seven was consecrated coadjutor to Bishop Provencher in 1851, taking over as bishop of St Boniface in 1853. He was made archbishop in 1871 as metropolitan of all British territory west of Ontario, and took a central role in the settlement of the Red River rising which led to the creation of Manitoba in 1870. See Benoit, *Vie de Monseigneur Taché*.

Catholic community in Manitoba, Taché was of necessity concerned with a whole range of problems that would bear heavily on any solution to the controversy. Perhaps most significant among personal factors were the archbishop's relations, first with those who were not Roman Catholic, secondly with his own non-French, Roman Catholic subjects. There was every indication that Taché enjoyed high personal prestige with the Manitoba population in general. Even during the height of the tension, opposition journalists treated him with deference, particularly compared with the treatment given his successor, Archbishop Langevin. Perhaps most remarkable of all were the cordial relations between Taché and Lieutenant Governor John Schultz, his old enemy of the 1870 rising. Politically, Schultz was strongly opposed to Greenway's Liberal government, and therefore had reason to ally with Taché on that score. However, even on the personal level friendship was quite evident. In a letter to Schultz in 1894, Taché spoke of 'your constant kindness to me,' and greetings, even gifts, often passed between the archbishop and the lieutenant governor's family.[17]

During at least the period preceding the school troubles, Taché seems to have had friendly relations with the infant University of Manitoba. This may have been largely because of the affiliation of the Collège St-Boniface to the university, although the affiliation itself must be regarded as remarkable for a French Catholic institution in that era. A letter of September 1891, in reply to an expression of regret by the university council at Taché's retirement from the Collège St-Boniface representation, revealed both growing estrangement and former harmony. The archbishop wrote that, in his view, the attitude evident in the recent school bill had spread to the university, with the result that he could not 'meet the promoters and supporters of such schemes with the same pleasure as I have hitherto done.'[18]

Probably more significant was the question of Taché's prestige with his Catholic subjects of other than French extraction, since it was not infrequently suggested during the crisis that the core of protest against the school bill was more cultural than religious. Although the French and Catholic factors in the struggle on the school question often merged, they were far from identical in Manitoba. The emphatic repudiation in 1895 of pro-Greenway John O'Donohue as a representative of Manitoba Irish

17 AASB, Taché to Schultz, February 1, 1894; Lady Agnes Schultz to Taché, February 10, 1894.
18 *Ibid.*, Taché to University of Manitoba Council, September 6, 1891.

Catholics by the principal non-French Winnipeg parish reflected a general attitude.[19] Extensive evidence exists that Taché's relations with his Irish-Catholic subjects in particular were far warmer than anything required by mere form. In December 1889, while the school bill was still in the discussion stage, a petition from the English-speaking Catholics of Winnipeg, and bearing the names of, among others, Daniel Smith, alderman, Nicholas Bawlf, merchant, and Gerald Brophy, barrister, was forwarded to the Manitoba legislature. The resolution stated that the proposed legislation was 'opposed to principles of sound government,' and declared the meeting's 'unalterable determination to maintain the separate school system.'[20] A similar resolution was submitted by the parishioners of St Augustine's in Brandon, on 24 March 1890.[21] Moreover, the general petition to the federal government of August 1890 contained at least a proportionate share of non-French names.[22]

On the personal level, when Taché was sick in Montreal during the winter of 1890–1, Father Fox of St Mary's, Winnipeg, wrote to him many times, and several times repeated the hope that the archbishop would be home in time to follow his custom of taking part in the St Patrick's Day festivities at the Winnipeg parish.[23] The letters of such laymen as John Barrett and Gerald Brophy of Winnipeg and W.J. Manbey of Oak Lake were frank and even confidential.[24] It was Taché who was responsible for obtaining an honorary LL D for Barrett from the University of Ottawa, and his concurrence in the choice of Barrett to make the legal protest against the school bill showed determination to avoid French and Catholic identification. Gerald Brophy's letter of June 26, 1891 was especially revealing, since it denied the Brandon *Times'* s rumour that he, Brophy, would oppose J.E.P. Prendergast in the next provincial election as candidate for Woodlands. Brophy told the archbishop that he might run in South Winnipeg, although this would involve considerable financial loss to himself, but his main point emphasized Catholic solidarity, irrespective of race:

19 See below, p.50.
20 AASB, Taché Papers, December 20, 1889.
21 *Ibid.*, March 24, 1890.
22 *Ibid.*, August, 1890.
23 *Ibid.*, Fox to Taché, Taché to Fox, January–February 1891.
24 *Ibid.*, Manbey to Taché, September 3, 1890. Manbey was an Irish-Catholic lawyer at Oak Lake; he wrote to Taché to stress the need for Catholics, French and others, to register for voters' lists to avoid being deprived of a vote at the coming elections.

I would look upon it as a great loss, if for any reason the minority were deprived of his services in the House ... I have no hesitation in saying that I believe that an English speaking Catholic in the House ... would be an advantage to our people, and though I do not personally presume to be that person, yet as I am aware that my name has been canvassed, it is only proper for me to express to your Grace that under no circumstances would I accept a seat in the Legislature if my so doing was to tend towards resulting in the exclusion from the House of an approved champion of our cause.[25]

The history of the two largest Catholic groups in Manitoba, the French and the Irish, has never lacked differences, as witnessed by the division of the archdiocese of Winnipeg from St Boniface in 1916. There is little evidence, however, that Taché contributed to the Irish-French quarrels, and the history of the school controversy at least under his administration revealed strong Catholic unity.

Like their Protestant counterparts, Manitoba Catholics were far from isolated. The immigration of French-speaking people had not come close to matching the influx of English-speaking immigrants from Ontario,[26] but strong emotional ties remained. Throughout the six years of the controversy, Ontario Roman Catholic bishops showed concern for their coreligionists in Manitoba, but they were reticent in comparison with their episcopal brothers from Quebec. And, among the Quebec bishops whose influence and ideas were vital to an appreciation of the church-state tension generated by the school question, none was more important than Louis François Laflèche (1818–98), Bishop of Trois-Rivières, former confrère of Taché on the Red River missions, and the man to whom the western prelate first turned for support. Not only did Laflèche represent an important focus of ultramontanism throughout Quebec,[27] but his political connections remained strong despite his age and his opposition to the Castor-Rouge

25 AASB, Brophy to Taché, June 26, 1891. The decision not to press the question of French language rights, although they too were being suppressed, emphasized the multi-racial consensus concerning the schools. As in the Riel case, reaction in both Ontario and Quebec did not always appreciate this complexity.
26 Considerable effort, without great success, was expended by Taché and others to bring more French to Manitoba in the early 1890s. A.I. Silver points out that Taché and other missionaries were partly to blame for the lack of enthusiasm among French-Canadians for the West. It must be admitted that their earlier warnings of rigours, physical and cultural, to be encountered, compared badly with the enthusiasm of emigration societies being formed in Ontario ('French Canada and the Prairie Frontier,' pp.11–36).
27 Ultramontanism may generally be described as the theory that placed strong emphasis on centralization and papal authority in the Church, although it was anti-nationalist in France

alliance under Mercier. On the federal level, the only practical possibility in his view was a combination of support for, and pressure on, the existing Conservative party, the Orange alliance notwithstanding. 'Je n'ai pas plus de confiance qu'il ne faut dans nos ministres Canadiens d'Ottawa et leur Chef, Sir J.,' Laflèche told Taché, 'mais ce que je crois, c'est que vous seriez encore plus maltraités si les libéraux étaient arrivés au pouvoir fédéral.' As for the upshot of Mercier's 'national' or 'centre' party, the realist in the bishop of Trois-Rivières saw only the splitting of the Conservative elements in Quebec, to the Liberals' advantage, and the stirring of counter-extremism in Ontario:

Cette recrudescence de fanatisme et la formation du parti des *equal rights*, n'est que l'écho du parti national bas-Canadien – qui est en train de mener notre province à la

and nationalist in French Canada. In the area of church-state relations, this school of thought gave clear pre-eminence to the church, as was evident in 'Le Programme Catholique' of the 1870s, inspired by Bishop Bourget (1840–76) of Montreal and by Laflèche. While the term 'ultramontanism' stressed the ecclesiastical dimension, the term 'Castor,' coined by Senator F.X. Trudel in 1882, stressed the political dimension of the same phenomenon. Like most labels, however, 'ultramontanism' and 'Castor' were applied to a number of individuals and to groups with less than perfect exactness. After the death of Trudel in 1890, the designation of 'Castor' champion was never worn with the same precision by any one person. J.P. Tardivel continued the vocal and abrasive individuality he had pursued in the 1880s. Over the quarter-century of his publication of *La Vérité*, Tardivel could be called the essential lay ultramontane, just as Trudel had been the essential Castor. On the political scene, Sir Hector Langevin never quite fitted the mold of Castor or ultramontane, despite his many ultramontane connections, and his rivalry with the favourite Castor target, Adolphe Chapleau. A.R. Angers and Alphonse Desjardins came closer to complying with the image. Other important political figures who may at least be grouped with 'la tendance ultramontaine' were Senator Philippe Landry, Flavien Dupont, M.P. for Bagot, Premier L.O. Taillon, and former premiers J.-J. Ross and Charles Boucher de Boucherville. Ecclesiastical counterparts in the ultramontane school added complexity to the picture. Most significant was the bitter criticism expressed by Bishop Laflèche, however much he might be considered the ultramontane patron saint, against those who had allied with Mercier. Among influential ecclesiastics, the individual who perhaps most closely approached the role of supporter of the lay political wing of ultramontanism was Monsignor C.A. Marois, vicar-general of Quebec. The work of Pierre Savard opens up several promising lines of investigation on ultramontanism. See Savard, *Jules-Paul Tardivel, La France et les Etats-Unis*; 'Jules-Paul Tardivel, un ultramontain devant les problèmes et les hommes de son temps.' See also, Rumilly, 'Monseigneur Laflèche et les ultramontains.' Further suggestions on the impact of Laflèche on the ultramontane movement are given in Crunican, 'Bishop Laflèche and the Mandement of 1896.' For the development of ultramontanism during the era of Bishop Bourget, see Sylvain, 'Liberalisme et ultramontanisme au Canada français,' in Morton, ed., *The Shield of Achilles/Le Bouclier d'Achille*, pp.111–38, 220–55.

banqueroute, et de là à l'union législative d'Ottawa, ou à l'annèxion aux Etats-Unis. Nos nationnaux [sic] de la Vérité et de L'Etendard, sont à mon humble avis, les hommes qui nous ont fait le plus de mal en jetant la division jusque dans les rangs du clergé, en soulevant les préjugés de race et de religion, et en se faisant les valets des libéraux.[28]

Whatever his opinion of the Quebec situation, Laflèche took for granted that the hierarchy should keep an active hand in politics, invisible if possible, public if necessary. Unfortunately, the bishop too easily identified all right-minded clerical thinking with his own. In practice, this meant that Laflèche was strongly partisan, reacting in particular against whatever helped the Liberals in any way. Once again, however, context was essential. The name 'Liberal' could evoke in his mind's eye little but continental European revolutionaries, Papineau-Dorion Rouges, Freemasons, the *Institut Canadien*, and, very vivid in his memory, the forces which had led to the division of his diocese in 1885. Thus Laflèche was ready to accept extreme statements against the Liberal party, such as the annexationist charge mentioned in the letter of 1890, as confirmation of his suspicions. Clearly his fears of the 'nationalist' movement sprang largely from the conviction that the net result could only be to become 'les valets des libéraux.'

Yet to see this side alone would be to distort the picture of the man. Laflèche, at least in 1890, believed quite strongly that Canada's remaining a nation was vital to the survival of the French Canadians and of the church within French Canada. It is true that some of his earlier words and actions seemed to have leaned dangerously toward the separatism which he condemned. Not a little of his opposition to Trudel and Tardivel may have been caused by the readiness of these laymen, however devout, to lecture the clergy. Nonetheless, Laflèche must be credited at least with the very clear view that the existence of a third party priding itself on being specifically French and Catholic would only bring similar counter-measures by the 'other half.' Moreover, it must be stressed that Laflèche was later to oppose the inclination in the direction of an ultramontane federal party by A.R. Angers in 1895.[29] Finally, the personal prestige which Bishop Laflèche enjoyed even among those who opposed his ideas must be remembered. Laurier, upon the death of Laflèche in 1898, was quoted as calling the bishop 'un fanatique, mais un saint prêtre,' and occupied the

28 AASB, Laflèche to Taché, May 19, 1890.
29 See below, p.114 ff.

front pew at the funeral.[30] Bishop Emard of Valleyfield, at the very time when he opposed Laflèche most strongly over the content of the episcopal mandement of 1896, insisted in renewing the invitation to the elderly bishop to preach the priests' retreat at Valleyfield in that year.[31] However much one might disagree with him, neither the opinions nor the person of Laflèche could be taken lightly; thus it was not by accident or simply because of old friendships that Taché turned to the bishop of Trois-Rivières when he looked for help from the East.

Many other individuals and factors heightened the tension surrounding the Manitoba crisis of the 1890s. The development of party loyalties in the province, the rise of the Patrons of Industry paralleling the crest of the Populists in the United States, the prolonged economic depression, the differences between the descendants of the French-speaking Métis and the few but important French who had come to Manitoba from Quebec during the Taché era – all had a bearing on the way in which the question developed both in Manitoba and on the federal level. In all, it was painfully clear that the context of the school question would not lend itself to a patient or generous solution on either the provincial or the federal level.

A TUG-OF-WAR OVER DISALLOWANCE

That the Manitoba school legislation posed dangerous problems for both major federal parties was evident as soon as the first rumours of the province's intentions were heard in the East. Both parties recognized the potential disaster of internal schism over the question. Interestingly enough, the Conservatives seemed to be the least worried, perhaps because of John A. Macdonald's traditional 'old tomorrow' attitude, perhaps because they were confident that either the courts or the voters would hobble Joseph Martin without direct federal action. At all events, despite the efforts of Lieutenant Governor Schultz to get Macdonald to approve reservation of the school measure, the prime minister adamantly refused, and directed Schultz to sign the bill.[32] From a quite different point of view, Archbishop Taché – although he later indicated that he knew Schultz was under federal pressure to sign the bill[33] – was quite convinced that the lieutenant governor could and should have reserved it. After referring to

30 Rumilly, *Histoire de la Province de Québec*, IX, p.56.
31 AEV, Emard to Laflèche, March, 1896.
32 PAC, Macdonald Papers, Macdonald to Schultz, March 28, 1890.
33 AAQ, Taché to Ouimet, March 14, 1894.

the petitions of the French MLA s to Schultz on 27 and 28 March, Taché's later account stated that the case clearly called for the use of the lieutenant governor's discretionary power. 'Le moins que l'on puisse dire,' the archbishop wrote, 'c'est qu'au 31 mars 1890, il y avait un doute sur la constitutionalité des actes qui enlevaient à la minorité les droits et privilèges dont elle jouissait par rapport aux écoles et à l'usage de la langue française.'[34] Nonetheless, the bills were not reserved and, having failed at Winnipeg, Taché began to look more and more to Ottawa.

Every report coming back from the East indicated that Taché's hope for immediate federal action would not be met. The bitter federal-provincial battles of the 1880s and the 1889 furor over the Jesuits' Estates Act, as well as the opposition stirred up by the veto of Manitoba's railway legislation during the same decade, were far from forgotten. Even more directly pertinent to the case against disallowance were the disturbing events that surrounded the recently concluded debate on the Northwest Territories. On January 22, 1890, D'Alton McCarthy moved a bill to delete clause 110 of the North West Territories' Act, which provided for the duality of language in the courts and in the proceedings and records of the Assembly. His motion stated that it was 'expedient in the interest of unity that there should be community of language.'[35] Only a compromise amendment by Sir John Thompson, minister of justice, reduced sufficiently the tension to avoid the breaking of party allegiance and the threatened division of Parliament along racial lines.

Among the Liberals, recognition by the federal party of the danger to their unity and to Laurier's position as leader because of his race was reflected in letters sent to Laurier soon after Martin's proclamation became known.[36] Laurier's letters to former Liberal leader Edward Blake and to Toronto *Globe* editor John Willison revealed the extent of his concern over the problem, going so far as to urge his own replacement.[37]

Blake made one important contribution in the handling of the school

---

34 Taché, *Une Page de l'Histoire*, p.98.
35 *Canada, House of Commons, Debates*, 1890, p.38.
36 See PAC, Laurier Papers, Edgar to Laurier, August 19, 1889; Cartwright to Laurier, August 9, September 3, 1889.
37 PAC, Willison Papers, Laurier to Willison, June 26, July 4, 1890; Laurier Papers, Willison to Laurier, June 30, 1890; Blake to Laurier, June 2, June 18, 1890. As Neatby and other Laurier students have noted, the 'wish-to-resign because-I-am-French-Catholic; theme was a recurring echo at several crises in Laurier's career. Without impugning Laurier's integrity, the psychological historian might suggest that this was a 'persecution weapon' which Laurier had no firm intention of ultimately using.

problem. This was the so-called 'Blake Resolution' of April 29, 1890, which prescribed an appeal to the judiciary in all cases of federal-provincial disputes over education. The key to Blake's argument was that the executive should not arrogate to itself judicial powers. Therefore, it should not disallow a provincial act simply because it considered that act *ultra vires*. If an act were *ultra vires* and against justice or federal-government policy, it might be disallowed, but once again the judicial method was to be preferred as less inflammatory.

Blake's resolution clearly reflected the general Ottawa reluctance to give encouragement to Taché's pleas for disallowance. At the same time, both parties agreed that the recourse to the courts called for by the resolution did not mean that the federal government abdicated all responsibility for action. Blake stated that he did not wish to absolve the federal cabinet of real duties that it might have; Macdonald was even more explicit when he backed Blake's resolution. 'The Executive is not freed from all responsibility by the reply of the Tribunal,' Macdonald stated, 'the reply shall be simply for the information of the Government. It may be that the Government does not approve of that decision and it could be its duty not to approve it, if it does not accept the conclusion arrived at by the Tribunal.'[38] The Blake resolution was incorporated in a measure presented by Justice Minister Thompson on July 9, 1891, and on September 30, 1891, the law was passed unanimously.[39]

These parliamentary developments did not prevent Taché from pressing his case for disallowance in every possible quarter.[40] Probably to emphasize the nonpartisan character of the protest against the Manitoba government action, J.E.P. Prendergast, late of the Greenway government, was sent to Ottawa to make contact with anyone who might support disallowance. Prendergast encountered attitudes ranging from indifference to polite refusal. The arrival of a personal delegate from Taché, however, along with the stimulus provided by several impassioned letters from the

38 *Canada, House of Commons, Debates*, 1890, p.4086ff.
39 *Ibid.*, p.4170–82.
40 It should be remembered that Archbishop Taché's health was not very strong during this period. Father Allard, his secretary, felt obliged to warn some of his Grace's correspondents to withhold all but the most necessary information. On May 29 the archbishop's letter to Bishop Laflèche included an apology for having to use a secretary to write the letter; mention was made of an illness which had already lasted six weeks (AASB, Taché to Laflèche, May 29, 1890). The school legislation was not calculated to revive Taché's spirits, but it is possible that he might have been more effective in countering it had he been in better health.

archbishop, prompted Justice Minister Thompson to spell out very carefully the case for pursuing judicial rather than political redress. Thompson's basic argument was similar to that underlying the Blake resolution, but focused on the difficulty of establishing the precise scope of the rights held 'by practice' at the time of Manitoba's entry into Confederation. 'A decision of the executive,' Thompson wrote, 'based on an *ex parte* statement of facts, as regards the practice existing at the formation of the province, would be open to be challenged by any person disagreeing with our decision.' Worse still, the justice minister argued, would be the parallels drawn, validly or invalidly, with the Jesuits' estates case. Disallowance of the Manitoba school law 'would be regarded, very widely ... as an interference with legislation of a purely domestic character ... and as influenced very largely by the fact that the legislation was distasteful to Roman Catholics,' whereas interference with the Quebec measure had been rejected 'although it was distasteful to a great number of Protestants ... Such a decision on our part,' Thompson concluded, 'instead of ending the struggle for the abolition of the separate schools in Manitoba, would only be a challenge to a fiercer and wider conflict.'[41]

Taché ultimately came to accept Thompson's position as inevitable if nothing more. But the minister of justice was not the only one the archbishop prodded. One of his earliest appeals had been to former Quebec Conservative 'Chef' Sir Hector Langevin and had not received an early reply.[42] Thus a doleful letter was sent to Taché's former missionary comrade, Bishop Laflèche, expressing disgust with the government's Northwest Territories' settlement, as well as its attitude in Manitoba. 'Je dois vous avouer,' Taché stated, 'que je crains que nous n'ayons rechauffé un serpent qui a profité de sa vie pour préparer les malheurs qui nous menaçent ... Les lois les plus odieuses et les plus inconstitutionnelles ont

41 *Ibid.*, Thompson to Taché, May 17, 1890.
42 One reason why Sir Hector might have been slow to answer and vague when he did was that he had things to worry him more pressing and personal than the fate of French and Catholic in Manitoba. The first rumblings of the so-called McGreevy-Langevin scandal were being heard. This scandal in the Public Works Department, involving Sir Hector Langevin closely enough to ruin him politically, was almost the private preserve of former Conservative J. Israel Tarte. It was Tarte's letters to Laurier during this period that kept insisting that the situation provided a particularly vulnerable spot for attack on the Conservatives. Not much was made of the issue until after the federal election of 1891, however. The subject is treated at length by LaPierre, 'Joseph Israel Tarte and the McGreevy-Langevin Scandal,' and by Fraser, 'The Political Career of Sir Hector Louis Langevin.' A good summary of Tarte's importance to Laurier and the Liberals during the early 1890s can be found in Neatby, *Laurier and a Liberal Quebec*, pp.59–62.

été passées contre nous, et à Ottawa on n'a pas l'air de s'occuper ni de désirer d'y apporter remède.' Taché begged Laflèche to contact Sir Hector and to stimulate if possible more than the lip-service support that had so far been in evidence. Taché feared that the Northwest bill, even as amended, meant the effective end of French rights in the Territories, and lamented that Langevin and other 'French champions' had voted for it. 'Pour ma part,' Taché wrote, 'j'aurais mieux aimé tout perdu sous le souffle haineux de McCarthy que de la perdre sous le vote mal emiellé de ceux qui devraient nous protéger.' Showing himself much more inclined toward the Catholic centre party notion than Laflèche was able to accept after the Mercier experience, Taché struck sharply at the results of the Tory alliance. 'C'est fort bien,' Taché pointed out, 'd'accuser le parti national, mais cette fois, le cri de guerre est parti des rangs des soi-disants conservateurs et les votes se comptent parmi eux. La province de Québec parait se soucier bien peu de nous; quand tous les avant-postes auront été saisis par l'ennemi, viendra le tour de la vieille forteresse.' Taché concluded his strong lament by asking Laflèche to write to other ministers as well as Langevin. 'De grâce, cher Seigneur,' he begged, 'rendez à vos anciennes missions le service de les protéger; écrivez fortement, écrivez promptement. Il n'a pas temps à perdre. Les nouvelles lois sont en vigueur depuis 5 jours, bientôt elles auront pris racine et qui sait?'[43]

Bishop Laflèche was stung into quick action. He dashed off letters to Langevin and the two other French-Canadian ministers, Adolphe Chapleau and Adolphe Caron. Laflèche echoed Taché's sentiments, speaking of the violation of the federal compact, of the attack on French-Canadian devotion to language and religion, and of dangers involved surpassing those of the Riel affair.[44] The bishop of Trois-Rivières, however, was soon won over to advocating judicial procedure instead of political intervention. At least a negative approval of the government position was evident in both Laflèche's letter of 19 May to Taché and in the notes he sent to cover the explanations put forth by the ministers. The politicians' replies were somewhat more positive, but each followed the same theme: recourse to the judiciary was the safest method and the one most likely to succeed.[45]

In the face of these pressures, Taché was brought slowly to accept the judicial way of dealing with the offending legislation. The mere statement

43 AASB, Taché to Laflèche, May 5, 1890.
44 *Canada, Sessional Papers*, 1891, no.63, pp.68–9, Laflèche to Chapleau, May 12, 1890.
45 AASB, H. Langevin to Laflèche, May 16, 1890; Chapleau to Laflèche, May 23, 1890; Caron to Laflèche, June 5, 1890.

that appeal to the courts was the best way of assuring redress was, however, a far cry from actually putting that plan into effect. At the very beginning of the procedure, with the archbishop so reluctant to envisage anything but disallowance, the delicate problem arose of deciding who was to take the lead, and precisely what steps were to be taken.[46] From the government's point of view, the situation was symptomatic of a predicament which it would face again and again throughout the heat of the school question: could it remain clear of the complaint of the minority while at the same time controlling the political explosives involved?

While preparations were being made to begin a solid legal case, several events took place which indicated that Taché, after his initial disappointment over the refusal of this disallowance, was regrouping his forces to keep the school issue in the public eye. First he called a 'Congrès national' at St Boniface beginning June 4, 1890. Although this meeting was without doubt under the direction of the archbishop, Taché wanted to be sure that the clergy would not take the lead in the official discussions of the delegates from each parish of the diocese. Moreover, although this 'Congrès national' did not issue a separate petition in 1890, it was a substantial enough institution to petition apart from Taché in 1892.[47] Two other major steps were taken by the archbishop in 1890: a pastoral letter and a widely circulated petition. The pastoral letter was worded in general terms and its main object was an attack on the action of the Manitoba government. The core of the letter was a sarcastic parody on what the province had done.

While destroying our old scholastic system to establish a new one, the State says to you: Have your children educated the way we direct, then we will help you and your school taxes will turn to the benefit of your children; but if you do not accept the school from which we banish all that is Catholic, you Catholics shall have no share in the moneys given by the State, though you are as much entitled to it as your fellow citizens; you will not only be deprived of your share of the legislative grant, but will be obliged to pay, out of your own pockets, for the education of those who

46 W.T. Shaw discusses the introduction by a Winnipeg French Canadian, Noah Chevrier, of the St Joseph school case, a confused appeal based on a fictitious situation. Thompson called it a 'sham,' and Ewart worked on the case only reluctantly, omitting any reference to it in his later writings on the subject. In any event, the case was heard before Justice Bain of the Queen's Bench on June 11, 1890, and judgment reserved. The plea was withdrawn soon after reservation, and attention concentrated on the much more solid ground of the Barrett case (Shaw, *The Role of John S. Ewart in the Manitoba School Question*, pp.78–113).
47 Taché, *Une Page de l'Histoire*, p.103.

attend the schools we call 'Public' and which we make Protestant; if, after all this, you will still wish to have your children educated, you will pay the entire expenses and we shall not diminish in the least the cost we impose on you for the education of the children of others.[48]

As for the petition, a note to Chapleau on September 20 indicated that this general statement of protest against the Manitoba government's action had just been sent, signed by Taché and 4266 Catholics of Manitoba.[49] As had been the case in April, the September plea did not demand disallowance, although the words 'subversive of the rights of the Catholics of Manitoba' were used to describe the school bill. The petition simply asked that the Governor-General-in-Council 'give such directions for the hearing and consideration of the said appeal as may be thought proper,' that the statutes be declared prejudicial, and 'that such directions may be given and provisions made for the relief of the Roman Catholics of the Province of Manitoba as to your Excellency in Council may seem fit.'[50] Despite the mildness of the petition, it at least served to remind the federal government of a fact which it would repeatedly face as time went on – an adverse decision from the courts would not mean the end of Catholic efforts to have their school rights restored.

THE BARRETT CASE BEGINS

There seemed, at this stage, little reason to fear that a judicial decision, however long it might be in coming, would be adverse to the minority. As early as April, while the St Joseph case was still alive, preliminary steps were taken through the legal firm of J.S. Ewart and Gerald Brophy to construct another appeal. The petition was filed by J.K. Barrett against the Winnipeg municipal by-law which, under the new school legislation, required him to pay taxes to the public schools. Barrett's case was heard by Mr Justice Killam on November 24, 1890 and the appeal leaned heavily on the words 'or practice' in subsection 1 of section 22 of the Manitoba Act.[51] The judge dismissed the application, holding that the statute under which the by-law was passed was valid. The case was then taken before the

48 AASB, Pastoral Letter, August 15, 1890.
49 Ibid., Taché to Chapleau, September 20, 1890.
50 Ewart, The Manitoba School Question, pp.28–30.
51 See Appendix 1; see also Ewart, The Manitoba School Question, p.11. The arguments presented in this and the subsequent court cases are treated in detail by Shaw in 'The Role of John S. Ewart in the Manitoba School Question.'

Manitoba Court of Queen's Bench. As predicted by Ewart and Brophy,[52] the judgments of Chief Justice Taylor and Justice Bain upheld that of the Winnipeg magistrate. This dismissal of appeal came on February 2, 1891, but it was accompanied by the dissenting opinion of Justice Dubuc.[53] Barrett immediately wrote to Taché, naturally enough praising Dubuc's opinion and saying that 'the protestantism of Taylor and Bain was too strong for their justice.' In the eyes of the chief justice, wrote Barrett, 'the words "by practice" merely guaranteed to us that we could not be prevented from supporting our own schools in the same manner that we did prior to entering confederation, but that it did not grant us immunity from paying taxes to the support of the state schools.' As for Bain's opinion, Barrett said there was such similarity in the wording of statements that he was 'morally certain that he had Taylor's judgment before him when he was writing his own.'[54]

John S. Ewart, Gerald Brophy's partner and the lawyer who was to play such an important role in the case from this point on, was somewhat less ready than Barrett to impute unworthy motives. Ewart was nonetheless emphatic in his conviction of the weakness of the Killam, Taylor, and Bain judgments. Ewart told Taché that 'instead of feeling disheartened, I am more confident than ever of final success.' Ewart said that nowhere in the court judgments was there an answer to his key question on the positive meaning of section 22 of the Manitoba Act: 'I find that it does not mean this & that, but no affirmative answer at all. I insist that it has a meaning. Let them but grant that & then join in the search for what it is & I do not fear the outcome.'[55]

Ewart quickly discovered that his hopes for an early hearing of the appeal by the Supreme Court of Canada were premature. The delay was an easy matter for the Manitoba government, since it simply involved denying a special request on the part of Ewart and Brophy. The request was that the rule be waived which required that appeals to the Supreme Court be set down at least a month in advance of the opening of the court session. Such a request needed the consent of both parties to the case, and Joseph Martin quite arguably stated that he was too busy with the current federal election, in which he was a candidate, to give time to a court case. Ewart and Brophy

52 AASB, Ewart and Brophy to Taché, January 1891.
53 Ewart, *The Manitoba School Question*, p.11.
54 AASB, Barrett to Taché, February 2, 1891.
55 *Ibid.*, Ewart to Taché, February 11, 1891.

informed Taché in Montreal of the unavoidable delay, but added that everything else was being done to prepare for the case.[56]

ELECTION INTERLUDE, 1891

The general election to which Martin referred was set for March 5, 1891, and was the first major federal event in which the Manitoba school question was a potential issue. The time for disallowance was rapidly disappearing, since the school law was nearly a year old. Whether for this reason or simply to bring more general pressure to bear on the federal government, Archbishop Taché, although ill in Montreal and in the hospital a good deal of the time, was planning a letter to be addressed to the Governor-General-in-Council to effect by one means or another the restoration of Manitoba's Catholic schools. His intent was to have the letter signed by all the Canadian bishops, making the project of major concern to both federal parties, but the letter was not sent until after the election, and the school question was not an election issue. At the same time, the efforts of various politicians to exclude the problem were revealing. They foreshadowed more strenuous, though less successful, efforts to get around the question in succeeding years.

Laurier and the Liberals were willing to keep the school question outside the range of issues in the election, partly because the case was still before the courts, but also, as already suggested, because the problem revived Laurier's doubts about his role as party leader.[57] Laurier's championing of unrestricted reciprocity in the election of 1891 is well known. For this study, the main point to be noted is that the Liberal leader's thinking on the subject was far more political than economic: it was the one policy on which Laurier felt he could get some kind of united party behind him. In Quebec in particular, reciprocity served to distract the electorate from the potential issue of race and religion.[58]

Whatever Laurier's motives were, the Conservatives were more than a little successful in tarring the policy of unrestricted reciprocity with the brush of disloyalty. The flag-waving cry would obviously not be as

---

56 *Ibid.*, Ewart to Taché, February 15, 1891. Martin failed to win the Selkirk riding, and was replaced as attorney general by Clifford Sifton on April 18, 1891. He won a federal seat in the fall of 1893, and was later premier of British Columbia for a short time.

57 See above, n.36.

58 Neatby, *Laurier and a Liberal Quebec*, p.48.

significant in Quebec as in the rest of Canada. Yet other arguments might and did come into play in the French province. If the vision of the clutches of the American giant did not bring much Quebec response in terms of loyalty to Britain, it could bring such response in terms of French-Canadian interests and, above all, 'survivance.' One incident in which this precise argument was brought into focus involved Archbishop Fabre of Montreal, and evoked the nemesis of the church in politics, which Laurier was trying hard to avoid in his first election as leader. Less than two weeks before the elections scheduled for March 5, Fabre delivered an address in Montreal in which he spoke strongly against any move toward annexation to the United States. The Conservatives gleefully took this to mean a direct condemnation of the Liberals and were quoting the archbishop to this effect. Thus L.O. David, Liberal MLA for Montreal East, hastened to protest against both the speech and its interpretation in a letter to Fabre on February 26. 'Vous avez des amis devoués,' David wrote, 'qui sont irrités à un point que vous ne soupçonnez pas. Vous avez ressucité la vielle guerre religieuse et soulevé des esprits qui feront bien du mal à la religion et aux âmes.' David's conclusion was that he had taken it upon himself to assure Laurier and Liberals from other provinces 'que vous n'aviez pu avoir l'intention de soulevér les catholiques contre le parti Libéral dans un moment où il a tant de droit aux sympathies du clergé.'[59]

David's letter revealed, as did the editorial columns of the Conservative *La Presse* and *La Minerve*, the ease with which an episcopal voice could be interpreted as being anti-Liberal.[60] It also re-emphasized the point that in Quebec the political dimension of the reciprocity issue was indeed more vital than was the economic. Whether Fabre had been convinced by Conservative friends to strike a veiled blow at the Liberals is not known; his vicar general, Abbé Maréchal, issued a denial of any political intent in the letter. Moreover, if the comments and actions of the Montreal archbishop during the 1895 and 1896 elections were indicative, it must be concluded that he was not inclined to get involved in party fights. Finally, comments in letters to and from Liberals immediately following the 1891 election would indicate general gratification with Quebec results. Although the incident was an ominous foreboding, no major quarrel with the clergy over political interference developed at this time.

Conservative dealings with the clergy preceding the 1891 election were both more positive and more significant. On one hand, Macdonald was, as

59 AAM, Fabre Papers, David to Fabre, February 26, 1891.
60 *La Presse*, February 23, 1891; *La Minerve*, February 23, 1891.

ever, not slow to view the Catholic vote as important and to use influence to align it in his favour.[61] On the other, very definite steps were taken in order to keep the potentially dangerous Manitoba school question from becoming an election issue. The most important government action involving the clergy in the period immediately before the 1891 election was Adolphe Chapleau's visit on 14 February to Archbishop Taché, still recuperating in a Montreal hospital. The leader of the French-Canadian Conservatives went to the archbishop with his mind gravely troubled by both political and personal problems. To Sir John Thompson, on December 22, 1890, Chapleau had sketched a bleak picture and sounded a warning that Quebec might easily be 'dismantled.'[62] His February 14 statement to the archbishop, later the cause of bitter controversy, did nothing to make his position easier. Chapleau recalled the New Brunswick school case of the early 1870s and quoted Cartier as having said that the inapplicability of section 93 of the BNA Act to New Brunswick was the reason why the federal government could not interfere there. Now, said Chapleau, precisely the opposite was true.

La position actuel dans le Manitoba est la question du Nouveau-Brunswick renversé: c.à.dire que si nous avons été obligés de laisser maltraiter des catholiques pour garder la constitution intacte, aujourd'hui le gouvernement d'Ottawa est tenu de protéger la minorité contre les actes de la législature de Manitoba, au sujet des écoles séparées et de la langue française, également s'il tient à conserver intact l'Acte de la Confédération. Il doit trouver, dans les pouvoirs que lui donne la constitution un remède efficace contre le mal dont la minorité se plaint à juste droit.

Chapleau then proceeded to give what was probably the strongest personal commitment made by any political figure during the entire school crisis:

Je ne suis pas le Premier Ministre, et je ne désire pas usurper son nom ni son autorité. Je ne parle donc qu'au point de vue général de notre politique. Mais ce que je puis dire en mon nom, le voici: Jamais je ne consentirai à laisser la minorité dans la province de Manitoba, dépouillée de ses droits et privilèges en matière de langue et d'éducation – pas plus que je ne consentirais à enlever à la minorité de la Province de Québec ses droits et privilèges en pareille matière. Tous les ministres catholiques dans le cabinet, j'en suis sur, me soutiendront chaleureusement et

61 See, for example, PAC, Macdonald Papers, Macdonald to Bishop O'Connor (Peterborough), November 26, 1890.
62 PAC, Thompson Papers, Chapleau to Thompson, December 22, 1890.

énergiquement sur cette question. Et je vous livre ce mot qui renferme tout mon avenir politique: Si, malgré mes protestations, le pouvoir fédéral, gardien naturel des droits des minorités dans les provinces, et le gardien spécialement indiqué en ce qui ragarde les droits et privilèges de la minorité dans Manitoba, n'apporterait pas de remède efficace contre cette législation injuste, je sortirai sans hésiter du cabinet avec la mission de faire redresser par mon travail en dehors, une injustice aussi criante et une inconstitutionalité aussi évidente.

Chapleau added a personal note for Taché to cover his formal declaration on the Manitoba schools and to indicate the limits he wished to place on its use:

Malgré que ma lettre soit confidentielle (je veux dire ma déclaration) je m'en rapporte à votre Grace pour ce qui peut en être communiqué à quelques personnes dont vous connaîtriez la discrétion: mais vous comprenez aussi bien que moi que la publication de ce document ne doit être permise que dans l'éventualité, savoir, si je manquais à l'engagement solennel que j'y prends.[63]

Chapleau had indeed made a serious commitment. Moreover, it later became clear that he had made it with Macdonald's knowledge, though perhaps without his support. How much this declaration had to do with Chapleau's departure from the cabinet in the fall of 1892 remains open to speculation.[64] From Archbishop Taché's point of view, the statement increased both his hopes and his dependence on the federal Conservatives. It is little wonder, too, that it ultimately increased his disappointment.

Despite strong pressure on Taché from several sources, notably the ultramontane,[65] no formal episcopal petition to the federal authorities was made before the election of March 5. It was significant, however, how closely the arguments of Laflèche and others in 1891 foreshadowed the Liberal rationale of 1895 and 1896. The danger of provoking action against separate schools in other provinces by a too-strong federal policy anchored

63 AASB, Taché Papers, Chapleau to Taché, February 14, 1891.
64 See PAC, Thompson Papers, Chapleau to Thompson, December 22, 1892 and Neatby and Saywell, 'Chapleau and the Conservative Party in Quebec,' A letter from Chapleau to Dansereau when Tupper was trying to form his new Cabinet in 1896 affirmed Macdonald's acceptance of Chapleau's promises to Taché. See below, p.240.
65 AASB, Henri Trudel to Taché, February 11, 1891; Abbé George Dugas to Taché, February 20, 1891.

the case in both instances.[66] Yet it would be unfair to equate precisely the two situations. In 1891, there was still the very real prospect of relief through court action; in 1895 and 1896, political action was the last and only recourse.

What the result would have been had a petition been presented during the 1891 campaign cannot be known. It is generally agreed that the Conservatives won the election largely on their success in branding as annexationist the reciprocity program of the Liberals and by their emotional appeal for a last loyal vote for Sir John A. Macdonald. Two points had particular bearing on subsequent events connected with the school question. The first was Laurier's relative success in Quebec – not overwhelming, but a continuation of the post-Riel shift evident in the 1887 election. In 1891, Laurier got thirty-four Quebec seats compared to twenty-nine Conservative and two Independent. As one ardent Conservative supporter complained to Senator Alphonse Desjardins, the Liberal leader was more and more assuming the role of 'le sauveur de nos destinés. C'est une idée qui flatte l'orgeuil national, mais si la presse conservatrice est assez outillée pour la lutte et pour pénétrer dans les masses d'ici à six mois, notre population verra probablement les dangers de la politique libérale et la manque de patriotisme de son chef.'[67] If indeed Laurier lacked patriotism as the writer suggested, the people of Quebec either were not convinced or did not particularly care. In any case, 1891 can be seen as a definite step forward for Laurier on the road to the victory of 1896.

A further point to be noted in the 1891 election concerned the Liberal failure in the Maritimes. Once again the loyalty cry was the main rock of the Conservative victory, but Liberal stalwarts saw other factors. First were the standard, only hazily verifiable, accusations that Sir Charles Tupper had reinforced the loyalty appeal with 'boodle.' G.W. Mitchell of Arichat, Nova Scotia, lamented to Laurier that 'the Liberals, as usual, appealed to the honesty and intelligence of a people not overburdened with either, while the Tories, true to the hereditary instincts of the tribe, appealed to the lower and sordid interests of the people and won.'[68] But there also ap-

66 AASB, Laflèche to Taché, February 16 and 17, 1891; Boucher de la Bruère (Quebec Legislative Council) to Taché, February 14, 1891.
67 ACSM., Desjardins Collection, J.L. Archambault to Desjardins, January 30, 1891 (this letter and others from this collection kindly made available by Reverend P. Desjardins, S.J.).
68 PAC, Laurier Papers, Mitchell to Laurier, March 23, 1891.

peared a remarkable number of complaints of pro-Conservative clerical interference, involving in particular Archbishop O'Brien of Halifax and Bishop Cameron of Antigonish.[69] At the very least it could be said that the Manitoba school question was drawing the clergy into the political arena, and not in Quebec alone.

TACHE'S 1891 PETITION: THE SPECTRE OF POLITICAL PRESSURE

For the immediate fate of the school question, the chief result of the 1891 election was that the renewed, though reduced, majority allowed the government greater freedom, whether from Liberal attack or episcopal pressure. The Liberal threat was blunted not only by the election defeat, but even more by the confusion resulting from Edward Blake's 'West Durham Letter.'[70] Archbishop Taché, leaving himself open to charges of collusion with and control by the government, withheld until after the voting the petition it was known he had prepared. On March 6, the day after the election, he circulated to all the bishops of Canada the document to be sent to the Governor-General-in-Council. An accompanying letter expressed the conviction that 'a petition addressed to His Excellency the Governor-General in Council and signed by the whole Canadian hierarchy would have great weight with the Federal Government.' Adding just a touch of coercion, Taché expressed his certainty that no bishop would refuse, and concluded that 'if the present attack against the Catholic rights in Manitoba were allowed to pass unchecked, the natural consequence would be that sooner or later, other attempts will be made, with the result of shaking Confederation at its very basis.'[71]

Twenty-eight of the twenty-nine bishops signed the petition, and many returned their copies with letters of encouragement.[72] A telegram of

69 See, for example, L.H. Davies, Charlottetown, to Laurier, March 27, 1891. For a more sympathetic view of clerical activity in the election, see Hopkins, *The Life and Work of Sir John Thompson*, pp. 175–80.
70 This manifesto to the electors in Blake's riding of West Durham berated the Conservatives for failure to rescue the country from depression, but equally and more spectacularly rejected the official Liberal platform of unrestricted reciprocity. The details of the letter and its effects are too well known to require review here, except to note that the resultant disarray within Liberal ranks undoubtedly contributed to the large number of Liberal losses in by-elections during the next three years.
71 AASB, Taché to English-speaking Bishops of Canada, March 6, 1891.
72 *Ibid.*, for example, Bishop O'Connor, Peterborough, to Taché, March 12, 1891.

March 17, however, brought a friendly but firm refusal from Bishop Rogers of Chatham, New Brunswick. Referring to his unhappy experiences of the 1870s, Rogers wrote that 'all the episcopate of Canada expressed sympathy with us against the New Brunswick school law, but no benefit resulted. The leaders of the French Acadian National Party have been slandering the episcopate of our ecclesiastical province, especially myself, without cause – hence my attitude of charitable reserve.'[73] There followed an exchange of letters between Rogers and Abbé Beaudry, who was acting as Archbishop Taché's secretary in Montreal. The bishop disclaimed any wish to question the motives or judgment of the twenty-eight bishops who had signed the petition. Nevertheless, in a long printed document of March 19 and in a letter of March 25 Bishop Rogers spelled out his reasons for refusal, some general, some peculiar to the New Brunswick situation. Reflecting again the racial complications of the presumably religious separate school question, Rogers stated that he could not feel justified in petitioning for change in Manitoba while nothing was being done in New Brunswick, and that more harm than good seemed to come from petitioning governments. Citing the case of the Massachusetts convent burning in the 1840s, Rogers concluded that it was 'sometimes ... best to bear our lot in patience.'[74]

In spite of these objections, the bishops' petition was presented to the secretary of state on March 24.[75] The governor general, Lord Stanley, sent an acknowledgment of reception of the petition to Taché on March 31. He stated that he had already seen Macdonald and Thompson, and 'j'apprends que la petition officielle a été reçue par le Conseil, et qu'elle sera considérée avec soin.' Taché was later to complain that the petitioners never did discover what actual attention was given to their document.[76] Perhaps the most noteworthy point in the petition was that it did not specifically demand disallowance, although this was still possible until April 10. So clearly was the cabinet expecting that the episcopal document would specify disallowance that Thompson could only express amazement when he wrote to Macdonald on March 26. 'In Council on Tuesday I only looked at the signatures to the petition from the Episcopate,' Thompson said. 'Today I *read* the document for the first time and see that it *does not ask for disallowance*.'[77] The deputy minister of justice, Robert Sedgwick, re-

73 *Ibid.*, Rogers to Taché, March 17, 1891.
74 *Ibid.*, Rogers to Taché, March 25, 1891.
75 *Canada, House of Commons, Sessional Papers*, 1891, no.63, p.2.
76 AAQ, Taché to Ouimet, March 14, 1894.
77 PAC, Macdonald Papers, Thompson to Macdonald, March 26, 1891 (italics Thompson's).

vealed equal surprise when he reported a Montreal interview he had had with Taché to Thompson. Sedgwick went so far as to ask Taché to make a positive statement to the effect that disallowance was not expected. This the archbishop was unwilling to do, but Sedgwick sounded highly gratified at Taché's general attitude.[78]

On April 6, a letter from Chapleau to Senator Desjardins indicated that the question of disallowance was now definitively laid to rest. It also reflected Chapleau's feeling that the absence of a demand for such a remedy in the bishops' petition had been a great relief; conversely, it suggested that a specific request for the radical move would have been taken very seriously and have caused some difficulty. 'Il n'y aura pas de désaveu,' Chapleau wrote. 'Les évêques ne le demandent pas dans leur petition au Gouvernement (reçue il y a une dizaine de jours) mais nous avons insisté sur des mesures de remédiement et je dois nous féliciter sur le bon esprit qui a paru animer tous nos collègues.'[79]

J. Israel Tarte was not so convinced. The journalist–politician still had many hurdles to overcome in his switch from Conservative to Liberal, but his letter to Thompson of April 7 exemplified the attitude of those who felt that the end of the period of possible disallowance meant the end of any hope for effective relief for Manitoba Catholics. Tarte blended compliment with sarcasm in his request for a copy of Thompson's report to the Governor-General-in-Council:

I may be permitted to say that I have a great deal of confidence in your sense of justice and in your legal science, but the Manitoba Act of 1870 seems so clear that I am anxious to know what reasons you have found to allow the law of 1890 to go into operation. Of course the final result will be that my countrymen and the Catholics of Manitoba are going to be deprived of the rights which were guaranteed to them by the constitutional instrument of 1870, sanctioned by the Crown.[80]

The Thompson report referred to by Tarte was dated March 21, and in it, as in his private correspondence on the subject, the minister of justice stressed the greater wisdom of allowing the courts to handle the case. On the other hand, Thompson did indicate that a court declaration that the law

78 PAC, Thompson Papers, Sedgwick to Thompson, March 30, 1891.
79 ACSM, Desjardins Collection, Chapleau to Desjardins, April 6, 1891.
80 PAC, Thompson Papers, Tarte to Thompson, April, 1891.

was *intra vires* would leave the way open for action by the federal government, and he left no doubt that, in his view, remedial action was constitutionally possible.[81]

The event that reduced all others to relative unimportance in the period following the election of 1891 was the death of Sir John A. Macdonald on June 6. Macdonald's passing removed from the scene the man who, over a period of nearly forty years, had managed better than anyone else the political necessities demanded by Canada's tensions, bicultural in particular. That there was a growing cleavage between the French Catholics and the extreme Protestant wing of the party was more than evident. Nonetheless despite government scandals and the recurring leadership crises from the Abbott through the Thompson to the early Bowell administrations,[82] the Conservatives increased their parliamentary majority from twenty-seven to fifty-eight through by-election successes between 1891 and 1894.[83] Economic conditions, although difficult, were not as calamitous as in other nations at least until 1895, partly because Canada did not have as far to fall; Conservative federal scandals were offset by the Mercier débâcle in Quebec and the disarray among the Liberals prior to their national party convention of June 1893.[84]

THE BARRETT DECISION

Whatever the potential political danger posed by the school question during the four years from the election of 1891 to the beginning of 1895, the federal government was somewhat insulated from major loss by the tortuous process of judicial testing. In brief, the decision of the Manitoba courts in the Barrett case was, on October 28, 1891, unanimously reversed in the Supreme Court of Canada, only to be reversed again by the Privy Council

81 Ewart, *The Manitoba School Question*, pp.31–4.
82 The story of the leadership problem within the Conservative party had been studied in detail by L.C. Clark, to some extent revising the views of J.T. Saywell and H.B. Neatby. See Clark, 'The Conservative Administrations,' pp.127–42; Neatby and Saywell, 'Chapleau and the Conservative Party in Quebec'; and Saywell, 'The Crown and the Politicians: The Canadian Succession Question 1891–1896.'
83 Clark, 'The Conservative Administrations,' pp.73–80.
84 Mercier's dismissal by Lieutenant Governor Angers in December 1891 and his subsequent electoral defeat on March 8, 1892, is discussed at length in Rumilly, *Histoire de la Province de Québec*, VI, pp.262–95.

in England on July 30, 1892. The factors that led to the Privy Council's overturning of the Supreme Court's judgment were complex, but the major ones were clear: the failure to obtain the services of Edward Blake and Sir Horace Davey, the non–participation of J.S. Ewart in the argument, the intrusion of the Logan case, the carelessness of the English counsel, Sir Richard Webster, the ambiguities in the ruling of Justice Patterson of the Canadian Supreme Court, and the lack of familiarity of the Privy Council with Canadian conditions.[85] Ewart's reports from London to Father Adélard Langevin, Taché's vicar general in St Boniface, bore out the impression of insurmountable hurdles faced by the Catholic case in England. On June 19, 1892, Ewart told Langevin that he had seen Sir Richard Webster, and that, in view of the imminent English elections, the attorney general was giving little attention to the Manitoba Catholic case, even though he was to present the lead argument. Ewart insisted, however, that he was determined to leave no stone unturned. He talked a second time to Webster's assistant and was preparing a new brief for the attorney general. Ewart concluded with code words by which he would let Langevin know the result of the argument, and with this prophetic line: 'We can of course count on Mr. Blake for a good argument, but the Attorney-General will be the leader; and if he fails to impress the court, it will be almost impossible to do so in following.'[86]

On July 14, Ewart sent a pessimistic account of the case which had just been pleaded with judgment reserved:

The result must be considered very doubtful. Six judges sat, viz. Lords Watson, Morris, Couch, McNaughten [*sic*], Hannen and Shand. From the outset, the two first were in our favour but the two last were against us. McNaghten and Couch said very little and I cannot say to which side they incline. The argument lasted three days. If we had had Sir Horace Davey instead of the Attorney-General, I am satisfied that it would have helped us very much. The latter is no doubt a very able man, but he has not the easy pleasant way of handling the Court, of which Sir

85 These factors and others are dealt with in detail by Shaw, 'The Role of John S. Ewart in the Manitoba School Question,' pp.226–62, and by Clark, *The Manitoba School Question*, pp.98–117. The Logan case was an appeal for Anglican school privileges to parallel Roman Catholic, but was manifestly inspired by the Manitoba government to complicate and weaken the Barrett case. The Blake who did assist in the appeal was Edward's brother, Samuel.

86 AASB, Ewart to Langevin, June 19, 1892.

Horace is undoubtedly a master. On the contrary, the Attorney has little tact and antagonizes them when there is no necessity of doing so. Then he has been so much occupied with politics he had not time to study the case, as it required to be studied. Mr. Blake did very well indeed and made me feel much happier than the Attorney had left me.

It is expected that the decision will be given very soon.[87]

And so it was; on July 30 came the single-word cablegram: 'Defeat.'[88]

In delivering the judgment, Lord Macnaghten adopted the position enunciated by Justice Killam in the original decision, holding that the word 'practice' in section 22 of the Manitoba Act was 'not to be construed as equivalent to "custom having the force of law."' The unanimous decision of the Canadian Supreme Court was given some attention, but two points in that judgment were held to be at fault: the consideration of the period 1871–90 to throw light on the previous period, and the acceptance that public schools under the 1890 law were in reality Protestant schools. 'The legislature has declared in so many words that "the public schools shall be entirely unsectarian,"' Macnaghten stated, 'and the principle is carried out throughout the Act.' Finally the Law Lord added an important *obiter dicta*:

With the policy of the Act of 1890 their Lordships are not concerned. But they cannot help observing that, if the views of the respondents were to prevail, it would be extremely difficult for the provincial legislature, which has been entrusted with the exclusive power of making laws relating to education, to provide for the educational wants of the more sparsely inhabited districts of a country almost as large as Great Britain, and that the powers of the legislature, which on the face of the Act appear so large, would be limited to the useful but somewhat humble office of making regulations for sanitary conditions of school houses, imposing rates for the support of denominational schools, enforcing the compulsory attendance of scholars, and matters of that sort.[89]

It is difficult to read this final judicial comment without suggesting that their Lordships were saying in so many words that they agreed with the thinking behind the schools act of 1890. Ewart's confidence that section 22 of the

87 *Ibid.*, July 14, 1892.
88 *Ibid.*, July 30, 1892.
89 *Canada, House of Commons, Sessional Papers*, 1893, no.33a.

Manitoba Act 'has a meaning,' had been disappointed. He had not counted on what has been persuasively described as 'probably the most extreme example of judicial amendment of the Canadian consitution.'[90]

It should be noted that the Manitoba government delayed its appeal to the Privy Council until a provincial election campaign could at least be launched. Evidently expecting that the Privy Council would uphold the Canadian Supreme Court, the Greenway government argued that it had to be returned 'in order to resist the encroachments of the Dominion Government.' The election of July 23, exactly a week before the Privy Council decision was announced, returned twenty-eight Liberals, eleven Conservatives, and one Independent.[91] With J.E.P. Prendergast retaining St Boniface for the Liberals, it was significant that the French vote had not been entirely alienated by the Greenway administration.

Whatever the strengths and weaknesses of the Privy Council decision, for the Catholic minority seeking redress it was a crushing blow. Not only did it reverse the unanimous ruling of the Canadian Supreme Court, but it placed the presumption of the law, thus far seeming to favour the minority's privileges, on the side of the Manitoba government. Any further appeal would encounter not only the status quo, but also, at least in the popular mind, the majestic wisdom of the Empire's supreme judicial body. In English-speaking Canada, while the Montreal *Gazette* remained open to the possibility of redress for Manitoba Catholics, the relatively moderate editorials of the Toronto *Empire*, to say nothing of more radical anti-French and anti-Catholic journals, took it for granted that nothing further could be done from the federal level.[92] While the legal mind saw that the Barrett decision affected only one aspect of sections 93 and 22, the political mind realized that the protection provided by later sub-sections of the two acts would be little more than an illusion without further word from the Privy Council. Thus came the long interlude of the 'Brophy' case, involving a petition from the Catholic minority, a hearing before cabinet members sitting as a sub-committee of the Privy Council, and the submission of six questions on the possibility of federal action to the Supreme Court of Canada and the Privy Council.

90 Schmeiser, *Civil Liberties in Canada*, p.162; see also Waite, *Canada 1874–1896; Arduous Destiny*, p.249.
91 Dafoe, *Clifford Sifton in Relation to his Times*, p.66.
92 See, for example, Toronto *Empire*, October 8, 1892.

THOMPSON, TACHE, AND TARTE: 1892–4

During this period, the two steadiest men were Sir John Thompson and John Ewart. As might be expected, Taché and others continued to press Thompson, before and after he became prime minister in December 1892, for relief without further delay.[93] At least equal pressure was brought to bear from the opposite direction. As N.C. Wallace put it to Thompson just prior to the formation of the new ministry, 'no remedial legislation and Sir John Thompson for Premier will be my standing ground.'[94] With Principal George Douglas of Wesleyan Theological College in Montreal and Dr Albert Carman, superintendent of the Methodist Church, assailing him as a 'Jesuit' and 'Papist,' Thompson was compelled to be extremely, perhaps excessively, cautious in his response to Catholic claims.[95] Despite the conflicting demands put upon him, however, Thompson showed calm determination to carry the Brophy case through in order to establish a firm legal foothold for any political action. John Ewart exhibited equal tenacity, combined with more than a little forbearance in containing Archbishop Taché's exasperation as one hope after another seemed to fade away. That Ewart spent time and energy on the case beyond the duty of legal counsel was proven many times over in written work, public addresses, and even monetary contributions to the Catholic schools' attempt to carry on.[96]

The move of Adolphe Chapleau from the federal cabinet to the lieutenant governorship of Quebec, when the Thompson government was formed, was at least partially connected with the school question. One interpretation stresses a combination of disappointed ambition and opposition from Ontario as the chief reason for the termination of Chapleau's federal career.[97] Yet Chapleau's letter to Thompson over the wording of the cabinet sub-committee report on the Brophy case insisted on far greater commitment to possible federal action than his English colleagues wanted

---

93 Ewart, *The Manitoba School Question*, pp.35–42.

94 PAC, Thompson Papers, Wallace to Thompson, October 7, 1892.

95 L.C. Clark's verdict is that Thompson in fact did his co-religionists 'less than justice' ('The Conservative Administrations,' p.249.) With the exception of the political prejudice which excluded Edward Blake from the Barrett case, and the unfortunate sequence of events which lost Sir Horace Davey to the opposition, it is difficult to see how Thompson could have more directly favoured the Catholic cause with any reasonable hope of success.

96 See Shaw, 'The Role of John S. Ewart in the Manitoba School Question,' pp.296–329.

97 Clark, 'The Conservative Administrations,' pp.491–3, 540–5.

to make.[98] Later personal statements revealed a genuine desire on Chapleau's part to keep faith with promises made to Archbishop Taché in 1891.[99] It can be argued that Chapleau's departure for Spencer Wood was the first of several mortal blows which the Manitoba school question inflicted on federal Conservative strength in Quebec.

In 1893, the most significant event on the federal level involving the school issue was J.I. Tarte's motion of censure against the government for its handling of the problem and the subsequent parliamentary debate between March 6 and 9. Tarte's motion was defeated by 120 to 71, but the most remarkable feature of the debate, beyond Tarte's charges of an official pact between Taché and Chapleau before the 1891 elections, was the diversity of support for the censure. Giving a strong premonition of what would come in 1895 and 1896, the condemnation was backed on the one hand by Quebec Liberals proclaiming their Frenchness and Catholicism, and on the other by radical anti-Catholic speakers such as D'Alton McCarthy. From Wilfrid Laurier, the debate brought declarations of a pro-minority stand far more positive than he was later going to find acceptable to his Ontario supporters.[100] Tarte's 'conversion,' too, however welcome and important it might be to Laurier, was not easily or quickly digested by Ontario Liberals, John Willison and the *Globe* in particular.[101]

One sequel to the parliamentary debate was that Archbishop Taché was drawn into a journalistic exchange over the dealings between himself and the federal government in 1891. Beginning on May 18 in *L'Electeur*, Tarte renewed the charges that the Conservatives had promised Taché disallowance and then had reneged.[102] Attempting to justify himself without canonizing the federal procedure, Taché answered in two open letters in June and July. Tarte made full and clever use of rebuttal.[103] In short, the debate was viewed in Liberal circles as simply confirming Taché's pro-Conservative stance.[104] That Taché had no intention whatever of taking the pressure for redress off the federal government was clear from his

98 PAC, Thompson Papers, Chapleau to Thompson, December 22, December 29, 1892.
99 See below, p.241.
100 *Canada, House of Commons, Debates*, 1893, pp.1762–2090.
101 See PAC, Laurier Papers, Willison to Laurier, January 29, 1894.
102 *L'Electeur*, May 18, June 2, 1893.
103 *L'Electeur*, June 27, July 13, July 28, 1893. Rumilly points out that Tarte's campaign was less against Archbishop Taché than an attempt to remove pressure from Laurier in the period of the critical June Liberal convention (*Histoire de la Province de Québec*, VII, pp.108–10).
104 PAC, Laurier Papers, O. McDonnell to Laurier, July 13, 1893.

subsequent letters to Thompson.[105] But, added to Laurier's failure to take any positive stand on the school question at the Liberal convention in Ottawa in June, the incident ended any faint possibility that Taché might turn to the Liberals.

On the electoral front, too, Catholic prospects were declining. Hugh John Macdonald, son of the late prime minister, resigned his Winnipeg federal seat in the fall of 1893. Macdonald had been pressing for this release for more than a year, making it clear to Thompson that he would have to oppose any potential federal remedial action 'tooth and nail.'[106] When the resignation did come, Joseph Martin rushed to contest the riding for the Liberals. Despite Laurier's apprehension and hints about alternative candidates, both Sifton and party organizer Isaac Campbell insisted with the federal leader that local exigencies had to prevail over vague national policy party fears about Martin's danger to the Liberals in Quebec.[107] In the vote taken on November 22, Martin won quite easily, but the campaign revealed that Conservatives as well as Liberals in Manitoba accepted the Barrett decision as ending the argument for federal interference on the school issue. Martin's victory marked a turn in Liberal fortunes in by-elections. At the same time, combined with Sifton's selection as a party vice-president during the June 1893 convention, Martin's arrival in Ottawa deepened Catholic suspicions of growing anti-Catholic influence in national Liberal councils.[108]

No study of the impact of the Manitoba school question on the federal level can neglect the problem of the Northwest Territories' schools during the period of judicial review. Despite the compromise arrived at under the Thompson amendment of 1890, D'Alton McCarthy each year reintroduced a resolution in Parliament for the abolition of separate schools and the dual-language system in the Territories. The most protracted and acrimonious debate over McCarthy's attempts came in 1894. Bitterness was added because the Territorial Assembly in Regina, under the leadership of Frederick Haultain, had moved to reduce Catholic school privileges in December 1892. Despite Taché's protests of unfairness, Thompson was

105 PAC, Thompson Papers, Taché to Thompson, September, 1893.
106 PAC, Thompson Papers, Macdonald to Thompson, November 8, 1892.
107 PAC, Laurier Papers, Sifton to Laurier, October 27, 1893; Campbell to Laurier, November 21, 1893.
108 Ibid., L.G. Power to Laurier, November 11, 1893; C.R. Devlin to Laurier, January 1, 1894.

persuaded by cabinet colleagues, George Foster and T.M. Daly in particular, not to disallow Haultain's school ordinances.[109]

Furthermore, Manitoba's School Amendment Act of 1894 was allowed to stand. This amendment, despite Lieutenant Governor Schultz' attempts to prevent it, reduced the possibility of circumventing the 1890 act in Catholic rural areas.[110] One major result of Thompson's refusal to disallow these measures was the added impulse it gave Quebec to move away from the traditional Conservative alliance, if only because it gave Tarte ammunition to promote the moderate Bleu movement toward Laurier.[111] Archbishop Taché, now in the last few months of his life, was exasperated enough to despair that even a favourable Privy Council decision would enhance the possibilities of effective federal relief, particularly when in the Brophy case the Canadian Supreme Court decided against the minority's position. The archbishop refused to be identified with the appeal to England, and spent his last energies in further remonstrations with Thompson over the federal government's mishandling of the schools in Manitoba and the Northwest.[112] Taché died on June 22, 1894. Thompson survived him by less than six months, struck down by heart failure on December 12 during an official visit to England.

Despite Taché's hesitations, his fellow bishops had not remained idle. After a good deal of consultation, an official petition requesting disallowance of the 1894 Manitoba emendments and protesting the Northwest Territories ordinances of 1892, was submitted to the Governor-General-in-Council in May 1894.[113] In response, the federal government sent a cautiously worded order-in-council to the lieutenant governors and legislatures of Manitoba and the Territories, expressing confidence that 'any well-founded complaint or grievance' would be quickly redressed.[114] Ignoring a September parade of Catholics to the Manitoba Legislature with a petition signed by more than five thousand,[115] the Manitoba government

---

109 Clark, "The Conservative Administrations," pp.306–15 and AASB, Taché to Thompson, December 6, 1893.

110 PAC, Thompson Papers, Schultz to Thompson, February 17, 1894.

111 PAC, Laurier Papers, Tarte to Laurier, January 30, 1894; February 5, 1894.

112 AAQ, Taché to Thompson, Taché to Ouimet, March 14, 1894.

113 *Canada, Sessional Papers*, 1895, no.20B. Interestingly, Bishop Emard of Valleyfield was the prelate to take the lead in obtaining consensus and signatures for the petition (see AAQ, Lacombe to Marois, April 16, 1894). Bishop Rogers, who had demurred in 1891, added his signature to the others in 1894.

114 *Canada, Sessional Papers*, 1895, no.20B.

115 AASB, Petition to Manitoba Provincial Government, September 11, 1894.

calmly replied in October that no reason could be found to alter either the original or the amended school legislation.[116]

THE BROPHY DECISION: BACK TO THE POLITICAL ARENA

At the same time, despite delays and difficulties, the Brophy case made its way through the Supreme Court of Canada to the Privy Council. Considering, as did Archbishop Taché for opposite reasons, that the entire procedure was pointless, the Manitoba government declined to argue the case before the cabinet sub-committee or the courts; thus the federal government appointed counsel to present the Manitoba position against the brief of J.S. Ewart. The six questions formulated in May 1893 for judicial decision focused on three main points. First was the basic question of whether the minority had indeed a well-founded grievance involving rights acquired after the union (sub-section 3 of section 93 of the BNA Act and sub-section 2 of section 22 of the Manitoba Act); the second point was whether the decision in the Barrett case had ended all possibility of appeal; and the third was whether the federal government had the power to take remedial action, executive or legislative.[117] The 3–2 decision of the Supreme Court against the right of appeal and the federal power of remedy, especially the opinion of Justice Henri Elzéar Taschereau, turned on the second point, the definitive impact of the Barrett decision.

The Canadian judgment, which one writer describes as a 'somewhat chilling dismissal from the highest tribunal in the Dominion, yet sufficiently conflicting as to offer some hope,'[118] had one particularly intriguing sequel. Two days after the Supreme Court judgment was handed down on February 20, 1894, Judge Taschereau, who was being condemned in French-Catholic circles as 'ce catholique sans coeur,'[119] wrote in haste and agitation to his friend Father Adélard Langevin in St Boniface. With several large inscriptions of 'confidentielle,' the judge took a position which seemed to contradict his official judgment.

116 *Canada, Sessional Papers*, 1895, no.20B.
117 Clark, 'The Conservative Administrations,' pp.267–82, gives an excellent summary of this stage of the case.
118 Shaw, 'The Role of John S. Ewart in the Manitoba School Question,' p.329.
119 AASB, Lacombe to Taché, February 22, 1894.

Je crois de mon impérieux devoir de vous demander *d'insister* auprès de Sa Grace Mgr. Taché et des intéressés sur le sujet à ce qu'un appel soit porté au Conseil Privé de la décision de la Cour Suprême, rendue avant-hier. J'ai des raisons spéciales de vous en écrire ainsi, malgré que je ne puisse, pour le présent du moins, les communiquer. Je vous autorise, si vous le croyez nécessaire, à vous servir de mon nom auprès de Sa Grandeur, à condition qu'à part vous-même et Sa Grandeur, personne ne sâche que j'ai écrit à ce sujet.

As tangible evidence of his sincerity, the judge offered to contribute fifty dollars to what he presumed would have to be a private fund to carry the case to England.[120] Whether the letter signified that Taschereau's judgment had been the result of political pressure or strategy (with the Privy Council tendency to reverse Canadian decisions in mind), or simply that he had been frightened by reactions after the decision was announced, the judge's advice turned out to be perspicacious. With Edward Blake finally brought in to help argue the minority case with J.S. Ewart, the appeal was made with success before the Privy Council on December 11, 12, and 13, 1894.[121]

A crucial section in the judgment delivered on January 29, 1895, referred to the 1892 Privy Council decision in Barrett's case. Lord Watson, the Lord Chancellor, stated that in the earlier judgment 'the sole question raised was whether the Public Schools Act of 1890 prejudicially affected any right or privilege which the Roman Catholics by law or practice had in the province at the Union.' He admitted that the negative answer given in 1892 had narrowly restricted the protection afforded by sub-section 1 of section 93 of the BNA Act. Watson suggested that the representatives of the Manitoba Roman Catholics and those who had drawn up or agreed to the provisions of that act had understood it to provide more protection than the justices of the Privy Council had judged to be the case. Moreover, Watson continued, 'the question is, not what may be supposed to have been intended, but what has been said.' In any case, the legal point of sub-section 3 was quite different from that of sub-section 1. Watson's conclusion was that 'their

120 AASB, Taschereau to Langevin, February 22, 1894. A rather substantial campaign for funds to finance the appeal to the Privy Council was in fact undertaken. Letters to and from Conservative contributors revealed both the tensions and the presumptions created by these donations. A.R. Angers, for one, was prepared to argue that these 'sacrifices personnels' deserved repayment in the form of the votes of his compatriots. (ASTR, Angers to Laflèche, February 27, 1895. Items from this collection kindly made available by L.L. LaPierre.)
121 *Canada, Sessional Papers*, 1895, vol.28, no.10, pp.190–325.

Lordships have decided that the Governor-General in Council has jurisdiction, and that the appeal is well founded.' The key point was that the Privy Council had decided not only a question of law (that a right to appeal existed under the constitution despite the Barrett decision), but also a question of fact (that the minority had sustained an injury serious enough to justify an appeal).

Having established the existence of sufficient grievance to form the basis of an appeal, Lord Watson went beyond the scope of the six questions asked. He insisted that a response to the appeal on the part of the governor general or subsequent action on the part of the federal Parliament would be discretionary and ultimately would be political.

I apprehend that the appeal to the governor is an appeal to the governor's discretion. It is a political administrative appeal and not a judicial appeal in any proper sense of the term, and in the same way after he has decided, the same latitude of discretion is given to the Dominion Parliament. They may legislate or not as they think fit.[122]

There was no escaping the burden thus placed on the shoulders of the federal government. The day of political reckoning could no longer be postponed. Watson's final 'obiter dicta' explicitly narrowed the possibilities of escape. He stated that redress of grievances did not necessarily involve repeal of the Manitoba School Act of 1890; he equally indicated that refusal on the part of the Manitoba government to make satisfactory adjustments would place responsibility back on federal shoulders. Just as the Privy Council judgment in the Barrett case had cast the majesty of the law against the hopes and attempts of the minority for redress, the Brophy decision swung the pendulum in the opposite direction. Even Clifford Sifton admitted that, however much it involved an over-simplification of the Court judgment, remedial action could now be presented 'not as the political act of a government ... but as the ... formal carrying out of an instruction by the Queen herself ... based upon the recommendations of the Imperial Privy Council, to oppose which would be treasonous and disloyal.'[123]

---

122 *Canada, Sessional Papers*, 1895, no.20, pp.1–12.
123 Dafoe, *Clifford Sifton in Relation to His Times*, p.72.

2
From courtroom to politics

Very nearly five years had gone by since the Manitoba government had passed its controversial school legislation. Political considerations had precluded the use of disallowance, the first line of defence available to the aggrieved minority. The slow and sometimes bizarre majesty of the judicial process had required four years to reduce the field to the unsheltered confrontation of political entities, the federal and provincial governments.

Certainty that a political move should be made did not mean clarity on the manner of making it. Colonel Alphonse Audet of Ottawa wrote to Archbishop-elect Langevin in St Boniface that the court decision, despite the fact that it was expected, had caused 'une profonde émotion dans les cercles politiques et dans la presse. On discute les effets; on en calcule des conséquences probables pour chacun des partis.'[1] The main pressure of course was being felt by the new prime minister, Mackenzie Bowell, and it quickly became evident that the situation was too much for him. Justice Minister Sir Charles Hibbert Tupper wrote gloomily to his father, Sir Charles, the Canadian high commissioner in London: 'I fear our govt. is very weak. All on account of want of good men in it. Departmental business is sadly neglected, and everything is in a mess.'[2]

---

1 AASB, Audet to Langevin, January 30, 1895. Colonel Audet, a close friend of Langevin's, archivist at the Secretariate of State in Ottawa, became one of the archbishop's chief sources of 'inside' government information.
2 PAC, Tupper Papers, C.H. Tupper to C. Tupper, February 13, 1895. The confusion and

A preliminary irritant was the question of the possible disallowance of the 1894 amendments to the Manitoba school law. Audet and a Winnipeg pastor, Father Cherrier, both mentioned the subject in letters to Langevin,[3] yet it was clear that nothing would be done about it. As Public Works Minister J.A. Ouimet put it to Desjardins, the disallowance tactic at that juncture would deepen enmities without giving much relief. Only a remedial bill would give the minority 'un remède complet à leurs griefs, tandis que le désaveu de l'acte de 1894 ne serait qu'un remède partiel.' But Ouimet's letter showed that pressure for such disallowance had appeared and had further weakened the cabinet position: 'Nul doute que les libéraux vont faire feu et flammes sur cette question de désaveu et que, supportés par Tardivel de la Vérité et quelques autres de nos amis qui ne verraient peut-être pas toutes les difficultés de la position, l'opinion publique va être pour un instant ébranlé ... Inutile de dire que la position n'est pas rose.'[4]

On the question of immediate action to be taken in view of the Privy Council decision, and of the concomitant question of holding a session of Parliament or of dissolving and going to the country, Bowell exhibited what Lady Aberdeen called his 'characteristic indecision.'[5] He stalled off Senator Bernier's inquiry on February 5.[6] On February 16 he notified Lord Aberdeen that the decision had been made to hear a formal appeal from the Manitoba Catholics before the cabinet, sitting as a special judicial committee of the Privy Council.'[7] The governor general faced Bowell with the question that concerned him directly as representative of the Crown: would there be a session or dissolution?[8] Bowell replied on February 17, in a letter that was a marvel of circumlocution, that dissolution had been decided upon in cabinet, though with as yet no fixed date.[9] According to

difficulty occasioned by Thompson's death and the selection of Bowell to succeed him are discussed at some length by Saywell, *The Canadian Journal of Lady Aberdeen*, Introduction, pp. xli–xlv, and Clark, 'The Conservative Administrations' (thesis), pp. 323–332. Lady Ishbel Aberdeen, wife of the Marquess of Aberdeen who had become governor general in 1893, provided many 'inside' views of Ottawa happenings through her voluminous *Journal*.

3 AASB, Audet to Langevin, February 17, 1895; Cherrier to Langevin, February 27, 1895
4 ACSM, Desjardins Papers, Ouimet to Desjardins, February 28, 1895
5 *Journal*, February 22, 1895, p. 200
6 ACSM, Bernier Papers, Bowell to Bernier, February 5, 1895. Senator T.A. Bernier of St Boniface and A.A. LaRivière, MP for Provencher, were Archbishop Langevin's 'Natural' contacts in the Senate and House. But neither demonstrated great ability or influence during the crisis.
7 PAC, Aberdeen Papers, Bowell to Aberdeen, February 16, 1895
8 *Ibid.*, Aberdeen to Bowell, February 16, 1895
9 *Ibid.*, Bowell to Aberdeen, February 17, 1895

Lady Aberdeen, the prime minister and the governor general conferred at length on the following day, and a dissolution followed by a May election seemed a relative certainty.[10] Yet within four days Bowell informed the governor general that the decision on session or dissolution would have to wait until the appeal of the minority had been heard.[11] This was indeed logical, yet Bowell had had the same facts before him when he had confidently announced dissolution a week earlier.

Bowell's bewilderment on the subject was understandable in view of the bombardment he was receiving from various sides. C.H. Tupper reflected the pro-dissolution position in his February 13 letter to his father: 'I learn that some of my colleagues want a session. Our duty is clear. Come to a decision on Schools. Go at once to the country for authority to act.'[12] The opposing position was upheld by the representatives of the Manitoba minority and by many from Quebec. The Quebec sentiment was echoed by two Conservative organizers who wrote to Bowell on February 12. One of these, N. Rosa of St Hyacinthe, stated that if no session were held, there would be no answer to Liberal charges that the Conservatives did not want to do anything for the Manitoba schools. His conclusion was that failure to meet Parliament would 'display weakness and indolence. If the elections come off before a session we will not engage in the struggle when defeat shall have been prepared. Please note that if I speak thus, it is because I have visited several counties recently.'[13] The pressure from Manitoba was even more direct. Langevin's directive to Senator Bernier was very pointed: 'Il nous faut, vous le savez, *une session et une loi réparatrice.*'[14] The senator came with John Ewart and Father Cherrier to Ottawa on February 25. Archbishop Duhamel of Ottawa reported their position to Bishop Laflèche:

Mr. Ewart est arrivé ici hier soir, avec Mr. l'abbé Cherrier et Mr. le Sénateur

10 *Journal*, February 17, 1895, p.198
11 *Ibid.*, February 22, 1895, p.200
12 PAC, Tupper Papers, C.H. Tupper to C. Tupper, February 13, 1895. C.H. Tupper from the beginning took the lead among non-French members of the cabinet in favouring redress for the Manitoba minority. The Toronto *Mail and Empire*, newly combined from *The Mail* and *The Empire* on February 6, 1895, temporarily provided more moderate discussion of the possibility of some federal action than had seemed possible in the anti-French heyday of *The Mail*. The amalgamation and the general attitude of the Ontario Conservative press is reviewed in Clark, 'The Conservative Administrations' (thesis), pp.354-9.
13 PAC, Bowell Papers, Rosa to Bowell, February 12, 1895
14 ACSM, Bernier Papers, Langevin to Bernier, February 23, 1895

Bernier. Ces deux messieurs (Cherrier et Bernier) me disent que les catholiques et le clergé de leur province demandent absolument une autre session afin de régler definitivement la question des écoles separées de Manitoba. Ils combattent tous les arguments en faveur d'une élection, même après communication d'un arrêté en Conseil ordonnant à la Legislature de Manitoba de remédier à l'injustice commise à l'égard des Catholiques.[15]

Cherrier himself in his report to Langevin on February 27 told of the meeting with Archbishop Duhamel, and in particular of a session with J.A. Ouimet, in which the minister of public works told them that the majority of the cabinet was in favour of dissolution and elections. Cherrier gloomily reported that neither he nor Ewart could see the logic of the government argument, 'si ce n'est la faiblesse, en règle générale, d'une administration gouvernementale, qui touche à son terme.'[16]

That Ouimet and A.R. Angers, minister of agriculture, had been at least tactically won over to the idea of an immediate election was evident from their letters. Ouimet's position was spelled out in a letter to Senator Desjardins on February 28. The main argument, which he presented as that of 'la majorité du Gouvernement,' was that a session might very well weaken the government position without helping the Manitoba minority. On the attitude of the members of the cabinet, Ouimet stated that he was convinced 'qui mes collègues sont parfaitement sincères dans leur désir de se conformer au jugement du Conseil Privé.'[17] In view of what would happen within a year, this was indeed high confidence. Even more remarkable was the assurance expressed by Angers, the Castor representative in the cabinet. In a letter to Bishop Laflèche, Angers repeated his earlier contention that even in the case of an election before a remedy was attempted it ought to be evident that Conservative ministers should be trusted above the Liberals. Pointing not too subtly at the ecclesiastical pressure he expected would be placed on voters in case of an election, Angers outlined what he felt was an open and shut case for the Catholic citizen. 'Doivent-ils moins espérer de nous qui par des sacrifices personnels avons obtenu le dernier jugement du Conseil Privé,' Angers asked, 'que de M. Laurier et M. Martin, qui sont reconnus comme partisans des écoles neutres?'[18]

15 AAO, Duhamel to Laflèche, February 26, 1895
16 AASB, Cherrier to Langevin, February 27, 1895
17 ACSM, Desjardins Papers, Ouimet to Desjardins, February 28, 1895
18 ASTR, Angers to Laflèche, February 27, 1895

Bishop Laflèche hardly needed convincing on Angers's last statement, but at least at this juncture he was also ready to reject the Conservatives should they fail to bring justice. On February 22 he sent a long letter to Archbishop Duhamel, which was forwarded by the latter to the three other French archbishops, Fabre of Montreal, Bégin of Quebec, and Langevin (whose consecration was set for March 19). Laflèche wrote that he had been visited during the week by both Angers and Laurier. He stated flatly that, although he retained personal esteem for the Liberal leader, this did not extend to Laurier's policy: 'Je suis demeuré convaincu que cette solution ne peut venir que du parti conservateur, et que si le parti libéral arrivait au pouvoir, elle serait définitivement entérée.' Laurier was evasive, Laflèche said, refusing to say what he would do if elected. Laflèche admitted that Laurier made it clear that he would oppose the existing schools if inquiry proved that they were in fact Protestant. However, he interpreted Laurier's position as favouring neutral schools where the Bible might be read and religion taught in such a way as not to proselytize. Laflèche concluded that he was sure Laurier would do nothing for the Catholics if elected.[19]

Predictably enough, Angers's assurances looked better to Laflèche. The minister had stated that the federal government, after hearing the formal appeal, would first approach the Manitoba government by an order-in-council before proceeding to remedial legislation. On the question of dissolution, Angers had not committed himself, but had admitted that dissolution, while likely, would indeed be dangerous in Quebec. Laflèche was disposed to accept Angers's declarations, but concluded that the Conservatives no more than the Liberals should be allowed to dodge their responsibilities:

S'il arrivait que le gouvernement fédéral ne donnât pas suite à cette arrêté, il serait, dans mon humble opinion, du devoir de tous les ministres catholiques et canadiens-français de donner leur résignation et de sortir d'un tel ministère, en s'efforçant de former un nouveau parti qui aurait pour programme le maintien et le respect de la constitution qui garantit la liberté de conscience et d'éducation à tous les membres de la confédération et de rendre justice égale à tout le Puissance, sans distinction de nationalité, de langue et de religion.[20]

19 AASB, Laflèche to Duhamel, February 22, 1895
20 Ibid., Laflèche to Langevin, February 22, 1895. It should be remembered that Laflèche earlier had opposed and later backed away from the third party idea. See below, p.114.

There is no record of Archbishop Fabre's reaction to Laflèche's suggestion of the formation of a third party, although from other remarks he was less likely than the other recipients to be in agreement with Laflèche. Duhamel replied that he too had seen Angers, and 'je partage l'opinion que V.G. [Votre Grandeur] exprime dans sa lettre.'[21] Bégin seemed more disposed to give Laurier some benefit of the doubt. In a note to Langevin commenting on the Laflèche letter, the coadjutor-archbishop of Quebec reported that 'M. Laurier, pressé par ses partisans catholiques, a du faire hier soir, me dit-on, une déclaration propre à satisfaire les catholiques.' He added (whether in sincerity or sarcasm is not clear), 'J'ai hâte de voir cela.'[22]

In late January, Bégin had been visited by Auguste Choquette, Liberal MP for Montmorency. In a letter to Choquette on the day following the interview, Bégin left open the question of the two parties' policies, although he leaned to the Conservatives:

Après nos longues et sérieuses entrevues au sujet de la question scolaire Manitobaine, vous devez être convaincu que je n'en fais pas – non plus que mes collègues – une question politique. C'est tout le contraire qui est la vérité. Je vais me mettre en relation immédiatement avec Mgr. Walsh, archévêque de Toronto, afin de connaître sa manière de voir sur cette question et surtout ce dont nous avons parlé hier et ce matin et spécialement au sujet de la fameuse commission d'enquête.[23]

21 AAO, Duhamel to Laflèche, February 25, 1895
22 *Ibid*., Bégin to Langevin, February 26, 1895. Louis-Nazaire Bégin (1840–1925) combined broad scholarship with a special talent for reconciliation. A founding member of the Royal Society of Canada, his nomination as Bishop of Chicoutimi in 1888 was looked upon as another Cardinal Taschereau imposition over the Laflèche wing in the Quebec ecclesiastical world. In 1891, as Taschereau's health failed, Bégin became coadjutor and later administrator of the archdiocese of Quebec. Yet by 1895, despite the gap which still existed between himself and the ultramontane group represented by Laflèche and his own Vicar-General Marois, Bégin was often the confidant, personally as well as by status, of both wings of the Quebec hierarchy. His distaste for excessive personal clash was revealed by the statement of his secretary in later years, the future Bishop Langlois of Valleyfield, that Bégin as an elderly Cardinal could not recall without tears some of the bitterness of the school crisis, especially the subsequent difficulties which led to the mission of Merry del Val (personal interview with Bishop Langlois, 1959). The fact that Bégin's primacy among the bishops was one of honour and not fixed by constitution or formal agreement was responsible for some of the difficulty over concerted action during the crisis. One result was an increasing number of admissions, sometimes grudging, that an Apostolic Delegation ought to be established in Ottawa.
23 PAC, Laurier Papers, Bégin to Choquette, January 30, 1895

One point was clear among the cross-currents evident in these letters: the pressures were already at work that would influence Bowell to change his mind on the question of a session a few weeks later.

THE CABINET HEARING AND THE FEDERAL REMEDIAL ORDER

First, however, came the formal hearing of the minority appeal. The date originally set by Bowell was Tuesday, February 26. When that day arrived, D'Alton McCarthy requested a delay of the argument on behalf of the Manitoba government; later in the session he said that not enough notice had been given to prepare. Ewart insisted that a delay should not prevent the Manitoba government from considering the order-in-council which might come from the federal government in view of the argument. He suggested that only enough time be allowed for someone to come from Manitoba with the documents which McCarthy said were needed. Bowell agreed to a brief delay until Monday, March 4.[24]

When the hearing was finally opened, Ewart led off with a broad review of the basis for the minority's appeal for federal intervention. He concentrated on the obvious intent of the Manitoba Act and subsequent provincial legislation to create and protect separate schools, rather than on the legal technicalities added by the court decisions in either the Barrett or Brophy cases. Ewart supported strongly the contention, many times advanced by Archbishop Taché, that the post-1890 Manitoba public schools were in fact Protestant. He concluded his main presentation with a series of scathing criticisms, quoting a former inspector of Protestant schools in Manitoba, Dr J.H. Morrison, against both the motives and tactics of the Greenway government.

McCarthy opened his case by presenting John O'Donohue of Winnipeg as a Manitoba Catholic who opposed separate schools. O'Donohue was emphatically repudiated as a representative of Manitoba Catholics, French or Irish, in a resolution sent to Ottawa by a large meeting of his own parish, St Mary's of Winnipeg.[25] McCarthy spent the bulk of his time disputing the 'Fourth Bill of Rights' presented by the delegates of the provisional government of Red River in 1870, claiming that fraud had been used in obtaining the separate-school guarantees in the Manitoba Act. McCarthy's most telling point, however, was his insistence that the cabinet members hearing

24 AASB, Angers to Laflèche, February 27, 1895
25 *Canada, Sessional Papers*, 1895, no.20, pp.104–5

the case could not escape their political identity. Even the elaborate judicial trappings of the hearing could not disguise the fact that it was these same Ministers, acting as advisers of the governor general, who would decide whether or not to bring federal action against Manitoba.[26]

As was to be the case repeatedly during the ensuing months, the 'grey eminence' who was insisting on the political dimension and who was succeeding in making events come his way was Clifford Sifton, attorney general of Manitoba. In his letter thanking McCarthy for his handling of the Ottawa hearing, Sifton pointed out that 'from the first I anticipated difficulty in making it clear to the public that the legal aspect of this question had passed away and that it was now purely a question of Government policy ... I think that we have sufficient ground now to go upon and they have gone so far in admitting our contention that they cannot very well get back.'[27] The development of events was rapidly confirming Sifton's estimate.

In the story of the federal involvement in the Manitoba school question it seems inevitable that Bowell be cast as a leader unequal to his task; perhaps the situation would have been too much for a far more forceful chief. At the same time, the courage and sense of justice Bowell exhibited when his old comrades-in-arms of the Orange Lodges tried to appeal to unalloyed anti-Catholicism should not be ignored. The prime minister insisted that he appreciated the feeling among Orangemen on the school question and that he did not fault the strong sentiment involved. What he did object to was their utter failure to use even basic logic. 'I am quite convinced,' Bowell told one supporter, 'from the utterances made by most of the Brethren in the press and on the platform, that they do not understand the question, nor draw the distinction which exists between this matter and the Jesuits' Estates Act.'[28] Whatever may be said about his lack of dexterity in handling the case, there would seem to be little doubt concerning Bowell's personal commitment to follow at least the minimum requirements of the Privy Council decision.

It was equally clear that Bowell was willing to use every means available to get Manitoba to give acceptable measures of relief without involving federal government action. His letter to Lieutenant Governor Schultz on March 7 combined hope with veiled threat. Bowell was replying to a note of February 20 from Schultz and wanted the lieutenant governor to use the

26 *Ibid.*, 1895, no.20
27 PAC, Sifton Papers, Sifton to McCarthy, March 11, 1895
28 PAC, Bowell Papers, Bowell to Clarke, March 21, 1895

tactic of trying to drive a wedge between Greenway and Attorney General Sifton. Bowell admitted that in view of Sifton's position, Greenway might be adamant, but he wanted Schultz to 'test them.' His conclusion pointed, in Bowell's characteristic uncertain phrases, to remedial action. 'I do not say that any remedial legislation will be passed; but the probabilities are that something will be done, and it would be much better to have it done with their concurrence, and in a modified form, than to force any measure upon them.'[29]

Nothing came of Bowell's suggested pressure on Greenway, and the 'probabilities' of the letter to Schultz became a reality on March 21. On that date, a remedial order, based on the March 19 report of C.H. Tupper, minister of justice, and accompanied by a minute-of-council reviewing the court case, was given formal sanction by the governor general. The key point stressed in the remedial order was the apparent duty which the Privy Council decision had placed upon the federal executive power to effect the restoration of Manitoba's Catholic school rights. No abrogation of the 1890 law or the 1894 amendments was demanded. Three fundamental rights, however, were stated as the points which had to be granted to the Manitoba Catholics in order to comply with the Privy Council decision: the right to 'build, maintain, equip, manage, conduct and support' schools in the manner provided for in the statutes in force before 1890; the right to a share in the school grants from public funds; and exemption from public-school taxation for denominational school supporters. Whether federal legislation would follow would depend upon the compliance or refusal of the Manitoba government.[30]

Concomitant with the remedial order came Bowell's decision to hold another parliamentary session rather than face an immediate election. Reaction to both moves was not slow in coming. On the clerical side there was general gratification, typified by a letter from Bishop Moreau of St Hyacinthe to J.A. Ouimet. The bishop congratulated the minister on the remedial order, saying that not only Catholics but all true friends of the country would be pleased by such courageous action. As for the session, this was also praised as an act of courage in which the school issue would have to be squarely faced, and in which 'sera prononcé pour nos honorables ministres la sentence de vie ou de mort.'[31]

For Bowell, however, the French-Catholic reaction was far too en-

29 *Ibid.*, Bowell to Schultz, March 7, 1895
30 *Canada, Sessional Papers*, 1895, no.20, pp.17–27
31 AESH, Moreau to Ouimet, March 22, 1895

thusiastic. After such a long wait and so many delays, it was natural that the remedial order would be greeted as a 'victoire catholique.' But that very phrase, splashed across the front page of Montreal's *La Minerve* on March 22, caused Bowell to write glumly to Caron:

I do not know anything that is more likely to provoke hostile feelings than boasting of this kind. The very fact of their claiming it as a victory for the Catholics instead of an adhesion to the Constitution, is sufficient to intensify the violent opposition which we already see in Ontario and the North West.[32]

For the time being, the Ontario wing of the Conservatives remained in line. There were continued protests from Orange lodges and journals, but the policy of cautious cooperation adopted by Clarke Wallace, controller of customs and the most active Orangeman in the Bowell government, set the pace. Wallace remained in his position, but Bowell was either consciously or unconsciously glossing over the problem when he wrote to Robert Birmingham of Toronto that Wallace's presence in the government caused no embarrassment. Instead of the rift reported by the *Globe*, which had prompted Birmingham's inquiry, Bowell replied that Wallace continued to do good work in the customs department, something which the prime minister very much appreciated:

The very day that the *Globe* said we were quarrelling, Wallace was lunching with me in my room. I have seen him only once since. If there is any feeling, it is with him although he never exhibited it to me. It used to be the difficulties between Chapleau and myself, which really never existed, and now they are trying to suggest jealousies between Wallace and myself.[33]

Bowell was either deceived or deceiving; either spelled trouble.

In any case, Bowell had a far more immediate and more important cabinet problem on his hands than Clarke Wallace. Immediately after the adoption of the remedial order, Charles Hibbert Tupper resigned the justice portfolio in protest against Bowell's decision to hold another parliamentary session without calling an election. Bowell argued that opting for an immediate election, 'while the political heather was ablaze throughout the country, would be a piece of political folly, inexcusable in any

32 PAC, Caron Papers, Bowell to Caron, March 23, 1895
33 PAC, Bowell Papers, Bowell to Birmingham, March 22, 1895

public man.'[34] Tupper countered that political fires were more likely to spread than to abate, and that the seriousness of the remedialism issue required 'a direct mandate from the people.'[35] Tupper withdrew his resignation and resumed his cabinet post on March 28, after the influence of his father, Governor General Aberdeen, and the CPR were brought to bear.[36]

Tupper's re-entry into the cabinet was, understandably enough, a great relief to Bowell. On March 29, the prime minister told his returning rebel that he would simply consider that the resignation letter of March 21 had never been written. Such compulsive covering over of differences was in itself a confession of weakness. Bowell's letter once again indicated that Tupper's main concern had been that a session without an election might scuttle remedial action, but the prime minister was no more definite than before as to what would in fact be done. He repeated that the federal government could legislate only if Manitoba rejected the remedial order. Therefore, he suggested, at the opening of the session 'it might be stated what the policy of the Government is upon the question of Remedial legislation, or, what to my mind would be better, to wait until the action of the Manitoba Government was known, and that after defining such policy, should it be found that the House did not approve, an appeal could be made to the people, or, if events justified it, an appeal could be made even though the House should approve.'[37] It was hardly an enlightening statement. On the matter of a projected date for an election, the closest the prime minister came to a statement of clear intent was a personal note to a supporter vacationing in Bermuda: 'Our present intention is to make the session as short as possible, and then take the best opportunity for appealing to the people in the Fall, when I hope that, to a very great extent, the excitement may have abated.'[38] Bowell was playing for time, but there was little hope, in the circumstances, that delay would improve the situation.

In any case, during his negotiations to get Tupper back Bowell was either unwilling or unable to let the remedial order stand on its own merits in Manitoba. Again trying to work through Lieutenant Governor Schultz, he sent a telegram in code on March 25 which thoroughly toned down the

34 *Ibid.*, Bowell to C.H. Tupper, March 23, 1895
35 *Ibid.*, C.H. Tupper to Bowell, March 25, 1895
36 See PAC, Aberdeen Papers, C.H. Tupper to Aberdeen, March 28, 1895, and the balanced summary of this crisis by Saywell in his introduction to *The Canadian Journal of Lady Aberdeen*, pp.xlvi–xlix.
37 PAC, Bowell Papers, Bowell to C.H. Tupper, March 29, 1895
38 *Ibid.*, Bowell to Judge Gowan, April 2, 1895

strong language of the order-in-council: 'Newspaper telegrams say Greenway and colleagues express opinion that order cannot be modified. This is
mistaken. Any arrangement he can make will be acceptable.'[39] This was
followed up by letters during the subsequent week in which Bowell asked
Schultz to intercede with both the Manitoba government and the Catholic
authorities. Specifically, Bowell asked Schultz to contact Father Albert
Lacombe, the famous missionary, to act as intermediary. Bowell also tried
to bring pressure on the newly consecrated Archbishop Langevin through
people as diverse as Senator Bernier and Hugh John Macdonald.[40] Despite
these moves, the main impression which emerged from the prime
minister's efforts during this crucial period was one of vacillation. He gave
the impression of not realizing the severity of the remedial order when it
was first issued, then of casting about frantically to reduce its impact. At all
events, Bowell's attempts to placate all parties was unsuccessful and, as
Liberal sources revealed even more clearly, he failed completely to prepare for what was coming from Manitoba.

THE LIBERAL REACTION

For the Liberals, the problems occasioned by the Privy Council decision
were different but no less perplexing than those faced by the Conservatives. Clifford Sifton coolly summed up the coming danger in a comment
sent to Laurier several weeks before the decision was handed down. His
reading of the argument and the justices' remarks led him to conclude that
the verdict would favour the right of appeal and the federal power to restore
Catholic privileges. 'It is a matter of great regret,' he said, 'that the decision
should be on this line. Not from a Manitoba standpoint because I fancy it
will make little difference to us here, but from the standpoint of Canadian
politics generally.'[41] Laurier too saw the clouds forming. Writing to Willison after hearing the same news from Edward Blake, he said that he was

39 *Ibid.*, Bowell to Schultz, March 25, 1895
40 *Ibid.*, Bowell to Schultz, March 28, March 30, 1895; Bowell to Macdonald, March 28,
   1895; ACSM, Bernier Papers, Bowell to Bernier, April 1, 1895. It was ironic that at the very
   time Bowell was trying to enlist Schultz to influence Greenway, he was obliged to inform
   the lieutenant governor that political necessity required that Schultz be replaced by J.C.
   Patterson. 'The difficulty which made Patterson's appointment necessary,' Bowell wrote,
   'arose at the formation of the Government in December last, and had to be dealt with' (PAC,
   Bowell Papers, Bowell to Schultz, March 30, 1895). Patterson succeeded Schultz on
   September 2, 1895.
41 PAC, Sifton Papers, Sifton to Laurier, January 4, 1895

not surprised: 'I cannot see that the BNA Act can be interpreted in any other way.' Laurier admitted that the situation would be 'a subject of great embarrassment to all,' but felt that 'the Government will feel it more than we will.' Laurier above all wanted Willison and the *Globe* 'not to venture any opinion until the Government have shown their hand and told what they are going to do.'[42]

Before the government did 'show their hand' in the remedial order, a good deal of pressure was put on Laurier to show his. Having visited the West in the autumn of 1894, Laurier knew quite clearly what the Manitoba Liberal stand would be. Isaac Campbell of Winnipeg wrote on March 13 that 'in this province our friends cannot recede from their position on the School Act,' and that to secularize the schools would please no one.[43] Provincial Secretary J.D. Cameron was even more adamant. 'With us compromise is impossible,' he wrote to Willison. 'There can be no solution of this question but the one and that is the formal and final abdication by the Dominion Government and Parliament of the right to interfere.'[44] Sifton was his usual analytic self. He told Laurier that he regretted having had to make a very strong public statement against any change in the Manitoba schools because of a resolution for redress made by James Fisher, former president of the Manitoba Liberal Association. But he did not hesitate to suggest that Laurier turn Tory anti-remedialism to the Liberals' advantage. In fact, Sifton concluded, it could well be argued that if the Conservatives were returned to power, their Protestant members from the provinces other than Quebec would refuse to fulfil the promises which they had made to the Quebec representatives before the election and, 'the election being over and another not in sight for five years, there will be a repetition of the treatment which was accorded to Archbishop Taché on a previous occasion.' Such concern by Sifton for his welfare might well have amused the late archbishop, especially when the Attorney General concluded that his line of argument ought to nullify the political effect of the remedial order in Quebec 'outside of course of direct clerical influence.'[45]

In Ontario, J.S. Willison and the Toronto *Globe* became the focus of the controversy over the stand to be taken by the Liberals. G.W. Ross, minister of education in Oliver Mowat's Ontario government and future premier of the province, encouraged Laurier to believe that some degree

42 PAC, Willison Papers, Laurier to Willison, January 7, 1895
43 PAC, Laurier Papers, Campbell to Laurier, March 13, 1895
44 PAC, Willison Papers, Cameron to Willison, March 4, 1895
45 PAC, Sifton Papers, Sifton to Laurier, March 2, 1895

of interference with Manitoba might be supported by his Ontario colleagues.[46] The quarry was the English-Catholic vote in general and Archbishop Walsh of Toronto in particular. J.D. Edgar was the chief exponent of the sheer political necessity of paying close attention to Ontario Catholics,[47] and shortly after the appearance of the Privy Council decision in 1895, had sent an excellent summary and analysis of the decision to Archbishop Walsh. He left no doubt in his synopsis that he understood that a Catholic appeal was admissible, and concluded that unless the whole question could 'be treated by all with moderation, firmness and patriotism, alas for Canada.'[48]

In his correspondence with Laurier concerning the *Globe* editorials of early March, Ross indicated that he was following Edgar's lead in paying close attention to the English-Catholic reaction. Of the *Globe* position, Ross said, 'the Catholic Register of this city, the exponent of the views of the papacy, writes somewhat deprecatory [*sic*], but on the whole satisfactorily.'[49] In a second letter to Laurier, Ross reported on an interview with an unnamed 'friend,' clearly Archbishop Walsh, in which there had been a very frank exchange of views. The archbishop, said Ross, had made five observations. It appeared that Walsh was convinced that the Liberals would win the next general election. The archbishop also agreed that it would be a mistake for Laurier to come out openly in favour of remedial action because, 'the effect ... in his opinion, would be to arouse public feeling in Ontario and greatly prejudice the Liberal party in this Province.' Walsh was prepared to leave the whole matter to the people of Manitoba, because he thought that 'their sober second thought will redress the wrongs they inflicted upon the minority.' The Toronto archbishop, Ross reported, did not require any pledge from Laurier as to the future, but 'leaned to the view that if in the course of a reasonable time, Manitoba did not act, Parliament should interfere.' As the last of his observations, Walsh confided to Ross that, should Laurier lead the Liberals to victory in the next election, 'Greenway and yourself could by mutual agreement remove every objectionable feeling in the Manitoba legislation without public irritation.' Ross was sure that Walsh would advocate 'moderation' and 'non-interference,' because a 'religious agitation would, in his opinion,

---

46 PAC, Laurier Papers, Ross to Laurier, February 27, 1895
47 *Ibid.*, Edgar to Laurier, November 25, 1894. For Edgar's work as a chief Ontario Liberal organizer and strategist, see Stamp, 'The Political Career of James David Edgar' (thesis).
48 AAT, Walsh Papers, Edgar to Walsh, February 18, 1895
49 PAC, Laurier Papers, Ross to Laurier, March 8, 1895

give Dalton McCarthy a prominence which would be unfortunate in the present crisis.'[50]

Laurier could only be cheered by such a report concerning Archbishop Walsh, but the news from other sections of the country was not so encouraging. In Nova Scotia, Colin McIsaac, former member of W.S. Fielding's provincial cabinet and now Liberal candidate in the by-election in Sir John Thompson's old riding of Antigonish, wanted Laurier to take at least as strong a stand on the school question as would the Conservatives. McIsaac felt that he had an excellent chance unless Bishop Cameron of Antigonish could use the Manitoba situation against him. McIsaac's rival would be Joseph Andrew Chisholm, a brother-in-law to Sir John Thompson's widow, and there was no doubt that Cameron favoured the Conservative. 'The extent of his interference,' said McIsaac, 'will depend largely on the reasons he can get for taking a part in the contest. He will willingly take a strong hand if this question affords the slightest pretext, in which case our chances of winning the county will be gone.'

McIsaac reinforced this opinion with that of a cleric, 'perhaps ... the most prominent priest in our diocese and who is a strong personal friend of mine with liberal convictions.' This priest, said McIsaac, had never before interfered in politics. However, he had now felt it his duty to warn McIsaac 'in time, lest our party should make any mistake.' McIsaac sent Laurier an extract from the priest's letter. After re-emphasizing his record of neutrality in political contest, the priest had stated that in the current case 'religion will be affected.' Therefore, he would 'by word and vote support the party that will give my co-religionists fair play ... You have to make up your mind if you wish to run successfully, to give them in Manitoba at least as much as the tories will give.' McIsaac's conclusion was blunt: 'I feel that I will be obliged to retire from the contest if I have to make an uneven and hopeless fight against the Hierarchy and the government.'[51]

L.G. Power of Halifax, an influential Catholic Liberal senator, strongly backed McIsaac's view in a letter of March 4.[52] A third Maritime Liberal, clearly a Protestant, D.C. Fraser of New Glasgow, Nova Scotia, saw the problem as more complex than did either McIsaac or Power, but was not unmindful that justice was involved. Fraser felt that, although the question had not affected the Maritimes to the same extent as Ontario and Quebec,

50 *Ibid.*, Ross to Laurier, March 13, 1895
51 *Ibid.*, McIsaac to Laurier, March 8, 1895
52 *Ibid.*, Power to Laurier, March 4, 1895

on the one hand Catholics were getting excited, and on the other, many Protestant Liberal supporters would be lost by a Liberal statement favoring coercion. 'Still,' he said, 'we must act generously and justly with the minority.'[53]

From Manitoba, Augustin Richard, hoping to run against La Rivière in Provencher, wrote that he had been to see Archbishop-elect Langevin for approval. Langevin had given his endorsement, he said, but

Malheureusement, me dit-il, je ne puis avoir la même confiance en votre chef, c.a.d., c'est probablement le politicien le plus honnête, le plus honorable, le plus distingué, mais sur cette question des écoles et de l'éducation, je le crois imbu du liberalisme de la vieille école des Dorions & jusqu'à preuve du contraire je ne puis changer d'opinion.

Furthermore, said Richard, 'c'est le clergé qui déterminera le résultat d'une telle lutte.' Richard added that he had tried to get Langevin to see that Laurier could not make a declaration, given the existing situation, but nothing he could say had changed Langevin's attitude, although the latter promised to see him again.[54]

Back in Ontario, the Ottawa Valley demanded attention, and again involved the clergy. On February 16, Laurier heard from a prospective Valley candidate deeply concerned with episcopal opinion. Frank Anglin, a Roman Catholic Toronto lawyer, who was later to be Chief Justice of Canada, wrote that he was willing to contest the traditionally Conservative South Renfrew seat, and that he had obtained Archbishop Walsh's blessing. 'The Archbishop of Toronto, although of well known conservative tendencies heretofore,' Anglin stated, 'fully approves of the selection and is now inclined to assist us in every legitimate way ... He further stated that he believed I would be thoroughly acceptable to the other prelates of the Province as a Catholic representative.' Anglin said that he had considered entering the contest in North Essex, but had decided against it, specifically because Bishop O'Connor of London was known to be a strong Conservative. As for South Renfrew, Anglin believed that the key might well be held by Bishop Lorrain of Pontiac (later Pembroke) and Archbishop Duhamel of Ottawa. As if to illustrate Edgar's contention, Anglin stated that most of the Catholics in the riding had hitherto voted Conservative, 'so that if a couple of hundred Catholics could be got to support a Catholic Liberal, the

53 *Ibid.*, Fraser to Laurier, March 11, 1895
54 PAC, Laurier Papers, Richard to Laurier, February 16, 1895

difficulty would be overcome.' Even here Walsh was seen as important. 'At the suggestion of our Archbishop, who has allowed me to use his name for the purpose,' reported Anglin, 'I have written as strong a letter as I possibly could to Mgr. Lorrain asking whether if nominated by the Reformers, he would give me his assistance in the election.' Anglin then asked Laurier himself to write to Bishop Lorrain, 'giving assurances as to the position which if elected I should occupy – and also giving such assurances as you could venture to give that Catholic interests will be safe in the hands of a Liberal Government.'[55]

Archbishop Duhamel of Ottawa posed a more difficult hurdle, not made easier by Bishop Laflèche's report of February 22.[56] Anglin's February 27 letter to Laurier spoke of seeking an interview with Duhamel on the following day. In an undated letter (probably March 1 or 2) Anglin sent the Liberal leader a long report of the meeting. The Ottawa archbishop was very friendly, said Anglin, but had stated that he could not give any encouragement to a Laurier supporter, since he 'knows positively that you, if returned to power, will refuse to do anything toward restoring Separate Schools – your policy being – he is assured – the establishment of non-sectarian, neutral schools.' Anglin then posed the question which was to face Laurier many times during the coming year, a question which involved both principle and political strategy: 'Could you not state to them privately that if returned to power, you are prepared to grant redress – and that as soon as the govt. is pledged to this policy, you will give a similar pledge?'[57]

Inevitably, whether Laurier could or would give such a pledge was going to be heavily influenced by his own crucial province. And there was little doubt which way the wind was blowing there. As if there were not enough pressure from Catholic power sources in Quebec, Henri Joly de Lotbinière, Huguenot, highly respected for integrity, and hero of many jousts with Conservatives both federal and provincial, had to be reckoned with. His opinion on the Manitoba school situation was widely known and was summarized in a letter to W.F. Luxton of *The Manitoba Free Press*. Joly spoke of his 'painful surprise' that the religious exercises in the post-1890 schools copied the pre-1890 Protestant program. He was sure that 'very few among the Protestant majority are aware of the great injustice committed towards the minority; if they knew of it, they would protest against it at once.' His own preference was for 'religious education satisfactory to all

55 *Ibid.*, Anglin to Laurier, February 16, 1895
56 AASB, Laflèche to Langevin, February 22, 1895. See above, p.48.
57 PAC, Laurier Papers, Anglin to Laurier, March, 1895

creeds;' if, however, separate schools were the only alternative, they should, in his opinion, be restored.[58]

Roman Catholic opinion from Quebec was a good deal more emphatic. C.E. Pouliot wrote that he would run against the Conservative Grandbois in Temiscouata riding, although he foresaw that it would be at considerable cost to himself; he stressed that it would only be personal regard for Laurier that would induce him to run. But he left no doubt about his attitude toward the school question:

Maintenant, mon cher M. Laurier, si je me présente, je dois vous déclarer bien franchement que je serai bien explicite sur la question des écoles – c'est ma conviction intime que le système d'écoles neutres établi au Manitoba est une injustice pour nos compatriotes et un fleau pour un pays – il faut l'enseignement religieux dans les écoles.[59]

Jules Tessier, Liberal member for Portneuf in the Quebec Legislative Assembly, reinforced Pouliot's argument in greater detail. Tessier concluded that without a strong statement by Laurier against neutral schools, 'je crains que cela ait des effets désastreux dans nos comtés.'[60]

The pressure was not without results. On March 6, Anglin was able to send to Duhamel a confidential statement from Laurier that was aimed at contradicting the Conservative 'calumny' that the Liberal leader was 'in favour of secular Godless schools.' Anglin quoted Laurier as saying that 'personally I am certainly disposed to restore to the Catholics of Manitoba the right which it was certainly the intention of both the Canadian Parliament and the Imperial Parliament to invest them with.' As for the scope of this opinion, Laurier had said that 'at present I speak for myself and I can speak for the individual opinion of a good many others amongst the Protestant Liberals. At a later day, and *probably not a distant one*, I hope to be able to speak with the full authority of the party.' Anglin then called the archbishop's attention to the *Globe* of March 6, which contained a pro-minority speech given by Laurier at St Jerome on March 5, and a copy of Joly's letter to the Montreal *Witness* calling for just treatment of the Manitoba schools. 'I trust,' Anglin said, 'that these will sufficiently dispel Your Grace's idea that Mr. Laurier was pledged to the policy of secular or Godless schools.' Anglin also quoted several Ontario Liberals of high rank,

58 AASB, Joly de Lotbinière to Luxton, February 19, 1895
59 PAC, Laurier Papers, Pouliot to Laurier, February 14, 1895
60 *Ibid.*, Tessier to Laurier, February 26, 1895

specifically Cartwright, Edgar, and Mulock. 'All agree,' he said, 'that Separate schools must be restored to Manitoba, while all are persuaded that the most effective method of settling the question will be through such an arrangement as they believe can only be effected by the Dominion Liberal party with the Liberals of Manitoba.' As for 'coercive legislation,' the opinion of the three gentlemen quoted was that it would likely 'lead to open resistance in Manitoba.'[61]

Anglin was quite prepared to use every argument with Duhamel to prove that the Conservatives rather than the Liberals were the real obstacles to justice for the Manitoba Catholics. He cited two factors in particular as proof that the existing government was unwilling to grant relief: they would not disallow the amendments of 1894, and they were apparently not prepared to hold a session and at least introduce remedial legislation as a government measure. As has been seen, it was very much this final argument from the Quebec side which induced Bowell to go through with a session against the strong opinion of C.H. Tupper and others. As for the accuracy of Anglin's statements to Duhamel, he was either misinformed or bluffing with regard to Mulock and, to a lesser degree, Cartwright.[62]

Whatever his political inclination, Duhamel must have smiled at the equally great confidence, exhibited by Anglin on the one hand and Angers on the other, that justice was safe with one party only. The archbishop was probably too ready to side with the Conservative version and to suspect the sincerity of the Laurier statement. As in Bowell's case, however, it must be wondered whether Laurier was as single-minded as Anglin portrayed him. Laurier's letter to Sifton of December 3, 1894 had given a different message. Following his trip to Manitoba earlier in the fall, the Liberal leader wrote to the Manitoba attorney general that during his western tour the subject of making the schools entirely secular had been mentioned many times. Laurier was emphatic that such a solution would be political folly. It would alienate the Presbyterians, 'a very important body, who, as a rule, are strong liberals,' and 'would not in any way mitigate the opposition of the Roman Catholic Hierarchy to the existing law.' Laurier told Sifton that in his opinion the clerical complaint about the Protestant nature of the schools 'was not well put from their own point of view. Sooner or later,' he insisted, 'they will come back to the position, which they have always held, that they are entitled to Catholic schools, and that whether the schools are protestant or secular, so long as they are not catholic, they will pretend

61 AAO, Anglin to Duhamel, March 6, 1895
62 See below, pp.69, 121.

they have a right to complain.' Laurier's conclusion was to advise Sifton to avoid any changes in the law in the direction of secularization, 'which while not satisfying those who are, at present, dissatisfied, would dissatisfy those who are, at present, satisfied.'[63]

Thus it seems clear that Laurier accepted that the Manitoba schools were Protestant, and was prepared to discuss this as a political factor; it is equally certain that one of his main concerns in making the request to Sifton was to avoid a new clamour for disallowance. Yet the second Privy Council decision had intervened between the letter to Sifton and the statement given to Archbishop Duhamel. The question of which was the real Laurier still remained, and it is against this background of some duplicity that the Liberal debate in the tense struggle which followed the issuance of the remedial order must be viewed.

LIBERALS AND THE REMEDIAL ORDER: WILLISON
'TURNS' LAURIER

As it had been for the Conservatives, so also for the Liberals was the remedial order a definite turning point. Naturally enough, the shock waves were felt most immediately in Manitoba. Premier Greenway had been receiving letters and resolutions of encouragement to stand fast even before the publication of the order; once it came they multiplied in number and virulence. Outside of Manitoba the main sources were Ontario Orange lodges and American Protective Association councils from various parts of the United States. Perhaps most colourful was the March 26 telegram from the Boston Council of the American Protective Association: 'Greeting, sympathy, backing. Resist the pope's insolent minority by force of arms if necessary – No Surrender!'[64] From Ontario during March and early April many similar resolutions arrived. Typical was the resolution of the Loyal Orange Lodge No. 439 of Carp, Ontario:

Whereas the Roman Catholic Ecclesiastical authorities are attempting to force Separate Schools on the Province of Manitoba, therefore be it resolved, – That we the members of this Lodge pledge ourselves to support no candidate at the ap-

63 PAC, Sifton Papers, Laurier to Sifton, December 3, 1894
64 PAM, Greenway Papers, Boston APA Council to Greenway, March 26, 1895. On the American Protective Association and its influence on the formation of the Protestant Protective Association in Canada, see Higham, *Strangers in the Land*, p.83ff. Watt gives a balanced discussion of the PPA in 'The Protestant Protective Association,' in Hodgins and Page, eds. *Canadian History Since Confederation*, pp.244–60.

proaching election who will not openly pledge himself to oppose any interference with the Legislative rights of Manitoba.[65]

Greenway could hardly help but be flattered. Answering a supporting letter of Thomas Gibson of Toronto, member of the Ontario provincial Parliament, Greenway wrote that Gibson's evaluation of the Manitoba schools situation had indeed been correct. 'Had it not been for the Clergy,' the premier insisted, 'the agitation would not have been kept up and the Public schools would have been accepted long ago.' Greenway went on to point out that the Manitoba legislature was adjourned until May to allow plenty of time for deliberations on the remedial order. However, Greenway stated, 'I cannot believe that the Parliament of Canada will ever crystallize into law such a demand as that which the Dominion Government has made upon us.'[66]

An opposite influence was being brought to bear, however. The Bowell–Schultz correspondence of late March implied that Schultz believed that Greenway personally might be moved away from a totally adamant position.[67] It is possible that Schultz was simply hoodwinking Bowell, but Schultz did make one significant move which indicated that he himself believed Greenway might be persuaded. While in Ottawa in early April, Schultz sought and obtained a written opinion of the constitutional aspects of Manitoba's position in view of the remedial order from Dr J.G. Bourinot, regarded as the leading constitutional expert in Canada. Word of the existence of the opinion was quickly spread around Ottawa, but it was clearly meant for Greenway and his cabinet. Schultz sent the twelve-page document to Greenway on April 19, calling it 'an independent opinion on the recent executive action of the Dominion Executive.'[68]

Bourinot's own words in his introduction were that he intended to give his own views of the question 'from the standpoint of a constitutional student who has no connection with political parties.' After a detailed review of the steps through which the case had gone, including the issuance of the remedial order, Bourinot summarized:

(3) That the legislature of Manitoba is now constitutionally bound to decide whether it will allow the subject matter of Education, so far as the circumstances of

65 PAM, Greenway papers, LOL No.439, Carp, Ontario, to Greenway, March 9, 1895
66 Ibid., Greenway to Gibson, April 1, 1895
67 See above, p.55.
68 PAM, Greenway Papers, Schultz to Greenway, April 19, 1895

this case require, to pass out of its direct control, or will in accordance with the letter and spirit of the constitutional law, as judicially determined, adopt such remedial measures as will remove the admitted grievances of the Roman Catholic minority of Her Majesty's subjects in Manitoba. The constitutional law in my opinion gives them full power to deal with the whole question in its present aspect.

(4)   That by such course the legislature of Manitoba will remove a difficult question from the arena of political and sectarian animosities, exhibit their desire to do full justice to every class ... at the same time give conclusive evidence of their readiness to submit to the deliberate judgment of the courts in every case.

(5)   That by failing to follow the course marked out for them by the law of the constitution they assume a most serious responsibility; since it would involve necessarily the removal of the subject of Education from the jurisdiction where it must and should rest under ordinary conditions and the handing of it over in this special case to the authority of the Dominion Parliament ...

(6)   That the question at present demanding a deliberate and calm judgment from the legislature and Government of Manitoba is not a question of sectarian or non-sectarian schools. It is a question of restoring a right and a privilege of the Roman Catholic minority ... The constitution may be wise or unwise in its provisions in this regard – it may be the soundest principle to place the jurdisdiction over Education solely in the Provincial authority – without any limiting provisions whatever; but that is not the question now at issue.

In conclusion, Bourinot quoted the eminent British constitutionalist, A.V. Dicey, on the absolute need for the predominance of the judiciary in a federal state, and added that 'for myself I cannot believe that in so clear a case as the one before us the Government and the people of Manitoba are at all disposed to violate so fundamental a principle of federalism as that pressed upon his readers by a most judicious English constitutional authority.'[69]

Schultz was not the only one who believed that Greenway was susceptible to influence to move away from Sifton, or who at least was willing to make a major effort to explore the possibility. James Fisher, J.S. Ewart's law partner, who had been president of the Manitoba Liberal Association in 1888 and who had clashed with Sifton in the Manitoba Legislature earlier in March, wrote a long and careful letter to Greenway on March 30. It was marked 'strictly private and confidential' in many places, and stressed that if Greenway should see fit to adopt any of the points proposed, he should not quote Fisher as the source, lest other cabinet members, specifically

69 *Ibid.*, Bourinot to Schultz, April 17, 1895

Sifton, Cameron, and Daniel McMillan, be prejudiced. Fisher's letter was significant not only because he was a Protestant Liberal urging redress of Catholic grievances, but because of the arguments he used to press for settlement of the clash with Ottawa. Fisher used as his point of departure a theory of confederation which accepted both a provincial and a cultural compact. 'I do not believe that Quebec would for one moment remain in the Union and see that compromise done away with,' Fisher warned Greenway.[70]

There is no evidence in the Greenway papers or elsewhere that the premier made any move to follow up the course suggested by Schultz, Bourinot, and Fisher. In any case, the real power in the Manitoba government was not Greenway; the man behind the effective decisions continued to be the attorney general, Clifford Sifton. In his letter of March 11 commending McCarthy on the latter's presentation before the federal cabinet, Sifton spoke of his own commanding position with an almost incredible assurance, at the same time giving an inside look at the Manitoba government tactics:

I had thought somewhat of proroguing our legislature at once before the order was made. In consideration however, this seems to me inadvisable. It would look to my mind as though the Government had prorogued the Legislature in order to avoid meeting the question fairly and squarely. I think therefore that we will take no unusual action but pursue the same course that we would if the question were not up … There is no reason … why we should give our answer immediately after we receive a copy of the order. We are entitled to take a reasonable time to consider it, and will probably do so.[71]

Prime Minister Bowell at least suspected who held the reins of power when he commented on Sifton's intrusion into Ontario provincial politics in April.[72] Similarly, Archbishop Langevin was sure that Greenway was under Sifton's thumb: 'Greenway voudrait faire quelque chose, mais Sifton le guette pour le jetter par dessus bord,' Langevin wrote to Bégin.[73]

---

70 PAM, Greenway Papers, Fisher to Greenway, March 30, 1895. Fisher followed this with a similar message to Bowell. Although the letter is not extant in the Bowell Papers, it is clear from Bowell's reply that he received it and that he largely shared Fisher's apprehension (see below, p.86).
71 PAC, Sifton Papers, Sifton to McCarthy, March 11, 1895
72 PAC, Bowell Papers, Bowell to Fisher, April 23, 1895
72 AAQ, April 6, 1895

Greenway did nothing to give Langevin further encouragement; thus the policy of the Manitoba government remained as Sifton and Cameron had stated it before the remedial order.[74] Meanwhile, the order had made Laurier the focus of a renewed struggle in the East. *L'Electeur* sounded the note which would be the theme of Quebec Liberal reaction to all Conservative attempts at remedial action throughout the crisis: 'Il ne remédie rien du tout.'[75] From Nova Scotia on March 22, Colin McIsaac sent Laurier the near-ultimatum of a soldier heading for the trenches. Reinforcing the opinion he had expressed on March 4, McIsaac felt that in view of the government's declaration of policy on the Manitoba school question the Liberals could not hope to succeed 'without being able to show that you approve of the policy of the government on this question.' McIsaac said that it was important that he be able to speak with the assurance of Laurier's clear backing and concluded by requesting a letter from him approving remedial legislation. 'With such a letter,' he stated, 'I have no fear of the result; without it I do not think it wise to contest the county.'[76]

Premier A.G. Blair of New Brunswick did not want to advise Laurier on specific steps. He did, however, stress the absolute need to seek a policy which would reduce religious antagonism. At least he was pleased that a session rather than an election had been called to follow the remedial order. 'An election immediately upon this remedial order,' he wrote, 'would have set the whole Protestant part of the Dominion aflame, it seems to me – it certainly would have done so here in a large portion of New Brunswick.' As for a politico-religious conflict, he recalled the anguish of the New Brunswick school struggle in the 1870s and made a worried prophecy: 'I have been through one, although it was mild in its character compared with what I fear may be the case in this present instance.'[77]

On March 24 a long and articulate letter came from Benjamin Russell of Halifax, professor at the Dalhousie University Law School and future Liberal member of Halifax. He told Laurier that his object was not to impose his views, but to correct the impression which he believed had been

74 Sifton was also the recipient of a copy of the Bourinot opinion from Lieutenant Governor Schultz. His reaction was calm and noncommittal. On May 1 he replied to Schultz: 'I have pleasure in acknowledging receipt of your favor of the 26th ultimo enclosing a copy of Dr. Bourniot's [*sic*] opinion in regard to the school matter which I have perused very carefully.' (PAC, Sifton Papers, Sifton to Schultz, May 1, 1895.) But this was the last reference to the constitutional expert in the Sifton Papers.
75 *L'Electeur*, March 26, 1895
76 PAC, Laurier Papers, McIsaac to Laurier, March 23, 1895
77 *Ibid.*, Blair to Laurier, March 23, 1895

given to the Liberal leader by a mutual friend, a Mr Forbes, that he, Russell, favoured opposition to the remedial action of the government. Russell stated that his initial reaction had indeed favoured such opposition, not out of Protestant feeling – 'I have not a particle,' he said – but 'that we should in the words of Mr. Blake, concede to the province "the right to do wrong," if she chooses.' He further believed that racial and religious tensions had been 'greatly aggravated by the Dominion Government's action, and that passions have been inflamed which it will be difficult to allay, perhaps in our lifetime,' and that Laurier could probably carry the country by flatly opposing the government action.

On thinking the matter over, however, Russell wrote, he had come to a quite different conclusion. First from the point of view of the long range good of the party, strong opposition to remedial action would leave Laurier 'supported by a phalanx of Orangemen inspired by no respect whatever for provincial rights – witness their action on the Jesuits' Estates Bill – but inflamed solely by a furious and fanatical Protestant bigotry.' Even if the Liberals wanted them, Russell doubted that such people would ever be a 'lasting and reliable source of strength … Still further, if the thing were possible, I very greatly doubt if this country would be worth living in, with its population divided into two bitterly hostile factions.' Russell's proposal was far from spectacular, but it contradicted the Sifton-Willison position: 'Acquiesce with as good a grace as we can command in the general remedial policy of the Gov't., steer clear if we can of anything that savors of dictation to the provincial authority, — let the rest of us resume the old fight over the tariff, the scandals, the combines and the general cussedness of the govt...' Russell admitted that the government might manage to take all the credit for remedial action in the Catholic constituencies, but felt this might be counter-balanced in other ways. Laurier might get the more important credit, Russell concluded, for 'a patriotic forbearance in not yielding to the temptation to accept the challenge and involve the Dominion in a war of religion and a war of races.'[78] The Halifax law professor thus represented the case of an important Liberal who had changed his mind on the best policy to follow, and, like David Mills, demonstrated that the division within the party was not simply a Catholic-Protestant or French-English split.

As had been the case before March 21, however, the most important exchange entered into by Laurier after the appearance of the remedial order was that with J.S. Willison. The *Globe* had immediately reacted to the

[78] *Ibid.*, Russell to Laurier, March 24, 1895

order-in-council with a series of strong attacks heavily overlaid with provincial rights' arguments.[79] In a warning note the day the document appeared, Laurier had requested moderation from the editor,[80] but Willison, supported by Mulock and Cartwright, insisted that Ontario Liberals would only accept a more belligerent stand.[81] David Mills, echoed by Frank Anglin, argued in precisely the opposite direction, and denounced the *Globe*'s 'drivel' as calculated to 'prevent the men in Parliament from fulfilling their duty,' and to 'drive all the Catholics into the ministerial camp.'[82] The essence of the debate between Laurier and Willison was contained in an exchange at the end of March. Writing from his home in Arthabaska, Laurier challenged the Toronto editor's provincial rights' stand in a carefully worded letter. The Liberal leader began with a statement of the need to adopt a 'governing principle' in framing a policy, and conceded that Willison had indeed done this in his adamant pro-province stand. In a dramatic series of questions based upon the provisions of section 93 of the BNA Act, however, Laurier attempted to undermine the logic of Willison's position. 'How is it possible,' Laurier demanded, 'to talk of provincial rights, when by the very letter of the constitution jurisdiction is given to the Federal authorities to review and override provincial legislation? What is the use of giving an appeal to the minority, if the appeal is to be heard only to be denied? ... It seems to me beyond doubt that in such matters the provincial sovereignty is abridged, and that this is not a case where provincial rights can be invoked.'

Willison answered Laurier's argument with an equally forceful letter on April 1. He agreed that the legal point of provincial rights was not the paramount issue; sound public policy and feasibility had been the objective sought by the *Globe*. 'Your own statement made to me more than once,' he reminded Laurier, 'was that when you had to decide you would decide for Manitoba.' Willison admitted that a case might be construed where federal power would have the duty to interfere. But effectiveness and the general interest of confederation had to be remembered.

I doubt very much if in any conceivable case federal interference in a province could be effective. The difficulty in the case of Manitoba is that the Privy Council

---

79 See in particular March 23, 1895
80 PAC, Willison Papers, Laurier to Willison, March 21, 1895
81 PAC, Laurier Papers, Willison to Laurier, March 22, 1895; Mulock to Laurier, March 25, 1895; Cartwright to Laurier, March 25, 1895
82 PAC, Laurier Papers, Mills to Laurier, March 28, 1895; Anglin to Laurier, March 26, 1895

declares, as it would not declare in the case of Ontario or Quebec, that is was within the competence of the Manitoba legislature to pass the Manitoba school law. The Dominion Parliament may give remedial legislation but it seems to me simply a matter of public policy and in this view I think I am sustained by the whole tenor of the argument before the Privy Council as to whether or not it would be in the general interest of Confederation that Dominion interference would be exercised.

Willison repeated that he was not trying to force Laurier's hand, and said that he could 'quite understand that you do not want to go to the length of positively declaring that there shall not be in any event, Dominion legislation for the relief of the Manitoba minority.' Nonetheless, Willison insisted, 'if Mr. Greenway resists Dominion legislation, it will be an ill day for the country when the attempt was made to exercise federal power in that province.'[83]

On the surface, the point at issue between Laurier and Willison was the degree to which the principle of provincial rights was to be allowed to be the deciding factor in the school case. For Laurier, at least, the problem was a good deal more complicated. As federal Liberal leader, he had to face the prospect of a small provincial party deciding not only the direction but even the fate of the national party. Finally, and however unspoken it remained during the exchange, was the racial and religious question. Laurier himself may not have faced the issue squarely even in his own mind, but it must be wondered how much of Willison's position depended on the fact that the minority right involved was French and Catholic. The editor repeatedly disclaimed any prejudice against separate schools or French privileges, yet it does not seem that he ever seriously grappled with the dilemma of the compromises of confederation, such as those suggested by Fisher to Greenway.[84] In any case, although the tone of the *Globe*'s articles may have been modified by Laurier's protests, Willison's position at least negatively won the day. Laurier's answers to Anglin in early April showed

83 PAC, Laurier Papers, Laurier to Willison, March 30, 1895; Willison Papers, Willison to Laurier, April 1, 1895
84 Paul Stevens, in his extensive coverage of this and subsequent Laurier–Willison confrontations, argues quite convincingly that the differences between the two men were largely attributable to their respective professions of politician and journalist ['Laurier and the Liberal Party in Ontario,' (thesis), pp.106–13]. Stevens' conclusion, however, that their division was 'more apparent than real,' does not seem sufficient to explain the sharpness of the exchange between the two men, particularly in view of Willison's account of the ordeal he was subjected to in Ottawa in an attempt by Laurier and others to 'turn' the *Globe* (Willison to Dafoe, March 7, 1923, quoted in Colquhoun, *Press, Politics and People*, p.40).

the degree to which the Liberal leader had been persuaded by the *Globe* editor. Laurier reminded his Irish-Catholic supporter how easy it would be for a strong pro-Catholic stance to evoke a Protestant counter-thrust, 'as weeds in an old pasture,' and even praised the *Globe* for recent efforts in promoting religious tolerance. Laurier encouraged Anglin to continue his contacts with Archbishop Walsh, 'by far the wisest and ablest of all the dignitaries in our church at the present time.' At the same time, the Liberal chief made it clear that he had now decided 'not to open my mouth until Parliament meets.' As for political strategy, Laurier told Anglin he was convinced that the government had, with the remedial order, 'exhausted their good intentions, and will never go any further.' As for a positive suggestion, Laurier was reduced to the point which would become his talisman for the coming year – an investigation. 'This may not be necessary for the Catholics,' Laurier concluded, but it could only be 'a great help with the Protestant community.'[85]

An important by-product of this first clash over remedialism was that Laurier again gave serious consideration to resignation as party leader. At the very time of the debate with Willison, the Liberal leader, recuperating from illness at his home, sent two long letters discussing his proposal to retire to C.S. Hyman of London. The impression of these letters and of Hyman's replies is that only with difficulty was Laurier persuaded to hold firm and await developments.[86] Whatever the seriousness of Laurier's vacillation, the conclusion which emerges from the mass of correspondence among Liberal leaders in March and early April 1895 supports Willison's claim to a major role in determining Liberal policy at this crucial juncture. According to the editor, Laurier later admitted with gratitude that the *Globe* had 'driven us into the course we have taken.'[87] J.I. Tarte's role in bringing Laurier to feel confident about Quebec despite Liberal opposition to direct remedial action clearly followed upon these first key pressures exerted above all by Willison.[88] At the very least it can be said that Willison's stance, despite compelling political and legal arguments to the contrary, succeeded in convincing Laurier to remain uncommitted for the moment and to begin his troubled but definite shift to the policy of non-interference. In comparison with the deteriorating position of Prime Minister Bowell, Laurier had passed through the first crisis over remedialism relatively unscathed.

85 PAC, Laurier Papers, Laurier to Anglin, April 2, 1895
86 *Ibid.*, Laurier to Hyman, March 28, 1895, April 1, 1895
87 Willison to Dafoe, March 7, 1923, in Colquhoun, *Press, Politics and People*, p.41
88 See LaPierre, 'Politics, Race and Religion in French Canada' (thesis), p.279.

3
Remedialism and clerical action: first skirmish

In the spring of 1895, two events took place in the clerical world which would influence ecclesiastical thought and action for the duration of the Manitoba school crisis. The first of these was the consecration by Archbishop Fabre of Archbishop Langevin on March 19 in St Boniface. Senator Bernier had doubts about the thirty-nine-year-old archbishop – 'inflammable, avec peu d'expérience,' he called Langevin – but hoped that the newly acquired responsibility would moderate his impulsiveness.[1] The ubiquitous Colonel Audet wanted Langevin to use the occasion of his consecration to rally the attending bishops to 'le vrai conservatisme,'[2] but most of the congratulatory letters the archbishop received expressed sympathy for the difficult situation which he was inheriting. On March 30 Langevin wrote to Bégin thanking the Quebec archbishop for attending the ceremony, then launched into a political commentary. He spoke of the opening of the Manitoba legislature, the absence of Greenway because of illness, a 'discours enragé' by Sifton on the school question and the remedial order, but also of the possibility that the provincial government might be ready to discuss a compromise. 'Un changement sérieux se fait chez nos ennemis; ils semblent commencer à comprendre que nous avons

---

1 AASB, Bernier to de la Bruère, March 24, 1895
2 *Ibid.*, Audet to Langevin, February 28, 1895

réellement des droits,' Langevin stated.[3] However, as the degree of Sifton's control became clearer, the young archbishop did not long retain much optimism about the Manitoba government.

A second event of importance for its church–state implications was the arrival in Canada of a letter from Cardinal Ledochowski, secretary of the *Congregatio Pro Propaganda Fide* at the Vatican. The letter was dated March 14, arrived on April 3 or 4, and was individually addressed to all members of the Canadian hierarchy. The Roman cardinal warmly approved the efforts of the hierarchy to obtain justice for the Catholics of Manitoba. Above all it was explicit in its condemnation of 'neutral schools': 'Il y a une doctrine, évidemment fausse, qui a cours chez quelques-uns, à savoir qu'il n'y a aucun danger dans les écoles qu'ils appellent neutres, et que ces écoles peuvent être fréquentées sans péril par les enfants catholiques. Doctrine fausse.'[4]

The letter itself did not indicate that it was being sent to all bishops; thus many prelates sent copies to their confreres along with their comments. Bishop Gravel implied that it had been somewhat at his prompting that the Roman letter had been sent.[5] Archbishop Fabre felt that it would encourage not only the Canadian bishops but also those American bishops who had been somewhat dismayed at the Faribault decision of Archbishop Satolli in 1893.[6] Archbishop Langevin, apparently prompted by a quick letter from Bishop Laflèche, suggested that the Ledochowski message might be published or at least made the occasion for a joint statement on the Manitoba school situation by the whole Canadian hierarchy.[7]

The Ontario bishops, however, had other ideas. Apparently before hearing from anyone else, Archbishop Walsh countered anticipated arguments in an anxious note to Bégin. 'I think it would not be wise,' he said,

3 AAQ, Langevin to Bégin, March 30, 1895
4 *Ibid.*, Ledochowski to Canadian Bishops, March 14, 1895
5 *Ibid.*, Gravel to Bégin, April 4, 1895
6 *Ibid.*, Fabre to Bégin, April 4, 1895. The 'Faribault school settlement' was a compromise with the public-school system worked out by Archbishop John Ireland of St Paul and approved by Satolli, apostolic delegate to the United States. Learning that the arrangement he had made was being quoted against the restoration of Catholic school privileges in Manitoba, Ireland hastened to assure Taché that the Minnesota compromise had been dictated by the presumption of 'Church-State separation' in the American constitution. 'Si Mgr. Satolli parlait aux évêques du Manitoba, ou d'autres parties du Canada,' Ireland insisted, 'il tiendrait certainement un langage tout différent.' (AASB, Ireland to Taché, January 24, 1893)
7 AAT, Langevin to Walsh, April 6, 1895

'at this critical juncture of affairs, to publish it in the newspapers, as it would infuriate the Protestants even more than Mercier's Jesuit bill.'[8] Archbishop Cleary was even more explicit. In reply to Langevin's letter, the Kingston archbishop urged that ecclesiastical trumpets remain silent at least for the moment, a remarkable statement in view of Cleary's acknowledged fearlessness. Cleary's rueful estimate of the Ontario atmosphere was that 'the bigots here do not believe that the hierarchy ever does anything publicly, more especially about election times, except for political party purposes.' He warned Langevin that the probable result of an official church statement would be that 'one party would be directly arrayed against us and you in the contest; whereas the question now stands upon the firm basis of the constitution, irrespective of parties.'[9]

Bégin communicated Walsh's opinion to Fabre on April 7, and to Emard and Langevin on April 8. In each case he stated that he agreed with the Toronto archbishop, adding his own exhortation in Langevin's case. He told Langevin that fanatics would say once more that the Pope was trying to take over Canada, but added that the part of the letter on neutral schools might be privately communicated to members of Parliament, especially 'les flottants.'[10] Monsignor J.O. Routhier, vicar general of Ottawa, presumed that a similar opposition to publication of the Roman letter would be very strong in the federal cabinet. He wrote to his friend Sir Adolphe Caron for confirmation of this opinion, adding that the letter had 'quelques paroles d'éloge pour le Conseil Privé & pour le Gouvernement Fédéral.' At the same time, Routhier observed, 'J'ai pensé que cette lettre, si elle était publiée, ferait tort à vos collègues protestants qui sont déjà accusés de se laisser conduire par Rome.'[11] Bishop Emard feared that Archbishop Langevin might make a hasty move and communicated his worry to Bégin:

En même temps que votre lettre du 8 courant, j'en recevais une de Mgr. de St. Boniface qui me parait hésiter en présence des exhortations pressantes de Mgr. Laflèche. Celles-ci, je crois, ne s'accordent pas absolument avec la demande formulée par Mgr. Walsh, qui a l'air de demander du sang froid et de la prudence.

8 AAQ, Walsh to Bégin, April 5, 1895
9 AASB, Cleary to Langevin, April 9, 1895
10 *Ibid.*, Bégin to Langevin, April 8, 1895
11 PAC, Caron Papers, Routhier to Caron, April 8, 1895. Routhier was the elder brother of Judge A.B. Routhier, who was later to be named one of the federal delegates to work on the Laurier-Greenway agreement. The Ottawa monsignor was among those who regarded as disastrous the clerical support being given to the 'Castor' faction in the Conservative party. See below, pp.311–12.

Thus, said Emard, the pressing need was for a general meeting of all the Canadian bishops, from which might issue a firm but moderate statement.[12]

Meanwhile, Emard had sent a letter of thanks to Cardinal Ledochowski for the Vatican directive, leaving no doubt that the Quebec episcopate considered that the question had become a direct federal responsibility. Praising the remedial order, Emard stated that 'il contient explicitement la reconnaissance authentique de droits lésés des catholiques, et logiquement il met le gouvernement fédéral dans l'obligation d'agir et de remédier à un ordre de choses illégal et illégitime si le gouvernement local refuse de le faire lui-même.' Concerning episcopal determination to speak out if necessary, Emard sounded as adamant as Laflèche.[13] By April 10 Emard had concluded that the 'révendications' he had spoken of to Ledochowski did not include publication of the Roman letter or an appeal to the electorate by the bishops. The opinions of archbishops Cleary and Walsh had had their impact, and Emard posed some searching questions for Langevin's consideration in a letter which revealed some apprehension over the new archbishop's impulsiveness.

Cet appel à l'électorat a besoin d'être bien étudié. Est-il nécessaire pour faire connaître la pensée des Evêques? donne-t-il du poids à leurs réclamations? ne jettera-t-il pas contre nous sans profit toute la masse protestante? ne déroutera-t-il pas les catholiques eux-mêmes par suite des déclarations ambigues des candidats? nous-donnera-t-il un homme de plus en chambre? ne nous enlevera-t-il pas quelques-uns du coté protestant? Questions bien graves, qui demandent à être discutées plus qu'elles ne l'ont été.

Emard renewed his insistence that if anything were to be done, it should be by the bishops of all the provinces together. 'Vous savez,' Emard wrote, 'il y a des tempéraments ardents et qui croient qu'il faut toujours soulever le public; mais à quoi tout cela peut-il aboutir quand on cherche un dénouement constitutionnel?'[14]

There was little doubt concerning the sympathies of Bishop Laflèche. A letter to Archbishop Fabre showed that he wanted to remain firm in episcopal support of the Conservative remedial order, and that if a public statement were necessary to counter any opposite impression, there should be no hedging. A Montreal ecclesiastical journal, *La Croix*, im-

12 AAQ, Emard to Bégin, April 10, 1895
13 AEV, Emard to Ledochowski, April 4, 1895
14 AASB, Emard to Langevin, April 10, 1895

mediately following the issuance of the remedial order, had published an article criticizing the order and the government as ineffective in bringing justice to the Catholics of Manitoba. Laflèche protested against this would-be voice of the clergy attacking the order-in-council without sufficient reflection, and wanted Fabre publicly to disavow the article.[15] Fabre found it difficult to devise a happy solution. He sent a letter to his priests, describing the *La Croix* article as 'maladroit,' and forbidding pulpit discussions of the political situation. Yet even this was considered too mild by Conservatives, since it did not condemn the Liberals.[16]

THE VERCHERES BY-ELECTION

Further correspondence made it clear that the key to the urgency in the Laflèche letter was the by-election soon to be held in the riding of Verchères. This riding, one of four to be contested on April 17, included sections from two dioceses, Montreal and St Hyacinthe. There was no doubt that the vote would be regarded as a test of French-Canadian reaction to the government's Manitoba school policy. As Bishop Emard put it to Archbishop Langevin, 'l'élection de Verchères, il ne faut pas dissimuler la chose, aura une grande influence sur la question de vos écoles.' At the same time, Emard added, 'cette élection se fait dans de très curieuses conditions.'[17]

The 'curious conditions' centred on the question of how much politicians would pressure bishops, and how much ecclesiastical pressure would be placed on voters. One of the key figures approached was Archbishop Langevin himself. His friend Colonel Audet had no hesitation in urging the prelate to appeal for full ecclesiastical support for the Conservative candidate, F.J. Bisaillon, against the Liberal, C.A. Geoffrion, brother of the late deputy for the same riding. Audet reminded Langevin that there were only four Catholics as against eleven Protestants in the cabinet. What would happen, he asked, if clear support did not come from Catholic Quebec? If, on the other hand, the bishops threw their weight clearly behind the Conservative candidate and the long-time Liberal stronghold of Verchères were taken, the episcopal bargaining position would be very strong.[18]

Colonel Audet did not discuss what would happen to the episcopal

15 AAM, Laflèche to Fabre, March 23, 1895
16 PAC, Caron Papers, Fabre to Routhier, April 9, 1895
17 AASB, Emard to Langevin, April 12, 1895
18 *Ibid.*, Audet to Langevin, April 3, 1895

position if they failed, but Langevin was sufficiently impressed to send strong letters to his Quebec colleagues, Bégin, Duhamel, and Fabre. It was not that Langevin was prepared to accept the Conservative policy without criticism. To Bégin he explained, 'Il faut que le Gouvernement d'Ottawa comprenne qu'il doit en faire une question de gouvernement, son affaire!' A few days later he wrote, 'Ouimet aurait dit à Montreal que le Gouvernement n'interviendra pas durant cette session;' then, heavily underlined, '*Mail il faut qu'il intervienne absolument* – nous sommes étranglés ici, voilà bientôt cinq ans que nous souffrons!' On the other hand, Langevin did not hesitate to choose between support for the Conservatives as against a possible Liberal alternative.[19] In a letter to Duhamel, Langevin repeated the same reservations on Ottawa's timidity that he had expressed to Bégin, but he did not hesitate to endorse the political deal expected by the government; he echoed the same sentiments in attempting to influence Archbishop Fabre.[20]

It was much against his will that the centre of attention and pressure fell on Fabre of Montreal. Prime Minister Bowell revealed a good deal when he wrote a short note to J.A. Ouimet on April 6. Among other things, Bowell seemed to presume that the remedial order involved a frank 'quid pro quo' deal with the bishops for their support and that he feared that the Liberals were attempting the same tactic.

I have just learned that Geoffrion has made arrangements with the Bishops and Clergy that he is to go to Vercheres and denounce Laurier for his silence on the Manitoba School Question, and on that condition they accepted him. If this be true, it seems that they are playing us false. You had better attend to it.[21]

Both Ouimet and Caron quickly moved to 'attend to it.' Ouimet contacted Bishop Moreau of St Hyacinthe and received an encouraging reply. Moreau first mentioned two pastors of his own diocese whose parishes were in Verchères; 'ce qu'ils pourront faire, ils le ferront,' he told Ouimet. Moreau then turned his attention to Archbishop Fabre, and assured Ouimet that the Montreal prelate was solidly on the Conservative side.[22] Archbishop Fabre's own letters showed him to be a good deal less confident than Moreau portrayed him. To Archbishop Bégin on April 5,

19 AAQ, Langevin to Bégin, April 12, 1895
20 AAQ, Langevin to Duhamel, April 6, 1895; AAM, Langevin to Fabre, April 11, 1895
21 PAC, Bowell Papers, Bowell to Ouimet, April 6, 1895
22 AESH, Moreau to Ouimet, April 10, 1895

Fabre wrote that the by-election was something he would like to ignore but was not being allowed to:

L'élection de Verchères nous donne de l'ennui. La Presse prétend que j'ai eu une entrevue hier avec M. Geoffrion a 2h. Or j'étais à la Longue Pointe dans ce moment-là. Je crains que les conservateurs attachent trop d'importance à cette élection. Ce comté est rouge depuis plus de trente ans ... Le candidat Geoffrion est le frère de celui qui representait le comté depuis tant d'années. Il est du comté, puis possède la confiance comme homme de loi de presque tous les habitants ... Le candidat conservateur est un étranger au comté.[23]

This may have been a good analysis of the political situation in Verchères, but it was not enough for Adolphe Caron. Through Monsignor Routhier, Caron communicated his thoughts to Fabre in what can only be described as raw political pressure. Routhier told of a meeting with Caron, in which the postmaster general had conveyed 'ses secrets et ses craintes au sujet de l'élection de Verchères.' Routhier's argument tightly identified the interests of party and religion; he went so far as to suggest that Fabre should use his 'influence extraordinaire' to persuade Geoffrion to withdraw from the contest.[24] That Caron and Routhier should have even attempted such an overture with Fabre revealed that the Conservatives were either out of touch concerning clerical potential in elections or, what is more likely, were clutching at straws to avert disaster in Quebec.

On the same day as he sent this letter to Fabre, Routhier dashed off a note to Caron in which he expressed doubts about the Montreal archbishop's political leanings. He enclosed a quotation from Fabre's controversial letter to his priests on the *La Croix* article, in which the Montreal prelate spoke of the obligations which would fall on the federal government, without mentioning the silence of the Liberal opposition. Taking for granted that the Liberals ought to have been condemned, Routhier quoted Fabre's outline of visible alternatives, now that the order-in-council had been given: 'quoiqu'il en soit, son [Manitoba's] refus d'adopter une mesure que réclament, de l'aveu de tous, la justice et le respect de la constitution, donnerait le droit au pouvoir fédéral, et lui imposerait le devoir d'intervenir directement et de remédier lui-même à l'état de choses actuel.'[25] Clearly the problem from Routhier's point of view was that Fabre, instead of taking

23 AAQ, Fabre to Bégin, April 5, 1895
24 AAM, Routhier to Fabre, April 8, 1895
25 PAC, Caron Papers, Routhier to Caron, April 8, 1895

sides against the Liberals, had required from his priests 'un silence absolu sur cette question brûlante et délicate.'

Fabre's reply to Routhier was an eloquent regret that he had been dragged into the political arena at all. The Montreal prelate was a little sad, a little reproachful, that the government of Canada felt that he could and would directly interfere in an election.

L'affaire de Verchères me préoccupe autant que tout autre et peut-être plus, parce qu'il a plu aux conservateurs de prétendre que je puis faire l'élection. Pour la première fois de ma vie, j'ai vu plusieurs ministres fédéraux et quelques ministres locaux. Ils croient, à tort, que j'ai de l'influence sur M. Geoffrion. N'ayant jamais parlé politique avec lui et de fait n'ayant que des rapports assez rares avec lui, je ne puis pas prétendre être tellement influent que de la détourner d'une élection quand il est déjà sur les rangs.

Fabre said he had seen Geoffrion socially on New Year's Day and that, on earlier occasions, their contacts had been mostly over legal matters. To Fabre, the whole affair had been magnified beyond all proportion, and he reminded Routhier that 'on voudrait me pousser à faire une démarche que l'on blâmerait dans toute autre circonstance.'[26]

Fabre's letter had some effect. As soon as he had received it, Routhier sent it along to Caron with the comment: 'Je m'empresse de vous communiquer la lettre de Mgr. Fabre. Mgr. n'est pas si coupable que je le pensais et que les journaux le disaient. Le comté de Verchères a toujours été rouge. Espérons cependant encore au succès. La défaite dans Verchères sera bien la condamnation des libéraux sur la question des écoles.' Routhier did not say what a Conservative defeat would mean, but he concluded with a lament which would have been a fitting ecclesiastical refrain for the entire school crisis: 'Il est si difficile de conduire le peuple.'[27]

On April 10, Fabre wrote again to Bégin, indicating that Geoffrion had explicitly supported remedial action. 'Il n'est pas facile d'intervenir,' Fabre insisted. 'Ce serait plus aisé s'il s'agissait d'une élection générale. Dans le cas actuel, M. Geoffrion a parlé en faveur de l'ordre en conseil. Que dire alors? Il faudra le prendre comme membre de l'opposition.' Finally, as in his letter to Routhier, Fabre indicated that the irony of the situation did not escape him. 'J'avais coutume d'être ignoré du ministère fédéral,' he

26 PAC, Caron Papers, Fabre to Routhier, April 9, 1895. A copy of this letter was sent to Routhier's superior, Archbishop Duhamel.
27 *Ibid.*, Routhier to Caron, April 9, 1895

wrote. '*Cette fois il n'en est pas ainsi* ... Les ministres fédéraux et locaux ne manqueront pas d'en parler à Votre Grandeur.'[28]

A subsequent letter to Bégin concerning Ouimet showed how concentrated that gentleman's pressure on Fabre had been, and how little Fabre had cooperated. Speaking of Ouimet, Fabre said:

Quoique ce Monsieur m'a toujours temoigné beaucoup de confiance ... je dois dire qu'il n'a pas été content de moi dans l'élection de Verchères. Jusqu'à présent j'étais ignoré à Ottawa. Cette année trois ministres m'ont fait visite et ont voulu me pousser à faire un acte imprudent en prenant le devant pour combattre M. Geoffrion. Je leur ai dit que la chose était impossible. M. Ouimet a été plus contrarié que les autres.[29]

The barrage of visitors and letter-writers managed to get one move from Fabre. Apparently to counteract the impression that his first letter to his priests had been a veiled criticism of the remedial order, as Routhier and others had concluded, Fabre sent a second private letter to his clergy. The archbishop stated that the earlier prohibition applied only to public pronouncements from the pulpit and did not preclude private expressions of support for the federal remedial order. Routhier was quick to pass on this second letter to Caron, saying that it was 'autant que j'attendais.'[30]

On April 16, the day before the election, Routhier sent Caron another note. He was pessimistic enough to feel compelled to defend himself over the Fabre affair. 'La circulaire de Mgr. Fabre fait bien du bruit, mais j'espère au succès. Elle arrive peut-être trop tard, mais ce n'est pas ma faute,' he wrote.[31] The Conservative newspapers continued to insist that Catholic rights could be upheld only if Conservatives were supported. The Liberal journal, *L'Electeur*, in particular, recognized the bishop's right to speak, because 'c'est une question plutôt religieuse que politique,' but they roundly denounced the Conservative attempt to get episcopal endorsement for one party against the other.[32] *La Minerve*, on the other hand, stated with pious detachment on election day that 'nos lecteurs savent que Mgr. Fabre, archévêque de Montreal, Mgr. Moreau, évêque de Sainte-Hyacinthe, et Mgr. Decelles, son coadjuteur, approuvent hautement

28 AAQ, Fabre to Bégin, April 10, 1895 (Fabre's italics)
29 *Ibid.*, Fabre to Bégin, August 4, 1895
30 PAC, Caron Papers, Routhier to Caron, April 11, 1895
31 *Ibid.*, Routhier to Caron, April 16, 1895
32 April 16, 1895

l'ordre en conseil remédiateur adopté par le gouvernement fédéral. Nous sommes en position de dire que l'opinion exprimée par ces éminents prélats est partagée par tous les autres membres de l'épiscopat canadien.'[33] Whatever the truth of the Conservative newspapers' claim about episcopal support, the result of the vote on April 17 was what had been expected by the realists on both sides; the Liberal Geoffrion defeated the Conservative Bisaillon.[34]

The significance of the Verchères by-election was more far-reaching than the difference of a single seat in the House. The Conservatives had been willing to employ heavy pressure to exploit church influence for political gain. The correspondence showed that some clerical influence was mobilized, although not nearly as much as the Conservatives would have liked, nor enough to bring sustained Liberal protest. The result indicated that, at least in a traditionally Liberal Quebec riding, reaction to the existing state of the school question was not enough to bring a substantial gain to the Conservatives.

ANTIGONISH AND HALDIMAND: MORE TROUBLE FOR THE CONSERVATIVES

Meanwhile, two of the other by-elections were being strongly affected by the school question and the federal remedial order. One of these was Antigonish, Sir John Thompson's former riding, and the scene of battle described by Colin McIsaac in his March letters to Laurier. Once again the Conservatives showed no hesitation in seeking episcopal support for their candidate. In Bishop Cameron of Antigonish, Prime Minister Bowell knew he would find a willing supporter, but he wanted to leave no stone unturned. Thus he wrote to A.R. Dickey, secretary of state, who was visiting his mother in Amherst, Nova Scotia, asking the cabinet minister to call on the bishop. Once again the main theme was the 'Catholic vote'; if it were not forthcoming, the presumption would be heavily against pursuing remedial action in favour of Manitoba Catholics.

In the opposing political camp, pressure was being continued on Wilfrid Laurier for a statement which would offset somewhat the pro-coercion speeches being made by Conservatives in Antigonish in early April. As he

33 April 17, 1895
34 L'Electeur, April 18, 1895. The evidence presented here substantially revises the picture of a fairly active and enthusiastic pro-Conservative intervention on the part of Archbishop Fabre suggested by Rumilly, Histoire, VII, p.216–18.

and the Liberal candidate, Colin McIsaac, had done in March, Senator
L.G. Power of Halifax begged Laurier for a declaration in favour of restoring Catholic rights in Manitoba. Power reminded Laurier of the latter's
statement that he did not want to gain office on the school issue. He said
that the Conservatives were making the Manitoba school question 'an issue
and substantially the only issue in Antigonish and I presume also in Verchères and the other Quebec constituencies where elections are to be run
before the session.' The result, in his judgment, was that 'if you remain in
your present attitude, which is understood here to be non-committal, we
shall certainly lose Antigonish, and probably the majority of the constituencies both at the by and general elections.'

Power admitted that the evident source of trouble was the 'indefensible
conduct of the Manitoba government,' and he felt that the obvious solution
was to 'settle with the Catholics and take the matter out of Dominion
politics.' This would allow the federal Liberals to 'deal with the Government on their general record where we would be sure to beat them.' But
facts could not be wished away, and Power's conclusion was to stress again
the gravity of the situation:

I may be mistaken, but if I am, so are the majority of your friends here and in
Antigonish. Tupper is to be challenged at the meeting tomorrow as to the government policy, and his answer may modify the position a little; but in my opinion our
policy is to stand by the rights of the Catholics as recognized by the constitutional
act of Manitoba.[35]

There is no record of Laurier's reply or of any formal statement from the
Liberal leader of the kind requested by Power. Nevertheless, both Power's
and McIsaac's letters indicated that they endorsed remedial action, if not
the remedial order devised by the government. On April 17, McIsaac was
elected by a margin of 118 votes, reversing the 222-vote majority which the
riding had given Sir John Thompson in 1891.[36]

Concerning the third riding in which the school question was an important factor, Haldimand in Ontario, Laurier received two significant letters
on April 3. The first of these was from Alexander Smith, secretary of the
Ontario Liberal Association. Smith first of all assured Laurier that his
position as the leader of the party was being questioned less and less in
Ontario. The policy of keeping quiet on the school question was also

35 PAC, Laurier Papers, Power to Laurier, April 5, 1895
36 Toronto *Globe*, April 18, 1895

receiving wider acceptance, Smith reported. As others had done, Smith informed Laurier that several Conservatives had told him that they believed the federal government would not bring in remedial legislation during the coming session and that this gave Laurier even better grounds for saying nothing. As for Haldimand, Smith felt strongly that it would be a mistake to send a Liberal candidate into the struggle at the last moment. D'Alton McCarthy had entered a candidate on a straight anti-interference platform. Surely it would be better, Smith said, to let the Conservatives and McCarthyites fight it out. Clifford Sifton and Stewart Mulvey of the Manitoba Orange Lodge were coming down to help McCarthy. Why not leave them alone, Smith suggested, and thus avoid taking a definite stand when the likelihood of gain was very small?[37]

A second letter reinforced the position urged by Smith. This was from Edward Farrer of the *Globe*, a journalist whose booklet on the reciprocity and annexation problem had caused high excitement during the 1891 federal election.[38] While he did not suggest an overt alliance, Farrer indicated how McCarthy might be useful to the Liberals both in ideas and practical cooperation. In the journalist's opinion, the Liberals had no choice but to work with the Barrie lawyer, since 'without doubt the remedial order has greatly strengthened McCarthy.'[39]

In any case, no Liberal candidate was presented in Haldimand. Sifton campaigned for the McCarthyite candidate, Jeffrey McCarthy, in a manner which was hardly characterized by restraint. So steeped in anti-French and anti-Catholic sentiment were Sifton's speeches, that the *Mail and Empire*, now moderated though hardly pro-Catholic, found it easy to charge the Manitoba attorney general with extreme prejudice and simple falsehood.[40] At the same time, the Conservative candidate, W.H. Montague, seems to have presented the remedial order as the probable end to federal action, and Laurier had no hesitation in charging the Conservatives with such a minimal interpretation when he discussed the matter with Archbishop Langevin in May.[41] Despite Sifton's presence, Montague won the seat by a margin of 594 votes.[42]

The fourth by-election held on April 17 was in the riding of Quebec West. Here the school question does not seem to have been such a burning

37 PAC, Laurier Papers, Smith to Laurier, April 3, 1895
38 See Waite, *Canada 1874–1896*, p.222.
39 *Ibid.*, Farrer to Laurier, April 3, 1895
40 April 16, 1895
41 *Ibid.*, April 12, 1895. See below, p.90.
42 *Ibid.*, April 18, 1895

issue. The result was the defeat of R.R. Dobell, running as an Independent, by the Independent Conservative, Thomas McGreevy, the man who had been involved in the patronage scandal which had ruined the career of Sir Hector Langevin.

The outcome of the by-elections of April 17 showed two Liberal victories and two Conservative. Once past, however, the Conservatives were much less inclined to view the tests of strength as the 'question de vie ou de mort' which had been presented to Archbishop Fabre by Caron and others before the contest. Prime Minister Bowell made a virtue out of necessity and made excuses for the losses in a letter to Adam Brown of Hamilton. 'Antigonish,' he wrote, 'has always been Liberal until captured by Sr. John Thompson, and although we thought there was a good fighting chance, still we had little hope of carrying it.' Verchères was a similar case, Bowell said, and in Quebec West, Dobell in many ways would have been preferable to McGreevy and the lingering unsavoriness connected with the latter, his brother and Sir Hector Langevin. In any case, Bowell argued, 'Haldimand more than counterbalances all the others. The slap that our good friend Dalton has got in the face, I hope will do him good. However, we will see what he will do next. He has lost his head, and worse than that I am afraid he has lost any principles he ever had.'[43]

Whatever the comfort gained by retaining the Haldimand seat, the situation within the Conservative party was deteriorating, and the other by-election defeats, especially that in Verchères, had speeded up the process. The McCarthyite wing and its sympathizers still within the party were the main problem on the English side; the divisions within the French contingent were, if anything, more ominous. Even before the by-elections Bowell had been compelled to make a number of statements to insist that the representative of the 'Castor' wing in the cabinet, A.R. Angers, was not 'on the block.' To Senator J.J. Ross, member of the Quebec Legislative Council and former premier, Bowell wrote in agitation that he could not be responsible for every rumour started by the Liberal press, 'nor can I help the talk of those who no doubt would like to see the change to which you refer. Of one thing I can assure you. There is no one in the Cabinet for whom I have a higher respect, and in whose party fidelity I have more confidence, than our friend Mr. Angers. Under the circumstances, it is not at all likely that he will be sacrificed by me.'[44] The events of July and

43 PAC, Bowell Papers, Bowell to Brown, April 19, 1895
44 *Ibid.*, Bowell to Ross, April 11, 1895. J.J. Ross, 'whose Scotch name and French tongue bore witness to the assimilating effect of generations of French mothers' (Skelton, *Laurier*, 1, p.478), had been, since 1891, speaker of the Senate. Not unimportantly, he was also known as a good friend of Bishop Laflèche.

August would provide an interesting commentary on this statement, but the rumour was not isolated. Bowell was obliged to make a similar denial to Alphonse Charlebois, Quebec City organizer, and to reveal that he had received several other challenges on the same subject.[45]

Colonel Audet was prepared to blame Ouimet for the Verchères defeat. He wrote to Archbishop Langevin that the actions of the minister of public works and the rest of the Bleu wing of the Conservatives were leading to a general Liberal takeover in Quebec, 'la victoire des libéraux qui pourrait ruiner à jamais vos libertés.'[46] Arthur Dansereau, postmaster of Montreal and confidant of Adolphe Chapleau, saw the other side of the question. To him, Ouimet had been thrust into the Verchères fight much against his will and had been forced to proclaim things which were against his better judgment. Two of Ouimet's Quebec lieutenants, G.A. Nantel, MLA, and T.C. Casgrain, M.P., felt the same way and Casgrain had confided his disgust to Dansereau. Describing Casgrain's reflection on Ouimet's situation, Dansereau wrote pessimistically to Chapleau:

Il [Ouimet] nous a confié qu'il était de notre avis et qu'il a été envoyé dans le comté comme un chien qui va à la chasse malgré lui. Il n'y a pas de doute que Ouimet, avec son gros bon sens, sentait l'enormité de la bétise qu'on lui faisait faire, mais il a été entrainé par son mauvais entourage. Le fait est que les trois derniers jours de l'élection, il n'a pas mis les pieds à Montréal, ce qui montre assez son découragement.

Dansereau added that he believed Caron and Ouimet were with difficulty restraining themselves from attacking Angers and the Castors, especially since the Castor journal, *Le Moniteur de Levis*, had been pursuing Caron. 'Je me demande quelle belle vie de communauté ces messieurs vont mener durant la session,' he concluded.[47]

Once again it was evident that more had been at stake in the by-elections than a few votes in Parliament. If they were a test, particularly in Catholic areas, of the federal government's policy on the Manitoba schools, they showed that the policy was not gaining support. Remedial action itself was not necessarily rejected, but the Conservative handling of the question was not endorsed in the way party strategists had stressed as vital before the vote was taken. It was a portent for future results on a larger scale. And the bitter divisions among Quebec Conservatives had been widened at a time when even unanimity might not have saved the situation.

45 *Ibid.*, Bowell to Charlebois, April 11, 1895
46 AASB, Audet to Langevin, April 18, 1895
47 PAC, Chapleau Papers, Dansereau to Chapleau, April 19, 1895

STORM SIGNALS FROM MANITOBA: LANGEVIN MEETS LAURIER

The parliamentary session of 1895 opened on April 18, the day after the by-elections. The Speech from the Throne relegated the school question to a relatively minor place, making a simple reference to the Privy Council decision and the order-in-council sent to Manitoba. The speeches in the subsequent debate, however, did not leave the school issue in obscurity. Laurier referred to the growing divisions within the cabinet and deplored what he called the 'unfortunate language' of the remedial order.[48] George Foster, named government House leader after Thompson's death and Bowell's accession, retorted by pointing out what would be clearly a Liberal as well as a Conservative dilemma, a 'two-faced' policy on remedialism. Citing Tarte and Geoffrion in Verchères, Foster reminded Laurier that his Quebec Liberal followers were finding the order-in-council not dictatorial but too soft.[49] Since the next move belonged to Manitoba, however, the school question moved out of the parliamentary spotlight during May and June.

More than anyone else, Prime Minister Bowell had to be concerned with Manitoba's reaction to the remedial order. In striking contrast, if not contradiction, to the full restoration terms of the remedial order, several of Bowell's letters during April and May suggested that the Manitoba government might make certain minor concessions, and that this would absolve the federal government from further action. On April 23 Bowell sent a reply to James Fisher of Winnipeg, who was trying to arrange a 'gentleman's agreement' between Greenway and the federal government in spite of Sifton. Bowell said he would try to follow some of Fisher's suggestions in seeking a settlement. Referring to Sifton and the statements the latter had made in the Haldimand campaign, Bowell wrote that 'if I may judge your Attorney-General by his recent conduct in Ontario, I should say that he was a man of very little discretion or judgment.' The prime minister said that it had been understood that Sifton had come to Ontario officially to obtain legal counsel. 'Why ... he should have gone into Haldimand and there pledged his Government to a certain line of action, before they could have possibly come to a decision,' Bowell wondered, 'is somewhat incomprehensible. Such conduct, in any other Government, would, beyond doubt, have caused his resignation or dismissal.'[50]

48 Canada, House of Commons, *Debates*, 1895, p.35
49 *Ibid.*, p.51
50 PAC, Bowell Papers, Bowell to Fisher, April 23, 1895

On April 30 and May 1, three coded telegrams went from Bowell to H.H. Smith, a prominent Winnipeg Conservative, all dealing with an 'important letter sent Greenway by Governor General.'[51] Lord Aberdeen's letter included an invitation to Ottawa for a conference, with some hint of 'better terms' for Manitoba. Greenway accepted the invitation, but in his reply he was careful to insist that willingness to discuss the school question 'does not of itself involve any admission of an intent to compromise.' He equally rejected any 'bargain' involving a more favourable financial settlement, since this would 'in all probability lead to a misconstruction of the motives of both parties.'[52]

In any case, the point which emerged most clearly in the months of April, May, and June 1895 was that the Manitoba government and Sifton in particular were determined to do nothing, but to take as much time as possible in the delay. Sifton, once back from the hustings in Ontario, returned to his cool, precise manner,[53] and insisted that the strictest legal argument be used to uphold the Manitoba government position. In an interesting letter sent during the lull before the re-opening of the Manitoba legislature, Sifton explicitly abandoned the straight provincial rights stand. Writing to a supporter who had dwelt exclusively on the provincial versus federal argument, Sifton observed that 'I do not fancy that we can take the very high ground in regard to Provincial Rights that you seem to favor.' The Privy Council decision, he said, made it clear that 'the jurisdiction exists and the fact that the jurisdiction exists carries with it the conclusion that under some possible circumstances it should be exercised.' Sifton's position was that 'although a case might arise in which the jurisdiction should be exercised, yet no case for interference has been made in respect of our school system; in fact any evidence that has been produced goes to show that there ought to be no interference.' The one point to be established, therefore, Sifton concluded, was to show 'that no such case has arisen.'[54]

The Manitoba legislature met again on May 9, but quickly adjourned. Theophile Paré, MLA, wrote to Langevin that the new adjournment had been voted in order to further consider an answer to the federal remedial order. This was evidently part of Sifton's policy of delay, Paré said, and there was little prospect of a change in position; nevertheless, 'mon impression est que le gouvernement est fort embarrassé de la question.' Unhappily, Paré added, his fellow French-Canadian deputy, A.F. Martin, had

51 *Ibid.*, Bowell to Smith, April 30, 1895
52 PAM, Greenway Papers, Greenway to Aberdeen, May 11, 1895
53 For example, PAC, Sifton Papers, Sifton to Schultz, May 1, 1895
54 *Ibid.*, Sifton to John Crerar, May 1, 1895

blundered by talking too long, getting into a trivial argument with James Fisher, who was one of their best supporters, and making too many inflammatory remarks about Sifton's campaign in Haldimand. The result had been that Sifton was able to turn the situation to his own advantage. Paré's conclusion was not all pessimistic, however. 'Le public est fatigué,' he wrote. 'L'opinion se modifie à Manitoba.'[55]

Unfortunately, Archbishop Langevin was not the type to help modify opinion and emotion. Probably the most significant event in the school question issue in the weeks between the April by-elections and the Manitoba reply to the remedial order, was the visit of the St Boniface prelate to Ottawa in April and May and his discussions with government officials and with Wilfrid Laurier. Langevin sent a letter to Prime Minister Bowell on April 25 requesting a meeting, and received a courteous invitation in reply.[56] Bowell was less polite in describing Langevin to others. Hugh John Macdonald had written the prime minister informing him of Langevin's trip; Bowell reported the archbishop's desire for an interview, as well as his propensity for inflammatory public statements.[57] Perhaps at Bowell's suggestion, John Costigan, the New Brunswick Irish-Catholic member of the cabinet, wrote to the archbishop to emphasize that the purpose of the remedial order had been neither delay nor compromise. The only possible compromise, Costigan insisted, would be one which could be accepted by Langevin and the Catholics of Manitoba.[58]

On the Liberal side, the first important figure to contact Langevin was Henri Joly de Lotbinière. Joly wrote that he had informed Laurier of the archbishop's forthcoming visit to Ottawa and that a meeting with the Liberal leader might be arranged. Joly rejected Sifton's extremism, especially his Haldimand statements, yet urged moderation, rather than an equally extreme position in Langevin's reaction. Joly's eloquent plea concluded:

Il semble que cette question d'instruction religieuse devait être, plus qu'aucun autre, envisagée avec modération, sans prejugés et sans passion, que l'on devrait commencer par se mettre à la place de ceux dont les opinions diffèrent des nôtres et

55 AASB, Paré to Langevin, May 11, 1895
56 PAC, Bowell Papers, Bowell to Langevin, April 27, 1895
57 Ibid., Bowell to Macdonald, April 29, 1895. Lady Aberdeen's impression of the new archbishop was equally unflattering. Her Journal described Langevin as 'still under forty & very fiery on the School Question ... very full of anxiety. He also made unwise fighting speeches' (Journal, July 13, 1895, p.235).
58 AASB, Costigan to Langevin, May 6, 1895

se faire un devoir de considérer la question à leur point de vue, aussi bien qu'au nôtre.[59]

The meeting of Langevin with Laurier was arranged for May 8. Alphonse LaRivière, according to his own account, was the one who finally engineered the interview, to take place in a private office at the University of Ottawa.[60] Langevin wrote Laurier three days later to thank him for the meeting, but also to make more explicit certain points which he felt had not been completely clear in the discussion. The archbishop began with a compliment on Laurier's rejection of certain 'doctrines impies et anti-sociales,' but quickly added reservations. Langevin took as his point of departure the amiable generality on which he and the Liberal leader had parted. 'Quand, au moment où vous vous leviez pour partir,' Langevin wrote, 'je vous ai demandé si nous pouvions compter sur vous, je ne me suis pas bien expliqué et je comprends que votre reponse n'ait pas été directe ... Je voulais dire que j'espérais vous voir parmi ceux qui approuvent publiquement l'ordre-en-conseil aussi bien que le jugement du conseil privé.' The archbishop then proceeded to a strong suggestion of guilt by association for those, especially Catholics, who would criticize the remedial order and did not hesitate to contrast the attitude of Bowell and other 'protestants éminents.' 'Je veux espérer encore que vous ne nous forcerez pas à dire que tout n'est fait sans vous – même malgré vous,' Langevin concluded. 'Je répète que quiconque ne recommande et même attaque l'ordre-en-conseil se montre notre ennemi. Celui qui n'est pas carrément pour nous est contre nous.'[61]

Acceptance of Langevin's position would have left Laurier with very little room to manoeuver. On May 14, the Liberal leader replied that he would be pleased to discuss the matter further if Langevin so desired but was obliged to differ sharply with the archbishop on the method of effective federal help. Laurier insisted that he had supported the duty of intervention from Ottawa long before the judicial decision had appeared. As for the existing remedial order, Laurier could only call it 'aussi faible de fond que violent de forme.' He reminded Langevin that the document was being interpreted in diametrically opposite ways by the supporters and opponents of separate schools in the Conservative party: 'Votre Grandeur est

59 *Ibid.*, Lotbinière to Langevin, May 3, 1895
60 *Ibid.*, LaRivière to Langevin, May 8, 1895
61 *Ibid.*, Langevin to Laurier, May 11, 1895. This document and the subsequent one are also found in the Laurier Papers.

satisfait de cet ordre tel qu'interprété à Verchères et à Antigonish. Elle ne saurait l'approuver tel qu'interprété à Haldimand.' Laurier conclut that the government would have to decide which was the authentic interpretation before Langevin could expect him to approve it.[62]

There is no record of any further meeting between Laurier and Langevin. However, the confrontation which did take place marked an important step. It meant that Laurier had had an extended opportunity to contact the young archbishop both by word and letter and to sense the unlikelihood that compromise would be reached in Manitoba. On the other hand, it meant that Langevin had encountered, and been swayed by, the Laurier charm without being convinced that any substantial Liberal help would be forthcoming for what Langevin wanted, effective federal interference. Finally, the exchange demonstrated how possible it was for Laurier to oppose a government policy which was already showing signs of being profoundly split.

The question still remained, however, of which direction Langevin would pursue, the accommodating or the adamant. Voices were not lacking on either side. John Ewart wrote on May 14 to inform Langevin that Greenway and Sifton were on their way to Ottawa and that he himself would be coming to Ontario. He told the archbishop of a lecture on the school question which he, Ewart, had given in the Congregational church in Winnipeg at the invitation of Reverend Pedley, and indicated that his suggestions of a compromise settlement had been well received.[63] Ewart wrote again on May 25 from Toronto, informing Langevin that he was available if needed, and underlining the clerical dimension of the opposing camp. 'I trust that some fair settlement may be arrived at,' Ewart said, 'some arrangement which will leave to your people all the control that is necessary for the conservation of the schools as Catholic schools, although of the National type, but which will be in some measure not altogether displeasing to the Protestant clergy.'[64]

Archbishop O'Brien of Halifax was in Ottawa at the same time and made a plea similar to Ewart's. He insisted that he was not trying to prejudge the case for Langevin, but used Lord Aberdeen's name to further his support for a compromise. 'I believe there is a very general desire to keep the question out of Dominion politics,' O'Brien wrote. 'Also, it seems to me that should Greenway offer certain measures of relief which might not,

62 *Ibid.*, Laurier to Langevin, May 14, 1895
63 *Ibid.*, Ewart to Langevin, May 14, 1895
64 *Ibid.*, Ewart to Langevin, May 25, 1895

perhaps, fully meet your views, there is a possibility that the House might consider them sufficient, and by vote or resolution decide that the Manitoba Gov't. had met the requirements of the Remedial Order. I have good reason to know that His Excellency is most anxious to see the question settled,' he concluded.[65]

On the other side, Bishop Laflèche saw to it that Langevin was not left to himself and to influences which might persuade him to give in. On May 15 the bishop of Trois-Rivières wrote Langevin that every point along the line had to be firmly maintained. 'Pour que les écoles soient véritablement séparées, il faut absolument que l'influence protestante ou infidèle n'y puisse pénétrer d'aucune manière, ni par inspection, ni par diplôme, ni par les livres.' Laflèche urged extreme wariness in the proposed Ottawa meeting with Greenway and Sifton, using a scriptural image for emphasis:

C'est maintenant qu'il faut à la simplicité de la colombe joindre la prudence du serpent. On nous concédera sans doute le principe et le nom des écoles séparées qui vous sont garantis par la constitution, le jugement de la reine et le 'remedial order.' Mais quelles conséquences en tireront ces messieurs? On vous assurera de même, le droit aux contributions des Catholiques et l'exemption de contribuer aux écoles publiques ou protestantes et aussi votre part aux allocations du gouvernement, mais dans quelles proportions?[66]

Laflèche repeated the same sentiments in a letter to Monsignor Marois, vicar general of Quebec, and urged the latter to use his influence on Langevin, whom he still feared might compromise.[67] On the following day, May 16, Laflèche again wrote Langevin to condemn a plan which the *Courrier du Canada* had published as the probable Greenway offer. 'C'est tout simplement le plan des écoles du N.O. auxquelles on a conservé la qualification d'écoles séparées, et qu'en realité on a remises aux mains des protestants.'[68] Another letter to Marois on May 28 indicated that Laflèche was still unsure of Langevin's steadfastness and once again showed his own opposition to even the slightest accommodation. In part, Laflèche wrote,

La rumeur de compromis proposé par Mgr. A.P. Langevin est démentie par les

65 *Ibid.*, O'Brien to Langevin, May 17, 1895
66 *Ibid.*, Laflèche to Langevin, May 28, 1895
67 AAQ, Laflèche to Marois, May 15, 1895
68 AASB, Laflèche to Langevin, May 16, 1895

journaux et serait compromettante si elle était vraie. Quand on a un droit certain garanti par la constitution, reconnu et protégé par le plus haut tribunal de l'empire, et par l'autorité royale elle-même, on n'a pas compromis à proposer, mais un droit à reclamer purement et simplement envers et contre tous ceux qui voudraient y porter atteinte.[69]

Laflèche's outlook, certainly of profound influence on the attitude adopted by the newly consecrated Langevin, was hardly calculated to lead to a settlement either with Greenway or with the federal intermediaries.

In point of fact, Langevin would not be offered even what Laflèche considered all too little. From St Hyacinthe Langevin sent to Bégin a pessimistic summary of the discussions in Ottawa held as a result of Lord Aberdeen's invitation to Greenway and Sifton.

Voici où en est notre grande question – permettez-moi cette brusque entrée en matière, je suis si pressé.

1. Le Gouverneur-général a donc fait venir Greenway et Sifton afin de les entendre et de se renseigner. Ils n'ont vu ni Bowell ni votre serviteur – le Gouv. Gen. n'y tenait point et eux non plus – Son Excellence craignait une discussion trop vive – Greenway et Sifton ont demandé que le Gouvernement leur fit des propositions.

2. Le Gouv.-General a vu Bowell avec MM. Caron, Costigan, Haggart, Foster et Daly– il leur dit ce que demandait Greenway & cie. – Bowell s'est faché et a dit que c'était trop fort, que cette conduite prouvait la mauvaise foi de Greenway et cie. 'Nous leur avons fait savoir,' dit-il, 'notre manière de voir – accepte-t-il l'ordre-en-conseil? Si oui, alors donc quelle mesure? – si non, qu'ils le disent carrément.'

3. J'ai parlé avec son Excellence à deux reprises. Je lui ai dit pourquoi je tenais ferme. Il m'a paru satisfait.

4. J'ai vu Bowell en particulier. Il m'a l'air d'être bien résolu à régler la difficulté, mais nous donnera-t-il assez? Greenway et Sifton sont repartis – vont-ils faire quelques propositions le 13 juin, jour de l'ouverture du parlement du Manitoba? Je ne sais, mail il est à craindre qu'ils proposent quelque chose d'impossible.

Alors que fera le Gouvernement d'Ottawa? Nous défendra-t-il? Je l'espère – oh! si Laurier venait à notre aide carrément! Quel [appui] il apporterait à la cause![70]

Thus can be seen the main outline of events surrounding the visit of the

69 AAQ, Laflèche to Marois, May 28, 1895
70 AAQ, Langevin to Bégin, May 26, 1895

Manitoba officials to Ottawa. Lord Aberdeen had been the chief intermediary, and had decided against a confrontation of the principals either
out of fear at the last moment or out of genuine conviction that no good
would result. Archbishop Langevin was more than ever thrown back on
federal action and in his own view needed Laurier's support at least as
much as that of the Conservative government. As far as accusations of
unworthy collusion were concerned, the Liberal press in Quebec was not
slow to attack Langevin, as long as the federal Conservatives were involved in the bargain. *L'Electeur* of Quebec suggested just such an agreement between Langevin and the Ottawa government in a report published
on June 6.[71] In reaction, an excited telegram was sent by the archbishop
from St Boniface to Monsignor Marois in Quebec:

Ce que dit l'Electeur du six courant sur une entrevue avec Daly et Tupper est
absolument faux. Je n'ai pas dit un mot des écoles. Nous avons parlé de la moisson
au nord-ouest et de la santé de l'honorable Tupper. Avertissez Courrier et
Evènement.[72]

There may have been no secret deal; the message equally revealed no
progress. All in all, the events of May and early June provided anything but
an improving picture for a quick and easy settlement of the school crisis.
After some long-range sparring, both the Manitoba government and ecclesiastical authorities had hardened their respective positions. Moreover,
the federal government was in a progressively worsening condition as the
avenues of escape closed off one by one. Once again Dansereau's mordant
wit described the situation. Returning from the capital he wrote to Chapleau at Spencer Wood: 'Si tu savais ce que c'est à ce moment à Ottawa!
Tout le monde se plaint des ministres, qu'ils trouvent faibles et insipides.'[73]
It was into this unhappy atmosphere that the reply of the Manitoba government to the remedial order came.

MANITOBA'S REPLY AND OTTAWA'S CONFUSION

The Manitoba Legislative Assembly was reconvened on June 13, delayed
from the originally scheduled date of May 9. Appearing in the press on June
15, the official reply of the provincial government to the federal remedial

71 *L'Electeur*, June 6, 1895
72 AAQ, Langevin to Marois, June 10, 1895
73 PAC, Chapleau Papers, Dansereau to Chapleau, May 15, 1895

order was sent to Ottawa under the date of June 25. Three major points were made in refusing to comply with the order. The first concerned efficiency:

Compliance with the terms of the Order would restore Catholic separate schools with no more satisfactory guarantee for their efficiency than existed prior to said date ... The said schools were found to be inefficient. As conducted under the Roman Catholic section of the Board of Education, they did not possess the attributes of efficient modern public schools. Their conduct, management and regulation were defective; as a result of leaving a large section of the population with no better means of education than was thus supplied, many people grew up in a state of illiteracy.

Coolly overlooking the debate which took place in 1890 prior to the Public Schools Act and the writings of Taché, Ewart, and others on the subject, the reply stated that 'so far as we are aware, there has never been any attempt made to defend these schools on their merits, and we do not know of any ground upon which the expenditure of public money in their support could be justified.' Next came the claim that insufficient investigation had preceded the federal order; thus, in the view of the province, much further inquiry was needed before attempting remedial action. 'We also believe,' the reply went on, 'that there was lacking the means of forming a correct judgment in the Province of Manitoba, as to the effect upon the province of changes in the direction indicated in the Order.' Finally came the reminder that local regulation was the long-range key to the situation. Reminiscent of the Stephen Douglas 'Freeport Doctrine,' the provincial statement warned that the federal government might be left with an administrative problem which it could neither handle nor get rid of. The conclusion of the Manitoba government was polite but chilling:

We respectfully suggest to Your Excellency in Council that all of the above considerations call most strongly for full and careful deliberation and for such a course of action as will avoid irritating complications ... We deem it proper also to call attention to the fact that it is only a few months since the latest decision upon the subject was given by the Judicial Committee of the Privy Council.[74]

There was no doubt of the skill of the reply, whatever its accuracy. John Willison's later descriptions were apt: 'for clearness, directness, simplicity

74 Canada, *Sessional Papers*, 1895, no. 20c

and dignity, nothing in the literature of the controversy excels the des-patches of the provincial administration in explanation and defence of its position.'[75] If ever Sifton's tactical and literary skill was in evidence, the Manitoba reply was a prime example.

The nature of the reply, as much as it may have been expected, threw the troubled federal government ranks even further into disarray. Prime Minis-ter Bowell was more than ever caught between two fires. A letter from Emerson Coatsworth, Conservative MP from East Toronto, illustrated the depth of feeling against remedial action in one wing of the party. Coats-worth was calm but factual; 'I trust you will not feel compelled to introduce any remedial legislation this session,' he wrote. 'The feeling against it in Ontario has grown so strong that with every desire to support the Govern-ment I (and I believe a large number of Ontario Conservatives are similarly situated) feel that it would simply be committing suicide politically to go in favor of such legislation.' Coatsworth cited numerous Methodist confer-ence resolutions against remedial action as 'some indication of the Protes-tant feeling,' and added simply that he had 'direct notice from my consti-tuency that I must oppose it or drop out.' He hoped that Bowell would again find a way of 'tiding it over for a time,' and reminded the prime minister of the lesson of the April by-elections. 'Judging from Verchères & Antigonish,' he wrote, 'it will not strengthen the government even in Catholic ridings.' Coatsworth concluded that he had no desire to add to Bowell's difficulties, but felt that facts had to be faced at all costs.[76]

Coatsworth's opinion was backed not only by the Methodist confer-ences which he mentioned, but also by many assemblies of other Protestant denominations, notably the Presbyterian. In a resolution passed at the General Assembly of the Presbyterian church in London in June 1895, it was held that, while parents and the church had the duty of detailed religious instruction, 'yet the system of public instruction should be based upon and pervaded by the principles of Christianity, and should give distinct place to the reading of the Scriptures and prayer.' On the other hand, separate denominational schools were declared to be an abuse; therefore federal interference in the Manitoba case was condemned. 'Such a course,' the resolution stated, 'could result only in evil which is not, we believe, demanded by a supposed compact between the Province and the Dominion of Canada, or between different classes of people in the province itself.' The final conclusion of the resolution was that a conference should

75 *Sir Wilfrid Laurier and the Liberal Party*, II, p.212
76 PAC, Bowell Papers, Coatsworth to Bowell, June 24, 1895

be held between Manitoba and the federal government to settle the dispute.[77]

Even among the supporters of remedial action on the Conservative side, there was deep division on the nature and timing of the action. The same questions which had led to C.H. Tupper's resignation in March had to be faced over again: should a bill be attempted immediately or should further negotiations be initiated with Manitoba? A cablegram, supported by a following letter, from Sir Charles Tupper in London to his son on June 21, indicated the direction in which opinion was running within the cabinet:

Do not think postponement although indefensable [sic] should under circumstances involve resignation. Three Provinces having at bye-elections supported remedial order, position completely changed. Strongly advise you to support remedial legislation in present House as Manitoba has refused, and resign if that policy not adopted by Government. Only defensible course. Commission of Judges now would stultify Cabinet passing Remedial Order.[78]

If Sir Charles was advising that the proposal to defer a remedial bill should at least be countenanced, the same was not true of the French-Canadian bishops. Even the most avid Conservative partisans in the clerical ranks were ready to threaten condemnation of the federal government if the Manitoba reply were not met immediately with a remedial bill. A promise of things to come was reflected in a letter from the Quebec chancery office to Langevin, written as soon as the first news of the contents of the Manitoba reply had filtered through. Abbé L. Lindsay, acting as secretary while Archbishop Bégin was on pastoral visitation in the country, wrote on June 17 that he was helping Monsignor Marois send out a large number of letters prompted by the disturbing news from Winnipeg and Ottawa. Thomas Chapais of the *Courrier du Canada* and minister without portfolio in the Taillon government in Quebec and his friend, Alphonse Charlebois, had hurried to see Marois on receipt of the report. These gentlemen, self-professed representatives of 'les craintes et les désirs des francs conservateurs, mais amis de la religion et de la Patrie,' although unwilling to go as far as having their own names mentioned as initiators, wanted 'une action commune de l'épiscopat vis-à-vis du gouvernment au sujet du "Remedial Order."' Significantly, the visitors'

77 PAC, Laurier Papers, 'Resolution of the General Assembly of Presbyterian Church,' June, 1895
78 PAC, Tupper Papers, Tupper to C.H. Tupper, June 21, 1895

argument was that only the bishops could effectively counter the pressure which was being exerted on the cabinet to again stall for time. 'On connait la signification de ce que les Anglais appellent "the six months hoist,"' Lindsay went on. 'C'est la mort et l'enterrement du "Remedial Order," et le "finis Poloniae" des écoles du Manitoba.' The urgent request of Chapais and Charlebois was, therefore, that the bishops should confront the government and firmly state: ' "Non, vous n'ajournerez pas ainsi le règlement de cette question vitale. Prolongez la session de quelques semaines, et rendez-vous justice." '[79]

A second letter on the same subject also involved Vicar General Marois, but this time referred to the hierarchy as the initiator of pressure to be brought on the federal government. H. Adjutor Turcotte, a Quebec Conservative lawyer, wrote to his brother Arthur Turcotte, MP, in Ottawa, on June 18, and reported some strong statements from Marois about the bishops' position. 'Ils ne veulent plus, disent-ils, être leurrés,' Marois insisted. 'Il y a cinq ans and plus qu'une criante injustice, reconnue par le Conseil Privé, existe ... Remettre la loi rémédiatrice à une autre session leur parait un leurre nouveau. Ils admettent la difficulté de la situation, mais il y a longtemps qu'elle est prévue; le Gouvernement a du s'y préparer; s'il n'est pas capable de la dominer, qu'il disparaisse. Il y a des limites pour les catholiques à faire les chiens couchants.' Turcotte continued to quote Marois; then, in the same vein reflected by Lindsay the day before, he reported the equally strong opinion of Thomas Chapais, especially noting the ironic importance of Bowell to 'la bonne cause':

Il est aussi carrément pour un règlement à cette session; il prétend que différer, c'est trop risquer – le Ier ministre peut être remplacé par un autre moins bien disposé; des causes peuvent empêcher une autre session sans loi rémédiatrice, & alors la défaite écrasante est certaine pour les conservateurs dans le province, le clergé unanime contre eux &c, &c.

Turcotte then added his own opinion, inserting an even stronger dash of political advantage and strategy against Laurier:

Ce sont là les vues qu'on m'a exprimées; je ne discute pas leur mérite. Mais si le gouvernement a des *raisons* pour ne pas procéder à cette session, il faut que ce soit des *raisons*; qu'il les fasse connaître au moins aux évêques, & à des hommes comme Mgr. Marois!! Dans tous les cas, mon opinion personnelle est que le mieux

79 AASB, Lindsay to Langevin, June 17, 1895

est d'en finir avec cette damnée question au plus vite. A quoi bon retarder, prenez donc le taureau par les cornes en braves, et vous le dompterez infailliblement ... L'Electeur de ce soir promet l'appui de Laurier & des libéraux catholiques. Vous devez être capables de faire votre procédure de manière à forcer Laurier à voter pour le gouvernement, ou à l'écraser à la prochaine élection.[80]

Nothing was more remarkable in these two letters than the almost compulsive desire to have the hierarchy take the initiative. There could hardly have been a more revealing proof of increasing conservative dependence on the bishops for effective political action.

One practical result of these discussions involving the clergy was that episcopal letters pressing for a remedial bill were sent to many cabinet ministers and members of Parliament. Characteristically, Bishop Laflèche's letters were first, most numerous, and most emphatic. A June 21 note from Abbé Béland, chancellor of the diocese of Trois-Rivières, to Marois, indicated that a hard-hitting statement had been sent by Laflèche to the following ministers, senators, and members at Ottawa: Angers, Caron, Ouimet, Costigan, Ross, de Boucherville, Landry, Montplaisir, Bernier, Sir Hector Langevin, Carignan, Desaulniers, and Legris. Béland enclosed a copy of the letter, and the main points were trenchant:

Le refus de la Législature Manitobaine de donner suite au 'Remedial Order' peut être un mal à plusieurs points de vue; il aura du moins cet avantage d'amener une législation que le pouvoir provincial ne pourra attaquer ...

Permettez-moi de vous dire, Monsieur le Deputé, que pour ma part – et je suis sur d'exprimer ici le sentiment du plus grand nombre – je trouve qu'il n'y a nullement à retarder, et que c'est à la présente session que le Parlement du Canada doit faire cette loi réparatrice des torts causés et des injustices perpetrées, laquelle seule peut ramener la paix dans notre Confédération.

Qu'y a-t-il à gagner en retardant? Absolument rien.

Qu'y a-t-il à risquer? Tout ...

C'est tout de suite, et non dans quelques semaines ou quelques mois, Mons. de Deputé, qu'il faut répondre à ce refus provocateur et révolutionnaire de MM. Greenway et Sifton, par un acte d'autorité calme, prudent mais énergique, qui sera la fin du trouble et l'éloignement du danger par le rétablissement du droit.

Laflèche concluded by assuring his recipients that he was expressing the opinion of all the episcopate.[81]

80 PAC, Caron Papers, H. Adjutor Turcotte to Arthur Turcotte, June 18, 1895
81 AAQ, Laflèche to ministers and deputies, June 21, 1895

Whether all the bishops would have agreed to send such a strong letter to the legislators was a question which Laflèche did not discuss; in any case, Archbishop Bégin followed suit by sending a much briefer and milder letter on June 24 to Bowell, Angers, Caron, and Ouimet, simply insisting on remedial legislation during the current session.[82] Bégin also wrote to Archbishop Fabre, whom his secretary, Abbé Lindsay, had referred to as a possible stumbling-block in the June 17 letter. 'L'irrésolution de Mgr. Fabre, si exposé à se laisser circonvenir' had been seen by Lindsay as equally unsure in dealing with the Conservatives as with the Liberals in the April by-elections. The Bégin letter reinforced the impression of the division of cabinet opinion reflected in C.H. Tupper's message from his father; it also illustrated the much gentler approach of the Quebec archbishop compared to that of Laflèche. Bégin wrote in part to Fabre:

D'après mes informations le Ministère Fédéral serait porté à renvoyer à une autre session la présentation d'une mesure législative en faveur des catholiques manitobains.

Ne croyez-vous pas, Monseigneur, qu'il serait utile d'écrire au moins privément à nos principaux ministres Fédéraux pour les presser de régler sans retard cette question si importante? Je leur écrirai aujourd'hui même. Des lettres dans le même sens, venant de tous les évêques ou au moins d'un bon nombre, ne demeureraient peut-être sans efficacité.

Je me permets de suggérer cette idée à Votre Grandeur; Elle en fera ce qu'elle voudra.[83]

A similar request was sent to Archbishop Duhamel of Ottawa by Langevin on June 25, along with a worried note about the relative weakness of the Manitoba representatives who should have been the Catholics' greatest hope.[84] Once again it seemed a case of episcopal strength being required to shore up political impotence. There is no record of letters to deputies from either Fabre or Duhamel, although they may have made private verbal efforts. In any case, the really strong clerical ultimatums did not come until early July.

Meanwhile, in late June an embarrassing element was added to the already complicated church–state picture, by the publication of a letter

82 AASB, Bégin to Langevin, July 2, 1895; PAC, Caron Papers, Bégin to Caron, June 24, 1895
83 AAM, Bégin to Fabre, June 24, 1895
84 AAQ, Langevin to Duhamel, June 25, 1895. Not knowing that the Quebec archbishop had already done so, Langevin asked for a similar intervention on the part of Bégin (AAQ, Langevin to Bégin, June 25, 1895).

from Bishop Gravel of Nicolet to his clergy.[85] The circular included two documents: the March letter from Cardinal Ledochowski to all Canadian bishops, and a memorandum prepared for the same Ledochowski by Gravel in 1894. This memorandum, after reviewing the legal and historical case of the Manitoba school controversy, made a suggestion on the manner in which the Vatican Secretary of the *Propaganda Fide* might assist in settling the case. Whether it was meant as an object lesson for the Nicolet clergy in influencing politicians in the current crisis was not made clear, but Gravel implied that influence had been attempted and had had some effect on the Privy Council decision of January 1895. The key section of the memorandum had posed the question of how the Roman tribunal might exert influence. The answer was not calculated to improve the image of either ecclesiastical lobbyists or an impartial judicial decision.

It might perhaps, through the intervention of His Eminence Cardinal Vaughan, represent, among other things, to the Colonial Minister in London, that his predecessor Lord Carnarvon, had given, in his own name, and in the name of Her Majesty the Queen, the assurance to the Catholics of Manitoba that they would have their separate schools, that consequently, the Crown is bound in honour to fulfil these solemn promises, if it does not wish to alienate the heart of the Catholics of Canada. An intimation of this nature might have a good effect in reference to the judgment, which the Privy Council will render within a few months upon the question, which the Canadian Government has submitted to it.

As a comment in the letter to the clergy, Gravel had added that Ledochowski 'at once placed himself in communication with Cardinal Vaughan, and it may be reported that his intervention has contributed on his part to create in English official world an opinion favorable to the Catholics of Manitoba.'[86]

Bishop Gravel certainly did not contribute to favourable opinion in

---

85 PAC, Laurier Papers, June, 1895. Bishop Gravel to the clergy of Nicolet. Texts of the Gravel letter and Ledochowski memo were published by the *Montreal Star*, June 19, 1895, and quickly appeared in newspapers across the country.

86 Emphatic denial of any effective ecclesiastical influence on the Privy Council decision came from one of the presiding judges, Lord Herschell, via Sir Charles Tupper. Writing to his son on August 6 Tupper said, 'Lord Herschell told me in the presence of Sir Donald Smith that there was not the slightest ground for the statement that the Judicial Committee had been approached by anybody re the Manitoba School Question. He said he had never exchanged a word on the question before the judgement was delivered except with the court & counsel in open court.' (PAC, Tupper Papers, C. Tupper to C.H. Tupper, August 6, 1895.)

Canada. The appearance of this ready-made grievance during the tense days following the Manitoba government reply gave the anti-remedialist forces an added weapon. On June 29 Clifford Sifton wrote to D'Alton McCarthy for a 'copy of Bishop Gravelle's [*sic*] letter which has been causing so much commotion.'[87] Several of Archbishop Langevin's correspondents mentioned the trouble being caused by the Gravel publication, but LaRivière added that it could be somewhat offset by an article by the Reverend Dr George Bryce of Winnipeg, in which the latter boasted of influencing the Privy Council in their 1892 decision on the Barrett case.[88] Langevin saw something almost diabolical in the way things seemed to be combining against a favourable school solution. 'La publication de la lettre de Mgr. Gravel et du Card. Ledochowski fait du mal, mais j'espère que tout va bien tourner. Evidemment l'enfer est en furie,' he wrote to Bégin.[89]

Bishop Laflèche added his contribution to the tension. Several Conservative newspapers reported with approval that the Trois-Rivières prelate was again blaming Laurier and the Liberals for making the school question a political issue. In turn the Liberal press made its counter-attack, culminating in *L'Electeur*'s unflattering remarks:

Dire au public que Mgr. Laflèche a plus de confiance en l'orangiste Bowell que dans le catholique Laurier pour la protection de nos droits religieux, c'est tout simplement faire soupçonner que le prélat est affaibli par l'âge, et inviter les catholiques à se chercher d'autres guides que ceux que l'Eglise leur désigne.[90]

THE JULY CABINET CRISIS: HEAVY CLERICAL SHADOWS

Meanwhile the question burned at Ottawa: would a remedial bill be presented or not? As T.M. Daly put it, somewhat ungrammatically, in an urgent note to Bowell, confusion and vacillation dominated the public image being presented to the electorate, and this was losing supporters

---

87 PAC, Sifton Papers, Sifton to McCarthy, June 29, 1895
88 AASB, La Rivière to Langevin, June 29, 1895. George Bryce (1844–1931) was among the most prominent Presbyterian clerics of Manitoba, having organized several congregations in Winnipeg and in rural areas after his arrival from Ontario in 1871. He was the principal founder of Manitoba College, and took part in the creation of the University of Manitoba in 1877. He served as Winnipeg school inspector in the 1870s, and was the author of several historical works on Manitoba and the northwest. On several occasions he entered into journalistic debate against Taché and Ewart on the school question.
89 AAQ, Langevin to Bégin, June 25, 1895
90 June 28, 1895

every day: 'It is the *repudiation* of the O.C. or failure to do anything in the face of that O.C. having been passed in March, that in combination with the other matters is going to be so hard for us to justify and get our friends to rally. I can assure you that if the position was not so serious I would not be so urgent.'[91]

The first indications that Langevin received from Ottawa after the Manitoba reply had arrived were that a remedial bill would indeed be attempted during the current session. A June 20 telegram from LaRivière said that he believed the cabinet was ready to move almost immediately.[92] On June 24, J.S. Ewart wrote Langevin that he had submitted a preliminary draft of a remedial bill to Ouimet and C.H. Tupper,[93] and Langevin in his note to Duhamel on the following day indicated that he was satisfied that the proposed bill gave sufficient control of schools to the church.[94] Ewart took a somewhat different approach in the letter he sent to Tupper along with the bill, and which the latter passed on to Caron. Ewart urged that the compromise nature of the proposed statute should be stressed, and that in fact such compromise features did exist. In his somewhat diffuse style, Ewart wrote that he had 'paid special attention to the removal of such features of the old system as really constituted difficulties and defects in its operation.' Ewart admitted that he was 'very little of a politician,' but felt that great advantage could be gained by stressing the aspects of the bill that did not completely meet Archbishop Langevin's demands.[95]

As late as July 3, Langevin was receiving some encouragement that the bill would indeed be presented at the current session of Parliament. Archbishop Cleary of Kingston wrote that he had been to Ottawa and had seen several ministers and members. Although he did not mention the date on which the statement was made, Cleary quoted Costigan in particular to the effect that a bill would come within the week. Cleary added some of his own views on what the bill should contain, concluding that the Ontario system plus compulsion on the Catholics to support their own schools should be sufficient.[96] On July 4 Langevin wrote to Ewart with further suggestions on details of the bill, still presuming that it was the nature and not the fact of legislation which was in question.[97]

91 PAC, Bowell Papers, Daly to Bowell, June 24, 1895
92 AASB, LaRivière to Langevin, June 20, 1895
93 *Ibid.*, Ewart to Langevin, June 24, 1895
94 AAQ, Langevin to Duhamel, June 25, 1895
95 PAC, Caron Papers, Ewart to C.H. Tupper, June 23, 1895
96 AASB, Cleary to Langevin, July 3, 1895
97 *Ibid.*, Langevin to Ewart, July 4, 1895

Even during the last week of June, however, there were many signs pointing in the opposite direction. Bégin's note to Fabre on June 24 mentioned a private but strong doubt.[98] The following day, Dr Séverin Lachapelle, MP, one of Langevin's Ottawa sources of information, wrote the archbishop that he had seen C.H. Tupper, who had informed the doctor that at least it had been decided that there would be no election in 1895. 'La dissolution du Parl. qui devait se faire au printemps dernier est donc remise à l'an prochain,' said Lachapelle, and concluded that this probably meant the bill was being postponed, although he did not quote Tupper to this effect.[99] Even the enthusiastic LaRivière was troubled by contradictory reports about happenings within the cabinet. Still hopeful about 'le projet de loi préparé par M. Ewart et soumis au gouvernement,' LaRivière wrote on June 29 that Ouimet was making suspiciously uncertain statements.[100] Several sources revealed that some forty English Conservative MPs led by Chief Whip George Taylor were threatening to abandon the government if a remedial bill were presented.[101]

On July 2, Bégin informed Langevin that Ouimet and Angers had answered his plea of the previous week with brief statements that they were not going to turn back from doing justice.[102] Within little more than a week, however, they were to take very different roads in putting that promise into practice. On July 6, Bowell informed Lord Aberdeen at Quebec that the cabinet had decided to postpone legislation and requested authority to announce a special January session to present a remedial bill.[103] On July 8, Finance Minister Foster read a brief statement on the floor of the House of Commons. He began by saying that the government had given 'careful deliberation' to the Manitoba reply of June 19. Foster's summary of the current state of the question tried to dispel trouble with dispassionate language. He promised a further 'olive branch' communication with Manitoba, but stated categorically that if the Greenway government failed to make 'a satisfactory arrangement,' the federal government would, in January, 'introduce and press to a conclusion such legislation as will afford an adequate measure of relief to the said minority.'[104]

But the fire in the heather, as Bowell had called it, was far from extin-

98 AAM, Bégin to Fabre, June 24, 1895
99 AASB, Lachapelle to Langevin, June 25, 1895
100 AASB, LaRivière to Langevin, June 29, 1895
101 Cf. Rumilly, *Histoire*, VII, p. 222.
102 AASB, Bégin to Langevin, July 2, 1895
103 Lady Aberdeen, *Journal*, July 13, 1895
104 Canada, House of Commons, *Debates*, 1895, p.4062

guished. As soon as the official policy of the government had been announced, the Castor representative in the cabinet, A.R. Angers, resigned. He was soon followed by the two other French ministers, Caron and Ouimet. On July 10 the situation looked so desperate that Bowell informed the governor general, now back in Ottawa, that his government would be in a minority in the House and would have to resign.[105] Before this happened, however, Caron and Ouimet withdrew their resignations. Angers steadfastly refused to return, but the government regained sufficient equilibrium to survive the debate on Foster's official statement of policy.

The reasoning within the cabinet which led to their official decision, and that which impelled Angers, Caron, and Ouimet to act as they did, remained far from clear.[106] There were several versions of the genesis and propriety of the decision to postpone legislation, but there was no doubt that ecclesiastical pressure had entered a new and tougher phase. When the first report of the cabinet decision became known, two of the strongest examples of clerical pressure on politicians during the entire school controversy were thrust at the French ministers. The first came from Monsignor Marois on July 6. The Quebec vicar general stated that the Conservatives could and would lose clerical support if remedial legislation did not come during the current session.

Les libéraux nous crient depuis le commencement que nous assistons à une comédie montée par le parti conservateur, et nous ont mis en garde contre tout ce qui arrive aujourd'hui. Ils ont été prophètes, et nous ne pourrons jamais excuser les conservateurs. Il faudra donc être contre eux, et *nous le serons*.

Puis, qu'ont-ils à gagner avec tous ces atermoiements, tous ces retards, toutes ces faiblesses? ... Il se tressent un fouet pour se faire flageller, et ils tissent la corde qui les pendra. Ils refusent de se couvrir d'honneur et de gloire pour revêtir le manteau de l'ignominie, de la duplicité, du mensonge et de la trahison! Nous avons fini d'être leurrés.

Je t'en prie, fais comprendre à Arthur qu'il doit tout faire pour urger l'action dès cette session, ou c'en est fait de notre confiance au parti.[107]

105 Lady Aberdeen, *Journal*, July 13, 1895
106 Two undated notes in the Bowell Papers indicate that a shift took place in majority opinion within the cabinet in the meetings between July 3 and July 6, with Smith and Costigan being brought to accept a further approach to Manitoba and, if necessary, a January session.
107 PAC, Caron Papers, Marois to Landry (or H.A. Turcotte), July 6, 1895. The letter in the Caron Papers is incomplete; Arthur is clearly A. Turcotte, MP.

In the face of such an ultimatum, it is hardly surprising that Caron and his colleagues were moved to go as far as resignation.

A similar statement was contained in an uncompromising letter from Bishop Laflèche to Angers and Ouimet on July 7. The essence of the bishop's letter might be summarized as follows: pass the law or go down fighting. In a fiery conclusion, Laflèche stated:

On pourrait succomber dans cette tâche que le fanatisme rend à la vérité difficile, mais au moins, s'il le fallait, que l'on ne soit pas dupé et que l'on tombe avec honneur comme les Rois qui reçoivent un coup d'épée en pleine poitrine et se relèvent toujours, et non point comme ceux qui tombent d'un coup de pied ailleurs, et ne se relèvent jamais, ainsi que le disait Louis Veuillot.[108]

It cannot be known for certain just how much this clerical pressure helped to bring on the cabinet crisis. It surely strengthened Angers in his resolution, and may well have been the reason that Caron and Ouimet at least went through the motions of resignation. When it came to a defence of the various lines of action, each of the Roman Catholic principals involved – Angers, Smith, Costigan, Caron, and Ouimet – made significant statements. Although not making a public pronouncement immediately after his resignation, which might have precipitated the fall of the government, Angers later explained his stand in the Senate. Echoing C.H. Tupper's arguments on how to treat political fires, Angers accused Bowell of both fear and foolishness.[109] More detailed and more critical of the four other Roman Catholic ministers was the defence of his resignation sent by Angers to Bishop Laflèche. In a letter not unlike a report of a subordinate officer to a commanding general, Angers began with an admission of defeat and a straightforward accusation of the architects of that defeat. Referring to Laflèche's strong letter of July 7, Angers stated,

Je n'ai pas répondu avant aujourd'hui à votre lettre du 7 courant. J'ai fait tout en mon pouvoir pour faire accepter la législation remédiatrice à cette session, mais je me suis rompu à la tâche. Si mes quatres collègues catholiques avaient persisté jusqu'à la fin dans la résistance, vous auriez vu triompher vos opinions.

Angers then moved to a description of the sequence of events. Smith and

---

108 AAQ, Laflèche to Angers, July 7, 1895; Laflèche to Ouimet, July 7, 1895
109 Canada, Senate, *Debates*, 1895, pp.658–64

Costigan were the first to buckle, Angers reported: 'Deux de nous ont abandonnés presqu'au premier instant,' he said. Then came the description of Caron and Ouimet, with a detailed condemnation of the policy of delay which they were now supporting:

Deux autres après s'être démis, se sont ralliés à politique qui porte, je crois, le coup fatal aux écoles séparées, et qui consiste à réouvrir les négotiations avec le gouvernment Greenway, non obstant le refus de la Législature de Manitoba de se conformer à l'ordre remédiateur. Ces nouvelles négotiations, suivies de reponses évasives, ou de promesses peu sincères, augmenteront la mauvaise volonté du parlement d'Ottawa. Dans l'intervalle entre la présente et la prochaine session l'excitation ira croissant. Le Parlement, qu'on a représenté comme hésitant aujourd'hui, en janvier prochain aura peur. La politique d'inaction du ministère a, je crains, mis en péril pour toujours la solution favorable de cette question des écoles. Si la législation avait été adoptée à cette session, celle-ci suivie d'une autre l'hiver prochain, avant la dissolution du parlement qui a lieu en avril, le fait accompli aurait été accepté par la majorité bien pensante des Protestants, et la question serait sortie du domaine de la politique, avant même que nous fussions allés aux élections générales. Ces vues, Monseigneur, n'ont pas prévalu, et je n'ai pas voulu accepter la responsabilité de mettre ainsi en péril les droits des Catholiques.

Je regrette que les événements des deux derniers jours soient venus me donner raison. La presse d'Ontario, au lieu de préparer l'opinion publique à adopter la législation nécessaire en janvier prochain, est entrée en campagne sur tous les points pour empêcher cette législation d'être présentée.[110]

Perhaps most interesting about Angers's accusations was their similarity to the charges of procrastination which would be used by Laurier, Tarte, and *L'Electeur* in the spring of 1896.

Like Angers, Sir Frank Smith defended his action in the Senate debate. His main argument was that it was the clear desire of the representatives of all the provinces except Quebec to once again attempt conciliation with Manitoba. He insisted that his motive was not to dodge responsibility for remedial action, but to avoid if possible a fight on racial and religious lines.[111]

110 ASTR, Angers to Laflèche, July 14, 1895. Lady Aberdeen felt that Bowell had deceived Angers and had misled the governor general in the matter of cabinet unanimity about deferring legislation. She described Angers as 'a good true straightforward little man – somewhat ultramontane in his views but quite sincere. He is of course, quite sore,' she added (*Journal*, July 14, 1895).
111 Canada, Senate, *Debates*, 1895, p.665ff

John Costigan's account was written some four years later, at the time when he transferred his allegiance from the Conservative to the Liberal party. In an apologia apparently destined for several English-speaking bishops, Costigan made several startling statements concerning the cabinet session where delay of the remedial bill had been decided upon. He defended the delay for the same reasons Smith had given, but he accused Foster and others of double-dealing, and stated that Angers had in fact agreed to postponement during the cabinet meetings.[112]

The most concise expression by Caron of his reasons for returning to the cabinet was a speech given about a month after the crisis at Baie-des-Pères in Pontiac county. Without saying anything about his reasons for resigning in the first place, Caron defended his own course of action and that of Ouimet as compared with that of Angers.[113] A more personal apologia for his action was sent by Caron to J.S. Ewart. This was a letter asking for an endorsement of the course of action taken by himself and Ouimet, and revealed the degree of sympathy for the Angers's position which was being generated in the province of Quebec:

If you believe that Ouimet and myself were right in accepting the pledges and assurances given us in the most positive manner by our colleagues, with the knowledge of the Governor General, what would you think of writing me a letter stating that you consider that the action taken by my colleague and myself is in the interest of the settlement of that vexed question and must meet with the approbation of the minority?

Caron gave the assurance that the letter would be used only privately, if Ewart so desired, and then returned to a résumé of his argument. 'I am firmly convinced,' he said, 'that if we had not taken the stand which we did, the school question of Manitoba was relegated to oblivion for years to come.' In direct contradiction to the line of argument used by Angers in his letter to Laflèche, Caron stated his conviction that January would bring a solution if Manitoba did nothing. He was very sorry to see Angers go, Caron said, and he regretted splitting the French-Canadian ministers, but Angers would agree to nothing except immediate legislation. In any case, concluded Caron, 'we can do in January what he has done now.'[114] Caron

112 PAC, Costigan Papers, Costigan to 'Your Lordship,' n.d. (c. May, 1899). Copies of this document, which has the strengths and weaknesses of a personal defence and which contains several inaccuracies perhaps attributable to the passage of time, may be found in several collections in the Public Archives of Canada including the Laurier Papers.

113 See Rumilly, *Histoire*, VII, 232–3.

114 AASB, Caron to Ewart, as related in Ewart to Langevin, July 18, 1895

seemed conveniently to overlook the fact that he and Ouimet had in fact resigned as had Angers, and thus gave further evidence that their brief journey into political limbo had been little more than a quick bow to ecclesiastical pressure.

Ouimet's defence, much like that of Caron, was outlined in the parliamentary debate on the school question which followed the cabinet crisis. Lady Aberdeen had an interesting comment on the interplay among the three French-Canadian ministers during the crisis, particularly on the unhappy position of Alderic Ouimet. 'One could not help being sorry for poor Ouimet,' she wrote. 'He looked so battered and torn with the conflict. It is said that Sir Adolphe stayed out so as to be sure of ultimately bringing Ouimet in and not leaving him to Angers' influence.' To what degree money and promises of money had to do with the reconciliation was, in July as it had been in April, not certain. Lady Aberdeen was convinced that CPR funds constituted more than a minor factor when she referred to Senator Drummond as 'peace-maker and purse-bearer.'[115]

LIBERAL REACTION AND PARLIAMENTARY DEBATE

In the Liberal camp, Laurier managed to maintain the noncommittal policy which he had defended against Archbishop Langevin in May. With the debate under way in the House and Senate, John Willison followed up his hard arguments of March and April with a message of gentler tone to Laurier, revealing the editor's awareness of the pressures the Liberal leader was facing from the French and Catholic side. 'I don't want to preach to you,' Willison wrote, 'but I cannot refrain from telling you that if you can avoid any declaration in favour of remedial legislation it will be an enormous advantage in Ontario. Be sure that this province will destroy any party that attempts arbitrary interference with Manitoba and the feeling has grown enormously strong.' The *Globe* editor assured Laurier that 'the Liberals are gaining in Ontario steadily and that nothing can save the Tories if you can maintain your present ground, and all depends on you.' Willison concluded by quoting Ontario Provincial Secretary A.S. Hardy, who had strongly opposed the *Globe*'s stand at the time of the remedial order. In Willison's words, Hardy was 'amazed at the feeling that has developed ... He is now satisfied ours was the wise course.'[116]

For his part, ultra-Protestant Liberal MP John Charlton wanted some-

115 *Journal*, July 13, 1895, p.238
116 PAC, Laurier Papers, Willison to Laurier, July 17, 1895

thing much stronger than neutrality from Laurier. In the Orangeman's Day entry in his diary, Charlton told of pressing the Liberal leader for a positive statement against federal interference at any time, in order 'to put an end to all suspicions that now existed against him among Protestant electors.'[117] Laurier's failure to comply provoked a July 16 entry in which Charlton lamented that 'we want a leader of sound principles, courage and iron will at this juncture and we do not have him.'[118] On July 19, however, Charlton claimed that Laurier and Tarte had gone so far as to give private assurances which 'amounted to a pledge that we would oppose the Remedial Bill and remedial legislation.'[119] The conclusion may have been premature on Charlton's part, but it did indicate the direction being taken, however slowly.

Many of the later reactions to the mounting crisis, French-clerical in particular, were coloured by what was said during the July debate in the House and Senate. Except perhaps for a violent McCarthy-LaRivière battle, these 1895 exchanges were more cogent and restrained than the interminable wrangles of the following spring, although the emotional content was heightened by fiery Orange speeches and parades in Ottawa and elsewhere. The Commons debate came in two bursts. The first was on July 11 and 12 following a Laurier motion to adjourn.[120] The second lasted from July 15 through 17 on the Liberal leader's motion of non-confidence, despite which Laurier managed to be perfectly neutral as to positive action of his own. Each motion was easily defeated, although a few Angers's supporters broke with the government in the division.[121] French Conservatives as well as Liberals did not hesitate to make hostile remarks about Tory Whip Taylor's 'forty friends.'[122] In the Senate, the debate was notably chiefly for the harsh light which Angers threw on the futility of delay if the object was to obtain compromise from Manitoba.[123] Perhaps the most interesting aspect of the whole July debate was the ironic fact that the extremists on both sides agreed on one vital point, that the Manitoba government was not going to budge.

117 John Charlton, *Diary*, June 12, 1895
118 *Ibid.*, June 16, 1895
119 *Ibid.*, June 18, 1895
120 Canada, House of Commons, *Debates*, 1895, pp.4187–250
121 *Ibid.*, pp.4411–640.
122 *Ibid.*, p.4242. L.C. Clark presents a judicious survey of the debates, and rightly concludes that the chief significance of the exchange was the 'divisions it revealed in the Conservative ranks' ['The Conservative Administrations,' (thesis), p.394].
123 Canada, Senate, *Debates*, 1895, pp.658–64

Along with a dramatic illustration of the impact of ecclesiastical pressure, the French bloc in the July crisis had once more demonstrated a basic fact of Canadian politics: the French could not push through a major point of policy without help from outside the fold. The outcome differed, but there were overtones clearly reminiscent of the dilemma faced by Caron, Langevin, and Chapleau after the Riel hanging almost ten years earlier. On the other hand, if the July experience had demonstrated the impotence of an isolated French contingent, it had even more graphically revealed the weakness of an administration which failed to hold them together. The vacillating government, which had left a flank open to clerical coercion, could and would become an entity which depended on clerical support for survival. From the point of view of the clerics, if it was their pressure which had been in part responsible for the cabinet resignations, the abortive outcome of that protest had left them in the middle of the arena holding a broken sword. They had little choice but to make the best of a bad situation. In contrast, and however easier his task may have been, Laurier had kept his restive team manageably united.

The federal follow-up to the July session did little to change the situation. On July 27 a 'pipe of peace' was held out to Manitoba in the form of a statement which maintained the federal power to pass remedial legislation, but begged the province to make it unnecessary. It threatened by citing Foster's promise of a January session, but suggested that Manitoba could avoid the thunderbolt. Unfortunately, the federal statement presented no additional facts or reasons such as any variation of an investigation, which might impel Manitoba to change the position adopted in its June reply. Moreover, admirable as it might be in its restraint when compared with the remedial order of March, the message conveyed the unmistakeable impression of federal retreat in the face of the province.[124] Time, instead of healing wounds, seemed to be aggravating them.

124 Canada, *Sessional Papers*, 1895, no. 39

4

Between the sessions:
a narrowing of choices

The events of July left Bowell's 'fire in the heather' more than ever out of control. Clifford Sifton, modestly avoiding reference to his own contribution to the crisis, saw the development of factors as clearly as anyone. In a letter to D'Alton McCarthy shortly after the resignation crisis and the government promise of a special January session for remedial legislation, Sifton thanked McCarthy for his telegram announcing the postponement of the bill, and said he was gratified to hear 'public sentiment in the East has grown much stronger of late against any proposed interference with our school laws.' Sifton felt that the open discord among the Conservatives was a great boon and would 'present a very strong temptation to the Liberals to vote against any Bill that the Government may bring in.'

The news that Caron and Ouimet had returned and that legislation had been explicitly promised in January if Manitoba did not move, had, in Sifton's view, made Manitoba's defence much easier. 'The Government,' he said, 'has made a much more serious blunder than any of the numerous ones which they have made hitherto.' Such a specific pledge, Sifton believed, 'would have a very strong effect in arousing sentiment in Ontario, and the Government would have stood a much better chance of getting a Bill through before adjournment or prorogation than they will at any time in the future.[1] What should be particularly noted in Sifton's cool analysis is

1 PAC, Sifton Papers, Sifton to McCarthy, July 12, 1895

that he thoroughly agreed with the Angers position on one point – that delay made remedial legislation unlikely – and thoroughly disagreed with him on another – that a split in the Conservative ranks would be a crucial factor in wrecking remedial hopes.

The opinions of French-Canadian journalists during and after the July crisis reflected the confusion produced by the government's temporizing. Liberal papers called the session useless, generally ignoring Angers while condemning the capitulation of Caron and Ouimet. Conservative journals were deeply divided in their reaction to the drama involving the three French ministers. Predictably, the ultramontane *Le Moniteur de Lévis* and *La Vérité* were outspoken in their support of Angers. Writing on July 20, J.P. Tardivel called the quick return to the cabinet of Caron and Ouimet 'une humiliation nationale,' and insisted that, 'sans la fermeté de M. Angers, qui rachète quelque peu la faiblesse des deux autres, nous serions la risée du monde civilisé.'[2]

Abbé David Gosselin, editor of *La Semaine Religieuse de Québec* and generally considered to reflect the opinion of Archbishop Bégin, spoke openly of the possibility of a substantial Quebec shift to the Liberals. Gosselin clearly favoured Angers's action over that of Caron and Ouimet. But this was not the main issue. Much more serious in Quebec eyes was the report of the threatened bloc opposition by Ontario Conservatives to any remedial measure. If this were true, Gosselin stated, 'alors il ne restait plus qu'à briser l'alliance de 1854 pour en contracter une avec d'autres éléments.' It might well be time to remind Ontario Tories of some hard political facts:

Ces messieurs sont au pouvoir, depuis quarante ans, grâce au parti conservateur de la province de Québec, et ils l'oublient, quand ce dernier a le plus grand besoin de leur concours. Eh bien! dit-elle, puisque c'est là tout le bénéfice de cette alliance, son utilité a cessé![3]

Even the normally pro-Government *La Presse* reacted at first in favour of Angers, expressing disgust at the power-hunger of Conservatives as well as Liberals.[4] By the end of the session, however, *La Presse* modified its position, accepting the argument of *La Minerve* and others that, had Caron and Ouimet remained out with Angers, the subsequent forced election would have been faced without French representation in the government.

2 *La Vérité*
3 *La Semaine Religieuse de Québec*, September 7, 1895
4 July 12, 1895

Such an event, *La Presse* admitted, could only be seen as 'le premier acte d'un conflit de races, dont il est impossible de calculer les résultats.'[5] Significantly, since it clearly would not espouse a position opposed to Bishop Laflèche, *Le Trifluvien* sided with the government rather than the ultramontanes. Above all, it rejoiced that the crisis had been resolved in time to thwart Liberal schemes for grasping power.[6]

Like the comments of most of the French journalists, the initial reactions of the bishops to the crisis favoured the strong stand taken by Angers. On July 16, Bishop Laflèche wrote a brief letter of congratulations in reply to Angers's apologia sent two days earlier.[7] On the same day, Archbishop Bégin, once more on pastoral visitation in a rural area of his diocese, wrote back to Monsignor Marois at the chancery to say that he was pleased with Angers's action and dismayed by that of Caron and Ouimet; he added that he was not particularly surprised at Caron.[8]

Efforts were made immediately, however, to get a kinder ecclesiastical reception for the ministers who had returned to the cabinet after leaving. On July 12, Dr Séverin Lachapelle, MP, implying that he feared a strongly worded outburst from St Boniface, wrote to Archbishop Langevin to ask that he study both sides of the question. As for himself, Lachapelle said, he believed Caron and Ouimet were more to be praised than was Angers: 'Je suis d'opinion que les ministres qui nous sont revenus, ont plus fait leur devoir d'hommes d'état catholiques que celui qui est parti, malgré que je ne doute pas de la sincérité de ce dernier.' Lachapelle concluded with a rather hollow sounding optimism. 'Nous avons arraché des concessions nouvelles,' he stated, 'qui assurent le succès de notre cause, à moins que le gouvernement et ceux qui le composent ne consentent à un déshonneur sans nom … Accentuer la division est le seul danger du moment.'[9]

As already seen, Caron took up his own defence in a letter to Ewart which the lawyer then passed on to Langevin.[10] Ewart replied to Caron that he felt the returning ministers were in good faith just as much as was Angers, and hoped that the archbishop could give Caron the letter he desired, which Ewart as a lawyer felt he could not.[11] Whatever his initial feelings about the July crisis in Ottawa, Langevin seemed to have been

5 *Ibid.*, July 18, 1895
6 July 26, 1895
7 AAQ, Laflèche to Angers, July 16, 1895
8 *Ibid.*, Bégin to Marois, July 16, 1895
9 AASB, Lachapelle to Langevin, July 12, 1895
10 *Ibid.*, Caron to Ewart, enclosed in Ewart letter to Langevin, July 18, 1895
11 *Ibid.*, Ewart to Caron, July 18, 1895

somewhat convinced by the arguments advanced by Lachapelle and Caron. Trying to maintain a noncommittal position, however, the archbishop did not reply to Caron directly; instead Ewart was again the intermediary. A letter from the Winnipeg lawyer to Caron on July 30 pointed out how difficult it would be for Langevin to praise explicitly the line of action of either Caron and Ouimet or Angers. 'He feels sure,' Ewart wrote, 'that you have all acted to the best of your judgment for the best interests of his people here, but you will at once see that he could not take upon himself to reflect in any way upon Mr. Angers for the course which he thought proper to take, by commending that which you took.'[12]

Langevin's letter to Bégin on August 2 combined an acceptance of the situation with a hope that the delay would not be disastrous. As indicated in the letter from Ewart to Caron, the archbishop was disposed to interpret kindly the good will of each of the French cabinet members. Speaking of 'la cause,' Langevin said:

Elle est exposée aux vicissitudes d'un long retard. Quidquid sit, j'ai encore confiance. Nos ministres canadiens ont voulu, je crois, nous aider chacun à sa manière. Il faut bien accepter la position faite et en tirer le meilleur parti possible. Le grand point est qu'il n'y ait aucune agitation malsaine et que nous attendions en toute patience dans la tranquille conviction de notre droit, le mois de janvier. C'est alors qu'il faudra frapper un grand coup.[13]

Letters between Langevin and Laflèche further indicated that, by the end of July, Bishop Laflèche had either argued himself or been argued into accepting the good faith of both sides of the French bloc division. In a note of August 7, Laflèche wrote that he had received Langevin's letter and, like Langevin, was not disposed to condemn either position in the crisis. Using the Old Augustinian dictum 'In necessariis unitas, in dubiis libertas, in omnibus caritas,' Laflèche said he agreed with Langevin that the most important thing for the moment was to heal hard feelings and to restore unity. It had been, Laflèche admitted, a question of choosing different means to the same desired end. 'Si l'un avait raison,' he wrote, 'l'autre n'avait pas tort.'[14]

12 PAC, Caron Papers, Ewart to Caron, July 30, 1895
13 AAQ, Langevin to Bégin, August 2, 1895
14 AASB, Laflèche to Langevin, August 7, 1895

ANGERS AND THIRD-PARTY RUMBLINGS

Movements were attempted within clerical ranks to bring the warring factions of French Conservatives back together. Archbishop Bégin mentioned such an attempt in a letter to Archbishop Duhamel on August 1. Referring to an unnamed plan of action of Caron and Ouimet, Bégin said he would try to get Angers to cooperate. The archbishop expressed his doubts about this or any other scheme short of divine intervention.[15] Bégin also found it necessary to try to bring influence to bear on Ouimet. A reply from Archbishop Fabre to his Quebec colleague referred to a request made by Bégin to help pressure Ouimet into a certain compromise, again unspecified. As seen earlier in the treatment of the Verchères election, Fabre doubted his ability to influence Ouimet, since the latter in particular had felt let down by the Montreal prelate.[16]

Archbishop Langevin, too, had little reason to believe that a reconciliation would be effected, particularly from Angers's point of view. Although he had been quoted by *La Presse* as being against agitation,[17] the former minister of agriculture soon seemed intent on burning bridges rather than mending them. In a quick reaction to a critical article from the pro-Angers *Le Moniteur de Lévis*, Langevin wrote in bewilderment to Bégin:

Que veut dire M. Angers? Il est certain qu'il s'est conduit en vrai chevalier et en homme de coeur, et je regrette que son journal ait cru devoir m'attaquer ainsi que Mgr. Gravel (Le Moniteur de Lévis) Cui bono? ... Ce n'est pas ce qui fortifiera la position de M. Angers et de son parti. Je sais aussi que les autres ministres ont agi en vue du bien.[18]

By September, rumours and reports indicated that Angers was indeed moving in the direction of a third party. How serious this was, and how much a matter of political blackmail on the part of Angers, Senator Landry, and others, remains uncertain. Probably something of both elements was involved, as indicated in a disturbing communication received by Langevin from Ottawa on September 18. The writer was Abbé Corbeil, an old friend of Langevin's. Corbeil reported that he had met Landry on the train coming from Montreal to Ottawa, and that the senator had been quite talkative:

15 AAQ, Bégin to Duhamel, August 1, 1895
16 *Ibid.*, Fabre to Bégin, August 4, 1895. See above, p.80.
17 July 24, 1895
18 AAQ, Langevin to Bégin, August 11, 1895

Ce monsieur intrigue pour devenir ministre. Avec l'ex-ministre Angers, Belleau, etc., il a assisté à un caucus au St. Lawrence Hall, pour la formation immédiate d'un troisième parti politique dans lequel on cherchera à entrainer le clergé.

Corbeil said that he had tried not to be too communicative, since there seemed to be several things which the senator 'semblait trop désirer connaître.'[19]

If practical steps for a third party did not gain great impetus, Angers's prestige and influence after his resignation was evidently an important factor in preventing his replacement. Letters received by one of Angers's chief supporters in the Commons, Flavien Dupont, made this particularly clear in the case of L.P. Pelletier, provincial secretary of the province of Quebec. With at least as much suggestion of hurt dignity as of high principle, Angers described the effort to acquire Pelletier as an affront to himself. 'On croit entrainer le clergé,' he remarked darkly, and 'on nous traiterait comme une quantité négligéable.'[20] As suggested by Corbeil, Senator Landry was prominent in the manipulations. Landry and, according to later reports, Monsignor Marois of Quebec brought pressure to bear first against Pelletier and then against Desjardins, the man who finally filled the vacancy in January.[21] When Desjardins was first rumored as a possible successor to the resigned minister, Landry asked Dupont to impress upon the Montreal senator the importance of maintaining Angers's abdication as a protest until the cabinet honoured its promise to introduce remedial legislation.[22] That efforts to have Chapleau return to Ottawa were meeting the same stubborn resistance from Angers and his group was equally clear in Dupont's correspondence.[23] Finally, the ancient rivalry between Montreal and Quebec City was not absent from the impasse. On the whole, while the performance of the government that he had left can hardly be praised, the ultramontane 'strike' conducted by Angers to defend the school rights of the Manitoba minority failed at least in perspicacity, if not in integrity.

19 AASB, Corbeil to Langevin, September 18, 1895
20 Dupont, 'La Question Scolaire Manitobaine,' VIII, no.5, pp.368–79; Angers to Dupont, October 2, 1895
21 See below, p.153, n.62.
22 Dupont, 'La Question Scolaire Manitobaine,' IX, no.1, pp.33–41; Landry to Dupont, December 17, 1895
23 *Ibid.*, X, no.3, pp.168–77

CONSERVATIVE DISARRAY: SCHISMS WIDEN

That the general political situation was going from bad to worse was evident from many sources in the summer of 1895. As devoted a Conservative as Joseph Pope, Sir John A. Macdonald's former secretary, could write that Bowell was 'a man whose sudden and unlooked-for elevation had visibly turned his head,' and that 'public business during that unhappy summer was well-nigh paralysed.'[24] Lady Aberdeen's *Journal* reported one near-disaster after another. Among other events, there was the threatened resignation of A.R. Dickey, minister of militia, before the sessions ended.[25] Next was the fact that a cabinet minister, C.H. Tupper, had to be established as a quite extraordinary listening-post for the governor general and his wife on holiday in British Columbia.[26] Finally, Lady Aberdeen reported strong opposition stirred up in Winnipeg over the rumoured appointment of J.C. Patterson to replace John Schultz as lieutenant governor of Manitoba.[27] But the enduring disaster was clearly the prime minister himself. In Lady Aberdeen's view, although Bowell 'wants to be perfectly straight and as an Orangeman is undoubtedly plucky in his determination to do what in him lies to do justice to the R.C. minority of Manitoba,' he was characterized by 'weakness and consequent shiftiness.' Furthermore, he was 'altogether in the seventh heaven at being Premier and fancies that he can emulate Sir John Macdonald's genius in managing his party.' Unfortunately, Lady Aberdeen concluded, the only result was to create 'universal mistrust both amongst the Members of his Government and the party generally.'[28]

That Bowell lacked sureness and even a grasp of some basic factors was illustrated in an exchange of letters with Ewart at the same time that the 'olive-branch' reply was on its way to the Manitoba government in late July. On July 24, Bowell sent Caron a note that he had received from Emerson Coatsworth, the Toronto MP who had been so outspoken with Bowell before the debate in the House.[29] Coatsworth stated that the emphasis in the Ontario opposition to remedial legislation had shifted from outright opposition to separate schools to the argument that Manitoba Catholics no longer wanted such schools, an opinion apparently based on

---

24 *Public Servant*, pp.109–5
25 *Journal*, July 19, 1895, p.248
26 *Ibid.*, July 18, 1895, p.246

27 *Ibid.*, July 28, 1895, pp.254–5
28 *Ibid.*, July 18, 1895, p.245
29 See above, p.95.

John O'Donohue's testimony. Coatsworth was insistent that what the public thought was true was at least as important as the truth itself. 'If the general feeling prevails,' Coatsworth pointed out, 'that the Manitoba Catholics as a whole or in the main are satisfied with their public schools it will make remedial legislation so much more difficult.' In a covering note Bowell asked Caron for reassurances for Coatsworth. 'Would it not be well to put your people in Manitoba on the *qui vive*, and get them to make a general demand for Remedial Legislation?' Bowell wrote. Caron had simply forwarded both letters to Ewart.[30]

On July 30 Ewart somewhat wearily answered Caron and returned the two letters. With the implication that Caron and particularly Bowell should have known these facts for themselves, Ewart pointed out that Coatsworth had 'entirely overlooked the fact that the petition upon which the Government has proceeded in granting the remedial order is signed by 4267 Roman Catholics in Manitoba.' Ewart added that since the total Catholic population was at most twenty thousand, 'this proportion is as large as anyone could reasonably require, and at all events as large as could by any reasonable exertion be obtained.'[31]

The strongest proof of the government inability either to direct a national policy or to keep its own house in order was the case of Clarke Wallace, controller of customs. Though not of cabinet rank, his position was 'of the Ministry,' thus important enough to make his outspoken criticisms of the government's remedial policy a point of great embarrassment. His dissent was well known during the parliamentary session, but it was his pronouncements at later public meetings that paraded government divisions most graphically. On July 30 several newspapers reported a statement by Wallace at an Orange convention in Halifax in which he condemned the restoration or maintenance of separate schools as 'wholly incompatible with that absolute divorce of Church and State which we hold to be essential to the well being of the community at large.'[32]

C.H. Tupper lost no time in sending a strong protest against Wallace to Prime Minister Bowell. It was unmistakeable, Tupper said, that Wallace was 'opposed tooth and nail to that feature of our policy formally declared in Parliament. If Mr. Wallace longer remains a member of the Government,' Tupper went on, 'our position will be everywhere discredited and in

30 PAC, Caron Papers, Coatsworth to Bowell, July 23, 1895; Bowell to Caron, July 24, 1895
31 *Ibid.*, Ewart to Caron, July 30, 1895
32 Montreal *Gazette*, July 30, 1895

the end I fear will become intolerable. Intelligent Protestants in common with our Catholic friends will lose all confidence in our sincerity while we dare to allow even one "enemy" within the gates.'[33]

Tupper also wrote to Finance Minister Foster, who was then in Prince Edward Island. Foster agreed that the island province, like other parts of Canada, showed that a political explosion was not far off, and that a cabinet meeting was needed as soon as Manitoba's answer to the second federal message was officially received. As for Wallace, Foster tried to be non-committal and said that it was 'undoubtedly a question for the Premier to deal with.'[34]

Predictably, the prime minister was not prepared to deal with such a burning problem. His reply to Tupper was that the news reports were too meagre to be fully trusted. Bowell said he understood Tupper's annoyance in view of the latter's speech in Parliament, adding that 'the most serious feature, to my mind, is the fact of his [Wallace] putting the resolution, condemning the Government of which he is a quasi-member.'[35] But Bowell gave no indication of willingness to censure Wallace in any way.

The late summer correspondence between C.H. Tupper and his father in London was revealing. The senior Sir Charles was more articulate than ever in his ambition that his son should profit from the existing confusion eventually to become prime minister. The younger man was less sanguine, in particular because of the unresolved Wallace situation and the increasing virulence of the Ontario Tory press.[36] C.H. Tupper had in fact struck a tender and crucial point. A radically different direction was being pursued by Ontario Conservative papers from that espoused by other party journals, notably the Montreal *Gazette*. The *Mail and Empire* was inconsistent, but never accepted remedial legislation as a genuine possibility. The more extreme papers such as the Toronto *World* simply enlarged on the Sifton-Wallace thesis of hopeless incompetence in past or potential Catholic schools.[37]

33 PAC, Bowell Papers, C.H.Tupper to Bowell, July 31, 1895
34 PAC, C.H. Tupper Papers, Foster to Tupper, August 7, 1895
35 *Ibid.*, Bowell to Tupper, August 16, 1895
36 PAC, Tupper Papers, C. Tupper to C.H. Tupper, August 6, August 15, September 20, October 22, 1895; C.H. Tupper to C. Tupper, September 5, September 8, 1895
37 Enlarging on his earlier treatment of this subject, L.C. Clark presents repeated evidence on the gravity of the Tory journalistic schism, 'The Conservative Administrations' (thesis), pp.403–7.

LIBERAL TENSION AND COMPROMISE:
SUNNY WAYS AND TORRES VEDRAS

Meanwhile, the Liberals were not without their share of difficulties. During the parliamentary session Laurier wrote to Willison protesting an article which had appeared in the *Globe*.[38] The letter, also dated July 17, said that the *Globe* was within its rights to claim liberty of action, but Laurier felt that the article was 'as much an attack on the Liberal Party as on the Conservative Party.' In an unusual burst of sarcasm, Laurier complained that 'the Globe seems to be of the opinion that the whole of Canada is composed of one province.' He reminded Willison of the absolute necessity in Canada of accepting diversity and of 'an honorable acknowledgement of those differences with the view of effecting a compromise of the same.' The *Globe* article, Laurier concluded, could only be regarded as 'a very serious reflection on me personally, and it has been a most painful surprise to me.'[39]

By July 24 Laurier had calmed down. He assured Willison of his friendship and said that he realized that his policy of remaining uncommitted until the government made a definite step was not enough for many. 'I am not satisfied with it myself,' he said, yet insisted that 'under the circumstances it was impossible to take a bold and well defined attitude without breaking the unity of the party.' Laurier frankly admitted that such a rupture might eventually come, 'but to exhibit at this moment the spectacle of a divided opposition would have been simply playing the game of the government.' Laurier assured Willison of his continued esteem, but, in this and in a letter a week later, showed that he could not accept the unqualified provincial rights stand adopted by the *Globe*.[40]

Further strong voices pressed Laurier to oppose remedialism. A spokesman for Premier Blair of New Brunswick stated that a visit by Laurier to that province would do 'more harm than good' until a satisfactory statement could be made.[41] A similar warning regarding a proposed Ontario tour came from J.D. Edgar.[42] But Laurier first had to placate Quebec. The Toronto *Mail and Empire* printed the statement made by the Liberal leader at Sorel and elsewhere in Quebec, that some substantial

38 July 17, 1895
39 PAC, Willison Papers, Laurier to Willison, July 17, 1895
40 *Ibid.*, Laurier to Willison, July 24, August 2, 1895
41 PAC, Laurier Papers, Mitchell to Laurier, July 27, 1895
42 *Ibid.*, Edgar to Laurier, July 26, August 1, 1895

concessions had to be offered to Catholics by the Manitoba government.[43] William Mulock quickly wrote Laurier that such a position could never be acceptable to Liberals in Ontario, insisting that the only compromise possible was the application of the Public Schools Act worked out in Manitoba itself. Mulock quoted the *Mail and Empire* article, and warned Laurier against any further statement that could be interpreted as favouring federal interference.[44]

Sir Richard Cartwright's approach was cast much more in terms of pure political strategy. Writing to Laurier on September 16, Cartwright said that he feared 'work it how we will, we will lose something in Manitoba. The only consolation is that our opponents will probably lose more.' Sir Richard then outlined what he felt was the best course as far as Ontario was concerned. 'We should,' he said, 'state frankly that the perverse folly of Government had so complicated matters that nothing remained but to negotiate and that you had no doubt you could arrange a satisfactory settlement.'[45] Cartwright's suggestion would surely not be well taken by the Quebec hierarchy, but the defensive strategy he proposed would help to confirm Laurier's own inclination.

A further actor in the piece in the autumn of 1895 was Principal Grant of Queen's University. Grant visited Manitoba in the late summer, and a long report of his tour appeared in a series in the Toronto *Globe* during September. In this account and other statements, Grant was clearly of the opinion that the Catholic minority had grounds for complaint against the Manitoba government. 'They are little comforted on being assured by people who live thousands of miles away, that they have no grievances,' he said. At the same time Grant strongly held that, for the good of all concerned, an investigation was a prime necessity.[46] Grant's effort earned him, among other reactions, the title of 'enemy of the national system' in F.C. Wade's pro-Manitoba booklet on the school question.[47] In any case, the widespread publicity of Grant's sympathy for the minority, combined with his pre-eminence as an educator who had had several well-known clashes with Archbishop Cleary of Kingston, would give his support of an inquiry weight with both Catholics and Protestants. The point was not lost by Laurier.

43 September 7, 1895
44 PAC, Laurier Papers, Mulock to Laurier, September 10, 1895
45 *Ibid.*, Cartwright to Laurier, September 16, 1895
46 Toronto *Globe*, letter by Principal Grant, September 21, 1895
47 *The Manitoba School Question*, pp.110–11

Laurier well knew that he would need all the support he could get. Despite the conflicting advice he had received and the increasing tempo of newspaper controversy over his position or lack of position as leader of the opposition, he scheduled a speaking tour of Ontario for October. As a preliminary, Laurier sought to enlist in a more vocal form the support of Senator Richard Scott, whose reputation as a moderate Catholic diplomat in school problems went back to the act of 1863 which bore his name. After discussing several other party problems, Laurier moved on to the core of his letter, a clear adoption of Grant's inquiry proposal. Pointedly referring to Scott's clerical connections, Laurier begged the senator to have his 'voice heard in high quarters.' Not ignoring the question of political advantage, Laurier reminded Scott that 'even from that point of view there is everything to be gained, by insisting at this juncture, that the true solution is by the joint investigation of the whole subject under the auspices and action of the two governments.'[48]

It was at Morrisburg, Ontario, on October 8, that Laurier proposed the two happy images which would serve him well for both present and future policy. For his future treatment of Manitoba, if he were to come to power, Laurier used the familiar fable from Aesop of the contest between the wind and the sun to remove the traveller's coat:

Well, sir, the government are very windy. They have blown and raged and threatened, but the more they have threatened and raged and blown the more that man Greenway has stuck to his coat. If it were in my power, I would try the sunny way.

As a rationale for his immediate policy of not presenting a detailed plan of action, Laurier seized on an even more appealing precedent, that of the Duke of Wellington against Napoleon's armies. He was not responsible for the current battle, Laurier stated, but neither did he want to shirk it. He reminded his audience that 'war has to be waged in a certain way':

When the Duke of Wellington was in Portugal, as those of you will remember who have read that part of the history of England, he withdrew at one time within the lines of Torres Vedras, and there for months he remained, watching the movements of the enemy. The French at that time were commanded by Marshall Massena, and Massena said: 'I want that man to come down from his lines; let him come down into the plain and I will thrash him, but I cannot assail him within the lines.' Gentlemen, I

48 PAC, Scott Papers, Laurier to Scott, October 1, 1895

am within the lines of Torres Vedras, I will get out of them when it suits me and not before.[49]

Glossing over the fact that there might be some difficulty in the exact application of the military metaphor, Laurier had found in the 'lines of Torres Vedras' a slogan to arouse sentiment from Ontario British hearts and, if nothing more, grudging acceptance of the strategy from the French.

As had been the case in March, David Mills took up a position quite different from that of most of Laurier's influential Ontario supporters. On October 12 Mills wrote Laurier a long and worried letter. He said that he very much regretted not being able to join Laurier for at least a few of his Ontario speaking engagements, but was restricted by his law lectures, of which he was giving twelve hours a week until Christmas. Moreover, he wanted to be free for meetings during the holidays and be ready to take his seat at the January session, should it come.

Obviously the Manitoba school question loomed large in Mills's mind, and he was afraid that party strategy might have taken over from principle in Ontario. Mills was not prepared to accept all the claims of Archbishop Langevin, but he was convinced that federal action was necessary. He confessed to 'great uneasiness' about the school question, yet he had 'no doubt whatever in regard to the Constitutional right of the minority in Manitoba, nor of the Constitutional duty of Parliament to protect that minority.' Worse still, Mills added, 'every hour's delay increases the difficulty of obeying the law and keeping faith.' As to the proposed strategy of 'Torres Vedras,' Mills was very frank. 'I can't help but feel,' he said, 'that the course taken is not one dictated by prudence but by timidity. Every day prejudice is more and more settling into a conviction of right, and the time must soon come when, looking at the course taken by the press, that it will be impossible for any Government in Manitoba to keep faith and live.' Characteristically, Mills derided the position taken by the *Globe* and ridiculed its publication of the booklet on the school question by F.C. Wade as 'most discreditable.' As a final ironic comment on party advantage, Mills stated that only the presence of Wallace had prevented the Irish Catholics from going over in a body to the Conservatives.[50]

The tour and the policy of 'Torres Vedras' nevertheless went on, though not without continued controversy within the Liberal ranks. A particular irritant was the presence of J. Israel Tarte on the Laurier team. Laurier felt

49 Toronto *Globe*, October 9, 1895
50 PAC, Laurier Papers, Mills to Laurier, October 12, 1895

that the Ontario Liberal attitude to Tarte was both unfair and unwise, and said so in a letter to Willison on November 3:

On the whole it was far better that Tarte should come to Ontario. It does good here, even if the result will be nil in Ontario. I do not however understand the sensitiveness of our friends. Tarte has done good, excellent service since he has joined us, and even if he be now charged with having done wrong while he was in the high councils of the conservative party, he deserves all the more credit for having broken away from them.

Laurier in the same letter took the opportunity to discuss the case of Honoré Beaugrand of *La Patrie*, the radical Rouge Montreal journalist whom Laurier had recently felt obliged to reject as a spokesman for the Liberal party. Laurier said that he realized his action gave the Tory press a chance to cry that he was playing for the clerical vote. On the other hand, the Liberal leader told Willison, it would have been much worse to have ignored Beaugrand's statement that *La Patrie*, while returning to the principles of *L'Avenir* of the old Rouge party, was still the voice of the Liberals in Quebec. Laurier was sure that had he not disavowed Beaugrand, cries of anti-cleric and pro-annexation would have been raised against him perhaps beyond control.[51]

Either not being conscious of or choosing to ignore the criticisms of his presence on the Ontario tour, Tarte wrote a cheerful letter to Willison on November 4 in which he dismissed Beaugrand even more thoroughly than had Laurier. Beaugrand had sent a letter to the Hamilton *Times*, accusing Laurier of being led by men of the Mercier tradition of over-deference to ecclesiastics. On this Tarte commented that 'Beaugrand has been for years a source of trouble and weakness for the Liberal party, as everyone in Montreal will tell you. He is a radical and a fool,' Tarte went on. 'A more selfish man you have never met ... Believe me, it is better to have Beaugrand against us than for us,' Tarte concluded, and asked Willison to refute the Beaugrand letter by a statement in the *Globe*.[52]

That there was no serious breach over the Tarte role was shown by the fact that both Laurier and Tarte continued to call on Willison for support on various matters during November. Whatever private apprehensions Willi-

51 PAC, Willison Papers, Laurier to Willison, November 3, 1895
52 *Ibid.*, Tarte to Willison, November 4, 1895. The situation involving Beaugrand was clearly the reason for establishing *Le Soir* as a more official Liberal voice in the Montreal area in April 1896. The new journal, however, survived only four months.

son may have had about Laurier's Ontario trip, the *Globe* was publicly confident that the results were all to the good for the Liberals. 'The Liberal party was never more united than at the present time,' the newspaper declared. 'From the chief down to the humblest man in the ranks there is permeating the party the spirit that presages victory.'[53]

At the same time as this controversy developed over personalities and immediate policy, Laurier tried to meet a more important long-range problem. If he was to enter a national electoral struggle with the school question threatening to ruin him in Quebec, Laurier had to be sure of a solid team to carry the rest of the country. Thus, on November 5, the Liberal leader wrote to Premier Fielding of Nova Scotia, offering him a portfolio in the government he hoped to form. After summing up the confusion and uncertainty resulting from the school question about as well as anyone ever did – 'it may break the opposition, or break the government, or break both the opposition and the government' – Laurier offered these comments on election prospects:

It is now evident that the government are going to make a strong bid to capture the Roman Catholic vote, by introducing remedial legislation, that is to say setting aside the school law of Manitoba, and substituting a law of their own. That they will capture the Roman Catholic vote is not at all certain, for I know for a certainty that the most intelligent and far seeing among the Roman Catholics – both clergy and laity – dread the action of the government as likely to conduce not to the reestablishment of separate schools in Manitoba, but to agitation for the abolition of separate schools in all the provinces.

Defending his own position calling for an investigation, Laurier said he felt it ultimately would be accepted. Yet it had to be admitted that 'when you come to deal with those questions, in which religion is concerned, it is always safe to look to unforeseen consequences.' Probably expressing more confidence than he felt, Laurier added that 'I do not apprehend them in this case, but I just point out the situation such as it is, with its advantages, and its possible dangers.'[54] Fielding's cautious reply, sent on November 25, indicated his consent to join the Laurier team, presuming the concurrence of 'other leading Nova Scotia Liberals.'[55]

During the struggle at Ottawa, members of the Manitoba government

53 October 29, 1895
54 PAC, Laurier Papers, Laurier to Fielding, November 5, 1895
55 *Ibid.*, Fielding to Laurier, November 25, 1895

were far from idle. Premier Greenway continued to receive many communications urging him to stand firm against federal interference, but the pressure on him was by no means from one direction only. Several of the letters he received from people in high places urged moderation and compromise. For instance, on November 27, 1895 Senator Charles Boulton of Manitoba urged 'some mode of negotiation by which a conciliatory attitude on both sides may be brought about.' The senator, a man with more impeccable anti-Riel credentials than even Schultz, added that he feared complete intransigence on Manitoba's part would mean playing into Mackenzie Bowell's hands.[56]

However, as had been clear during the aftermath of the remedial order of March, Greenway was not the one who was making the binding decisions in Manitoba. Clifford Sifton, as acting minister of education (his primary cabinet post was that of attorney general), carefully avoided inflammatory statements and actions, but used many expedients to publicize a 'no-compromise' position on the part of the Manitoba government. On August 9 Sifton sent a copy of his own outline of the case to Dr Albert Shaw, editor of the *Review of Reviews* in New York and on August 17, sent another copy to the London editor of the same review.[57] More significantly, Sifton was active in circulating the booklet by F.C. Wade on the school question. This highly partisan, sometimes scurrilous, booklet, was published in full in the Toronto *Globe*,[58] and many of Sifton's subsequent 1895 letters mentioned his enclosing the work to his correspondents.[59] The extent to which the booklet was being used, as well as the degree of collaboration between Sifton and D'Alton McCarthy, was illustrated by a long November letter. Referring to McCarthy's request for speakers for the December by-elections in Ontario, Sifton regretted that no one could be sent from the Manitoba government. Literature, however, was another matter. Five hundred copies of Wade's booklet had already been shipped, and 'if any more can be made use of to advantage they will be forwarded immediately.'[60]

CONSERVATIVE AND CLERICAL MANOEUVRES

Rents in the Liberal fabric, however, were minor compared to those in the

56 PAM, Greenway Papers, Boulton to Greenway, November 27, 1895
57 PAC, Sifton Papers, Sifton to Shaw, August 9, 1895; Sifton to Stead, August 17, 1895
58 September 17ff, 1895
59 PAC, Sifton Papers, Sifton to Alfred Hunter, Toronto lawyer, December 11, 1895; Sifton to Rev. Thomas Webster, Newbury, Ontario, December 23, 1895
60 *Ibid.*, Sifton to McCarthy, November 27, 1895

Conservative. On September 26, Fred L. Jones, parliamentary correspondent for the Toronto *Globe*, delivered a few items of Ottawa gossip to Laurier, still at his home in Arthabaska. Jones reported that Ouimet had said that Angers might still be invited and persuaded to return. He quoted an unnamed Conservative cabinet minister in praise of Laurier for his tact thus far in handling the Manitoba question. Jones's comments on Bowell were, as might be expected, not flattering. The prime minister had recently made a brief trip through Manitoba and the Territories. There was no doubt, said Jones, that the object of Bowell's visit had been to see Greenway. It was equally clear that Bowell had made no headway with the Manitoba premier.[61]

The Conservative view of their own situation was, if anything, even less congratulatory than that painted by their Liberal opponents. If strength had been looked for from the Conservative provincial government of Quebec, a loss in a Montreal by-election in October dampened any possible optimism from that direction. Arthur Dansereau commented, as only he could, on the Montreal reaction against Premier Taillon in a letter to Lieutenant Governor Chapleau in Quebec:

Ce soir, grande excitation dans les rues de Montréal. Le vote anglais a été presque général contre le gouvernement. Ne cherche pas de midi à quatorze heures. On va te dire que c'est la nomination de Curran: erreur. Ce peut être le prétexte; mais non la cause. C'est un vote personellement hostile à Taillon. Pour comble de malheur, ceux qu'il a fidèlement soutenus en chambre contre le sentiment de la ville de Montréal, tels que Bond, G.W. Stephens, Hague, Thomas, ont tous, comme un seul homme, enrégimenté leurs forces dans cette élection contre lui. Ce qu'il a de flair! Et n'oublie pas que c'est à peu près la même chose partout. Cette bonne et honnête nature croit qu'on peut conduire le monde avec des prières.[62]

Needless to say the Dansereau report was not calculated to prompt Chapleau to return to the active Conservative team, federal or provincial.

Perhaps the most scathing description of French-Canadian Conservative leaders, particularly of the moderate or Bleu persuasion, came from the pen of Colonel Audet in a letter to Archbishop Langevin on October 10. Audet began his litany of condemnation with Laurier, saying that the Liberal leader was left with only two choices, to be 'un radical ou un lâche.' But Audet then lashed out even more violently in the opposite direction. 'Du coté des conservateurs, notre marchandise est-elle de meilleure

61 PAC, Laurier Papers, Jones to Laurier, September 26, 1895
62 PAC, Chapleau Papers, Dansereau to Chapleau, October 22, 1895

qualité?' he asked. His answer was not very hopeful. 'Si les principes sont meilleures, l'applaitissement et la vénalité sont les mêmes,' he complained. Audet felt that Angers was an exception, but, whether one looked to Ottawa or Quebec, the rest of the Conservative picture was black indeed:

Caron, Ouimet, Chapleau, Beaulieu, Nantel, Pelletier, et le reste, qu'avons-nous sous ces noms? On ne peut répondre à ces questions en public, en présence des étrangers, mais entre nous, en petite comité, les portes bien fermées, tout bas, il faut bien nous avouer que ces hommes ne sont pas honnêtes ni de sentiments, ni d'actions; qu'ils s'entourent de voleurs et de crapules; que ce sont tous dês goinfres et pour la plupart des vulgaires ivrognes; qu'ils exploitent le pouvoir, le parti et les amis du parti comme des brigands le feraient d'une forêt impénétrable. Et ces admissions, ces aveux, nous couvrent le front de honte, nous noient le coeur dans le dégout et le découragement.[63]

Whatever can be said for or against Audet's political and personal insight, his sweeping condemnation of the French Conservative leaders would hardly dispose his friend the archbishop to trust the fate of the Manitoba schools to the exclusive care of such a group.

Rumours flew thick and fast in early November about the quickening of a revolt within the cabinet. The practical outcome of the anti-Bowell movement was a scheme whereby Sir Charles Tupper, Senior, could return from England to replace the prime minister. Bowell was persuaded to invite Tupper to return to Canada to discuss plans for a fast North Atlantic steamer line. But the camouflage was at best flimsy. So unsettling was the cabinet 'palace intrigue' that even C.H. Tupper's formerly adamant stance on remedial legislation began to waver. At least he tried his hand at convincing the Manitoba Catholic party to press for a compromise which would make remedial legislation unnecessary. In a November 12 letter to Ewart, then in Ottawa, Tupper put into writing what he had apparently stated in conversation the night before. 'In my opinion,' Tupper wrote, 'any fair settlement of the School question now is in the interest of the minority rather than a reliance on the Federal Parliament.' Tupper cited several compelling reasons: the bill's details had not yet even been discussed in cabinet despite the proximity of a session; the actual presentation of a bill would probably bring on a cabinet crisis, despite his own wish to avoid that if possible; it did not seem that the vacancy in the cabinet was going to be

63 AASB, Audet to Langevin, October 10, 1895. It is interesting to note that by the time of the January cabinet crisis, Audet would include Angers in his list of accusations (AASB, Audet to Langevin, January 6, 1896).

filled; finally, Laurier, in opposition, was pledged to further delay. 'For this and many other reasons,' Tupper concluded, 'pray carefully consider any compromise before insisting on the full enactment from us as all may then be lost.'[64]

Unhappily, the prospect of substantial accommodation was decreasing on all sides. For one thing, the one Quebec bishop whom outsiders seemed to consider as a possible ambassador between Catholic forces and the Manitoba government was unwilling to thrust himself into such a thankless and probably fruitless task. Bishop Emard of Valleyfield, in a revealing reply to Father Wagner, dean of Windsor, Ontario, said that he would not have any official status if he did go to see Greenway, as Wagner and others had suggested. In Emard's view, such a visit would have been looked upon with disapproval by other bishops because of the national repercussions of the Manitoba question and of everything done to try to solve it. In a remark clearly aimed at Angers and other ultramontanes, Emard reminded Wagner that the problem was 'singulièrement compliqué par les exigences de la partisannerie politique, et elle a été rendue bien difficile à résoudre par les indiscrétions tapageuses de certains hommes qui étaient le plus tenus au calme et à la prudence.' Finally, said Emard, he would be leaving himself open to charges of 'l'ingérence étrangère,' a commodity which seemed to be increasing on all sides.[65]

Even further reducing the likelihood of compromise, Archbishop Langevin continued to receive strong journalistic support from Conservative newspapers in Quebec. That he appreciated and continued to reinforce this support was shown by his correspondence with several editors in early November. To L.Z. Joncas of *L'Evénement*, Langevin wrote to recommend an article in *Le Manitoba* condemning the 'enquête' proposed by Laurier. The archbishop insisted that 'Greenway n'a rien fait et ne veut rien faire – proposer une enquête c'est faire le jeu de nos plus implacables ennemis.' Langevin added a postscript with exclamation marks that left little room for adjustment, with or without an inquiry. 'Il n'est nullement question d'un compromis!' he proclaimed.[66] Letters in a similar vein went to T. Chapais of *Le Courrier du Canada* and J. Royal of *La Minerve*. A capsule assessment of Laurier's motives left little room for accommodation. 'Le malheureux Laurier nous trahit pour arriver au pouvoir,' Langevin concluded.[67]

64 PAC, C.H. Tupper Papers, C.H. Tupper to Ewart, November 12, 1895
65 AEV, Emard to Wagner, October 31, 1895
66 AASB, Langevin to Joncas, November 2, 1895
67 *Ibid.*, Langevin to Royal, November 2, 1895

Joncas's November 6 reply to Langevin reflected the solemn tone of the Quebec right-wing journals and certainly encouraged the archbishop to remain adamant.[68] But if it was true that the Conservative spokesmen were willing to support Langevin's no-compromise policy, it was equally clear that they expected a return. At least they did not want any weak links in the ecclesiastical chain. Royal made this quite clear to the archbishop in a letter concerning a Father Page of St Boniface who apparently had advised his family in Quebec to support Laurier. Worst of all, Royal complained, Page had quoted Langevin as authority for his position:

Cette lettre fait le tour de la famille Page qui est très conservateur et est exploitée par les autres ...

Voilà un monsieur prêtre qui est bien imprudent pour ne rien dire de plus et je suis sur qu'en portant le fait à la connaissance de Votre Grandeur le dommage fait aux frères de M. Page par un tel avis sera réparé en temps opportun.[69]

As for actual negotiations on a possible negotiated settlement, news of several attempts to devise an acceptable formula came from Ottawa to Langevin in late November. J.S. Ewart reported his contact with C.H. Tupper and said that he had delayed leaving Ottawa in order to be available for consultation. Commenting on various plans that he had thus far heard proposed, Ewart said they were 'not at all such as Your Grace would sanction and I am inclined to think that they will not be much improved.' On the one hand, it was certain that Greenway would not make 'sufficient advances.' On the other, Ewart's confidence in the federal government was disappearing. 'Whatever may be given to the public, I feel assured that there is the very greatest difficulty and disagreement in the cabinet,' he observed. 'Not only about the school case but upon other points, the relations of the ministers seems to be very much strained and I am apprehensive that it may be impossible for them to agree upon a bill giving relief to the minority.'[70]

68 *Ibid.*, Joncas to Langevin, November 6, 1895
69 *Ibid.*, J. Royal to Langevin, November 2, 1895
70 *Ibid.*, Ewart to Langevin, November 18, 1895. An interesting sidelight on Ewart's continuing role in the school case was the fact that he had a rather substantial bill for legal fees which had not been paid and yet he was unwilling to press Archbishop Langevin for the same. Ewart had sent his bill to Alex Ferguson, who was handling the finances of the case for the federal government. Ferguson forwarded it, though after a month's delay, to Caron, and suggested a total payment from the federal government of $1000 to cover Ewart's bill and Ferguson's own expenses. Ewart's letter was also important because it

Beginning with an attitude quite different from Ewart's near-pessimism, Senator Bernier, on his arrival at Ottawa, wrote that he would do his best to insist on existing gains rather than consent to any compromise. On November 17, Bernier told Langevin that Ewart was inclined to give in too easily.[71] A week later, Bernier reported that although no detailed proposal had come to light, 'il parait toujours qu'il y a quelque raison de croire à un mouvement de rapprochement de Greenway et de son gouvernement.'[72] A third letter of November 28, however, showed that Bernier was now inclined to share Ewart's unhappy view.[73] Alphonse LaRivière held out the hope that, while the first Greenway offer was not enough, it might be amended satisfactorily. He asked if this was possible from Langevin's point of view, but then gave a strangely accurate prophecy based on his estimate of public opinion:

L'opinion générale ici, est que Laurier s'opposera à la loi réparatrice en proposant un enquête, et qu'il aura l'appui de tous les libéraux et d'un nombre suffisant de conservateurs anglais pour empêcher l'adoption de la mesure. Advenant ensuite son arrivée au pouvoir nous n'attendrions pas plus que ce qui nous est offert aujourd'hui, avec le rappel du 'Remedial Order.'[74]

LaRivière and Bernier, however, were not the major source of worry. On November 30 C.H. Tupper stepped up the pressure he had begun three weeks earlier with Ewart. The specific prelude was a note from Langevin

revealed the difficulties encountered in financing the surviving Catholic schools. Bompas, Bischoff and Co. of London had apparently reduced their charges by $250 after Ewart's objection. In particular, however, Ewart stressed that Langevin was in no position whatever to bear outstanding costs: 'I would further press upon you not to ask for any further reduction because the only effect of it would be to make us charge it up against the Archbishop here. Perhaps you are aware of the extremely straightened circumstances in which he finds himself at present. For the last five years he has had to strain every nerve and appeal not only to his flock here, but to seek very largely outside assistance in order to keep up his schools in this Province. His exchequer is completely depleted, and as you may have known, he is endeavouring to raise some money in Quebec by means of a lottery. The small item of $794 is really nothing at all to the men with whom you deal, whereas it would be a matter of very great importance to our people here. I may say confidentially that the embarrassment for funds is here so great that I have had to contribute, as well as some other Protestant friends very considerably towards the Winnipeg schools' (PAC, Caron Papers, Ewart to Ferguson, November 8, 1895; Ferguson to Caron, December 4, 1895).

71 AASB, Bernier to Langevin, November 17, 1895
72 *Ibid.*, Bernier to Langevin, November 23, 1895
73 *Ibid.*, Bernier to Langevin, November 28, 1895
74 *Ibid.*, LaRivière to Langevin, November 29, 1895

congratulating the Nova Scotian on his continued statements favouring relief for Manitoba Catholics. Langevin had not, however, confined himself to compliments. He pressed Tupper for continued vigour and warned that episcopal support for the Conservative party was not automatic. Langevin urged that 'surely ... we will not be delivered up into the hands of our enemies with a simple concession of detail ... A nominal settlement would be worse than a flat denial of justice,' he went on, 'and it would expose us to lose for ever faith and confidence in a party that have assumed the noble mission of protecting what the Hon. Lords of the Hon. Privy Council of England call the Parliamentary Compact.'[75]

Tupper replied to Langevin that negotiations were still going on at Ottawa and thanked the archbishop for his compliments. Echoing his words to Ewart, however, Tupper stated that he was now 'favourable to compromise if the essential elements of equality and justice were secured for the minority.' Tupper's rationale for his change of position was strongly tinged with complaint:

I am drawn to this by the evident apathy of Catholics. Our Government ever since the espousal of their cause, has had no accession of strength. We lost a Catholic county in N.S. A Catholic candidate is now found fighting us in an Ontario constituency and a Catholic deserted us in the Cabinet.

A catholic leader (from Quebec as well) dares to advocate a commission for further delay and enquiry, and to argue (at Renfrew, Ont.) that after all, the grievances of the Manitoba minority are simply those which every minority has, and which are redressed only when under the condition it becomes a majority.

In view of these facts, Tupper believed, the alternative to a negotiated compromise would be 'defeat in Parliament and afterwards in the country,' which would 'leave the minority without any redress, and our constitution dishonoured and ignored.' Tupper assured Langevin that Bowell, if pressed to the limit, would not back down from his formal pledge, 'but it is hard to realize, as I am doing, the faint support he is obtaining from Catholics in the face of desperate efforts to wean from him the strength of his quondam Protestant friends.'[76] Tupper dramatically revealed the problem caused by the identification of the church with one party's program; there could be no mistaking the pressure he was putting on the archbishop.

With this letter before him, Langevin seems to have sent out warning

75 AASB, Langevin to Tupper, November 27, 1895
76 Ibid., Tupper to Langevin, November 3, 1895

signals that there was danger of LaRivière and Bernier capitulating; a December 6 letter from La Rivière was profuse in assurances to the contrary. 'M. le senateur [Bernier] et moi, nous accordons parfaitment avec vous, Mgr., à refuser quoique ce soit qui ne serait qu'un compromis, et non une restitution des nos écoles séparées.'[77]

Meanwhile, Archbishop Bégin had some significant news in Quebec. He was much happier with Tupper's performance than with that of Caron and Ouimet, and not all sure of Angers's current state of mind. 'L'Hon. Angers a, dit-on, tantôt des espérances, tantôt des craintes,' Bégin wrote. 'On me tient au courant de ses fluctuations d'idées.' More interesting, however, was Bégin's account of important meetings with Laurier:

J'ai eu deux longues entrevues avec M. Laurier; la dernière m'a un peu plus reconforté que la première. Il a toujours son projet d'enquête à mettre en avant pour former, dit-il, l'opinion protestante ou plutôt pour la réformer et la préparer à accepter de bon coeur une législation rémédiatrice. Il me dit que Mgr. Walsh, Arch. de Toronto, tout en ne se liguant pas avec le parti libéral, épouse cependant ses idées, même celle d'une enquête. J'ai toujours combattu cette idée qui me paraît être propre à remettre en question et à compromettre nos succès obtenus devant le Conseil Privé; il prétend que les Conservateurs, même s'ils font adopter une loi rémédiatrice, ne pourront pas la faire fonctionner, parce qu'on suscitera toute espèce d'entraves. Il m'a dit clairement, 'Mgr., c'est nous qui règlerons la question, et nous la règlerons de manière à donner satisfaction aux catholiques de Manitoba.' M. Choquette, son bras droit, m'a dit la même chose, il y a quelques jours. M. Laurier a ajouté qu'il pourrait obtenir du gouvernement Greenway plus facilement que les Conservateurs un abandon des mesures injustes prises vis-a-vis de la minorité. Je le crois bien – Il reconnait parfaitement que la minorité a des griefs fondés et que le Gouvernement Fédéral doit intervenir. Je lui ai conseillé d'aider les conservateurs à régler la question si épineuse du Manitoba afin qu'il n'ait pas à s'en occuper, s'il finit par arriver au pouvoir; le fera-t-il?[78]

Clearly, the Liberal leader was not yet ready to emerge from his 'lines of Torres Vedras,' and the July predictions of both Sifton and Angers that delay would bring little change were being borne out.

The position or confusion of position to which Langevin had been brought by these various influences was amply reflected in two long letters

77 *Ibid.*, LaRivière to Langevin, December 6, 1895
78 *Ibid.*, Bégin to Langevin, November 26, 1895. In this letter, as elsewhere, Bégin showed that he was hardly the active pro-Angers partisan suggested by Audet.

which he sent at the end of November to episcopal colleagues, Bégin in Quebec and Cleary in Kingston. To begin with, Langevin told Bégin, the Manitoba government itself had admitted that its schools were Protestant when, by way of compromise, the offer had been made to suppress 'tout ce qui est sectarian dans leurs écoles publiques ... et de permettre l'instruction religieuse dans les écoles après trois heures.' Langevin then spoke of Ewart's refusal to consider the Manitoba proposal and expressed renewed confidence in the hard-working lawyer. The archbishop also discussed the evident obstacle caused by the division within the cabinet. He then posed the problem of alternatives if the federal cabinet did not bring forth a bill. What, for instance, should the Catholic ministers be advised to do? Should they resign? Langevin showed that he was not yet a Laflèche; he at least wondered what was the best method of proceeding. 'Y aura-t-il lieu de lancer la sorte de manifeste dont parlait Mgr. Laflèche?' he asked, 'Y aura-t-il lieu de faire un programme pour le présenter à l'électorat et le faire signer par les candidats?'

The question of the impending by-elections was then discussed, Langevin asking Bégin if he could exert influence, particularly in Charlevoix. Finally, Laurier's noncommittal position, even as reported by Bégin, was again criticized. If Protestants were not already prepared for the law by the delay from the previous session, he said, they would hardly be more prepared by further delay. At the end of the letter came a few dash notes added on December 1:

Prendergast, notre député ici, me disait en confidence qu'il est dégouté de Laurier, que ce grand chef a perdu sa meilleure carte en ne prenant pas en mains la cause de nos écoles ... Le Lieutenant-Governor Patterson nous est favorable ici, mais il ne peut rien ... Lord Aberdeen m'a demandé s'il pouvait nous aider ... Ce qu'il nous faudrait, ce serait au moins un homme parmi nos ministres canadiens.[79]

From the beginning Langevin was clearly concerned that the struggle for school restoration be not a 'French-only' effort. During the crisis of the previous summer, he had written Bégin of his hope to involve the 'Irish' bishops (a racial classification which would have interested, if not amused, at least Bishop Cameron). 'Je tiens à avoir l'appui entier et formel de l'episcopat irlandais,' Langevin stated. 'A ce dessein, j'écris à Mgr. Cleary de Kingston et je lui envoie une copie du petit résumé dans lequel M. Ewart

79 AAQ, Langevin to Bégin, November 29, December 1, 1895

indique comme introduction au bill un sommaire des concessions faites.'[80]

With the same purpose in mind, Langevin sent another message to Cleary immediately after his letter to Bégin at the end of November. The first part of Langevin's letter discussed the remedial measure supposedly being prepared in Ottawa. Langevin spoke as if he were in constant contact with Ewart in the capital, and seemed to feel confident he could accept certain details and reject others in the proposed bill. He spoke of the danger of the lieutenant governor's nomination to the proposed school board of 'nominal Catholics, bad Catholics, like the freemason John O'Donohue of Winnipeg.' He said that he would insist on Catholic inspectors, since 'in the North-West our people are ill-treated by protestant inspectors who are altogether unfair toward the C. schools.' Regarding the problem of Catholics in districts where they were too few to have separate schools, Langevin said he had agreed that Catholic taxes should go to the public schools. 'Some find it too lenient on my part,' he added, 'because there is no vice-versa for the Protestants who will never pay taxes to the Sep. Schools. But Mr. Ewart, our legal advisor, told me that this concession would appear very liberal and give satisfaction to many people.'

Then came an excited postscript, added on December 2. 'Two great events' had taken place since the first part of Langevin's letter. 'First, the Greenway Government have communicated with the Federal Cabinet about some kind of a compromise by which we would be left entirely to the good will of our Protestant friends of the majority.' The 'compromise' Langevin found almost ludicrous. The only concession proposed was a permission to be granted to clergy of all faiths to teach religion after 3:30 PM in the existing schools. 'Evidently, we cannot even entertain the idea of adopting such a poor scheme,' the archbishop said. 'The second event,' Langevin added, 'is the mission given to V. Rev. Father Lacombe by your humble brother and his suffragants [sic], to go and see Our Rev. Brothers of the Hierarchy.'[81] Ironically, the conditions outlined with such care by Langevin in the early part of his letter turned out to be quite unrealistic; the briefly mentioned mission given to Lacombe proved to be of major significance.[82]

80 Ibid., Langevin to Bégin, August 2, 1895
81 AASB, Langevin to Cleary, November 29, December 2, 1895
82 Albert Lacombe (1827–1916) went west as a missionary immediately after his 1849 ordination at the age of twenty-two in Montreal. He soon came to know the youthful Bishop Taché, joined the Oblate order, and was sent directly to Fort Edmonton with the traders of the Hudson's Bay Company. Not only did he evangelize, but he became known as the

The five months between July and December had not greatly changed the argument or policy of either federal party. Strategically, however, the passage of time and events was clearly in the Liberals' favour. Laurier had found a way to prolong his refusal to take a positive stand on remedialism, thus allowing his party to remain at least externally united. The Conservatives, on the other hand, had only narrowed their choices and reduced their hopes of success under a leader they neither respected nor were willing to support. As Angers bitterly remarked about the team he had abandoned, 'Le gouvernement depuis juillet dernier n'a converti personne.'[83]

friend of both Cree and Blackfoot in the whole territory between the Bow and Peace rivers. All his life he promoted Indian training schools to ease the hard transition brought about by the white civilization. The year 1874 saw his completion of a remarkable Cree dictionary and grammar. On at least two occasions his was the crucial influence in preventing serious trouble between Indian and white, first in 1883 when the CPR was being rushed through Blackfoot territory, then in 1885 when he persuaded the majority of the Indians not to join the Northwest Rebellion. Not least among those who regarded Lacombe as the West's most important missioner, Catholic or Protestant, was William Van Horne, builder and later president of the CPR. When the first train arrived in Calgary in 1883, Lacombe was honoured by President George Stephen and Van Horne by being named president of the CPR for one hour during a dinner in the official dining car. Nor was he a novice at dealing with government officials. Between 1893 and the fall of 1895 he had been in Ottawa no less than four times to discuss the school problems, first of the Métis and Indians, later of the Catholics of Manitoba and the Northwest. Thus the legate chosen by Langevin lacked neither prestige nor practice in the art of lobbying. Lacombe's forty-six letters to his archbishop during his stay in the East, provided a constant, if highly personal and sometimes biased, insight into the political events of the period between December, 1895, and March, 1896. More significantly, Lacombe became the major source of information and attitude being fed to the bishops (especially Langevin), and thus an important factor in the formation of their policy.

Further biographical details on Lacombe may be found in Hughes, *Father Lacombe: The Black Robe Voyageur*, and J. Phelan, *The Bold Heart*. A treatment of Lacombe's Ottawa sojourn from his personal point of view is given in Crunican, 'Father Lacombe's Strange Mission,' pp.57–72.

83 Dupont, 'La Question Scolaire Manitobaine,' VIII, no.5, pp.368–79; Angers to Dupont, December 14, 1895

5
December by-elections and the January crisis: re-alignment without revival

Whether or not remedial legislation was actually to come after the new year, the Conservatives' immediate political objective of the last weeks of 1895 was the winning of several key by-elections, two in Ontario and two in Quebec, all formerly held by the party. Ontario North was to be contested on December 12, Cardwell, which included the Orangeville-Caledon area, on December 24; and the two Montreal ridings of Montreal Centre and Jacques Cartier, vacated by the judicial appointments of J.J. Curran and Désiré Girouard, were set for December 27 and 30 respectively.

The two Ontario ridings were considered as significant tests of the English-speaking Catholic vote,[1] but both parties sensed that the key battles would be in Quebec. A month before the elections, Laurier was already confident that the two Montreal Conservative strongholds were 'safe for us beyond question.'[2] On the other side of the political fence, Caron was appealing to Archbishop Langevin to use all possible influence in the Quebec contests. Caron called the situation 'très grave' in Judge Curran's former riding of Montreal Centre, and insisted that the crucial factor was to get the right candidate to run. The man in question was Dr Sir William Hingston, 'catholique fervent, professeur à l'Université Laval, bien vu des Anglais-protestants, Irlandais lui-même, ayant le confiance des

---

1 PAC, Costigan Papers, Costigan to Walsh, December 20, 1895
2 PAC, Willison Papers, Laurier to Willison, November 19, 1895

Irlandais et universellement respecté par tous.' Caron stated that Archbishop Fabre had agreed to approach Hingston to enter the contest. Now the minister of militia wanted Langevin to exert pressure as well, and drew in bolder lines the political syllogism which he seemed to forget had been used in Verchères in April:

Je n'ai pas besoin de vous expliquer que, si nous perdons Mont. Centre, les protestants qui nous appuient sur la question des Ecoles nous diront: La province de Quebec ne se préoccupe pas de cette question ou point que vous prétendez, puisque, à la veille de la lutte qui doit régler cette question pour toujours, ou retarder sa solution pendant des années, vous n'êtes pas capable d'élire dans le métropole de la province de *Québec, plus intéressée que* toutes les autres provinces à cette question, un homme pour combattre ce combat.[3]

Langevin was prompt in answering Caron's letter and showed himself more than willing to aid the government in persuading Hingston. At the same time, he did not hesitate to prod the cabinet to stick to its promises. 'Il n'a plus à reculer, les vaisseaux sont brulés,' he insisted. 'L'opposition elle-même, au moins la partie catholique si elle comprend son intérêt et son devoir, votera avec le Gouvernement.' By a long and effusive declaration that the Conservatives could never dream of considering 'cette lâche resource' of an inquiry, Langevin revealed apprehension that the cabinet might indeed be thinking of adopting Laurier's avenue of escape. The archbishop took special care to mention the duty of Costigan and Smith, 'les membres irlandais qui ont appuyé le retard dont nous souffrons tant et qui permet à nos ennemis de dresser leur batterie.'[4]

Langevin also wrote to Fabre to reinforce the pressure brought on Hingston.[5] Fabre was prompt but much less optimistic than Langevin in his reply concerning the doctor's candidacy, stressing Hingston's age and the unwisdom of the judicial appointments. Fabre made a further knowing lament about the difficulty and importance of the by-elections. 'Ces différentes élections partielles donnent plus d'embarras que les élections générales,' he commented. 'Tout le camp en même temps se jette sur un quartier et crée de grands embarras.'[6] Langevin's November 27 reply

---

3 AASB, Caron to Langevin, November 2, 1895, (italics Caron's)
4 *Ibid*., Langevin to Caron, November 7, 1895
5 AAM, Langevin to Fabre, November 5, 1895
6 AASB, Fabre to Langevin, November 9, 1895

simply expanded his argument on the duty of Montreal Catholics to support their Manitoba brethren by voting Conservative.[7]

The resignation of Clarke Wallace as controller of customs on December 12 was clearly a relief for the rest of the government. Certainly the French Conservatives did not hesitate to interpret the incident in their own favour. 'Voilà qui prouve,' a cabinet minister told Father Lacombe, 'que nous voulons coute que coute, aller jusqu'au bout dans les promesses que nous avons faites.'[8] With or without Wallace, however, and despite the immediacy of the by-elections, it was evident that the rifts in the Conservative team were widening. A squabble between two Quebec province cabinet members, J.A. Ouimet and W.B. Ives, acutely pointed up the problem. Ives, deputy from Sherbrooke, walked out of a cabinet meeting dealing with the elections, and told Bowell that any active role by Ouimet would be a distinct liability, particularly in Montreal Centre. 'The English people will have nothing to do with Mr. Ouimet,' Ives insisted, 'and the less he appears, the better, so far as they are concerned.'[9]

At the same time, the continued activity of Angers was doing further damage. The former minister of agriculture was proclaiming that the passage of time had proven correct the decision he made in July. To Bishop Laflèche, who had not favoured his action as much as he had hoped, Angers wrote on December 14 that Wallace's resignation did not represent a purification of the government but a proof of political failure. 'Depuis le huit juillet dernier à ce jour,' Angers stated, 'le Cabinet n'a fait aucun progrès pour amener ses partisans protestants orangistes à favoriser l'adoption d'une loi réparatrice.'[10] Angers was not content to make his position known only in private. On December 13, Lacombe reported a speech by Angers at Quebec City in which the ex-minister charged the government with treachery, and insisted that no real relief would be forthcoming. 'C'est sérieux,' the missionary admitted, 'la chose ne paraît pas brillante pour nous, dans la province de Québec.' The spectacle of Angers's activities brought Lacombe's wry conclusion: 'Ab amicis nostris libera nos, Dne.'[11]

On December 24 Lacombe reported that he had seen Angers personally

7 AAM, Langevin to Fabre, November 27, 1895
8 AASB, Lacombe to Langevin, December 12, 1895
9 PAC, Bowell Papers, Ives to Bowell, December 14, 1895
10 ASTR, Angers to Laflèche, December 14, 1895
11 AASB, Lacombe to Langevin, December 12 and 13, 1895 ('From our friends deliver us, O Lord')

and that the ex-minister had been, if anything, even more violent against the Conservative ministers:

Hier je voyais longuement l'Hon*ble* Mr. Anger [*sic*], qui maudit les Ministres conservateurs comme une bande de chanapands, qui seront toujours prêts à sacrifier les Catholiques de Manitoba, si ça fait leur affaire. Pour tout au monde, il ne voudrait retourner au milieu d'eux; cependant il fera tout en son pouvoir, pour aider, afin que le Bill réparateur soit voté.[12]

As for Laurier, while he refused to announce a specific Liberal remedy beyond an inquiry, he had no choice but to become more vocal on the school question during the by-election campaigns. His address in Montreal on December 8 promised to both 'do justice' and 'settle the question,' but equally insisted on the need for Protestant as well as Catholic support. Laurier stressed the point that he, with the support of Premier Mowat, was in a far better position to obtain a moderate attitude from Ontario than were the Conservatives. Glossing over the fact that such promises would hardly be endorsed by Willison and many other Ontario Liberal spokesmen, Laurier's conclusion was, once again, the need for an inquiry.[13] His reward from the Quebec Conservative press was, as before, denunciation as a traitor.

ELECTION RESULTS

The first of the constituencies to be contested, Ontario North, had been held by the Conservatives in 1891 by a margin of 254 votes. On December 12, 1895, the riding gave the government an even more impressive victory. J.A. McGillivray, who had been an unsuccessful candidate under Meredith in the provincial election of 1886, received 2085 votes against 1289 for the Patron candidate and 1096 for Gillespie, the Liberal.[14] The Conservatives

---

12 *Ibid.*, Lacombe to Langevin, December 24, 1895. Lacombe spelled Angers' name without an 's' throughout his letters

13 *Montreal Star*, December 9, 1895

14 Toronto *Mail and Empire*, December 13, 1895. The thrust of the Patrons of Industry candidates into rural federal ridings was an added complication for both major parties. A depression-born phenomenon not unlike the Populist movement in the Unites States, the Patrons were either courted, ignored, or opposed by the Liberals and Conservatives alike according to the advantage of the moment. Granted the strong free-trade emphasis of the movement, the Liberals were more endangered by the Patrons than were the Conservatives, but sometimes managed a *modus vivendi* with the third party. For example, in the

thus retained a seat in rural Ontario, increasing their margin in a three-way fight. But their winning candidate, McGillivray, opposed his party's remedial policy, and gave a foretaste of the radical Tory schism which would grow during the subsequent months.[15]

Two problems were obvious from the point of view of the Liberals: the split in the anti-government vote, because of the appearance of the Patrons, and the fact that the Liberal candidate, a Catholic, had run third. Tarte's analysis of the outcome, plus some revealing information about developments in the Montreal by-election picture, went out to Willison on December 13. Tarte admitted that no one had really expected the Liberals to win in North Ontario, but called the 'crushing defeat of the Liberal candidate ... a damaging blow for us.' He was convinced that half of the normal Liberal vote had gone to the Patrons, while the Tories had maintained party loyalty. 'Will you tell me privately,' Tarte asked Willison, 'why we cannot have more control over our friends?'[16]

Laurier's reaction was even more pessimistic than Tarte's, especially over the margin of the Conservative win. He complained to Willison that Ontario did not seem willing to approve the stand that he, Laurier, had taken against the Tory press in Quebec. 'I am now in terror as to this province,' the Liberal leader wrote. 'I have taken great risks on the school question ... If my views had been endorsed in Ontario, I would have been thereby greatly assisted in this province but if the coercive policy of the government is adopted by your people, what else than disaster am I to expect here?' Laurier concluded, however, that he had no regrets and that his stand on an inquiry was simply what he thought was right. 'It was the only course consistent with reason and justice,' he said, 'but reason and justice may cut a poor figure, if battered between the prejudices of Quebec and the prejudices of Ontario.'[17] Significantly, just as Tupper was complain-

---

1896 general election, the Liberals did not run in ten ridings where there were Patron candidates; only in three ridings did the Conservatives fail to oppose. The principle enunciated by Richard Scott as a lesson from the Ontario North defeat would thus seem to have been accepted by the Liberal strategists: 'Above all things a Patron and a Grit must both be defeated when pitted against a Government candidate.' The origin and fate of the Patrons of Industry are briefly discussed in Wood, *A History of the Farmers' Movement in Canada,* Morton, *The Progressive Party in Canada.*

15 The active support and speeches of N.C. Wallace promoting McGillivray during his campaign were strong evidence of this fact. McGillivray voted for the second reading of the Remedial Bill in March, but was classed as an anti-remedialist in the subsequent election campaign (see *La Minerve*, June 8, 1896).

16 PAC, Willison Papers, Tarte to Willison, December 13, 1895

17 PAC, Laurier Papers, Laurier to Willison, December 17, 1895

ing to Langevin about Catholic apathy in Quebec, Laurier was now saying the same thing in the opposite direction about Ontario.

Before the next by-election, in Cardwell, a particularly interesting exchange took place between Laurier and his old friend, Senator Richard Scott. Scott felt that the Ontario North contest had demonstrated 'an old feeling long dormant in Ontario that a considerable element of the Grits dislike voting for a Catholic.' As to the government remedial proposals, 'their determination to carry the s.s. Act must win over a considerable number of co-religionists who on all other issues would vote Liberal.' Scott's conclusion was that the quick passage of a remedial bill might be the only politically viable solution for the Liberals.[18]

Laurier's reply on December 24 agreed with Scott's objective, but not with the means suggested. Laurier agreed that if the school question could be taken out of the political arena 'from every consideration it would be a blessing to the party and to the country.' Yet his conclusion showed how far he had come from the position he had taken in his correspondence with Willison earlier in the year. Whatever he was to promise in public later on, Laurier at least in theory rejected remedial legislation, Conservative or Liberal, with or without an inquiry:

If the leading Roman Catholics in the country, who sincerely wish the restoration of Separate Schools, would only reflect, they would soon convince themselves that on the very day when they would have their Separate Schools restored by the power of the Federal Parliament, they would be further than ever from the actual restoration of those schools.

Laurier conceded that the Liberals would lose Cardwell, but reaffirmed that 'we are sure to win Montreal Centre and Jacques Cartier, unless they are bought away from us.'[19]

Laurier in fact spared no effort in the Montreal campaign. Mowat and Ross, with their pro-separate-school credentials, came from Ontario. Premier Fielding supplied a touch of Maritime prestige. *L'Electeur* goaded Archbishop Fabre into a declaration of neutrality by accusing him of partiality for the Conservatives.[20] *La Presse*, somewhat perversely playing the 'independent,' chose this moment to accuse Caron of doing nothing to prevent the bankruptcy of La Banque du Peuple because of that

18 PAC, Scott Papers, Scott to Laurier, December 21, 1895
19 PAC, Laurier Papers, Laurier to Scott, December 24, 1895
20 *L'Electeur*, December 24, 1895, cf. Rumilly, *Histoire*, VII, pp.258–60

establishment's Rouge directorate. The newspaper even charged that Caron 'a tout fait pour transformer la crise en désastre.'[21] These charges simply culminated the combination of bungling and misfortune which plagued the Conservatives during the Montreal by-elections. The unpopularity of the judicial appointments which had opened up the seats, the Ives-Ouimet squabble, the Castor attacks of A.R. Angers and Caron's immediate problems, all converged to provide the Liberals with easy targets. As for the school question, with the Liberals offering, realistically or otherwise, the hope of a better solution for the Manitoba minority, it was evident, as it had been in Verchères, that the Conservative handling of the problem was not generating any new sources of support in Quebec. The result was that on December 27 Montreal Centre gave a majority of 346 to McShane over Hingston; on December 30 Jacques Cartier went to Charbonneau of the Liberals by a margin of 574.[22]

In Ontario, meanwhile, Cardwell fell to the McCarthyite candidate William Stubbs. The vote was Stubbs, 1503; Willoughby (Conservative), 1296; Henry (Liberal), 544. Trying to assess this shocking Ontario result for the Liberals, Laurier and Willison exchanged reflections before the year ended. Laurier was shaken by the 'stampede from our ranks to McCarthy's';[23] Willison was deeply concerned about the absence of leadership among Laurier's Ontario lieutenants.[24]

The Liberal leader naturally was gratified by the Montreal victories, but he warned Willison not to be misled by the result. On the one hand, while the clergy had generally abstained from intervention in the current contests, they might well interfere 'with fatal effect' in a general election.[25] More important, Laurier emphasized that the Liberal message which had triumphed in Montreal was the very opposite to anything that would be acceptable in Ontario.[26]

On the Conservative side, too, there were several significant reactions to the by-elections. Prior to the Cardwell vote, John Costigan had tried

21 *La Presse*, December 21, 1895
22 Rumilly, *Histoire*, VII, p.261. The untimeliness of the appointments of Girouard and Curran was reflected by such diverse voices as Father Lacombe (AASB, Lacombe to Langevin, January 2, 1896), and R.D. McGibbon, prominent Conservative lawyer, who saw Curran's selection as a blow to himself and to English Montreal (Morgan, *Canadian Men and Women of the Time*, p.737).
23 PAC, Willison Papers, Laurier to Willison, December 26, 1895
24 PAC, Laurier Papers, Willison to Laurier, December 27, 1895
25 PAC, Willison Papers, Laurier to Willison, December 30, 1895
26 *Ibid.*, Laurier to Willison, December 31, 1895

unsuccessfully to enlist Archbishop Walsh's intervention for the Conservatives.[27] Despite the spectacular McCarthyite sweep in the largely Protestant riding, Conservative analyses were certain that the small Catholic vote had gone solidly to the Liberals.[28] Archbishop Langevin's reflection was that 'les Catholiques irlandais ne peuvent pas croire que le parti de Meredith qui a cherché à leur ravir leurs écoles soit sincèrement décidé à donner des écoles séparées aux Catholiques de Manitoba.' On the Montreal results, Langevin was equally interesting, if perhaps less accurate. 'C'est une victoire pour Angers, et non pour Laurier,' Langevin wrote Bégin.[29] The remark did less than justice to Liberal efforts, but accurately diagnosed the Castor-Bleu poison in the Conservative body.

Colonel Audet, with the evidence of the *La Presse* attack on Caron to support him, added more precision to Langevin's conviction about who had won and lost in Montreal. Saying that he had just returned from the Montreal campaign, Audet agreed that Caron and Ouimet had been the direct targets of a negative vote. Yet he reflected ruefully that it would be the idea of remedial action rather than the ministers personally that would suffer most in the long run. Audet's assessment of blame for the Montreal disaster was significant. In a letter which included the initial stage of the cabinet revolt, Audet first attacked the lieutenant governor of Quebec. 'L'histoire tiendra responsable de ce désastre national Chapleau qui a voulu rester à Québec,' Audet insisted. Then came 'Angers et sa clique qui ont persisté dans une grève insensée,' despite pressing appeals to the contrary. Finally, charged Audet, there was the clergy, guilty, not of too much interference, but of too little. Audet did have praise for two influences on the side of Hingston in Montreal, the Redemptorist Fathers and the superior of the seminary, but criticized 'les prédilections de Mgr. Bégin pour MM. Angers et consorts,' and 'l'inaction de l'évêché de Montréal.'

Audet's rationale for clerical intervention in politics led in his view to a clear case of support for the government in the current crisis:

Il est évident que le clergé ne doit pas s'inféoder à un parti politique: mais lorsqu'il s'agit comme dans les dernières luttes de l'éducation confessionelle de l'enfance et de la délivrance d'une minorité catholique, l'abstention de sa part me parait une faute énorme et comme ministres de l'Eglise et comme membres de l'Etat.[30]

27 PAC, Costigan Papers, Costigan to Walsh, December 20, 1895
28 AASB, Ouimet to Langevin, December 26, 1895
29 AAQ, Langevin to Bégin, January 2, 1896
30 AASB, Audet to Langevin, January 6, 1896

It seemed to escape Audet that Angers and his clerical supporters were using the identical argument in opposing the government.

The results of the December by-elections left a mixed impression on both parties, more negative than positive in each case. Each seemed to have more cause for worry than for optimism. The crucial facts in the unforgiving political balance sheet were that the Liberals had made no headway whatever in the two rural Ontario ridings and, by Laurier's own admission, had gained in Quebec only by projecting an image which would be political suicide in English Canada. The Conservative picture was even darker. Their one victory, out of four seats formerly in their grasp, was in a solid Conservative riding by a former Meredith man who was clearly anti-remedialist. More significantly, they had seen valuable ground slip away in Quebec, losing two traditionally solid seats. The Liberal wins in Montreal were, of course, a gratifying portent for that party's future, but the only unmistakeable advance in the December skirmishes was that scored by the McCarthyites.

THE SPEECH FROM THE THRONE AND
THE NEST OF TRAITORS

It was against this disintegrating background that the government moved to fulfil its fateful promise of the previous July. Manitoba's formal reply to the federal message sent after the summer session had been dispatched to Ottawa on December 21.[31] In a briefer form, the reply was a more unbending version of the one which had been sent in June. Clearly helping Laurier and hurting Bowell by supporting an inquiry and re-emphasizing the danger to Confederation of coercive federal action, the Manitoba statement left the federal government little choice. In the January 2 Speech from the Throne, Lord Aberdeen added the prestige of the vice-regal office to a straightforward announcement of remedial legislation.[32] The words were brave; but never had the decorous phrases of a governor general masked so unconfident a government. Two days after Lord Aberdeen gave voice to the cabinet intention of bringing in a remedial law, seven ministers resigned. The seven – Foster, Haggart, Montague, Tupper, Dickey, Ives, and Wood – English Protestants all, gave as reason for their action the prolonged failure of Bowell to fill the vacancy created by Angers's resignation.[33]

31 Canada, *Sessional Papers*, 1896, no.39, p.6
32 Canada, House of Commons, *Debates*, 1896, I, p.1
33 *Ibid.*, pp.9–10

It is true that Bowell had re-shuffled the cabinet late in December. After Wallace's resignation, the position of controller of customs was raised to cabinet rank and given to J.F. Wood. Wood's former office, controller of inland revenue, was also raised to cabinet standing and conferred on E.G. Prior. On December 21, W.H. Montague was appointed minister of agriculture, and J.A. Ouimet took Montague's former position of secretary of state on December 27 as acting minister.[34] None of these moves, however, compensated for the absence of a third French Canadian in the cabinet.

For Bowell, the ten days from January 3 to 13 say an amazing ebb and flow of fortune. As if the prime minister did not have enough problems, a new and almost unrelated squabble within the cabinet, the Caron-Montague affair, came to light just after the resignations were presented. Two anonymous letters accusing Caron of taking bribes had been sent to Lord Aberdeen. Caron had received these through Bowell and had engaged a handwriting expert to attempt to discover their source; the culprit seemed to be none other than Caron's cabinet colleague, W.H. Montague.[35] The press got wind of the story, and Montague wrote two vehement letters to Bowell to deny authorship of the letters and to criticize the prime minister both for giving any credence to the charges and for failing to inform him earlier.[36] Bowell sent Montague a lame and confused reply,[37] and the authorship of the letters as well as the accuracy of their contents remained a mystery.[38] Like the Ives-Ouimet crisis in December, a petty quarrel again revealed Bowell's incapacity as a leader, as well as profound trouble in the cabinet with or without him.

According to Lady Aberdeen's *Journal*, the first news of the cabinet revolt reached the prime minister on Friday evening, January 3, at Government House, where Bowell was conferring with Aberdeen. Haggart, spokesman for the rebels, had come to inform the governor general of their intention, and arranged for the senior Tupper to meet Bowell.[39] Bowell met with Sir Charles on Saturday and received the seven resignations that same afternoon, but refused to accept without a fight the alternative offices held out to him. The 'Memorandum of the Seven' for Lord Aberdeen stated that

34 *Guide to Canadian Ministries Since Confederation*, pp.22–4
35 PAC, Bowell Papers, Caron to Bowell, January 6, 1896
36 *Ibid.*, Montague to Bowell, January 3, January 6, 1896
37 *Ibid.*, Bowell to Montague, January 6, 1896
38 Both Caron and Montague expressed the desire to keep the matter from open discussion in the Commons when McCarthy tried to stir it up on January 15 (cf. Canada, House of Commons, *Debates*, 1896, p.68).
39 Lady Aberdeen, *Journal*, January 5, 1896, p.298

Foster, Montague, Tupper, Jr, and Dickey had each tried to persuade Bowell to give way to 'another member of the Conservative party,' and that it seemed to them that the prime minister had decided to resign. But Bowell changed his mind despite further urging even from Daly, who had not threatened revolt, and, after the conference with Tupper, Sr, proceeded to accept the seven resignations.[40]

Bowell lunched with the governor general on Sunday, and Lady Aberdeen reported that the prime minister was 'making an effort after reconstruction & says if he could get Chief Justice Meredith, he would snap his fingers at all the rest. He has sent Welldon [sic] down to Toronto with carte-blanche offers to Meredith of the Premiership & all, but is not hopeful.'[41] It was also clear that the Conservatives who wished to replace Bowell were not unanimous in favour of Charles Tupper, Sr, as his successor, with dissent coming from both extremes of the remedialist spectrum. Like many others trying unofficially to get the ear of the governor general, the anti-remedialist Alexander McNeill, MP, visited Lady Aberdeen on January 7, and suggested Meredith or Weldon as leader.[42]

For the time being at least, the sympathies of Lord and Lady Aberdeen were clearly on Bowell's side. Lady Aberdeen described the action of the bolters as 'a most extraordinary exhibition of treachery, when one thinks that these very men sat round the council table over the Queen's speech and amended it a few days ago.' On Sunday the Aberdeens urged Bowell to make every effort to reconstruct, and in particular to disappoint the plans of Tupper, Sr, – 'not to throw the country into the hands of one who would doubtless deal with it only in such a way as would suit himself.'[43] Despite the vice-regal encouragement, Bowell was unable to form a new team and on Monday sent a despairing note to Aberdeen. 'I see no change in the aspect of the situation,' he wrote, 'and fear that there [is] no solution of the present problem than for me to resign. I shall, however, defer final action until Wednesday next.'[44]

The likelihood of either reconciliation or reconstruction was hardly increased by the events of Tuesday, January 7. Taking the lead for the seven rebels in his statement to the House, Finance Minister Foster denied

40 Cf. Wallace, *The Memoirs of the Rt. Hon. Sir George Foster.* Further details of the role in the cabinet crisis of Governor General and Lady Aberdeen are related by Saywell in his introduction to *The Canadian Journal of Lady Aberdeen.*
41 *Journal*, January 5, 1896, p.299
42 *Ibid.*, January 7, 1896
43 *Ibid.*, January 5, 1896, p.300
44 PAC, Aberdeen Papers, Bowell to Aberdeen, January 6, 1896

both personal dislike for Bowell and personal ambition on his own part. He recalled his misgivings over Bowell's succession at the time of Thompson's death; he stated that all possible effort had been made to get the prime minister to complete the cabinet after Angers's resignation. Yet, said the minister of finance, 'we found ourselves face to face with Parliament having a Government with its numbers incomplete, and with no assurance that the present Premier could satisfactorily complete.' Foster was particularly careful to point out that the crisis did not concern remedial action. 'There is no disagreement between ourselves and the Premier,' he insisted, 'upon any question of public policy, trade or constitutional, with regard to which action has already been taken, or in respect to which an attitude has been assumed by the Government under the present Premier.'[45] Bowell's reaction to Foster's statement in the Commons was to approach the Liberal benches, shake hands with the leaders, and say for all to hear that it was 'such a comfort to shake hands with honest men, after having been in company with traitors for months.'[46]

A Conservative caucus scheduled for Tuesday afternoon was cancelled because of Bowell's refusal to have anything to do with the bolters.[47] Lord Aberdeen contributed to the frustration of the rebels by refusing to accept Bowell's resignation on two occasions on January 8 and 9. In a formal statement on January 8, Aberdeen insisted that it would be 'unfitting that the head of the administration responsible for the preparation of that speech [from the throne], should not have full opportunity to review the situation, and should he so determine, to test the feeling of Parliament thereupon.'[48]

Bowell's speech in the Senate on January 9 showed that he had not been able to surmount the obstacles. Just how much of what Costigan described as the 'tactics of stevedores' strike' had been employed by the bolters is not certain, but a deep sense of betrayal pervaded Bowell's words. The prime minister stated that he would resign if he could not form a government within three days, and re-emphasized that he would not back down in regard to remedial legislation.[49] Yet, while Lady Aberdeen and others

45 Canada, House of Commons, *Debates*, 1896, pp.9–10
46 Lady Aberdeen, *Journal*, January 7, 1896, p.301. According to Her Ladyship, Bowell had been with her in the House when Foster made his statement.
47 APQ, Chapais Papers, H. Langevin to Chapais; *L'Electeur*, January 7, 1896. Lady Aberdeen's description was that the party was so divided 'that they dare not call a caucus' (*Journal*, p.303).
48 PAC, Aberdeen Papers, Aberdeen to Bowell, January 8, 1896; cf. Lady Aberdeen's *Journal*, 304–5.
49 Canada, Senate, *Debates*, January 9, 1896

believed that Bowell's speech would be his last gasp before giving a third resignation which, according to her, would have been accepted,[50] within less than a week the prime minister had managed to reconstruct.

BOWELL AND LACOMBE: FIRST RECONSTRUCTION FAILS

Various accounts of the cabinet crisis present a remarkable disparity, not to say contradiction, of factors and decisive pressures operating throughout the episode.[51] Certainly a significant role at several key points in the crisis was played by Father Lacombe. Early in his mission Lacombe had attempted to define his own and the episcopal position in relation to the government with a nonpartisan proposal of policy to Langevin:

Donc ... Il est entendu chez vous, à Ontario et (je suppose) à Québec, que si le Gouvernement conservateur, fidèle à ses promesses, est défait, en voulant donner la loi rémédiatrice et finale, il devra être soutenu par Evêques, prêtres, &, &, quand il en appelera au peuple. Si au contraire il abandonne notre cause ou ne veut nous donner [que] ce que nous ne pouvons accepter, alors nous ferons notre possible pour aider à le renverser? C'est bien cela, n'est-ce pas?[52]

The impartiality of the manifesto was admirable, but Lacombe quickly found it difficult to maintain his detachment. After initial visits to bishops in Ontario and Quebec, Lacombe in late December was plunged into a much thornier matter. He was approached to serve as intermediary in the attempt to fill the Angers vacancy in the cabinet and described his acceptance in a December 30 report to Archbishop Langevin:

Hier, votre ami, le colonel Audet, venait ici, pour me supplier d'accompagner le ministre Costigan, afin d'aller offrir à L'Hon*ble*. Mr. Masson le portfeuille de Mr. Anger. Voilà encore une autre affaire scabreuse pour moi. J'ai répondu au colonel: 'Télégraphiez à Mr. Costigan que j'accepterai cette mission si délicate, si on m'assure que mon nom ne sera pas mentionné au dehors.'[53]

50 *Journal*, January 10, 1896
51 Note, for instance, the opposing interpretations given by C.H. Tupper in his letter to Father Burke (PAC, C.H. Tupper Papers, Tupper to Burke, February 3, 1896), and by John Costigan in his apologia (PAC, Costigan Papers, Costigan to 'Your Lordship,' n.d.; see above, p.139, n.112). Lady Aberdeen's *Journal* contains a detailed narrative of events as seen from Rideau Hall. Among modern analyses, the best accounts are those found in Saywell in his introduction to Lady Aberdeen's *Journal*, and in Clark, 'The Conservative Administrations' (thesis), pp.421–42.
52 AASB, Lacombe to Langevin, December 12, 1895
53 *Ibid.*, Lacombe to Langevin, December 30, 1895

Quite evidently Lacombe sensed the embarrassing publicity which would attend the sudden prominence he had been given. Yet the condition he stated was certainly not very realistic, and hardly lessened the responsibility of the step he was taking. For good or ill, Lacombe felt that he had no alternative but to push on. A second letter of December 30 was full of doubt and incredulity at his own position:

Je pars à l'instant pour aller offrir à Mr. Masson le portefeuille de Mr. Anger, et cela au nom de Bowell qui vient de m'écrire – O tempora! O mores! Ou sommes-nous? Ou suis-je? Est-ce que je rêve? Demain je partirai pour Ottawa. Costigan vient me rencontrer demain matin ... Je loue à gros jeu. Qu'est-ce que la Congrégation va faire de moi, sur mes vieux jours?[54]

Masson refused the plea of Father Lacombe on grounds of ill health, and the third letter from Montreal on December 30 showed that the die was being case even deeper for the old missionary:

Ma pauvre tête est bien fatigué ... Masson ... ne veut pas accepter à cause de sa santé, qui certainement est très précaire et très inquiétant pour sa famille.
    Mr. Costigan arrive ce matin pour me rencontrer. Que va-t-on décider? Hier soir je télégraphiais au gouvernement de m'attendre aujourd'hui, avant de prendre aucune décision. Il faut que je sois ce soir à Ottawa et presse Mr. Bowell d'ouvrir ainsi la session, sans s'occuper de remplir la vacance d'Anger; car il me menace de prendre un Anglais et un protestant, puisque les catholiques se montrent si apathétiques.[55]

It may have been unconscious on his part, but Lacombe's involvement was now so direct that he wrote as if it were he himself who was being threatened by the vacancy.

Lacombe's arrival in Ottawa did anything but relieve the pressure. 'Le gouvernement parait épouvanté de ce qui va arriver,' Lacombe reported. 'Ses amis d'Ontario menacent de l'abandonner, puisque les catholiques de Québec et d'Ontario semblent se tourner contre le passation de la mesure.' Thus Lacombe felt that he was obliged to do everything in his power to shore up the sagging French side of the government and proposed another candidate for the vacancy. 'M.M. Caron, Daly & [sic] venaient me rejoindre chez leur premier ministre,' he wrote. 'Masson ayant refusé à cause

54 *Ibid*., Lacombe to Langevin, December 30, 1895, no.2
55 *Ibid*., Lacombe to Langevin, December 30, 1895, no.3

de santé, je propose le Sénateur Desjardins qui va arriver ici de Montréal, dans quelques instants, et que j'accompagnerai chez Mr. Bowell. Vous voyez quel commerce je mène!!'[56] Well might Lacombe describe his activity as 'quel commerce,' since it seemed clear that it was he who was promoting Desjardins. Yet in this as in many other political steps he felt obliged to take, Lacombe in effect had asked himself what else he could do and had answered by stepping into the breach left by weak or disgusted compatriots. He would find it very hard to get out, even if he wanted to.

Lacombe's final sentence in his first letter from Ottawa on December 31 went so far as to promise full ecclesiastical support at election time should the government be beaten over the presentation of a remedial bill; the letter equally contained a straightforward government directive to Archbishop Langevin not to come to Ottawa:

Ici au gouvernement, on vous dit de ne pas pour le moment, vous éloigner de Manitoba, de surveiller les agissements de Greenway, en vous priant de tout faire pour aider the gouvernement, qui certainement veut sincèrement faire passer la loi. Je disais aux ministres, hier soir: 'Si vous êtes battus, en présentant franchement et loyalement, devant les chambres, *la loi*, aux élections générales, nous vous ramenerons au pouvoir.'[57]

In his second letter of December 31, Lacombe took more time and care than in the one written earlier in the day. He reviewed the events at Bowell's house on the previous night and the pathetic little scene of Desjardins' near-refusal:

De la je télégraphie à l'Honble. Alphonse Desjardins de venir. Aujourd'hui après deux heures, il arrivait: Sir Bowell, Caron, Ouimet et moi nous le rencontrons. On lui offre le fameux portefeuille. Pauvre Desjardins!! Il est tout tremblant! Il ne sait vraiment comment s'excuser – Il a des embarras personnels, et puis, et puis!! Demain il donnera de Montréal une réponse, qui sera sans doute négative. Donc tout probablement un anglais et protestant va prendre la place d'Anger.[58]

Lacombe returned to Montreal on New Year's Day and made another

---

56 AASB, Lacombe to Langevin, December 31, 1895, no.1. Senator Alphonse Desjardins was a Montreal businessman, a former mayor of the city, an organiser of the Papal Zouaves and of the 'Programme Catholique' of 1871, and had represented Hochelaga riding at Ottawa from 1878 until raised to the Senate in 1892.
57 *Ibid.*, Lacombe to Langevin, December 31, 1895, no.1
58 *Ibid.*, Lacombe to Langevin, December 31, 1895, no.2

attempt to bring in Desjardins. But this too failed, as did his proposal to consider Bernier for the vacancy. In his letter of January 2 the missionary came close to bitterness over the universal weakness he was encountering:

Vraiment je perds confiance dans mes compatriotes. Il y a comme un vertige, qui entraine nos hommes et nos populations, dans l'aberration. Que voulez-vous? Nous n'avons pas d'hommes. C'est décourageant. Que voulez-vous qu'on fasse avec Bernier et LaRivière? Sans énergie et la capacité voulue-quelle lutte peuvent-ils soutenir?[59]

Once again the strong impression was conveyed of a vacuum which Lacombe felt he had to fill or lose everything. At the same time, his temperament leaned toward taking the centre of the stage; at least some of the statements he reported were hardly those of one seeking obscurity. For instance, in this same letter of January 2, Lacombe spoke of strongly reproving the government for political blunders during the previous year. 'J'ai reproché *bien gros* au gouvernment,' he reported, 'd'avoir sans necessité nommé pour le moment les juges Girouard et Curran et ouvrir ainsi des élections qu'on perd. Et puis commier Shortis, ce qui exaspère nos gens! C'est une fatalité contre nous.'[60] Thus, despite his occasional qualms over the propriety of his position, Lacombe had very quickly become an ambassador taking a great deal of discretion into his own hands. In any case, it seems clear from his December letters that Lacombe had been given a major role by Bowell and had been unable to produce the vital replacement for Angers. Furthermore, Lacombe's entry into the picture added to the credibility of the 'official' explanation of the bolters, since the prospect of his eleventh-hour success may have postponed their revolt, and his failure may have confirmed it. No matter what their ultimate motives may have been, the seven dissentient ministers could point to the hard fact that, even with clerical influence brought to bear, Bowell had failed in a major effort to complete his cabinet.

Once the cabinet revolt became a reality, Lacombe re-entered the scene to help upset the plans of the bolters. On January 6, Colonel Audet wrote

59 *Ibid.*, Lacombe to Langevin, January 2, 1896
60 *Ibid.* In March 1895, Valentine Shortis, an Irish immigrant from a well-to-do family, killed two men in Valleyfield. There was strong evidence of insanity in the case, but Shortis was condemned to be hanged on January 3, 1896. After consultation with the Colonial Office, Lord Aberdeen, on his own discretion, commuted the sentence to life imprisonment on December 31, 1895. The reaction against this decision was particularly unfavourable in Beauharnois and Valleyfield and was a further weakening factor for the government in Quebec (Rumilly, *Histoire*, VIII, pp.51–2).

Archbishop Langevin that he had wired the missionary in Montreal to return immediately to Ottawa. 'A son arrivée demain,' Audet said, 'il pourra peut-être sauver la situation en réunissant tout le parti conservateur français, pourvu que Bowell n'ait pas encore cédé.'[61]

But Lacombe's initial prospects were not very hopeful. First of all, in his attempts to help Bowell find a replacement for the departed Angers, Lacombe could not and did not get anything like united clerical support, largely because of the continued sympathy in Quebec city for the stand Angers had taken. Lacombe's January 6 letter, written immediately after his return to Montreal from the provincial capital, summarized the matter with dismay: 'Mr. Anger a une foule d'amis, dans Québec.'[62] Colonel Audet also viewed the Angers position and the support it received from the clergy as little less than disaster. 'Angers reviendra-t-il au sens commun?' Audet wondered. 'J'en doute, il semble frappé de folie,' he told Langevin.[63]

Langevin in turn was equally pessimistic, but wanted Lacombe to bring even more pressure to bear on the Conservative leaders. Langevin followed with a wish which was easier to make than to accomplish:

Donc, que le cabinet soit formé à neuf et qu'ils passent ou cherchent à faire passer une loi scolaire avant les élections. Si le vieux Sir Charles Tupper voulait promettre de nous rendre nos écoles et si Bowell croyait pouvoir lui céder la place! mais tout cela est de l'incertain.[64]

How uncertain things were in Langevin's eyes was reflected in a note sent the following day to Fabre, in which Langevin showed himself willing to consider turning even to Laurier: 'Laurier voudra-t-il et pourra-t-il faire quelque chose?' he asked. 'La conduite des ministres lâcheurs justifie l'attitude de l'Hon. Angers. Nous sommes entre le mains du Bon Dieu!'[65] Lacombe's return to Ottawa on January 7 brought from him his strongest statement of dissatisfaction with the government and its factions. He said

---

61 AASB, Audet to Langevin, January 6, 1896
62 *Ibid.*, Lacombe to Langevin, January 6, 1896. That the most formidable stumbling-block to the completion of the Quebec wing of the cabinet continued to be a combination of Angers and important clerical supporters, in particular Vicar General Marois of Quebec, was suggested in the correspondence of Lacombe, Audet, Caron, Flavien Dupont, and Monsignor J.O. Routhier of Ottawa. See in particular AASB, Lacombe to Langevin, January 4, 1896, and Routhier to Langevin, June 28, 1896.
63 *Ibid.*, Audet to Langevin, January 6, 1896
64 AAQ, Langevin to Lacombe, January 7, 1896
65 AAM, Langevin to Fabre, January 8, 1896

that he was completely bewildered by the events which were taking place. He had just come from dinner at Bowell's house, and reported on the prime minister's follow-up to his 'nest of traitors' statement that afternoon. 'Il est dégouté de la conduite du grand nombre de ses collègues. Il n'y a pas à s'étonner, quand on a entendu ce qui s'est dit cette après-midi, dans la chambre. La déclaration de Foster est indigne d'un gentilhomme envers son chef.' Lacombe expected Tupper to be called but was apprehensive about the policy the latter would adopt and, once again, echoed Chapleau's importance. 'Pour moi, je pense qu'il [Tupper] n'en viendra pas à bout, s'il ne gagne pas Chapleau à venir le joindre,' the missionary stated.[66]

A BARE SURVIVAL

Bowell's January 9 address to the Senate, however, seemed to turn the tide. Lacombe's report to Langevin was ecstatic:

Je lui disais: 'C'est la plus belle et la plus noble page de votre vie.' Il s'est acquis, par son discours au Sénat, des masses de sympathie. J'étais près de lui, quand il a prononcé, avec énergie, son discours, *pro vita sua*. Il a été admiré et applaudi par les deux côtés de l'auguste auditoire. Je vous assure que c'était solonnel.

Lacombe's practical reaction to Bowell's statement was to return to Montreal that same evening and again to approach Desjardins. His report of success on January 10 was straightforward. 'Je pense que Alp. Desjardins aujourd'hui prend la place d'Anger,' Lacombe wrote. 'On a toute confiance que le cabinet va se réorganiser. Alors tant mieux pour nous.'[67]

In the tortuous process leading to Desjardins's decision to answer Bowell's plea and enter the cabinet, a further important influence beyond that of Lacombe was brought to bear. This was Lieutenant Governor Chapleau, presumed by many to be the only hope for a solid Quebec wing for either Bowell or Tupper. Chapleau had been visited several times by Lacombe, and, according to the missionary, continued heartily to support the principle of remedial action. He successfully resisted all attempts to have himself drawn back to Ottawa from the haven of Spencer Wood, but sent some revealing words of advice and encouragement in Desjardins in pressing the latter to enter the cabinet. Chapleau commended the federal government's intention, despite its confusion. 'Si cela manque de sanction finale,' he wrote, '[il] ne manque pas de clarté sur l'intention de votre

66 AASB, Lacombe to Langevin, January 7, 1896
67 *Ibid.*, Lacombe to Langevin, January 10, 1896

gouvernement.' At the same time, the lieutenant governor clearly echoed the image of unreliability projected in Quebec by the bolters:

Il ne vous reste qu'à surveiller l'attitude de vos amis politiques d'Ontario. Si vous êtes surs de leur loyauté à donner main forte à l'acte de justice réparatrice que votre loi préscrit, très bien! Si vous avez raison de croire que votre législation ne leur impose qu'une trève jusqu'aux élections, avec le droit de recommencer les hostilités après la session ou après les élections, alors vous n'aurez qu'a répéter le mot de Napoléon à Metternich: 'Des traités comme ceux-là, ne sont bons qu'à déchirer.'

As for himself, Chapleau concluded with a little political catechism which he felt had been learned the hard way. 'Quant à moi, mon cher ministre,' the lieutenant governor wrote, 'je suis dans *réserve*, et je vous verrai triompher de loin ... je vous souhaite la paix, la foi et l'espérance. [En politique la charité bien ordonnée commence par soi-même et ne finit pas par les autres.]'[68]

At the same time that Desjardins was being persuaded to accept office, the Aberdeens were given a new and more acceptable version of the cabinet revolt by C.H. Tupper. More specifically, the younger Tupper succeeded in shaking the Aberdeens' earlier assumption that the accession of his father to the leadership would spell the end of remedial legislation.[69] If the vice-regal prejudice against the elder Tupper was not entirely removed,[70] it was changed enough to prepare for subsequent events. Bowell balked for a time against taking back Foster, Haggart, and Montague, whom he considered the ringleaders,[71] but the prospect that Laurier would be called to form a government forced his hand.[72]

68 ACSM, Desjardins Papers, Chapleau to Desjardins, January 10, 1896
69 Lady Aberdeen, *Journal*, January 10, 1896
70 *Ibid.*, January 7, 1896. Evidence of the Aberdeens' prejudice against Sir Charles Tupper, Sr, may be found in Lady Aberdeen's *Journal* describing events following Sir John Thompson's death in 1894, (*Journal*, December 12, 1894) and during the cabinet crisis (*Journal*, January 5, 6, 7, 1896). The question is dealt with at some length in Clark, 'The Conservative Party in the 1890s,' and in his 'The Conservative Administrations,' pp.439–40.
71 PAC, Bowell Papers, Daly to Bowell, January 12, 1896. Actually, according to a postscript, this letter was mislaid before being sent by Daly. Daly discovered it under a blotting pad February 2, 1896. It was sent on to Bowell, however, since 'in light of subsequent events it might interest you.' Thus the letter did not actually play a part in Bowell's decision, but Daly's reasoning seems to have been the line of argument which persuaded Bowell to accept Tupper's plan.
72 That Lord Aberdeen seriously considered summoning Laurier is clear from Lady

Once again it was a near miss. So narrow was this particular escape from disaster that Lacombe could write to Langevin on Monday morning, January 13: 'Quand vous recevrez ces lignes, déjà le télégraphe vous aura annoncé sans doute la chute de notre ami, Sir Bowell et du Ministère.'[73] Yet the government did not fall and Bowell took back his 'traitors.' The agreement was that Tupper, Sr, would lead the House in attempting to pass a remedial law, then take over as prime minister for the elections. Officially, Lord Aberdeen would not accept 'any sort of arrangement or understanding about a change of Premiership,' and refused to promise a dissolution if the Conservatives were defeated on a remedial bill.[74] Tuesday, January 14, found Bowell in his office in the presence of Daly, Smith, Caron, and Ouimet, giving a formal promise to Desjardins that a remedial bill which met the approval of Lacombe and 'autres amis autorisés de la cause de la minorité du Manitoba' would be introduced. Equally, Bowell had to guarantee that the accession of Sir Charles Tupper, Sr, and the return of the bolters would not mean any essential changes in the law, and finally that the remedial measure would be put through even if the government of Manitoba passed a law giving the separate schools back to the minority.[75]

More than anywhere else, the floor of Parliament was the arena in which the government situation during the cabinet crisis was vulnerable to attack. When the seven resignations were first announced, a stormy two-day debate followed Caron's motion to adjourn until January 21 'to allow time to consider the gravity of the circumstances.'[76] A compromise adjournment until January 14 was achieved, but not without repeated charges by Quebec Liberals of government treachery toward Manitoba Catholics.[77] The exchange over the reconstructed cabinet on January 14 and 15, and the later debate on the reply to the Speech from the Throne, filled more than eight hundred pages of Hansard. The bulk of what was said simply covered

Aberdeen's *Journal*. The governor general went so far as to consult Dr Bourinot on the constitutional propriety of the step (p.305), and Lady Aberdeen concocted a skating-party interview between Laurier and Captain Sinclair, a vice-regal aide (pp.307–8). Laurier's excitement over the possibility of being called was revealed in the correspondence of J.D. Edgar (PAO, Edgar Papers, Edgar to Mrs Edgar, January 6, 10, 1896), and in Laurier's own January 11 letter to his friend and confidante, Mme Lavergne (quoted from private sources in Rumilly, *Histoire*, VIII, p.16).

73 AASB, Lacombe to Langevin, January 13, 1896
74 Lady Aberdeen, *Journal*, January 13, 1896, p.310
75 A detailed account of these stringent conditions can be found in a long memorandum written January 15 by Senator Desjardins (ACSM, Desjardins Collection).
76 Canada, House of Commons, *Debates*, 1896, p.7
77 *Ibid.*, pp.7–9, 53–55

familiar ground of charges and counter-charges. Probably the most significant speech on either side in the debate was that given on January 23 by J.I. Tarte. Despite his several utterances, Laurier was in effect still refraining from a definitive statement on the school question. Yet his shock-troop leader, Tarte, was now prepared to use the argument which would serve the Liberals well in face of the expected but still mysterious bill. This was the thorny problem of insuring finances for any restored schools in Manitoba. The speech was especially significant because it marked a shift of emphasis in Tarte's pronouncements from berating the government for its delay in coercion to warning of the dangers of such coercion. This shift may have helped pave the way for Laurier, but it earned Tarte irate reactions from Quebec clerics such as Canon Paul Bruchési, the future archbishop of Montreal. 'Révoltant!' wrote Bruchési to Bégin.[78]

For the reconstructed government, the final impression left by the long debate was one of profound vulnerability. The odour of venality and the tone of desperation in the 'reconciliation' were impossible to escape. Perhaps most ominous of all from the Conservative point of view was the accusation of 'la trahison du parti tory d'Ontario' on the matter of re-medialism by the normally Conservative *La Presse* of Montreal.[79] If the purpose of the revolt had been to seek renewed strength by reinforcing the Quebec section of the cabinet, the result had been precisely the opposite.

The sequence of events in the January crisis was reasonably clear. The motives and the inside picture of the influences at work remained, even after the spate of explanations which came in the debate and elsewhere, complex and confusing. Official statements of reconciliation watered down the bitterness of the break, but too much had been said and done to be patched over except in a very surface manner. After a great deal of uneasy manoeuvering over having to 'eat his own words,'[80] Bowell gave a formal note of exoneration for the rebel ministers to C.H. Tupper. The prime minister said that new facts brought to his attention since his harsh speech in the Senate had shown that he had been hasty in his accusations. He admitted that up to the day Parliament met it still appeared that he might fill Angers's position; thus he accepted the failure to do so as the reason for the resignations.[81] The statement sounded, and was, more than a little hollow. Almost ten years later, when the expression 'nest of traitors' which became

78 AAQ, Bruchési to Bégin, January 27, 1896
79 January 23, 1896
80 Lady Aberdeen, *Journal*, January 14, 1896
81 PAC, C.H. Tupper Papers, Bowell to Tupper, n.d., but probably c. January 15, 1896

the by-word for the crisis, was brought up in the Senate, Bowell showed that his opinion of the crisis had never changed. 'I do not remember having used the expression "nest of traitors,"' he said, 'but if I did not use it, I ought to have used it.'[82]

As for the view of the bolters after cabinet reconstruction, C.H. Tupper, the one minister who was left out in the re-shuffle (because of his father's entry), felt that the whole episode had concluded with nothing gained and much lost. Tupper had little good to say for the new arrangement except that the remedial bill would at least be presented. In a letter to a clerical supporter, he did not hesitate to lay the blame for the 'stalemate' on the ministers who had stuck with Bowell:

Ferguson, Costigan & Daly (not to mention Caron & Ouimet) or any one of them are responsible for Bowell's lunacy & the great injury done to our party during the 'crisis.' Had it not been for them, Bowell would gracefully have gone. Sir C.T. would have been Prime Minister & our victory would have been certain. These men however have played Turk (I refer to Ferguson & Daly) and having acted with us up to 'resignation' encouraged Bowell to play the fool until the cart was nearly upset.[83]

Sir Charles Tupper, Sr, described his version of the crisis in his autobiography some years later and made the process sound almost amicable:

When a majority of the members of the Bowell Cabinet had resigned and the party had been broken into pieces, I was reluctantly induced to come to the rescue on the meeting of Parliament in 1895. Asked by the recalcitrant members of the Cabinet to assume leadership, I refused, declaring that I would not do so except at the request of the Premier, Sir Mackenzie Bowell. It was not until all efforts on his part at reconstruction had failed that he requested me to become leader of the party. I told him I would do so if he was prepared to receive back all his colleagues, to which he assented.[84]

To say the least, Sir Charles's version did not reflect the complexity and violence of the eruption.

Bishop Laflèche's interpretation, like the initial reaction of the Aberdeens, was categorical; the basic motive for the resignations could only have been a plot to scuttle remedial legislation. 'Les défections,' the bishop

82 Canada, Senate, *Debates*, January 11, 1905
83 PAC, C.H. Tupper Papers, Tupper to Father Burke, February 3, 1896
84 *Recollections of Sixty Years in Canada*, p.308, confirming the account given to Sir William Van Horne (Tupper Papers, Tupper to Van Horne, January 6, 1896)

wrote to Marois, 'tout tristes qu'elles soient, auront l'avantage de séparer le mauvais grain d'avec le bon, et de démasquer les hypocrites et les traîtres de manière à ouvrir les yeux aux aveugles volontiers eux-mêmes.'[85] John Costigan and the Liberal opposition had joined in the same sweeping indictment of the motives of the bolters. In retrospect, these simplistic interpretations can hardly be maintained for all those involved in the revolt, particularly the Tuppers. A more probable view, and one which allows for a wide spectrum of motives among the bolting ministers, is that they were simply searching for a viable combination which would give them a chance for political survival, with or without remedial legislation.

At the same time, the revolt was more than a stratagem that failed. Irrespective of the motives of the various actors in the piece, remedial legislation had been delayed, and the team required to carry it through, even when re-assembled, was a suspect and shaky one, headed by a prime minister without credibility or authority. The event that dominated all else during early January was not, as Bowell had promised, a remedial bill, but an internal revolt involving more than half of his cabinet. It is true that Bowell had inherited a situation that was not of his making. He was pleasant, and anxious to be just, especially to the Catholics despite his Orange background. But he was clearly out of his depth. He either deliberately misled the Aberdeens about the circumstances of the revolt, or was so obtuse or vain that he did not or would not understand what was happening. Above all he failed where it mattered most for a prime minister, as a leader of men; in brief, he attempted to play Macdonald's 'old tomorrow' game without John A.'s ability to calculate what was coming or to command loyalty when it was most important.

Nonetheless Bowell was back, perhaps revealing as much about the weakness of the party which had not been able to get rid of its inadequate leader, as about Bowell himself. The church, in the person of Lacombe, had been deeply involved, and the involvement was not likely to lessen. As a prelude to the attempt to pass the most explosive piece of legislation in Canadian parliamentary history, a worse preparation than the January cabinet crisis could hardly be imagined.

WAITING FOR THE BILL

One of the factors that strongly conditioned the course of thought and action at Ottawa immediately after the cabinet crisis was the emphatic vote

85 AAQ, Laflèche to Marois, January 4, 1896. Even the faithful Conservative *La Minerve* (January 7, 1896) initially suspected treason on the parts of those resigning.

of confidence given the Greenway government in the Manitoba provincial elections on January 15. The standing in the forty-seat legislature after the election was: Liberals, 32; Patrons of Industry, 2 (committed to support Greenway's school policy); Conservatives, 6, of whom two, Marion and Paré, were French. That the school question was the central issue of the election was more than evident in Greenway's own election address to his constituents in the riding of Mountain. The premier spoke of the 'menacing attitude assumed by the Dominion Government' as the main reason for the election being held. At the very least, he insisted, the proposed federal action required a thorough formal investigation.[86] Showing the degree to which the Conservative as well as the Liberal candidates, except in the French ridings, were committed to a maintenance of the status quo on schools, Sifton and Cameron felt compelled to issue statements denying any hint of collusion with Laurier and the federal Liberal party or of prospective compromise with the Catholic authorities.[87]

Besides giving emphasis to Liberal warnings against coercing a clearly expressed provincial majority, the feature of the election which most affected the federal picture, especially on the clerical-political level, was the victory of J.E.P. Prendergast in the riding of St Boniface. Prendergast, although he had resigned in protest from the Greenway cabinet during the early days of the school crisis, had remained within the party, and again ran as a Liberal in the 1896 election. It was clear from Langevin's letters to various correspondents in Quebec that he had continued on good terms with Prendergast, and that the latter remained something like an ambassador between Langevin and the provincial government. But Prendergast was nonetheless a Liberal, and Conservatives who viewed their efforts to promote a remedial bill at Ottawa as a *quid pro quo* deal with the church, expected Langevin to work actively against Prendergast and were angered when he did not. The repercussions coming back to Langevin from Ottawa after the election were emphatic and were continued evidence of the price of political involvement by the church. LaRivière's reaction was moderate but still complaining. 'J'ai beaucoup de mal,' he wrote Langevin from Ottawa, 'à faire comprendre ici la raison de l'élection de Prendergast, lequel ayant fait partie de la conférence libérale, à Ottawa, avec Sifton et autres, est considéré comme un libéral avancé, ami du gouvernement local.'[88]

---

86 PAM, Greenway Papers, Election Address, January, 1896
87 Manitoba *Free Press*, January 4, 1896
88 AASB, LaRivière to Langevin, January 21, 1896

Senator Bernier was both more vocal and more bitter. He protested against Prendergast's candidacy on January 10 and complained about Langevin's failure to oppose the Liberal candidate in a letter of 21 January.[89] Writing on the matter on January 17, Lacombe told of a meeting with Bernier where the latter was so extreme in his criticism of Langevin and Prendergast that Lacombe could only say, 'Vous savez qu'on ne raisonne pas avec ce sénateur.' But Lacombe himself was hardly less critical. In a second letter, January 17, Lacombe reported that many other Conservatives were loud in their displeasure over Prendergast's election, and let his own feelings show rather clearly:

Au gouvernement, on me le répète *avec amertume*, on regrette ces élections de gens, 'qui aujourd'hui voteront avec le Gouvernement, au moins d'après ce qu'ils promettent, mais demain seront contre!' So it is for Prendergast, qui est un traitre et travaille avec Greenway. Hier un ministre, Sir Adolphe, me disait: 'Nous regrettons l'élection de Prendergast qui est élu à la porte de l'Archevêché et sous la protection de Mgr. Langevin ... Mgr. se compromet avec nous!!'[90]

Once again, an ecclesiastical goal in the political field was showing itself to have a substantial price tag; even neutrality on Langevin's part was being viewed as betrayal by the Conservative party command.

THREE BY-ELECTIONS: TWO EPISCOPAL RUBICONS

Three federal by-elections took place during this same period. The first, West Huron, was made necessary by the appointment of the Conservative, J.C. Patterson, as lieutenant governor of Manitoba. In the voting on January 14, the Liberal candidate M.C. Cameron won the seat, which he had held briefly in 1891, by a majority of 180. In contrast with the December by-elections, this represented an encouraging gain for the Liberals in Ontario. At the same time, because of the high degree of confusion at Ottawa while the seat was being contested, the West Huron election passed without great commotion over the school question.

The case was far different, however, in the remaining two by-elections. The first of these, Charlevoix, scene of the celebrated 'influence indue' case of 1876, lay mainly within the diocese of Chicoutimi, and deeply involved the head of that diocese, Bishop Labrecque. The seat had been

89 *Ibid.*, Bernier to Langevin, January 10, 1896
90 *Ibid.*, Lacombe to Langevin, January 17, 1896, letters 1 and 2

carried by the Liberals in the 1891 election by a majority of 307 out of a total vote of 2777.[91] The new Liberal candidate, Charles Angers, was a lawyer and an exemplary Catholic from La Malbaie, but the Conservatives were determined to win the seat back at all costs. Sir A.P. Caron sent seventy-five dollars expense money to Father Lacombe to encourage the missionary to go north and take an active part in the crucial campaign. 'Si nous perdions Charlevoix,' Caron wrote, 'je crois réellement que le sort des écoles est tout à jamais scellé.'[92] The minister of militia failed to mention that his own fate might well be sealed along with that of the schools; in any case he put Lacombe in an embarrassing position. In the wake of the two Montreal by-elections in late December, Lacombe had told Archbishop Langevin that he probably would go to Chicoutimi, 'pour m'entendre avec Mgr. Labrecque, au sujet de d'élection partielle de Charlevoix, qui aura lieu bientôt. S'il faut encore perdre ce comté!'[93] In a second letter, after taking Desjardins to see Bowell, Lacombe referred to further government pressure to enlist him and was more hesitant.[94] On January 2, Lacombe indicated that he would consult Archbishop Bégin and would follow the archbishop's advice. Bégin was not in Quebec when Lacombe arrived, but the missionary was persuaded by others not to go to Chicoutimi. His January 6 letter to Langevin described the influences which had dissuaded him:

Vous savez qui le gouvernement m'avait pressé d'aller dans le comté de Charlevoix, à Chicoutimi, afin d'obtenir la majorité du côté conservateur ... Après avoir consulté nos amis, Nossignors Marois, Hamel, Laflamme et le L. Gouverneur Chapleau, j'ai cru ne pas me rendre à la pression du Gouvernement: ça aurait été me compromettre et le clergé de la Province. Les ésprits sont si excités.[95]

Whatever Lacombe's decision was going to be, Bishop Labrecque felt that he himself had to get into the battle. On the one hand he showed that he was not blind to the possible repercussions of excessive episcopal action. 'Les événements sont tellement précipités,' he wrote to Langevin, 'que vraiment les évêques ont besoin d'user de la plus grande circonspection, s'il ne veulent pas faire plus de mal que de bien à la question des écoles que

91 *Canadian Parliamentary Guide*, 1891, p.187
92 AASB, Caron to Lacombe, January 1, 1896
93 *Ibid.*, Lacombe to Langevin, December 31, 1895, letter 1
94 *Ibid.*, Lacombe to Langevin, December 31, 1895, letter 2
95 *Ibid.*, Lacombe to Langevin, January 6, 1896

nous avons tous à cœur.'[96] This did not, however, bring the conclusion that he should stay out of the election. On January 6, Labrecque reinforced Caron's plea that Lacombe should come to Charlevoix.[97] By January 20, Lacombe gave the impression that he was being prevailed upon from all sides, but still refused to comply:

Mr. Pelletier, le secrétaire provincial de la Province, est venu me rejoindre à l'Archevêché et m'a supplié d'aller au secours du Comté de Charlevoix, que le gouvernement va probablement perdre. J'ai refusé de me mêler à la chose politique jusqu'à ce point. Je me fie sur Mgr. Labrecque pour aider notre cause, en autant que sa sagesse et prudence l'inspireront.[98]

The 'sagesse et prudence' which Bishop Labrecque decided to use came in the form of a pastoral letter sent out on January 24. He knew it was a serious step. 'J'ai tenu conseil avec les meilleures têtes de la cure et du Séminaire,' he wrote to Bégin, 'et j'ai franchi le Rubicon.' The heart of Labrecque's mandement, supposed to be read without comment, was as follows:

Nous ne voulons pas faire de politique, ni nous prononcer pour un parti plutôt que pour l'autre, mais il y a à régler une question religieuse, fort importante, la question des écoles du Manitoba. Nous regardons comme un grave devoir de conscience pour les électeurs de ne donner leur vote qu'à un candidat qui s'engagera formellement et solenellement à voter, durant la présente session, pour une législation réparatrice qui aura été agréé par l'autorité ecclésiastique, Veuillez remarquer, je le répète, en cette circonstance, d'un grave devoir de conscience.[99]

Clearly, the 'no commentary' rule was inserted to prevent variations of interpretation by individual curés. Labrecque tried to present his intervention as nonpartisan. His justification of his action to his metropolitan, Bégin, was that he had remained 'strictement sur le terrain religieux sans acception de personnes ou de partis. Que tout candidat, bleu, rouge ou indépendent, fasse la déclaration que je demande et que j'ai droit de demander, et il peut bénéficier de ce document tant qu'il voudra.'[100] The

96 *Ibid.*, Labrecque to Langevin, January 13, 1896
97 *Ibid.*, Labrecque to Lacombe, Janaury 6, 1896
98 AASB, Lacombe to Langevin, January 20, 1896
99 *Ibid.*, Labrecque's Pastoral Letter, January 24, 1896
100 AAQ, Labrecque to Bégin, January 24, 1896

difficulty, of course, was that the Conservatives had pushed for the statement and, once made, interpreted it as the clear and obvious sanction of the church in their favour. It was not enough, however. On January 27, the Liberal candidate, Charles Angers, apparently having taken the declaration required by the Labrecque letter, was elected by a majority of 176, a reduction of 131 from the Liberal majority achieved in 1891.[101]

The election brought two significant repercussions, beyond the fact that it had elicited the first official episcopal volley in a federal election involving the school question. The first result was predictable, a war of words between Liberal and Conservative newspapers. Tarte contributed to the ammunition available to both sides by his charge in Parliament of 'influence indue' by Bishop Labrecque. Once the result was known, L'Electeur's headline trumpeted: 'Le Candidat Libéral élu par une majorité de 176 sur l'argent, le whiskey, les orangistes et les curés!'[102] So violent was the Liberal paper's tone that Laurier felt obliged to at least mildly reprove the editor, Pacaud, for his excessive attacks on Bishop Labrecque.[103]

Naturally enough, L'Electeur's pugilism brought a sharp reaction from church authorities, particularly those in Chicoutimi. The newspaper got the best of a somewhat maladroit effort on the part of Bishop Labrecque to discipline editor Pacaud for the attack of January 28. On February 6, the bishop's secretary, Abbé Frenette, sent a threat that L'Electeur would be banned in Chicoutimi unless Pacaud printed a retraction which Frenette spelled out word for word. L'Electeur gleefully printed the retraction, without comment, along with the full text of Frenette's heavy-handed demand.[104] La Minerve felt compelled to come to Frenette's defence, styling Pacaud's manoeuver a 'suprème inconvenance' carried out 'dans un esprit de défis et d'insolence.'[105] L'Electeur assumed an air of injured innocence in its reply on the following day,[106] and La Minerve was obliged to admit that Frenette 's'était exposé à la mésaventure dont il a été la victime.' Nonetheless, the Conservative paper insisted, Pacaud had been guilty of a 'subterfuge indigne.' 'Il a voulu,' La Minerve concluded, 'avoir l'air de se rétracter, quand de fait il se moquait audacieusement de l'injonction épiscopale.[107]

Paralleling the squabble over the Frenette letter was a philosophical and

101 L'Electeur, January 28, 1896
102 January 28, 1896
103 PAC, Pacaud Papers, Laurier to Pacaud, January 30, 1896. See also below, p.177.
104 February 19, 1896
105 February 21, 1896
106 February 22, 1896
107 February 27, 1896

theological discussion concerning the right of the ecclesiastical authority to interfere as Labrecque had done. The pro-clerical apologist was Abbé L. Paquet of Quebec City. Once again, *L'Electeur* seemed to get the best of the exchange, suggesting that the extremely solemn Paquet was extending to *Le Courrier* and other Conservative journals 'la même foi qu'aux encycliques.'[108]

A second repercussion of the Charlevoix affair, beyond the journalistic one, concerned the vicar general of the Chicoutimi diocese, Abbé Bruno Leclerc, curé of La Malbaie, pastor and personal friend of the successful Liberal candidate, Charles Angers. In a circular marked 'strictement confidentielle' for his diocesan clergy only, Labrecque stated that he had issued the mandement only when convinced that the election was far more than a purely political contest, and that he had several times tried and failed to get a declaration in favour of remedial legislation from Angers. Instead, according to the bishop, Angers had declared in favour of Laurier's 'enquête.' Labrecque stated he would still have kept silence had not his vicar general, Leclerc, openly come out in favour of Angers, 'même en chaire (du moins c'est ainsi qu'on l'a compris) pour un homme que se déclare prêt à trahir la cause religieuse et nationale, un homme dont le premier pas dans la carrière politique est un acte de *libéralisme catholique* bien caracterisé.' Labrecque insisted that only after the report of Leclerc's statements had he taken the very serious step of publishing the mandement. The bishop's conclusion was curt. 'Le mal est fait, j'en laisse la responsabilité à son auteur,' he said, and added that Leclerc was now a man 'en qui il m'est impossible à l'avenir de reposer aucune confiance.'[109]

---

108 February 17, 1896. There was no lack of academic opinion brought to bear on the 'intervention' question. Even before the Charlevoix clash, Archbishop Langevin sought expert theological advice from at least three separate sources. Abbé L. Colin, superior of the Grand Seminary of Montreal, replied that Catholics were obviously bound to support just laws, including, in his opinion, the proposed remedial measure. Nevertheless, the obligation 'ne pourrait guère, présentement, être rappellée aux citoyens par l'autorité épiscopale, sans de graves périls' (AASB, Colin to Langevin, January 16, 1896). Père Froc, OMI, of the University of Ottawa, gave substantially the same opinion as Colin (AASB, Froc to Langevin, February 5, 1896). But Père Filiatrault, SJ, leaned more to the possibility of obliging Catholics in conscience to support the government, 'si le seul moyen vraiment efficace d'obtenir ce résultat consiste à faire adopter par les chambres d'Ottawa une loi réparatrice, reconnue suffisante par les évêques' (AASB, Filiatrault to Langevin, February 9, 1896). Langevin may have been more impressed by the latter 'hard-line' opinion, but the exhortations to caution on the part of the academics undoubtedly played a role in the decision not to send a letter to Catholic deputies before the debate on the bill. See below, pp.212–20.

109 AEV, Labrecque's circular to Diocesan Clergy, February 10, 1896. A marginal note, probably by Bishop Emard, on the copy of this letter found in the Valleyfield archives,

At least one prominent Quebec Conservative was convinced that the most significant aspect of the Charlevoix election was not the attempt at clerical intervention, but the fact that the Liberals were able to convince the voters that the Conservative government would delay remedial action out of existence. This was L.P. Pelletier, the pro-ultramontane provincial secretary of Quebec. In a letter to Caron shortly after the Charlevoix contest, Pelletier stated that, against his will, he was afraid that there might be something to L'Electeur's charges that the Conservative wall was far from mended, and that the Ontario members of the cabinet were indeed conspiring to assure that remedial legislation, though presented, should not go through. He said that he would not accept the charges until proven, yet several recent private letters had sown grave suspicions in his mind. Pelletier believed that the life of Parliament could be extended; above all he was convinced that the government could quickly bring the issue to a vote. If they could not, or felt they could not win when the vote came, the federal cabinet ministers ought to resign; they should refuse to contribute to a 'comédie impardonnable.'

Next Pelletier came to the reasons for taking his position. 'Je suis pour le règlement de la question des écoles avant d'être ami de parti et avant d'être conservateur,' Pelletier insisted. The 'farce' had gone on for six years; Charlevoix had been lost because the Liberals had with justice been able to point the finger at continued inaction. The best of ultramontane independence came out in Pelletier's tough conclusion:

Si je suis trompé, je ne contribuerai pas à avoir trompé le peuple. J'ai combattu Laurier en disant qu'au fond, il était contre les écoles catholiques; je ne soutiendrai pas un gouvernement conservateur qui au fond serait dans la même position.

J'ai réussi à convaincre nos évêques que le gouvernement était dans la bonne voie. Comptant sur l'engagement d'honneur que j'ai contracté envers eux pour le parti, ils ont pris une position qui leur a valu des injures brutales; je ne permettrai jamais qu'ils croient que j'ai contribué à les tromper et je dégagerai ma responsabilité de manière à ce qu'ils le comprennent.[110]

indicated that Leclerc escaped the ecclesiastical limbo to which Labrecque was apparently consigning him: 'M. l'Abbe Leclerc, V.G.,' the note stated, 'n'eût pas de misère à refuter des calomnies dont les politiciens l'avaient accusé auprès de Sa Grandeur; S. Gr. reconnait l'innocence de son GR.vic. et lui rendit son confiance, sans vouloir toutefois retirer cette lettre –: "Ca servira à vous punir de vos péchés passés."' It should also be noted that Charles Angers, although he refused to approve a remedial bill in advance of its appearance, was one of the six Quebec Liberals who voted for the bill and against Laurier when the test came in March.

110 PAC, Caron Papers, Pelletier to Caron, February 3, 1896

A further note from Pelletier on February 6 indicated that he had received Caron's letter assuring him that the duration of Parliament could and would be extended until June, and that the government staked its life on remedial legislation. Pelletier replied that his remarks on February 3 did not mean that he believed treachery would succeed, but that he was convinced that a scuttling scheme was being actively promoted.[111]

The Charlevoix affair showed that the lines were tightening still further. Labrecque had well illustrated the dilemma of the churchman trying to be nonpartisan, yet directly supporting one party's policy. Pelletier's misgivings indicated that the gravity of direct episcopal interference was beginning to be appreciated at least in some quarters. More important, Pelletier brought into sharp relief the most evident political lesson of the by-election: the Liberals could win in Quebec in the face of a hostile episcopal mandement, or at least could neutralize such a document through some clerical support, and by charging the Conservatives with treachery and promising a better settlement under Laurier. The lesson would not be lost in the hectic months ahead.

The Cape Breton by-election was arranged to obtain a seat for Sir Charles Tupper, Sr., and added its own fuel to the fire. The offer to make way for Tupper came from the sitting member, D. MacKeen, on January 8.[112] The Liberal candidate was George Murray, who resigned his seat in the Nova Scotia legislature in order to oppose Tupper. The first major reference to the school question during the campaign was made by Tupper at Boiesdale, Nova Scotia, on January 12. Sir Charles insisted that he had supported the Thompson procedure of exhausting attempts to deal with the matter through the courts. Since, however, the Privy Council had declared that a grievance existed, and since the Manitoba government had refused to rectify the situation though given every opportunity, he now believed that it was the duty of the federal government to enact a remedial law in order to uphold the constitution.[113] Tupper's continued concentration on justice and minority rights seems to have been at least acceptable to his constituents; on February 4 he was returned with a majority of 820 votes.[114]

111 *Ibid.*, Caron to Pelletier, February 5, 1896; Pelletier to Caron, February 6, 1896. The suggestion that the life of Parliament could be extended was based on the fact that the final writ for the Algoma election of 1891 was not returned until June 11. Apparently Lord Aberdeen was not impressed, and after consulting Bourinot, the governor general advised the cabinet that the case was not worth taking to the Supreme Court (Lady Aberdeen, *Journal*, March 19, 1896).
112 PAC, Tupper Papers, MacKeen to Tupper, January 8, 1896
113 Halifax *Morning Chronicle*, January 23, 1896
114 Toronto *Mail and Empire*, February 4, 1896

By far the most exciting aspect of the Cape Breton campaign, however, came on February 3 with the report of a letter from Bishop Cameron of Antigonish, in which his coreligionists who supported Laurier's proposal were described as 'hell-inspired hypocritical Catholics.' Although no great commotion over the letter was evident in the news reports of the campaign itself, the bishop's inflammatory phrase received more than a little attention in the immediate wake of the election. On February 4 the Halifax *Morning Chronicle* and on February 5 the Toronto *Globe* stressed the influence of the Cameron letter and expanded on its possible consequences.[115] Even Father Lacombe was upset by the furore. 'Je crains bien,' he wrote to Langevin, 'que l'intervention du clergé (pourtant légitime) dans cette élection ne fasse du mal à l'église. Mr. Laurier me menace d'une terrible réaction de la part des protestants et des libéraux de Québec.'[116] Archbishop Walsh was no happier about the possible repercussions in Ontario. 'S.G. [Sa Grandeur] regrette énormement la manière de Mgr. Cameron,' Lacombe reported to Langevin after a personal interview with the Toronto archbishop. 'En effet c'est sérieux de se servir de cette expression contre les libéraux: "hell-inspired hypocrites." That's a great mistake in the circumstances – Il craint bien que Mgr. Cleary n'en fasse autant à un moment donné.'[117] A week later Lacombe was able to write that the private nature of Cameron's letter had become known, and that the excitement, at least in Ottawa, was dying down.[118]

When Tupper was introduced as a new member to the House on February 11, there were a number of references to Cameron's role in the by-election. Cartwright, for instance, called the bishop 'the gentle and pious prelate to whom he [Tupper] owed his election.'[119] But no one seemed inclined to press the issue with much vigour; the basic reason for Tupper's presence in the House was clear to all. He was to provide an effective head for a government committed to federal legislation on the

---

115 Further details on the clerical factor in this byelection may be found in McLaughlin, 'The Canadian General Election of 1896 in Nova Scotia' (thesis), pp.45–55.

116 AASB, Lacombe to Langevin, February 4, 1896

117 *Ibid.*, Lacombe to Langevin, February 7, 1896

118 *Ibid.*, Lacombe to Langevin, February 13, 1896. Lady Aberdeen, in her *Journal* of February 11, cast doubt on the authenticity of the Cameron letter, although she observed that 'the expression is not withdrawn.' There seemed to be some doubt even about the precise phrase used, Lady Aberdeen reporting it as 'hell-bound hypocrites.' A statement authorized by Cameron himself in the Antigonish *Casket* of February 6 called the *Chronicle*'s report a 'garbled extract from a private letter marked as such.'

119 Canada, House of Commons, *Debates*, February 11, 1896, p.1526

Manitoba school question. Sir Charles was reminded of this hard reality in a note of congratulations on his election received from Langevin on February 7. 'Your manly declarations ... afford us great hopes and almost a certitude about the favourable issue of this much-vexed question,' the archbishop wrote. Tupper could only reply that he was 'deeply anxious for a satisfactory settlement,' based on 'the rights of minorities and the maintenance of the Constitution.'[120] The polite rhetoric on both sides only thinly disguised the obstacles which lay ahead. The newspaper reports of Tupper's first caucus can hardly have restored Langevin's confidence; even the presence of a forceful new leader left a substantial block of Ontario Conservatives adamant against remedialism.[121]

120 PAC, Tupper Papers, Langevin to Tupper, February 7, 1896; AASB, Tupper to Langevin, February 14, 1896.
121 Toronto *Mail and Empire*, February 12, 1896

6
'Les malheurs chevauchent en troupe':
a missionary as diplomat

Proof of Tupper's intent was the immediate introduction of bill 58, entitled
'The Remedial Act (Manitoba)' by the new minister of justice, A.R. Dickey. Both Lacombe and LaRivière had reported that the reason for the last
of many delays in placing the bill before the House had been to await
Tupper's election and arrival in Ottawa; dramatically, both Tupper and the
bill were presented on the same day. In his elaboration, Dickey stressed
that framing the bill had been 'a matter of very great difficulty,' and
expressed regret that copies were not yet available for distribution. Dickey
then outlined the main provisions of the bill, beginning with the somewhat
apologetic statement that it had been 'found impossible to restore to the
Roman Catholic minority in Manitoba those rights which it was thought
they were entitled to under the constitution without establishing a system
of separate schools.' There was to be a board of education for separate
schools, containing nine members, like the Catholic section of the pre-1890
board. The lieutenant governor was to make the appointments, or, if he did
not, the federal government would. Trustees would be able to tax all
Catholics for the new schools, except those who preferred to support the
public schools. Teachers would have to meet provincial standards 'in
secular matters,' and there was to be a double system of inspection,
Catholic for day-to-day matters, a second by the government from time to
time to check efficiency. The book clause had been extremely difficult to
settle, Dickey said, with the decision finally being left to the separate-

school board to choose from among books used by the Manitoba public schools and Ontario separate schools. To McCarthy's question on the financial arrangement, Dickey pointed out that the details of the provincial grant to separate schools would not be dictated. It would simply be stated that the Catholic schools had a right to such a grant, 'taking it for granted ... that the province of Manitoba itself will, after the system is established, supply that fund to the separate schools.'[1]

After Dickey's comments on the provisions of the bill, Liberal P.A. Choquette immediately asked if the measure had been 'approved by the religious authorities'; Ouimet interjected that Choquette should find that out for himself. Dupont asked for a French translation, and Caron replied that none was yet available. Laurier wanted to know if the date for the second reading of the bill had been fixed. If anything, the Liberal leader gave the impression of favouring delay, insisting that 'some time would be needed for the study of the Bill before the second reading.' To Mills's inquiry whether a copy of the bill would be sent to the Manitoba government, Dickey replied that he saw no objection although he did not consider it necessary. 'If it is considered more courteous it shall certainly be done,' Dickey concluded.[2] Although there were a number of questions during the succeeding ten days which seemed to reflect an unusual delay in getting copies of the bill circulated, there was no major discussion on remedialism until February 21. On that day Foster moved, with Laurier's agreement, that debate on the second reading of the remedial bill be made the first business of Tuesday, March 3, and that discussion continue 'on the following days until the debate thereon be completed.'[3]

The relatively mild exchange that accompanied the presentation of the remedial bill respected the tradition of Parliament for a first reading, but it barely hid the heavy infighting which involved both federal parties in late January and all through February. Once again, the focus of much of the

1 Canada, House of Commons, *Bills*, 1896, No.58; *Debates*, February 11, 1896, pp.1512–14. Dickey's statement about Clause 74, the section dealing with the provincial-education grant and which was to cause prolonged controversy during the debate, contained more than a little official mendacity. Father Lacombe and Sir Adolphe Caron, among others, were obliged to assure ecclesiastical authorities that any provincial recalcitrance over the school grant would be compensated for by an amendment to the Dominion Lands Act, with the federal government giving part of the land sales' fund directly to the separate schools (AAQ, Caron to Bégin, February 22, 24, 1896; AASB, Lacombe to Langevin, February 19, 1896).

2 Canada, House of Commons, *Debates*, 1896, p.1514
3 *Ibid.*, February 21, 1896, p.2095

tension was Father Lacombe. Although he managed to stay out of the Charlevoix fight, the role of the ambassador-missionary became more and more important. It is true that Lacombe himself was not unmindful of the anomaly of his position. 'Ah! mon Dieu!' he wailed to Langevin, 'est-il possible que sur mes vieux jours de sauvage, il m'était reservé d'être mêlé à de semblables questions de politique! Moi, pauvre missionaire du pauvre et l'ignorant, traitant et discutant aujourd'hui avec nos hommes d'état, les avisant et leur servant d'interprète ... Ca me paraît comme une comédie.'[4] Whatever else the settling of the cabinet crisis may have accomplished, however, it assured that a remedial bill would be forthcoming; and it assured that Lacombe, who had worked so diligently to help patch the cabinet in order to have such a bill presented, would leave no stone unturned to help the government put the bill through. His most irrevocable step came on January 20 in the form of a dramatic letter to Wilfrid Laurier. Here the old missionary seemed at one stroke to go beyond the limits of his commission and to demand what the Liberal leader would be almost certain to refuse. Without reservation, Lacombe claimed to speak 'in the name of our bishops, of the hierarchy and the Catholics of Canada,' and without qualification he asked 'the party of which you are the very worthy chief, to assist us in settling this famous question, and to do so by voting with the government on the Remedial Bill.' Nor was Lacombe content to leave the matter as a polite request; he moved on to a black-and-white ultimatum:

I must tell you that we cannot accept your commission of enquiry on any account, and shall do our best to fight it. If, which may God not grant, you do not believe it to be your duty to accede to our just demands, and if the government, which is anxious to give us the promised law, is beaten and overthrown while keeping firm to the end of the struggle, I inform you, with regret, that the episcopacy, like one man, united with the clergy, will rise to support those who may have fallen in defending us. Please pardon the frankness which leads me to speak thus.[5]

From the Liberal point of view at least, Lacombe might well excuse himself for his 'frankness'; frankness was a mild term for what they considered the letter to contain. It must be remembered that the public furore over Lacombe's ultimatum to Laurier did not come until a month later, when the text of the supposedly private letter was published in *L'Electeur*. Furthermore, Lacombe clearly believed, at least in January,

4 AASB, Lacombe to Langevin, January 10, 1896
5 AAQ, Lacombe to Laurier, January 20, 1896

that he had retained enough independence to be able to approach Laurier without fear of having prejudiced his position. Even if Laurier were to become prime minister, Lacombe wrote, 'je me conduirai avec lui, comme j'ai agi avec les conservateurs, c-à-d, franc et loyal, avec tout pouvoir dûment constitué.'[6] Whatever possibility this impartiality might have had before the January 20 letter, the ultimatum opened the breach between Lacombe and the Liberal leader almost beyond repair.

From the missionary's correspondence it was evident that the immediate influence in the composition and sending of the letter to Laurier was none other than Bishop Laflèche. Lacombe included Bégin with Laflèche when quoting to Langevin the authorities he had consulted before speaking in the name of all the bishops.[7] But Lacombe's own letter to Bégin on the same day as the ultimatum to Laurier, went to some length to inform the Quebec archbishop of his just-finished visit to Trois-Rivières, and of the language he would use with the Liberal leader. In particular, Lacombe cited Laflèche's approval of trying to put Laurier in a 'yes or no' position.[8] If it cannot be said that the ultimatum to Laurier was Laflèche's, it clearly was Laflèche-inspired. Moreover, although it spoke in the name of all the bishops of Canada, the letter was unknown at least to one, Bishop Emard, until it became public in mid-February.

In any case, Lacombe's subsequent letters showed that the ultimatum letter was the pretext for the growing barrier between the church hierarchy and the Liberal leader during the next month. As many as five meetings took place between the two men. Each time the gap seemed a little wider. Each time, according to Lacombe, Laurier took as his point of departure that the January 20 letter was a declaration of war. This was summed up in a conversation which Lacombe reported on February 15:

Grande entrevue de nouveau avec Mr. Laurier, que je rencontre dans les couloirs et qui m'entraîne dans sa chambre. Non, il n'y a pas moyen de le convaincre de nous suivre. C'est la guerre qu'il nous déclare, puisqu'on le pousse à cela. Ma lettre est son grand cauchemar. Il la montre à ses partisans et les consulte, sur la portée de ce document. 'Je l'ai toujours devant moi, sur mon bureau,' me dit-il. 'Donc c'est la guerre! – Et bien, vous l'aurez,' lui ai-je dit. 'L'Episcopat et le clergé veulent nous écraser!' a-t-il continué à reclamer ... Au moins il persiste à se déclarer contre nous. Que fera-t-il au dernier moment?[9]

6 AASB, Lacombe to Langevin, January 13, 1896
7 Ibid., Lacombe to Langevin, January 20, 1896
8 AAQ, Lacombe to Bégin, January 20, 1896
9 AASB, Lacombe to Langevin, February 15, 1896

It should be noted, however, that Lacombe could never bring himself to dislike Laurier personally, even though their differences over policy grew irreconcilable. As late as February 19 the missionary wrote of the Liberal leader: 'Pourtant c'est drôle, je suis porté à vouloir estimer cet homme. C'est bien regrettable qu'il ait embrassé cette ligne de conduite. Il est probable qu'il va encore chercher à me rencontrer. Que puis-je faire plus pour lui?'[10] Even after Laurier's March 3 speech, with which Lacombe could not have disagreed more profoundly, a spark of attraction still remained. 'Que c'était triste et regrettable d'entendre une si belle éloquence défendre une si mauvaise cause!' Lacombe lamented.[11] But as an indicator of the way the tide was running, Lacombe's admiration for and confidence in Bowell grew as his ability to find common ground with Laurier decreased. Shortly after the cabinet crisis, Lacombe spoke of Bowell as 'toujours le même, sincère et fidèle,'[12] and on February 4 the missionary described a chance meeting with the prime minister which revealed a good deal about their increasing friendliness:

Comme toujours, j'ai été très content et très satisfait de mon entrevue avec mon vieil ami, qui, quoiqu'orangiste, me témoigne tant d'intérêt et même d'affection. Ce matin, désirant le rencontrer, je m'en allais dans une belle voiture couverte, quand je le vis qui s'en allait à pied vers les bâtisses du parlement. Je descendis de ma voiture et j'allai l'inviter à monter avec moi, en lui disant: 'C'est l'Eglise qui vient chercher l'Etat.' 'Indeed you are too kind, my good Father confessor!' fut sa réponse. Et nous nous dirigions vers son office.[13]

In any case, the problem was far deeper than a question of personal likes and sympathies. Inevitably, it was the still-awaited remedial bill which drew the bulk of attention and energy in late January and early February. On January 25, Honoré Beaugrand of *La Patrie* accused Lacombe of having obtained a secret copy of the bill, and of manipulating the measure to suit the Quebec bishops, Laflèche in particular.[14] According to his January 6 letter to Langevin, Lacombe had indeed seen a 'draft statute' based on Ewart's proposal of the previous summer, and would try to get a copy for Langevin when he got to Ottawa the next day.[15] The cabinet crisis

10 *Ibid.*, Lacombe to Langevin, February 19, 1896
11 *Ibid.*, Lacombe to Langevin, March 4, 1896
12 *Ibid.*, Lacombe to Langevin, January 17, 1896
13 *Ibid.*, Lacombe to Langevin, February 4, 1896
14 *La Patrie*, January 25, 1896
15 AASB, Lacombe to Langevin, January 6, 1896

pre-empted all attention for the subsequent week, but the Desjardins memo of January 15 posed, as a condition of the senator's entry to the cabinet, that Lacombe see and approve the proposed bill. According to the same memo, Caron stated that Lacombe had seen the draft, although Bowell was not clear on the point.[16] On January 17, Lacombe himself indicated that he had not been shown the latest version of the bill and was worried about it. 'Il paraît que ce *bill* que je n'ai pu voir encore *in toto* est pas mal altéré depuis l'original de l'été dernier,' the missionary wrote.[17] Again on January 20 he stated that as yet he did not have a copy, but 'j'ai pu apprendre que probablement c'est la même chose que l'été dernier, tel que élaboré par Mr. Ewart.'[18] Regarding Beaugrand's charge of January 25, Lacombe's reaction was that 'heureusement que, à part l'effrontée "La Patrie," aucun journal n'a osé me toucher ni même me supposer quelque chose.' He was not blind to the growing sensitivity of his role – 'Mon Dieu! que va-t-il arriver? Dans quelle position délicate je me trouve! Je suis watché de tous côtés,' he wrote – but he felt he had no alternative but to push on. Once more Lacombe said that he did not yet possess a copy of the bill, but that he had had a long discussion with Ouimet and had been satisfied with the details outlined by the minister. Ouimet had indicated that the final draft should be ready that same day (January 28), and, although presentation would have to await Tupper's election and return to Ottawa, Lacombe hoped that 'ce soir ou demain matin avoir en secret une copie de cette loi.'[19] Lacombe clearly did obtain a copy of the law before it was presented in Parliament, and John Ewart, receiving a copy from the minister of justice, immediately returned to Winnipeg and delivered it to Langevin on February 4.[20] There is no evidence that the bill was changed before first reading at the behest of either Lacombe or Langevin, but it was equally clear that approval from St Boniface was a prime objective.

LIBERAL RIFTS

During the lull before the appearance of the bill, all was not orderly within the Liberal camp. In Parliament on the day on which Tupper was elected, February 4, Lavergne of Drummond-Arthabaska, Brodeur of Rouville,

16 ACSM, Desjardins Collection, Desjardins Memorandum, January 14, 1896
17 AASB, Lacombe to Langevin, January 17, 1896
18 *Ibid.*, Lacombe to Langevin, January 20, 1896
19 *Ibid.*, January 28, 1896
20 AASB, Ewart to Langevin, February 4, 1896

and Choquette of Montmagny all fired broadsides at the government for delaying the bill. Brodeur quoted Caron during the Verchères election as calling upon God that a bill would be introduced during the 1895 session. In 1896, Brodeur insisted, the opposition should not be left with the blame for obstructing a bill which would appear too late to be passed. 'Not only am I willing to have a Remedial Bill brought up, but introduced as soon as possible, and not indefinitely postponed, as the Government are trying to do,' Brodeur proclaimed. All three French Liberals pointed to Foster and the other bolters as the real obstruction, and all attacked the government for not being decisive enough in the direction of effective restoration. 'What is the reason why the Bill has not yet been introduced?' Brodeur asked. 'It is because certain Ministers have insisted upon the Bill being altered ... They intend, Mr. Speaker, to bring up a mutilated Bill.[21] Choquette claimed that he would support a really effective measure, but did not believe that one would be forthcoming. He therefore still supported Laurier's plan for 'a commission of arbitration between interested parties.'[22] Brodeur's remarks indicated, however, that at least some Quebec Liberals were not satisfied with the noncommittal stand their leader was taking. According to Lacombe and other observers in Ottawa, the focus of disaffection was Cléophas Beausoleil, member for Berthier. Notable among the reasons for the rumblings was the increasing prominence of former Conservative J. Israel Tarte. Tarte's speeches of January 23 and 28 had not only disturbed Liberals with pro-clerical sensitivities, but had marked him further as an upstart over old-line party members. In his February 1 letter to Langevin, LaRivière attributed some of the weaning process to Father Lacombe, and on February 6, after the Charlevoix affair had grown in excitement, elaborated on the situation. 'Beausoleil est à la tête d'un mouvement en faveur de notre loi,' LaRivière wrote. 'Dans le fond, on jalouse Tarte et l'influence que ce dernier exerce sur Laurier, et l'on veut le reléguer à l'arrière-banc.'[23]

The reported disaffection from the Liberals and adhesion to the remedial bill was not quite what LaRivière had portrayed. On February 14, the reportedly 'bolting' Liberal member sent one of the still rare copies of the bill to Canon Bruchési at the episcopal chancery in Montreal. Beausoleil said that his first impression was that the measure was 'incomplet dans une partie essentielle,' specifically because of the absence of any guarantee that

21 Canada, House of Commons, *Debates*, 1896, pp.1164–9
22 *Ibid.*, p.1178
23 AASB, LaRivière to Langevin, February 1, 1896

the Catholics would get the grants to which the bill said they had a right. Furthermore, said Beausoleil, there was no provision for the restoration of the property of Catholic schools confiscated by the 1894 amendments. 'Quand les Evêques ont demandé le désaveu du bill de 1894,' he observed, 'le gouvernement a refusé sous prétexte que la loi réparatrice ferait justice sur toute la ligne. Je ne vois dans le bill aucune trace de l'accomplissement de cette promesse.' Finally, Beausoleil feared the implications of what Bishop Labrecque had done in the Charlevoix by-election. Did it mean, he asked, that deputies had to support any measure approved by the church, no matter how ineffective the members judged it to be? 'Il y a beaucoup de députés qui trouvent la loi projetée presque nulle,' he wrote, 'et ils préféreraient laisser la question ouverte plûtot que de lui donner une solution aussi peu satisfaisante pour l'avenir.[24] Beausoleil in fact ended in March by voting for the bill and against Laurier, but he had raised the key question for a deputy faced with an ecclesiastical mandement in a political matter. In any case, the revolt was hardly as enthusiastic as LaRivière, indulging in some wishful thinking, had suggested.

Laurier was not unaware of the budding trouble within his party. Not only did he continue to see Lacombe, but he went to the extent of rebuking the excessive criticism of the hierarchy current in the Liberal papers over the Charlevoix election.[25] Laurier at least made the gesture and made sure that the right people knew about it. On February 5 Archbishop Bégin was able to assure Laflèche that many Liberals were looking for a pretext to support the remedial measure, and that 'on m'a montré hier deux lettres de M. Laurier qui déplore et reprouve les excès de langue de ses partisans dans la presse contre l'autorité religieuse.'[26] Nonetheless, the steadfastness of his Quebec supporters continued to be a major worry for Laurier.

24 AAM, Beausoleil to Bruchési, February 14, 1896
25 See above, p.164.
26 ASTR, Bégin to Laflèche, February 5, 1896. The letters referred to were almost certainly the two letters from Laurier to Pacaud of January 30 and February 5. The February 5 reprimand seems to have been calculated by the Liberal leader for discreet publication. If so, it was extremely clever, since it appealed to principle without indulging in an excess of diplomacy. Unless some very unlikely change took place, Laurier wrote, 'il n'y a plus de doute que le clergé va prendre fait et cause pour le gouvernement aux prochaines élections ... Nous allons avoir une nouvelle guerre ecclésiastique.' As a consequence, the Liberal leader insisted, Liberal spokesmen would be putting themselves in the wrong if they initiated quarrels 'par des écarts de langage ... Il faut au contraire, faire appel à la conscience des vrais catholiques et leur faire comprendre que sur cette question comme sur toutes les autres, nous n'avons aucune hostilité contre le clergé. Il faut arriver à l'éclairer et non à le froisser' (PAC, Pacaud Papers, Laurier to Pacaud, February 5, 1896).

On January 31, the Liberal leader wrote at length to C.E. Pouliot, the probable Liberal candidate for Temiscouata, and developed a quite detailed rationale for his inquiry proposal. Significantly, Laurier stressed that the main purpose would be to satisfy Protestants rather than to uncover unknown facts. Protestants, Laurier pointed out, 'ne veulent d'écoles athées, mais ils ne veulent pas non plus, d'enseignement dogmatique ... en imposant aux catholiques les mêmes restrictions qu'ils s'imposent à eux-mêmes, ils ne se rendent pas compte qu'ils sont coupables d'un acte d'intolérance.' Thus a prime requirement was that Protestants be shown that a Protestant system was in fact being imposed upon Catholics. Laurier stretched credulity when he said that this had been his consistent position for four years, but there was an air of urgency about the letter which could hardly be dismissed as mere diplomacy. Avowing his sincerity in working for the restoration of Catholic school rights, Laurier told Pouliot that he would try every argument to bring the whole party to accept this as a constitutional necessity, but that it could only be done by free inquiry and without clerical pressure. 'A toute événement, j'y mettrais mon orgueil,' Laurier concluded, 'et si je ne réussissais pas, je briserais volontairement ma carrière.'[27]

A further demonstration of Laurier's concern for a negotiated and unspectacular settlement was a letter he addressed to Clifford Sifton on January 28. Sifton had apparently written to alert the Liberal leader that federal government activity in the West pointed to an immediate election, possibly before the remedial bill was presented. Laurier agreed that Sifton's observation 'confirms the news which comes to us from all sides,' and stated that the government was 'uncertain as to the fate of the Remedial Bill.' But the Liberal leader hastened to reject any optimism which Conservative difficulties over remedialism might encourage. 'We are not any more certain than they,' he wrote. 'Moreover, whatever may be the result, that is the last question on which I would like the Liberal party to come into power. Unless this question can be settled by Manitoba itself, we will have it in federal politics for ten years at least, and it will be a perpetual thorn in

27 Groulx, *L'Enseignement Français au Canada*, II, pp.117–19. Letter furnished from private collection by J.F. Pouliot, MP, later Senator. Groulx finds the rationale for an inquiry given by Laurier in Proulx, *Documents pour Servir à l'Intelligence de la Question des Ecoles du Manitoba*, pp.170–1, more convincing than that given to Pouliot. The argument in the *Documents* was that any remedial bill would get embroiled in interminable legal wrangling. Moreover, Groulx feels that even the reason for inquiry given to Pouliot was preferable to that suggested in the remedial debate in the House, which implied that there were still unknown facts in the case.

the side of any government.' Laurier then asked Sifton to 'let me know frankly if you are prepared to make any concessions to the minority, and, if so, to what extent.' Laurier said that he believed public opinion in the East was showing 'a strong current of sympathy in favor of the minority,' although this current had been 'to a large extent stemmed by the harsh action of the Government.' In any case, Laurier concluded, 'any concessions which you would make to the minority would be welcome,' and he added the ominous refrain which he had coined the year before: 'The School question is an unknown quantity; it may break the Government; it may break the Opposition; it may break both the Government and the Opposition.'[28]

Sifton was unable or unwilling to offer any satisfactory compromise, either at the beginning of February or later in the month when Laurier wrote to him again. Concerning an unspecified suggestion made by Laurier in the latter correspondence, Sifton's reply was that 'my own view remains as it was, namely that the change referred to would in no way meet the views of the minority & would simply add another complicating factor to the already complicated problem.'[29]

ENTER THE ABERDEENS

While these tensions were building up within the parties, the efforts made by the governor general and his wife to head off the direct federal-provincial clash involved in remedial legislation were numerous and extraordinary. In a report to Colonial Secretary Chamberlain on January 25, Lord Aberdeen expounded forcefully on the futility of compulsion. 'No measure compelling Manitoba to act can possibly satisfy in any permanent manner the two parties (Protestants and Catholics)' he wrote. Moreover, he added, in a perceptive summary of the gravest danger of the case, 'the controversy will no more be confined to Manitoba than the Home Rule Controversy had been confined to Ireland.'[30] In December Lady Aberdeen had written to Archbishop Langevin imploring him to investigate every possible avenue toward a negotiated settlement.[31] During January both the governor general and his wife were in discreet contact with Laurier on the subject, and the Liberal leader's letter to Sifton on January 28 used argu-

28 PAC, Sifton Papers, Laurier to Sifton, January 28, 1896
29 PAC, Laurier Papers, Sifton to Laurier, February 20, 1896
30 PAC, Aberdeen Correspondence, Aberdeen to Chamberlain, January 25, 1896
31 AASB, Lady Aberdeen to Langevin, December 22, 1895

ments which, even in phrasing, were remarkably like those used by Lady Aberdeen in a letter of the same day.[32] On January 23, at a reception held at Rideau Hall in honour of Father Lacombe, the vice-regal couple valiantly tried to enlist the support of the missionary for a conference of all the principals involved in the controversy. As Lady Aberdeen reported in her *Journal*, she and her husband stressed the long-range danger involved in the quarrel. 'If this Bill is passed by the votes of the French Members from Quebec of both parties,' they argued, 'the cry against French ascendancy will become a yell & then what hope will there be for their schools in the other English pro[vinces]?'[33] Both Her Ladyship and Lacombe, however, indicated in their reports of the discussion that the missionary had remained convinced that it was too late for such a conference to have any hope of success.[34]

A further important auxiliary whom Lady Aberdeen tried and failed to enlist was H. Joly de Lotbinière.[35] Her most extraordinary effort, however, was directed toward Archbishop Walsh of Toronto. Conscious of the prelate's interest and influence, Her Ladyship sent Walsh a long and carefully worded entreaty on January 28. She stated that the governor general would like to go to Toronto to discuss the problem with Walsh, but could not do so at the moment without suspicion. She wondered if Walsh might come to Ottawa, and asked him to write Langevin again to propose an 'eleventh hour' meeting of federal, provincial, and ecclesiastical authorities, 'without of course mentioning His Excellency.' She repeated the arguments used with Lacombe on the danger of religious strife involved in remedial legislation. Then came an even more startling proposal. In a request which clearly involved the governor general, Lady Aberdeen ventured a suggestion which not a few Canadians would have found incredible:

And may we also venture to ask if His Holiness the Pope could not intervene at this time in the interests of the Church and of peace? Could not a message come from Rome or through even Cardinal Satolli, which would at least prevent the Church in Quebec from so openly exercising political influence & thus irritating the people elsewhere? Forgive me if I have written too freely ... we know you will understand His Excellency's motives in this communication.[36]

32 PAC, Laurier Papers, Aberdeen to Laurier, January 25, 1896; Sifton Papers, Laurier to Sifton, January 28, 1896; AAT, Lady Aberdeen to Walsh, January 28, 1896
33 January 24, 1896
34 *Ibid.*, January 29, 1896; AASB, Lacombe to Langevin, January 28, 1896; see also AASB, Aberdeen to Lacombe, January 24, 1896; here the governor general seemed to be trying to smooth over the most heated part of the previous night's discussion.
35 PAC, Aberdeen Correspondence, Joly to Lady Aberdeen, February 3, 1896
36 AAT, Lady Aberdeen to Walsh, February 3, 1896

There is no record of Walsh's reply to Lady Aberdeen. It seems clear that he did not make the request to Rome, but did write to Lacombe and Langevin to urge moderation. More significantly, Walsh also wrote to Laurier, opposing the latter's plan for an inquiry in Manitoba and suggesting instead the meeting of all principals. The same suggestion was sent by Walsh to Lacombe, Bégin, and Langevin. To Bégin he recommended the Ontario separate-school arrangement as the goal to be worked for in Manitoba. Such a compromise would not be wholly satisfactory, but in his opinion was 'the most feasible when the immense difficulties and embarrassments of the case are taken into account.'[37]

Predictably enough, Walsh's proposal satisfied neither side. Alerted by Langevin's apprehensions, Lacombe hurried to Toronto. Showing exhaustion even in his letters, Lacombe reported on February 7 that he was very satisfied with Walsh's reaction. 'C'est un frère pour nous,' Lacombe wrote, although 'je ne pense pas que son plan d'une conférence amicale avec les différents partis puissent [sic] s'effectuer.'[38] Lacombe was even more emphatic in his rejection of the suggested meeting when he got back to Ottawa, particularly because Caron and Ouimet were strongly against the idea. 'Pas d'affaire! disent-ils,' wrote Lacombe. '"Notre bill est prêt! Il a été promis – Et bien qu'il soit présenté. Cette conférence ruinerait la cause." – "Voilà ce qu'on a dit au conseil," me dit Ouimet.'[39] Even when Lord Aberdeen again pressed him to support the conference proposed by Archbishop Walsh, Lacombe remained adamant. 'Je lui ai dit franchement,' the missionary told Langevin on February 13, 'qu'on ne devait pas y penser, que la chose n'était plus possible, que personne n'en voulait, ni Archevêque de St. Boniface, ni conservateurs ni Laurier.'[40]

Laurier was angered by Walsh's proposal and letter because it seemed to him that the Toronto archbishop had reversed the position he had taken only four months earlier.[41] Lacombe's account of Laurier's reaction was dramatic. 'Il a contenu son émotion,' Lacombe wrote, 'et m'a dit que malgré le respect qu'il avait pour l'Archevêque Walsh, il soutenait et soutiendrait que S.G. avait *oublié*, parce que certainement, en octobre

37 AAQ, Walsh to Bégin, February 4, 1896; AASB, Walsh to Lacombe, February 3, 1896; Walsh to Langevin, February 7, 1896. The letter to Laurier is not found in the Laurier papers, but a copy was enclosed in Walsh's letter to Bégin.
38 AASB, Lacombe to Langevin, February 7, 1896
39 *Ibid.*, February 9, 1896
40 *Ibid.*, February 13, 1896
41 A letter from Bégin to Walsh on January 31, 1896, made it clear that P.A. Choquette, Liberal MP, had been quoting Walsh in support of the inquiry proposal (AAQ, Bégin to Walsh, January 31, 1896).

dernier, Elle lui avait dit qu'Elle approuvait son projet d'*enquête* ou commission ... En parlant du projet d'une conférence telle que entendu par
Mgr. Walsh, "je n'ai rien à proposer au Gouvernement," il m'a répondu.'[42]
Despite the failure of the proposal for a high-level meeting in February,
the vice-regal couple's efforts were not yet exhausted. Lady Aberdeen
indicated in her *Journal* that as early as January 24 she and the governor
general had discussed the matter with Sir Donald Smith, and that the latter
had agreed to go west 'to confer privately and on his own responsibility
with the leaders on both sides.' Despite illness, Smith, who, in Lady
Aberdeen's view, had 'more influence in Manitoba with all parties than
anyone,'[43] departed in mid-February without the knowledge or at least
without the official sanction of the cabinet. Smith's reaction as reflected
in Lady Aberdeen's *Journal* and newspaper interviews was quite
optimistic.[44] Editorially, however, the Liberal papers saw the move simply
as a new Conservative diversion. The *Globe* called the mission 'an attempt
to adopt Mr. Laurier's policy without seeming to do so.'[45] *L'Electeur* saw it
as another 'reculade' on the part of government to avoid doing real justice
to the Catholic minority.[46] More significantly, Smith's optimism was not at
all evident in the reaction of either of the protagonists in Manitoba. Langevin was by now clearly committed to getting an effective remedial law rather
than a compromise settlement which would depend upon the good will of
the provincial government. To Bégin, Fabre, and Walsh, Langevin wrote
that 'quelque ait été la mission de Sir Donald Smith (si mission il y a eu) il a
échoué complètement. Nos gouvernants ont trop excité les passions
populaires pour être libres de faire un pas en avant.'[47] To Lacombe, the St
Boniface archbishop dismissed Smith's efforts in brief and sarcastic fashion. 'Donaldus venit, vidit, nihil fecit,' he wired.[48] On the other side, a
telegram from Greenway to Smith indicated that the latter had indeed
interpreted the Manitoba reaction too optimistically. 'Must have misun-
derstood me,' Greenway telegraphed. 'Did not suggest conference. Am
willing to consider proposition for conference if received from Dominion
Government.'[49]

42 AASB, Lacombe to Langevin, February 9, 1896
43 February 3, 1896
44 *Ibid.*, February 25, 1896
45 February 26, 1896
46 February 26, 1896
47 AAQ, Langevin to Bégin, February 22, 1896; AAM, Langevin to Fabre, February 22, 1896;
   AAT, Langevin to Walsh, February 22, 1896
48 AASB, Langevin to Lacombe, February 22, 1896. ('Donald came, saw, and did nothing.')
49 PAC, Bowell Papers, Smith to Bowell, February 25, 1896

Despite the ineffectiveness of his overtures, Smith's 'unofficial' mission did pave the way for the much more official delegation which went to Winnipeg in late March. Perhaps the most interesting aspect of the interlude was the constitutional problem it raised. The very evident role played by Lord and Lady Aberdeen in the February exploratory trip later gave the Liberals the opportunity to protest a violation of responsible government. Tupper had no choice but to somewhat lamely accept responsibility for the vice-regal action.[50] In retrospect, the unconstitutionality of the governor general or his wife actively working to scuttle or at least parallel the announced policy of the government can hardly be denied. On the other hand, whatever may be said of the impropriety of their actions, Lord and Lady Aberdeen could not be accused of sitting 'with hands folded while bitter strife is fostered.'[51]

LANGEVIN'S OBJECTIONS, LACOMBE'S ULTIMATUMS

Although *La Patrie* could not substantiate its charges that Lacombe had been dictating the main lines of the remedial bill, there was no doubt that the government was counting heavily upon approval from St Boniface and upon Lacombe to insure that such approval was forthcoming. The lack of capacity of those who might have taken some of the burden off Lacombe's shoulders, notably LaRivière and Bernier, was evident both from their own less than penetrating letters to Langevin and from Lacombe's remarks. LaRivière lacked influence and Bernier lacked both tact and influence. The missionary's January 28 comment was revealing: 'Pauvres Bernier et LaRivière, quoiqu'ils si croient se importants, que font-ils? LaRivière ... au moins on peut lui faire des remarques ... mais l'autre! Attention!'[52] Thus, for good or ill, the main burden of intermediary continued to fall on Lacombe. Furthermore, Lacombe was quickly moving to the position that the alternative to accepting the proposed Conservative bill would be to get nothing at all. Laurier's objection might well be that Lacombe's 'diplomacy' would result in arraying ecclesiastical thunder on the side of a quite inadequate solution – ' "Ah! mes amis," me disait Laurier,' Lacombe reported, 'Mgr. Langevin criait partout qu'il n'accepterait pas de compromis et qu'il voulait ses écoles et rien que ses écoles ... Et voilà que *votre* bill vous en fait avaler en masse!'[53] But as early

50 Canada, House of Commons, *Debates*, 1896, pp.4132ff
51 AASB, Lady Aberdeen to Langevin, December 22, 1895
52 *Ibid.*, Lacombe to Langevin, January 28, 1896
53 *Ibid.*, February 9, 1896

as January 17 Lacombe was writing that 'le succès de notre question se dessine de plus en plus. Il faudra voter pour ou mourir; car c'est une question de vie ou de mort.'[54] By February 11 when the bill appeared the position of 'half-a-loaf-is-better-than-none' seemed to have been accepted as an indisputable fact of life by the old missionary.

In point of fact, however, Langevin was not prepared to accept the half-loaf. So much was this so that the subsequent barrage of Lacombe's letters revealed a near rupture between the archbishop and his delegate. The letters of February 13, 15, 18, 19, and 21 developed like a suspense novel; each made the existing remedial bill a less negotiable ultimatum. The note of February 13 set the stage. Lacombe reminded Langevin that the linchpin of ecclesiastical support for the bill in the East was Langevin's approval. 'Les Evêques d'Ontario et de Québec,' Lacombe wrote, 'm'ont assuré qu'ils seraient satisfaits du Bill et le soutiendraient une fois que l'Archevêque de St. Boniface et les autres intéressés auraient exprimé leur satisfaction et acceptation.'[55] The first of two letters on the 15th stated that 'j'ai dit quasi-officiellement que nous acceptions le Bill,' despite its evident imperfections. 'Ne vaut-il pas mieux céder,' he argued, 'sur certains points de détails, qu'on pourra régler plus tard, que de ne rien avoir du tout? ... Le Gouvernement et l'Episcopât du Dominion attendent cette déclaration de votre part.'[56] A second dispatch went out the same day, after Lacombe had received Langevin's objections to the book clauses of the bill in particular. The missionary stated that he would suspend action if so ordered, but warned that delay in approval might prove fatal.[57] On 18 February Lacombe was in Quebec City, so far committed to the bill that he had taken the liberty to leave the following statement for the absent Bégin in Langevin's name: 'Que nous acceptons, *en principe*, le Bill rémédiateur, dans la prévision que des amendements y seront ajoutés, lors de la discussion.'[58] Apparently Bégin had not remained sufficiently in line to suit Lacombe, going so far as to give Choquette a letter which left room for conscientious objection to the bill.[59] To bring pressure on the Quebec archbishop, Lacombe seems to have presumed Langevin's approval and thus drafted the statement of acceptance. Having thus burned his bridges at Quebec, Lacombe's reaction to Langevin's next move could only be one of

54 *Ibid.*, January 17, 1896
55 *Ibid.*, February 13, 1896
56 *Ibid.*, February 15, 1896, Letter no.1
57 *Ibid.*, February 15, 1896, Letter no.2
58 *Ibid.*, February 18, 1896
59 *Ibid.*, February 15, 1896, Letter no.2

consternation. Shortly after Lacombe had posted the report of his Quebec declaration, both he and Bégin received an outright veto of the bill from the western prelate. 'Legem ignoramus,' Langevin wired. 'Primae editiones de libris et taxatione displicent.'[60] In a letter following the telegram, Langevin poured out a litany of misgivings. Although he possessed an earlier draft of the bill, Langevin complained that 'il paraitrait qu'ils l'ont modifiée encore, et si les résumés des journaux (car on me laisse complètement dans les ténèbres et on ne m'a rien communiqué) sont exacts, il y a lieu de s'inquiéter.' The accumulation of doubts and objections, Langevin concluded, *'me rendent actuellement presqu'impossible l'acceptation du bill … Je veux bien reconnaitre le bon vouloir (un peu intéressé) du gouvernement d'Ottawa, mais qu'il nous donne une loi acceptable et pratique.'* Not that the Liberal alternative was any better. 'Sous prétexte de nous aider ils tentent de nous étouffer,' Langevin wailed. 'Mais les conservateurs ne sont pas sans tâche. O! comme politique que tu es méprisable!'[61]

One of the major influences on Langevin's hesitation at this point was Colonel Audet. During this crucial February period, at least two significant exchanges took place between the archbishop and his confidant at the Secretariat of State. On the 13th Langevin wrote that he had received Audet's 'declaration de principes en matière scolaire,' in which the colonel had expressed grave misgivings about the Conservative party. 'Vous dîtes que les écoles vous retiennent seules au parti,' Langevin replies. 'Cela dit énormément.' Langevin's own comment was that, 'tout en louant un parti qui est au pouvoir et pourrait y être longtemps, et qui défend nos droits en ce moment, il ne faudrait pas nous imaginer que tout conservateur est franc catholique.' As for Laurier, Langevin told Audet that he wished at least to leave a door open. 'Il ne faudra pas le provoquer,' Langevin wrote, 'afin de lui laisser une issue pour revenir au bon sens,' even though it seemed likely that the Liberal leader's final position would be 'jouer à la Papineau.'[62] Within a week, Audet stated that he had irrefutable evidence to the effect that Chief Whip Taylor had again tried to overthrow Bowell. He added that Costigan was more convinced than ever that the motive for these 'conspirations permanentes' was to wreck the remedial bill. It was not that Audet, any more than Langevin, had rekindled confidence in Laurier and Tarte.

60 AAQ, Langevin to Bégin, February 17, 1896 ('We do not recognize the law. The first drafts concerning books and taxation displease us'). The majority of Langevin's direct messages to Lacombe are not extant, but they clearly duplicated the statements sent to Bégin.
61 *Ibid.*, February 17, 1896
62 Groulx, 'Correspondance Langevin-Audet,' p.276; Langevin to Audet, February 13, 1896

'Pauvres hommes ceux-ci,' said Audet, 'esclaves des grits ontariens qui les forcent à combattre la loi rémédiatrice ... C'est la répétition de l'enchainement de Dorion et de sa petite clique rouge au char de George Brown.' What Audet feared was that Ontario Tories were imposing the same kind of bondage on their French-Canadian colleagues; thus even at this late date he was prepared seriously to propose forming a new alliance. 'Si donc aujourd'hui,' Audet wrote, 'encouragés par notre petit nombre (depuis 1887) les tories veulent nous faire faux bond sur cette loi rémédiatrice, ils rompent par là la pacte qui nous unit à eux, et nous chercherons d'autres alliés que nous trouverons facilement parmi les Anglais de la nuance Blake.' At the very least, Audet insisted, such a threat should be used in editorials and in conversations with English-speaking Conservatives, in order to bring wavering party men back into line.[63] With a rather different goal in mind, Audet's formula sounded not unlike that of J. Israel Tarte.

The net effect of Audet's opinions could only have been to convey a deeper suspicion of Conservative double-dealing than Langevin had yet faced. At the same time, Lacombe's letters were accumulating, demanding immediate approval. The message of February 19 acknowledged the 'Legem ignoramus' telegram and somewhat wearily explained how the objections concerning books and the method of financing might be met.[64] Finally, on February 21, the missionary was driven to a complete spelling-out of the case for an immediate and unqualified approval of the bill. The letter was accompanied by two urgent cipher telegrams, unblushingly paid for by J.A. Ouimet.[65] Lacombe had just returned from a tension-filled meeting with Caron, Ouimet, LaRivière, Bernier, and others, and presented the situation as an open and shut case:

C'est fini – Prenez votre parti – Voulez-vous tout ou rien? Si vous adoptez cette dernière résolution, alors la question est perdue et notre espérance s'en va. Rappelons-nous que nous ne commandons pas. Nos adversaires sont légions ... Pour moi, Mgr., malgré ce qui m'est réservé dans l'avenir de responsabilité, devant Dieu et devant les hommes, voici mon *ultimatum*: et cela après bien des réflections et des consultations avec ceux qui s'intéressent à notre cause. – Je vous dis, que nous devrions accepter le Bill, tel qu'il est, franchement, dans la prévision et l'espérance, que si le Gouvernement remporte le vote, alors on pourra facilement

63 AASB, Audet to Langevin, February 20, 1896
64 *Ibid.*, Lacombe to Langevin, February 19, 1896
65 *Ibid.*, February 21, 1896

amender certains détails, qui deviendront faciles avec le temps. Pour le moment, il faut accepter cette loi, telle quelle, supposé qu'elle soit acceptée par la majorité, à la seconde lecture ou bien nous allons jouer notre dernière carte et nous abandonner au pouvoir des libéraux, avec lesquels l'épiscopat est en guerre en ce moment, sur presque tous les points du pays. Si nous voulons courir ce risque, c'est votre affaire.–

C'est très bien et très brave de dire: 'Je ne veux pas de telle clause, je m'opposerai; il nous faut telle chose, on doit changer telle disposition &' – mais si nous perdons ce que nous étions loin d'espérer dès les commencements de la lutte, ne nous exposons-nous pas à tout perdre? quand nous allons voir les conservateurs vaincus et s'éloigner (un grand nombre de ceux des notres) de l'arène politique pour toujours? Je vous conseille donc d'écrire de suite à tous les Evêques de Québec, des Provinces Maritimes, d'Ontario et de votre province d'accepter, avec vous, la loi rémédiatrice, telle que formulée dans le présent Bill, et cela malgré l'opposition des libéraux, qui veulent faire du zèle. – Plus que jamais c'est le moment critique.

Soyez sûr que ma manière d'agir n'est pas dictée par mes sympathies pour le parti conservateur, mais pour la cause de nos écoles, qui me préoccupent jusqu'à me rendre malade.[66]

To Lacombe's barrage of letters and telegrams was added, on February 20, LaRivière's threat to resign from the Conservative party if the bill were not approved,[67] and, on the following day, Ewart's acceptance of the measure as 'very fairly satisfactory.'[68] The combination of pressures had the desired result.[69] On February 22, Langevin wired a clear, if somewhat less than classic Latin message, addressed to Lacombe at Ottawa University: 'Lex applicabilis, efficax, et satisfactoria. Probo illam. Omnes episcopi et veri catholici approbare debent. Vita in lege. Optima littera tua. Nihil vero de conciliatione.'[70] To Bégin the message was 'Mihi et advocato [Ewart] videtur applicabilis et efficax, pugna pro nobis.'[71] On the same

66 *Ibid.*, February 21, 1896
67 AASB, LaRivière to Langevin, February 20, 1896
68 *Ibid.*, Ewart to Langevin, February 21, 1896
69 The CPR running time between Ottawa and Winnipeg in 1896 was forty-nine hours (CPR Public Relations Division, Toronto). Thus, while Langevin would have received the February 21 telegrams, Lacombe's strong letter of that date would not have arrived before the archbishop assented.
70 AASB, Langevin to Lacombe, February 22, 1896. ('The law is workable, efficacious, and satisfactory. I approve it. All bishops and true Catholics ought to give approval. There is life in the law. Your letters are excellent. But let there be no conciliation.')
71 AAQ, Langevin to Bégin, February 22, 1896. ('[The law] seems to me and to our lawyer [Ewart] workable and efficacious – fight for us.')

day, February 22, letters went out to Fabre, Walsh, Laflèche, and Emard, all expressing Langevin's consent to the bill, but all containing the proviso that certain amendments be made when the measure went into committee after the second reading.[72]

Langevin's approval of the bill, however, did not equal canonization. There was no effective way to cover up the misgivings which had preceded his acceptance. While it could not be proven conclusively that the government had delayed the printing of the bill until ecclesiastical approval was forthcoming, *L'Electeur* did not hesitate to make such a charge.[73] In fact there had been a remarkable delay while the Langevin 'fiat' seemed so doubtful. It may at least be concluded that the growing panic in Lacombe's letters reflected not only fear that he had gone too far in his position as ambassador, but, more basically, fear within the Conservative party itself. Having staked its survival in power on a measure designed to satisfy Catholics, the last thing the government could afford was disapproval or even silence from the church. Mutual dependence and over-identification were growing quickly.

LIBERAL OVERTURES AND A BOMBSHELL

Naturally enough, the Liberals were not prepared to accept the remedial bill simply because Archbishop Langevin had finally given it his blessing. More than a little effort continued to be spent in mending their own ecclesiastical fences. Senator Richard Scott wrote to Archbishop Walsh on February 18, begging the Toronto prelate to consider the weaknesses of the remedial bill. 'I am satisfied that the cause of the minority will be injured rather than benefited by the proposed enactment,' Scott stated. He stressed that Walsh's contribution could be very great, 'not only in advising a reasonable consideration of this question, but in preventing very many exhibitions of Catholic dissentions in the coming elections.'[74] On February 22, P.A. Choquette wrote to Lacombe at Ottawa, thanking the missionary for an earlier interview, but insisting on his serious objections to the bill. In particular, Choquette objected to the inefficacy of the provincial-grant clause, and the failure to provide an alternative in case the

---

72 AAM, Langevin to Fabre, February 22, 1896; AAT, Langevin to Walsh, February 22, 1896; AETR, Langevin to Laflèche, February 22, 1896; AEV, Langevin to Emard, February 22, 1896
73 February 17, 1896
74 AAT, Scott to Walsh, February 18, 1896

province refused such a grant. Were the government to include such a clause, Choquette said, 'il ... me mettrait presque dans l'obligation de l'approuver ... Ceci prouverait la bonne foi du Gouvernement et ferait disparaître de mon esprit l'idée que ce bill n'est qu'un trompe l'œil et n'est mis devant la chambre que pour passer les élections.'[75]

On February 22 a delegation of seventeen high-ranking Liberals of the Quebec district, led by Sir C.A.P. Pelletier, François Langelier, MP, and Mayor Parent of Quebec City, paid an official visit to Archbishop Bégin to plead the Liberal cause. This visit was clearly connected with the publication of Lacombe's letter to Laurier; in any case, L'Electeur gave a very rosy account, even though it admitted Bégin's criticism of its own recent campaign against Labrecque and Abbé Paquet. 'Mgr. a parlé de façon à rassurer complètement les catholiques qui appartiennent au parti libéral,' the report ran. More than that, L'Electeur continued, Bégin had insisted that to him it was 'tout à fait indifférent que ce soit un parti plutôt qu'un autre qui gouverne pourvu que le pays soit bien gouverné.' The delegation left, the newspaper concluded, 'enchantée de la reception qui lui avait été faite et des paroles si conciliantes du distingué prélat.'[76] Predictably enough, other versions of the interview were less sanguine. In an attempt to clarify the situation and 'pour mettre fin aux différentes versions que la presse donne de la réponse faite,' Bégin's secretary sent a letter which appeared in L'Electeur and La Minerve on the 26th. The letter outlined five points, the last of which was that the Quebec Liberal papers might be denounced officially if their tone did not improve. Moreover, the letter indicated that the principle of remedial legislation ought to be accepted. On the other hand, it reserved judgment on the merits of the actual bill coming up before the House and repeated Bégin's refusal to be identified with any political party.[77]

Two days after the visit of the Liberal delegation to Bégin, Laurier reinforced their presentation of the case with a long and careful letter to the Quebec archbishop. He enclosed Senator Scott's critique of the bill, and hoped that the same freedom to oppose episcopal desires in a political

---

75 AASB, Choquette to Lacombe, February 22, 1896
76 L'Electeur, February 22, 1896. One of the documents which the Liberals apparently relied upon in the interview was Cardinal (then Archbishop) Taschereau's 1872 circular on the New Brunswick school dispute. Taschereau's directive left Catholics free to choose the means they judged best to achieve separate schools without disrupting religious peace. PAC, Tarte Papers, unsigned letter to Bégin, 18 February, 1896.
77 La Minerve, February 26, 1896. Bégin's statement also took pains to deny the rumour that a collective episcopal letter would be sent to all Catholic MPs. See below, pp.212–20.

matter would be extended to the Liberals as had been given the Conservatives in the case of the disallowance of the 1894 amendments. In particular, Laurier argued that the surest proof of the necessity of an inquiry, which he now called an 'étude préparatoire,' was the 'inefficacité absolue' of the bill which was being attempted without one.[78]

The most effective Liberal move of the period between the first and second reading of the bill was, however, a counter-attack against Father Lacombe. The weapon was none other than Lacombe's own January 20 ultimatum to Laurier. As seen in the missionary's accounts of his meetings with the Liberal leader, Laurier had, during early February, used the letter with his inner circle of advisers and as the hard core of his objections to Lacombe's entire approach. On February 20, the first public rumblings about the letter were heard in *L'Electeur*; the full text was published the following day. *L'Electeur* challenged Lacombe's right to speak as 'l'agent diplomatique de l'épiscopat canadien,' and stated that an archbishop (either Bégin or Fabre) had privately but strongly objected to the authority the missionary had assumed. Calling the letter 'insolente et pleine de menaces,' the Liberal newspaper particularly criticized the threat of 'des foudres de l'Eglise' over a bill yet unpublished.[79] On February 22, one of *L'Electeur*'s correspondents signing himself 'Un Membre de Parlement' (probably Dr Rinfret, deputy for Lotbinière) excused Lacombe somewhat on the grounds of inexperience, but nonetheless insisted that the missionary was 'absolument incapable de jouer le rôle politique qu'on lui a confié.' The article even suggested recourse to Rome to check Lacombe's activities.[80] *La Patrie* and *Le Cultivateur* enthusiastically joined the protest. Beaugrand concentrated on the clerical pretensions involved,[81] Tarte on the manner in which Conservative politicians had been able to use Lacombe as a puppet. 'Il s'est fait jouer de la plus incroyable des façons,' *Le Cultivateur* proclaimed. 'Il a servi d'instrument à des hommes qui se moquent de sa crédulité.'[82] More significant was the measured but stern rebuke which appeared in the usually pro-Conservative and widely read *La Presse*:

Les malheurs chevauchent en troupe, dit le proverbe. Au moment où nous perdons le dernier espoir au Manitoba, le R.P. Lacombe, missionnaire au Nord-Ouest,

78 PAC, Laurier Papers, Laurier to Bégin, February 24, 1896
79 *L'Electeur*, February 20, 1896
80 *Ibid.*, February 22, 1896
81 *La Patrie*, February 21, 1896
82 February 21, 1896

adressait d'Ottawa, à l'hon. M. Laurier, une lettre publique qui est, – comment, diable! exprimer cela? – on ne peut plus inopportune. Il est digne de remarque que, chaque fois que des membres individuels du clergé veulent diriger les événements politiques, ils commettent des erreurs de tactique impardonnables; la lettre du dévoué missionnaire ne déroge pas à cette coutume. Elle va rendre la position de M. Laurier bien plus difficile et donner des armes à nos ennemis. Ce n'est pas avec des menaces d'opposition qu'on peut espérer faire quelqu'impression sur un esprit aussi indépendant et aussi désintéressé que celui du chef de l'opposition; c'est avec un engagement d'honneur qu'il fallait de lier. Le langage du Père Lacombe peut se résumer à ceci: 'Apprends bien tes devoirs et tu auras du sucre; sinon, tu auras un bon fouet.' Cela peut être de mise avec les petits sauvages des écoles du Nord-Ouest que le R.P. dirige avec tant de zèle et de dévouement, mais ne peut que produire des résultats malheureux à Ottawa.[83]

On the following day, February 22, *La Presse* added that Lacombe's letter had placed many more than the Liberals in a difficult position, and was causing 'une pénible impression chez tous les partisans de la loi réparatrice.' The Montreal paper went to some lengths to demonstrate that Lacombe could not possibly have spoken in the name of all the bishops. Finally, it was pointed out that the inevitable result of such a threat was the kind of gathering of all anti-remedialists that was in fact being called on that very day in Toronto.[84]

La Minerve's first reaction was to defend Lacombe's action. J. Royal's ministerial paper stated that the distinctive characteristic of the letter was 'la franchise qui ignore les sous entendus et va droit au but.' Lacombe's plea to Laurier was called 'un appel touchant ... à la foi, au patriotisme et à l'esprit de justice d'un autre homme, son compatriote et un catholique comme lui.'[85] But *La Minerve* soon found itself obliged to shift emphasis to accusing Laurier of breaking confidence in allowing the letter to become public. Even on this point there seemed to be some doubt, with the Liberal delegation to Bégin and *L'Electeur* blaming 'un collègue du Rev. Père Lacombe' for releasing the letter.[86] *La Minerve* had little patience with such suggestions. 'La vérité est,' the Bleu newspaper insisted on February 24, 'que M. Laurier a laissé trainer cette lettre sur son pupitre durant quinze jours et l'a communiquée à tout le monde.' More serious was the question

83 *La Presse*, February 21, 1896
84 *Ibid.*, February 22, 1896
85 *La Minerve*, February 22, 1896
86 *L'Electeur*, February 22, 1896

of motive. 'Le but de cette indiscrétion est évident,' *La Minerve* concluded. 'Il s'agissait de soulever les ultra protestants contre la loi réparatrice et l'on a assez bien réussi.'[87]

Once again, *La Presse* seemed to strike the best balance. Replying to *La Minerve*'s criticism and Lacombe's own defence published in the ministerial organ, *La Presse* reminded both the missionary and *La Minerve* that the onus for making the letter public was not the key question. It was the merit of Lacombe's letter and of the obligation which it sought to impose that was the main issue. *La Presse* redoubled its assurances of respect for Lacombe as a missionary, but begged him to consider the result of his 'diplomacy.' 'L'adoption du projet de loi qui semblait assurée est devenue problématique depuis cette publication,' the editorial stated. 'Les adversaires ont redoublé d'ardeur et les amis sont devenus vacillants.' Worst of all was the narrow corner in which Lacombe had managed to place the bishops. They could neither disavow him nor openly support him without great danger. Once more *La Presse* could only conclude that 'son intervention ... a été des plus malheureuses.'[88]

Not unexpectedly, English-Canadian reaction, both Liberal and Conservative, was highly critical of Lacombe's attempt to pressure Laurier. The Toronto rally of February 23 at Massey Hall, already planned to protest the remedial bill, reflected ominous signs of the feelings which had been aroused. In their reports of the assembly, both the *Globe* and the *Mail and Empire* pointed out that well-known leaders of both parties had attended, giving unmistakeable evidence of cleavage on the lines of race and religion. The *Mail and Empire* named twenty-three Ontario Conservative MPs who had resolved now to vote against the remedial bill.[89] The *Globe*, generally adopting the same attitude as had *La Presse*, rejected Lacombe's complaint that confidence had been violated. 'The letter from beginning to end is political,' the Toronto paper observed, 'and he cannot complain if the discussion upon it has followed those lines.'[90] It should be noted that the language of Ontario Liberal news comment, apparently at Laurier's request, was sufficiently restrained to prompt *La Minerve* to compare it favourably with the virulence of the Quebec Liberal press.[91] Nonetheless, the impact of the Lacombe letter was unmistakeable in English Canada,

87 February 24, 1896
88 February 27, 1896
89 Toronto *Mail and Empire*, February 24, 1896
90 Toronto *Globe*, February 24, 1896
91 *La Minerve*, February 27, 1896

and the result was anything but favourable to the result the missionary had hoped to produce. The February 26 solemn resolution of the Manitoba legislature protesting the 'futile though unjustified attack' of the remedial bill, and the similar protest of the Ontario government of March 4, were clearly linked to the reaction against Lacombe's manifesto.[92]

Obviously crucial in terms of the significance of Lacombe's mission and of its long-range impact on the fate of the remedial bill, was the clerical reaction to the publication of his letter. Bishop Emard first learned of the letter from the newspapers and immediately wrote to Archbishop Fabre in consternation:

Puis-je demander à Votre Grandeur si quelqu'un a été, par qui de droit, chargé de représenter l'Episcopat auprès du gouvernement, et si l'acceptation faite par lui de la Loi Rémédiatrice *telle que proposée* doit réellement lier tous les Evêques? Les conséquences sont si graves que, s'il y a eu autorisation donnée et engagement pris au nom de l'Episcopat, j'ai été personellement tout à fait ignoré.[93]

Fabre, attempting to calm Emard's apprehensions in his reply, merely confirmed the conclusion that Lacombe's action had been very much on the missionary's own initiative. 'La lettre de Votre Grandeur est un mystére pour moi,' Fabre wrote. 'Je n'ai jamais entendu parler d'adhésion de la part des Evêques à l'acte du gouvernement.'[94] Bégin's position was uncertain. *La Presse* and others quoted him in criticism of Lacombe's letter, and his interview with the Liberal delegation of February 22 showed that he was not prepared to endorse the remedial bill as Lacombe had done.[95] On the other hand, the same interview revealed that Bégin was far from repudiating Lacombe, and the missionary's own letter to Langevin from Trois-Rivières on February 29 reported a very reassuring visit which he had just finished with the Quebec archbishop, currently in hospital:

S.G. m'a reçu avec sa bonté ordinaire. Après une longue explication, qu'on voulait avoir de ma bouche, os ad os, plutôt qu'une lettre, Mgr. m'a déclaré, comme il a dû déjà le faire dans une lettre à V.G., qu'il acceptait votre manière d'agir et l'approuvait, promettant de nous supporter jusqu'au bout. Sur mes remarques, Mgr. M'a rassuré me disant qu'il n'y avait rien de vrai dans ce que les libéraux

92 Winnipeg *Tribune*, February 27, 1896; Toronto *Globe*, March 5, 1896
93 AAM, Emard to Fabre, February 21, 1896 (italics Emard's)
94 AEV, Fabre to Emard, February 22, 1896
95 *La Presse*, February 22, 1896; *L'Electeur*, February 22, 1896

avaient publié, affirmant que S.G. désapprouvait ma conduite. 'Ne craignez pas un semblable acte de lâcheté et de trahison de ma part,' me disait-Elle.[96]

Abbé J.B. Proulx shared the general affection shown towards Lacombe, but also joined the critics. 'Que diable ce cher Père allait-il faire dans cette galère?' he asked his friend Abbé Payette of Trois-Rivières. 'Il demand à un homme de signer pour une loi qui n'était pas encore redigée; et s'il ne le fait pas, il le menace de l'opposition du clergé et de l'épiscopat; il se dit le représentant des Evêques du pays ... En sacrifice, c'est un héros, mais un enfant en diplomatie.'[97] Even Abbé Langis, vicar general of Rimouski, and Abbé Corbeil of the French-Canadian immigration agency, normally staunch clericalists, were quite perturbed by the all-inclusive nature of Lacombe's statements. Comparing the letter to an earlier celebrated faux pas, Corbeil told Langevin that 'elle sera le prétexte ... pour faire voter plusieurs députés contre la loi, comme celle de Mgr. Gravel a été pour le mois de juillet dernier.'[98] Colonel Audet and Lacombe himself, in their comments on the sequel, were reduced to protesting the public release of the letter rather than defending its contents.[99]

Whatever the exact sequence of events surrounding the publication of the Lacombe letter, the ultimate responsibility for bringing it before the public eye must be placed with Laurier. Yet, as La Presse and others continued to point out, it was not Laurier who had created the occasion. It was Lacombe, with Bishop Laflèche prominent in the background. It is clear from Laurier's notes to Willison and John Dafoe, then with the Montreal Star, that the Liberal leader had decided to oppose the remedial bill well before February 20.[100] But the uproar that followed the letter's release confirmed Laurier's resolution. He would not yet allow himself great optimism, but the reaction to Lacombe's demand gave him at least long-range political hope. On February 22, Laurier wrote Willison that his course was 'plainer yet to me perhaps than it ever was.' Laurier went on:

96 AASB, Lacombe to Langevin, February 29, 1896
97 ASST, Proulx Papers, Proulx to Payette, February 23, 1896
98 AAQ, Langis to Bégin, February 25, 1896; AASB, Corbeil to Langevin, n.d.
99 AASB, Audet to Langevin, February 27, 1896; Lacombe to Langevin, February 25, 1896
100 PAC, Willison Papers, Laurier to Willison, February 18, 1896; University of Manitoba Library, Dafoe Papers, Laurier to Dafoe, February 17, 1896. Earlier in February, Dafoe had written a letter to the editor of The Week in praise of Laurier, and the Liberal leader was writing to thank him and to encourage Dafoe's political journalism. See Cook, The Politics of John W. Dafoe and the Free Press, pp. 12–13. In his own biography of Laurier, Dafoe assigns to himself an important role in the 'calculated indiscretion' of releasing the letter (Dafoe, Laurier, p.38).

If we are to have a country at all, we must put down the threats of all factions, &
appeal with greater courage than ever, to the nobler sentiments of all Canadians. I
fully expect that the active hostility of the church may crush us just now; it will very
soon make us stronger. At all events, it must have that effect, if there be any
manhood left in Canada.

I do not disguise that I am passing through a very severe ordeal. The thought that
my action is to cost the political life of many of the noble fellows who support me so
loyally is rather painful and even distressing – but there is only one way open, & it
is very plain.[101]

There were many signs that the current in French Canada was indeed
turning toward Laurier and the Liberal position, perhaps more quickly than
the Liberal leader suspected. Even Lacombe's intense emotion did not
prevent him from seeing the trend. The missionary tried to get Bégin to
proscribe *L'Electeur*,[102] with the Quebec archbishop cooperating to the
extent of the warning found in his public letter of February 24. Lacombe's
greatest concern, however, was the erosion taking place in clerical sympathies. It was disturbing enough to hear a good Catholic lawyer warmly
supporting Laurier's point of view, Lacombe told Langevin on February
18, but 'je suis épouvanté de voir tant de prêtres (haut placés) pensants
comme les libéraux.'[103] The publication of his letter to Laurier evidently
did anything but stem the tide. Despite the 'bienfaisant soulagement' which
Lacombe felt as a result of Langevin's long-awaited approval of the remedial bill, the missionary could only lament that 'c'est à ne pas y croire
combien l'esprit du peuple est faussé! Quand je dis le *peuple*, j'entends
plusieurs de nos bons citoyens et de plusieurs prêtres et Curés qui mar-
chent avec la politique de Laurier.'[104] Ironically too, from Lacombe's
standpoint, during the furore which followed the publication of his letter,
ultramontane voices were heard, if not in support of Laurier, at least in
criticism of the efficacy of the bill and of the unqualified support Lacombe
was giving it. In his *Moniteur de Lévis*, Senator Philippe Landry expressed
strong opposition to the proposed system which would leave the Catholic
school board under the sway of the Greenway government.[105] Such 'aid
and comfort to the enemy' given by *Le Moniteur* and *La Vérité* prompted
Colonel Audet, despite his own recently expressed suspicions of the Con-

101 PAC, Willison Papers, Laurier to Willison, February 22, 1896
102 AASB, Lacombe to Langevin, February 18, 1896
103 *Ibid.*, February 18, 1896
104 *Ibid.*, February 25, 1896
105 February 22, 1896

servatives, to recall bitterly 'le zèle pharisaique des programmistes de 1871' and 'la vénalité haineuse des castors de 1883.'[106]

In their efforts at winning over ecclesiastics, the Liberals were probably not as successful as they had hoped, particularly in the case of Bégin. At the same time, combined with the reaction against Lacombe, they had made substantial inroads. Moreover, it must be concluded that, in the sequence of events Laurier and the Liberals played their cards well. Was the release of the Lacombe threat timed to coincide with Langevin's expected acceptance of the remedial bill? Or was it to counter the rumour of a more formidable ecclesiastical move, following upon Abbé Paquet's highly publicized defence of the right of episcopal interference? However calculated the publicity decision, and although Laurier's moves may have contained more high dexterity than high principle, the timing contrived to take much of the impact out of Langevin's approval, and to focus attention on a clerical move which was highly vulnerable to attack. It was not that the Liberals were less given than the Conservatives to burning the candle at both ends. If *La Minerve*, *La Courrier du Canada*, *La Monde*, and *L'Evénement* varied all the way from saying that the Lacombe letter was private to insisting later on that it be accepted as the most official of public documents, *L'Electeur* and *Le Cultivateur* treated Lacombe's manifesto, depending on the occasion, sometimes as the insignificant statement of an unauthorized person, sometimes as the formal challenge of the entire hierarchy. The important fact was that many signs indicated that the Liberal strategy was beginning to work. Without the Liberal leader being at all sure of it at the time, the brief period between the appearance of the Lacombe letter and the debate on the remedial bill must be viewed as a turning point in Laurier's political fortunes in Quebec. Whether the decision to oppose the remedial bill as directly as Laurier did on 3 March had been taken before the letter's publication is a moot point; Lacombe's own account of his 15 February meeting with Laurier suggests that this was at least under discussion. The broadcast of the Lacombe threat can thus be seen either as a trial balloon to test reaction, or as a move to get sympathy for a decision already taken. Either way, the response gave grounds for Laurier's increasing confidence.

Reading over what the Liberals and others had to say about him, Lacombe often said that he wished to be back among the Indians where they said he belonged; at least he could understand their savagery better than that encountered at Ottawa. In fact, with the exception of a brief but important part in the story of the projected letter to the deputies,

106 AASB, Audet to Langevin, February 24, 1896

Lacombe's role soon became that of a bystander, although a very excited one. Nonetheless, he had plunged deeply into the political cauldron of the country. Many times he repeated that he did not want to be a party man; his political creed was to support the government in power as long as that government was working reasonably for justice and equity, in this case the restoration of the lost school rights. But, whether he wanted it or not, in late December and early January Lacombe had been in the middle of patching a shaky Conservative cabinet. He had become the government's chief instrument in pushing Archbishop Langevin to the acceptance on February 22 of a bill against which the prelate had violently protested less than a week earlier. Finally, the missionary was the one through whom Laurier definitively broke with the episcopal position, or with what Lacombe said was the episcopal position. Willing or not, qualified or not, Lacombe had become at least as much a voice and arm of the Conservative government as he was of the bishops.

In many ways, the letter to Laurier may be taken as the symbol of both the strongest and weakest points of Lacombe's diplomatic mission. Unquestionably, it revealed courage and forthrightness; no one could ever accuse the missionary of a lack of energy or devotion to the cause of the schools. Moreover, if blame must be attached to the letter, Lacombe was not the only one involved. Laflèche, Langevin, and, to a lesser extent, Bégin, all had some responsibility. Yet the letter was Lacombe's, first and last, and its approach, like its author's entire attitude to the political situation, must at least be called naïve. To attempt to exert the kind of pressure which the letter implied, and at the same time to insist that the letter be kept private, was obtuse and unfair, if not actually impossible. The conclusion cannot be avoided that Lacombe did not in fact grasp the implications of the situation into which he was plunged, particularly of the complexities of the party system. His support, and through him the somewhat checkered support of the bishops for the Conservative remedial bill, involved upholding not only a bill of uncertain value, but the total program of a government which was crumbling under its own weight. As Abbé Proulx put it in his letter to Payette, 'on courrait risque de se lier imprudemment avec un corps qui, par son vice intérieur, avant longtemps deviendrait cadavre.'[107] Sixty-nine years old in February, projected, almost to his disbelief, into a world that was not his own, Lacombe spared nothing during his Ottawa mission. He was above all a man of action, who would far rather have been accused of having tried and failed than of not having tried at all. But the price of his decisive action came very high.

107 ASST, Proulx Papers, Proulx to Payette, February 23, 1896

7
Debate on the remedial bill, the Smith mission, and the great filibuster

TUPPER AND LAURIER IN THE HOUSE

The debate on the second reading of the remedial bill which began on March 3 added little to the already overworked arguments for and against remedial action. Yet much was added to the strategy and the tension involved, both for the contesting political parties and in the church-state interplay which was so close to the core of the problem.[1]

There could have been no clearer sign of the leadership that Tupper had assumed than his moving the second reading of the remedial bill. Like others who were to follow, Tupper voiced the feeling that this was the most important debate in Parliament since confederation. A review of the events and compromises which preceded confederation formed the first part of Tupper's address. He spoke of the conviction of the delegates to the Quebec Conference that the proposed scheme 'afforded the means of removing that antagonism of race and religion which had been found to act so fatally in reference to the interests of Canada.' Tupper's argument was built around the clear intent of section 93 of the BNA Act and laid heavy stress on Alexander Galt's sponsorship of the clause in order to protect Protestant school rights in Quebec. Tupper reconstructed the scene at the Westminster Palace Hotel Conference in London and called upon the

---

1 L.C. Clark, in 'The Conservative Administrations' (thesis), pp.454–79, has devoted an extensive review to the main speeches of the debate. Certain key statements, however, deserve particular attention in this study.

still-living members (Sir Hector Langevin was the only one in the House) to witness that there would have been no Confederation without the delegates' bowing to Galt's insistence on this limitation to provincial powers in regard to education. Tupper reviewed the familiar arguments about the obligation imposed on the federal government by the second Privy Council decision and quoted 'eminent divines' of many Protestant churches as 'ready to endorse the action of the Government of Canada.' Tupper cited especially Sir William Dawson, longtime superintendent of education for Nova Scotia, 'not only a Protestant but a Presbyterian of the sternest sect,' as having given a 'most clear and emphatic' signed declaration of his support for the proposed remedial bill. As he had in his election campaign, Tupper emphasized that the issue was 'not a question of separate schools,' but 'a question of the constitution of the country,' that the federal government proposed to interfere in the least degree possible, and that the Manitoba government was still invited to take action. He admitted that there had been great division and difficulty in drawing up the bill and that the government was still open to suggestions of means which might remove the necessity of going through with the measure. The point, Tupper concluded, was to end, not to begin, religious wrangling on the question.[2]

Laurier's turn came next. Just as surely as Bishop Labrecque had done a month earlier, Laurier now crossed his own Rubicon. Instead of simply opposing Tupper's motion for the second reading of the bill, Laurier in an amendment called for a six months' hoist. Both the tone of defiance and the arguments used in developing the Liberal leader's amendment were significant. Laurier claimed that there was no help for the minority in the government bill. Yet 'it would be a most violent wrench of the principles upon which our constitution is based.' Laurier took Tupper to task for his analysis of the history of Confederation. He suggested that the separatism which Tupper had encountered in Nova Scotia in 1866–7 had been focused more against coercion than against the idea of confederation itself. Turning to the later period, Laurier traced the recurring friction within the Canadian framework to attempts by one section to force another, giving as an example the New Brunswick school agitation and the Jesuit estates' case. Much more emphatically than he had in previous statements during the remedialist controversy, Laurier dwelt on provincial rights. 'The danger is all the more to be apprehended,' he stated, 'if, searching further on for the causes which have brought about this commotion, you find that on every occasion there abridges the independence, the sovereignty of the provin-

2 Canada, House of Commons, *Debates*, 1896, pp.2721–36

cial legislatures.' Commenting on Tupper's remarks on section 93, Laurier contended that this feature of the constitution which granted one legislature power over another was 'perhaps a great error.' The government clearly had the power to coerce, but this did not answer the question of how the power should be used. Thus Laurier recommended a 'full and ample inquiry ... conciliation ... coercion only as a last resort.' He insisted that a chief failure all along had been the lack of proper investigation; even with the decision of the Privy Council at hand there was still need for publication of facts. To Foster's impatient interjection asking what needed to be investigated, Laurier replied that he would inquire precisely into the main points of the petition of the Roman Catholic minority, that is, that there had been a compact between the Catholics and England at the time of Manitoba's entry, that the system of common schools was repugnant to their consciences, and that the Manitoba schools were in reality Protestant schools. As for the Donald Smith mission, Laurier felt that it had been a year too late, and that even now the government was disowning responsibility for this one measure of conciliation which had been tried. Instead, they were insisting on a highly offensive yet ineffective bill.

It was in the peroration, almost as an '*obiter dicta*,' that Laurier made his most startling move and effectively shifted the ground of the battle. 'Not many weeks ago,' Laurier stated, 'I was told from high quarters in the Church to which I belong that unless I supported the School Bill which was then being prepared by the government and which we have now before us, I would incur the hostility of a great and powerful body.' Calling this 'too grave a phase of this question for me to pass over in silence,' Laurier nonetheless insisted that 'no word of bitterness shall ever pass my lips against that Church.' As he had many times during his career, Laurier dissociated himself with the continental brand of anti-clerical liberalism, reaffirming his identity as a 'Liberal of the English school,' who believed that it was 'the privilege of all subjects, whether high or low, whether rich or poor, whether ecclesiastics or laymen, to participate in the administration of public affairs, to discuss, to influence, to persuade, to convince.' Then came Laurier's most memorable, and in the eyes of some, most vulnerable statement:

I am here representing not Roman Catholics alone but Protestants as well, and I must give an account of my stewardship to all classes. Here am I, a Roman Catholic of French extraction, entrusted by the confidence of the men who sit around me with great and important duties under our constitutional system of government. I am here acknowledged leader of a great party, composed of Roman Catholics and

Protestants as well, as Protestants must be in the majority in every party in Canada. Am I to be told, I, occupying such a position, that I am to be dictated the course I am to take in this House, by reasons that can appeal to the consciences of my fellow-Catholic members, but which do not appeal as well to the consciences of my Protestant colleagues? No. So long as I have a seat in this House, so long as I occupy the position I do now, whenever it shall become my duty to take a stand upon any question whatever, that stand I will take not upon grounds of Roman Catholicism, not upon grounds of Protestantism, but upon grounds which can appeal to the conscience of all men, irrespective of their particular faith, upon grounds which can be occupied by all men who love justice, freedom and toleration.

Having made his daring thrust, Laurier did not attempt to soften its impact by any summary or further argument. He simply renewed his call for an inquiry and moved the amendment that 'the Bill be not now read the second time but that it be read the second time this day six months.'[3]

It can hardly be overemphasized that the stand adopted by Laurier did not affect the logic but only the tactics of the debate on remedialism. His introduction of the Lacombe threat, praiseworthy or otherwise, was a deliberate and significant political move, only indirectly related to the merits or demerits of the bill at hand. Laurier's close personal friend, L.O. David, confirmed that the step was taken only after careful forethought, and with more than a little apprehension.[4] Precisely how much Laurier personally regarded the Lacombe letter as official church policy cannot be known with certainty. Laurier's communications with Bégin, the known misgivings of Emard and Fabre, and the emphatic reaction against Lacombe after the publication of his letter, suggest that the Liberal leader felt that there was sufficient doubt in the matter for him to risk the danger in French Canada against the obvious gains which could be made in English Canada. Laurier's letter to Willison thanking the editor for the *Globe*'s praise showed confidence that the gamble had been justified. 'I understand that this speech has been well received in Ontario,' Laurier said with proper reticence. 'In Quebec it has made the *Bleus* mad with rage, but I never saw our friends in better fighting condition.'[5] Inside Parliament, John Charlton, the North Norfolk Liberal member who had long been known for his emphatic Protestant and Anglo-Saxon outlook, exulted that Laurier's amendment was 'the most pronounced form of hostility to the Bill which

3 *Ibid.*, pp.2737–59
4 *Laurier et Son Temps*, p.77
5 PAC, Willison Papers, Laurier to Willison, March 9, 1896

could be adopted, while at the same time a politic move because all wings of the party opposed to the Bill for whatever reason could vote for this amendment.' Charlton was understandably elated by Laurier's challenge to ecclesiastical interference. He called the performance a 'magnificent stand – a defiance to the Catholic clergy of Quebec. Their enmity is now an assured matter. Laurier knew all of the consequences and the step he has taken is a heroic one.'[6]

On the other side of the political divide, Alphonse LaRivière wrote Archbishop Langevin that Laurier's speech had taken everyone by surprise. It had been widely presumed that Laurier would confine himself to a repetition of insistence on an inquiry and that D'Alton McCarthy, if anyone, would move the hoist resolution. LaRivière admitted that even he had been taken aback by the starkness of the Liberal leader's declaration. 'Laurier brûle ses vaisseaux,' LaRivière wrote, 'et son discours a été une véritable révolte contre l'influence cléricale ... telle qu'il a étonné même les protestants.' LaRivière recorded an interesting encounter with McCarthy: 'Après le débat je rencontrai McCarthy et lui dis: "Laurier has stolen your motion." A quoi il répondit: "He has not only done that, but he has stolen my title of champion of the Protestant cause." Et il avait parfaitement raison.'[7] McCarthy may have been speaking with tongue in cheek; quite clearly LaRivière was not.

As for the reaction of the man whose letter had occasioned Laurier's manifesto, Lacombe found it hard to restrain his bitterness. Recording his emotions as he listened to Laurier from the visitors' gallery, Lacombe wrote to Langevin on March 4:

Honte et ignominie à cet homme sans cœur, qui vient de décider son avenir comme homme publique. Donc c'est fini! Ce dont il m'avait menacé, il y a quelques jours, il l'a accompli hier, au milieu des applaudissements de ses partisans [sic]. Il a déclaré la guerre – Pendant une heure et demie, avec une éloquence entrainante, il nous a condamnés, les Evêques, le clergé et moi donc! Malgré ses protestations de catholicité et d'attachement à sa mère, l'Eglise, c'est fini, il s'est suicidé hier devant sa patrie et son église. Mon Dieu, que c'était triste et regrettable d'entendre une si

6 John Charlton, *Diary*, March 3, 4, 1896
7 AASB, LaRivière to Langevin, March 5, 1896. Willison later noted that Clarke Wallace had also risen to speak at the same time as had Laurier. Although it was in keeping with his role as opposition leader that he should have been given preference by the Speaker over a private member, Laurier might well have lost most of his dramatic impact had Wallace made the counter motion or amendment (Willison, *Reminiscences*, p.250). P.B. Waite views Laurier's shift of emphasis from his proposed inquiry to the negative 'six-months hoist' as, at best, 'somewhat hollow' *Canada, 1874–1896*, p.267.

belle éloquence défendre une si mauvaise cause! Mon cœur en pleurait! C'est fini! qu'il ne vienne plus me parler, je le renie – qu'il ait le sort des Mercier et des autres esprits *forts*!

For the key to the motive for Laurier's outburst, Lacombe was sure that it was not hard to find. 'C'est le pouvoir qu'ils veulent *per fas et nefas*,' he wrote.[8] Bishop Laflèche's reaction showed a self-revealing satisfaction, since the confrontation in Parliament had turned out much as he had predicted. 'Je suis satisfait du terrain sur lequel a été posée la question par les deux chefs de chaque parti,' he wrote Langevin. 'C'est un duel à mort, il faut vaincre ou mourir! Tant mieux! J'aime les situations claires et précises, chaudes ou froides, parce que l'eau tiède provoque le vomissement!'[9]

Principles or power-seeking, virtue or vice, Laurier's challenge turned out to be a master political stroke. He had deflected Lacombe's potentially dangerous letter into at least an incipient political advantage. Without doubt the motion for a six-month delay was 'less disruptive ... than any amendment could have been ... No constructive amendment could have satisfied the two sections of the party.'[10] Certainly no other move would have permitted the Liberal party to continue, as it did during the subsequent debate, to burn the candle at both ends and support Laurier for completely opposite reasons.

FOLLOWERS AND DEFECTORS: SECOND READING PASSES

That the Liberals would take advantage of the opening which Laurier had provided quickly became evident. Far from finding the bill too harsh, Geoffrion, Lavergne, Rinfret, Monet, and other Quebec Liberals proceeded to attack the government measure as totally insufficient. Geoffrion thought that further negotiation ought to be attempted, but 'if this parliament is to pass a remedial law, let it be stringent, let it be positive.' He repeated that he would vote against the bill 'not because I am opposed to remedial legislation ... but I have a strong faith that our leader will be able to succeed where the Government are sure to fail.'[11] Lavergne concentrated

8 AASB, Lacombe to Langevin, March 4, 1896
9 *Ibid.*, Laflèche to Langevin, March 6, 1896
10 Neatby, *Laurier and a Liberal Quebec*, p.69
11 Canada, House of Commons, *Debates*, 1896, pp.2847–53

on the Conservative failure to disallow the 1890 law, although he admitted that Liberals were generally opposed to the way Conservative governments had used disallowance in the past. Rinfret and Monet, like many French Liberal spokesmen, quoted at length from J.P. Tardivel's ultramontane *La Vérité* and came down hard on the inefficacy of the bill.[12] Even when on March 12 Colonel Amyot interrupted to read Archbishop Langevin's February 22 telegram to Lacombe, Monet was alert with the answer that if the archbishop could approve the bill from a religious standpoint, he and his fellow Liberals should have 'the same right to vote it down from a national standpoint.'[13] Colin McIsaac of Cape Breton, like his French Liberal comrades, attacked the bill as a retreat from the position taken in the remedial order, and said that it 'offers a dry and lifeless skeleton to the Manitoba minority ... a stone to those who asked for and were promised bread.'[14]

At the opposite end of the spectrum, Liberals such as John Charlton could and did wax eloquent against this or any other remedial bill as a violation of provincial rights and an imposition of an outworn system on an unwilling majority. Whereas J.D. Edgar and even Joseph Martin put the case more moderately and concentrated on the need for a careful inquiry in their attack on the bill,[15] Charlton rivalled McCarthy and Wallace in his denunciation of the iniquity of all remedialism. Revealing that Laurier was not slower than others to use every weapon available, Charlton wrote in his diary that the Liberal leader had approved the draft of his speech and had suggested that Charlton pursue the line that separate schools in Manitoba had, in the first instance, been abolished by popular demand.[16]

Not all Liberals, however, were able or willing to direct fire at the bill for contradictory reasons. Cléophas Beausoleil, focus of the Liberal 'revolt' rumour of February, in Rumilly's words 'ni ascète, ni clérical,'[17] announced his intention to oppose Laurier and vote for the bill. He began by recalling Laurier's repeated assertion that the Liberals did not wish to make political capital out of the school controversy. Thus, Beausoleil stated, the coming vote should be regarded as a non-party one. He repeated his support of Laurier on all other matters, his endorsement of the Liberal convention platform of 1893, and his regret at having to separate from his leader on the remedial bill. Nonetheless, despite his own feelings on the shortcomings of the bill, Beausoleil insisted that his solemn personal

---

12 *Ibid.*, pp.2866–79, 3153–72
13 *Ibid.*, p.3352
14 *Ibid.*, pp.3778–98

15 *Ibid.*, pp.2799–814, 3013–46
16 John Charlton, *Diary*, March 5, 1896
17 *Histoire*, VIII, 32

pledges and the unlikelihood of getting anything better compelled him to support the second reading and to oppose Laurier's amendment.[18] Beausoleil's stand, however, as the final vote was to show, did not produce the wave of changes among Quebec Liberals which Laurier had originally feared and Conservative partisans had predicted. Joseph Pope had estimated on February 29 that 'about twenty Grits will bolt from their party on the question.'[19] Reflecting the decline from his earlier high optimism as well as his continued lobbying in the matter, Lacombe informed Langevin after Beausoleil's speech that 'j'ai gagné Mr.Frémont, ancien maire de Québec, à se ranger de notre côté, mais je n'ai pu réussir avec l'Honble. Béchard.'[20]

Without the advantage of the negative position, the Conservatives did not have nearly as much room to manoeuver as did the Liberals. Thus a greater number saw no choice but to defect from party solidarity. A few English-speaking Conservatives, including Agriculture Minister Montague, abstained from speaking at all. Clarke Wallace's speech, immediately following Laurier's amendment, brought into sharp focus the ominous and significant fact that, with the possible exception of Charlton, the most virulent anti-French and anti-Catholic statements were coming from Ontario Conservatives. Wallace began with a tribute to Sir Charles Tupper's contribution to racial and religious harmony in Canada, but quickly switched to an insistence that the current bill was sure to bring religious war. He even opposed the idea of a commission of inquiry and pointedly asked Joseph Martin why he was supporting such a move. Declaring that he would oppose the restoration of separate schools at any cost, Wallace concluded by supporting Laurier's amendment.[21]

Government replies both to Wallace and to the Liberals emphasized constitutional duty and necessity in the case, although, understandably enough, a wide variety of approach was evident. English Protestants such as Dickey and Prior stressed their support of the bill despite personal disapproval of the principle of separate schools.[22] One group of French Conservatives, led by Caron, worked hard to reduce the emotional content of the debate. Caron dwelt on the bi-partisan support of the Blake amendment of 1890 and insisted that everything had been done to keep the

18 Canada, House of Commons, *Debates,* 1896, pp.2952–60
19 PAC, J. Pope, *Journal,* February 29, 2896
20 AASB, Lacombe to Langevin, March 13, 1896
21 Canada, House of Commons, *Debates,* 1896, pp.2760–73
22 *Ibid.*, pp.2773–96, 4115–22

question out of politics. Both Laurier and *L'Electeur* were quoted at length as having been against the government first for acting too slowly and now for acting too hastily. Caron concluded by reproving Laurier's 'painful reference' to the Lacombe letter.[23] Other French Conservatives such as Amyot and Joncas were a good deal less restrained, and combined bitter attacks against the Greenway government with ridicule of what they claimed to be Laurier's naked struggle for power.[24]

Even during the first week of debate on the second reading, it was evident that a substantial number of English-speaking Conservatives, nearly all from Ontario, were going to follow Wallace's lead and separate from the government. The speech of T.S. Sproule of North Grey typified this sentiment. Sproule stated that although he remained as much a Conservative member as he had been for seventeen years in the House, now, 'regarding this Bill as a most obnoxious one,' he was obliged to vote against it.[25] A more personal expression of the same sentiment was given by B. Rosamond, MP for North Lanark, in a March 9 letter to Tupper. Rosamond stated that the feeling against the remedial bill in his constituency was 'much stronger than I supposed,' that 'even Roman Catholic supporters are opposed to it or perfectly indifferent,' and that 'I could not honourably do anything but vote against the Bill.'[26] On the other hand, one of the most remarkable efforts during the first part of the debate was the speech of Finance Minister Foster. For all the accusations against him of backsliding on remedialism during and after the January cabinet crisis, Foster presented far more than perfunctory arguments favouring the bill.[27] Lacombe was effusive in his praise of Foster's performance,[28] and even John Charlton had to admit that 'Foster ... made a great effort to keep his party together.'[29]

Although the debate on the second reading of the remedial bill filled some fourteen hundred columns of Hansard, the impression of mere pad-

23 *Ibid.*, pp.2816ff
24 *Ibid.*, pp.2857–64, 3172–98
25 *Ibid.*, pp.2924–52. Other Ontario Conservatives who reflected the same mentality as Sproule were A. McNeill, T.D. Craig, W.F. Maclean and Colonel W.E. O'Brien. Chief Whip George Taylor tried to ride the fence by announcing that he would vote for the bill, yet would insist in Committee on a lessening of the 'separate' requirements (pp.3432–45). Taylor's remarks formed a strange duet with French Conservatives who were promising precisely the opposite to Langevin.
26 PAC, Tupper Papers, Rosamond to Tupper, March 9, 1896
27 Canada, House of Commons, *Debates*, 1896, pp.3472–515
28 AASB, Lacombe to Langevin, March 13, 1896
29 *Diary*, March 13, 1896

ding or filibuster was not yet paramount. Members who were rarely heard from on other subjects, such as T.E. Kenney of Halifax in support of the bill, and H.G. Carroll of Kamouraska supporting Laurier, gave carefully constructed addresses.[30] In fact, the third week produced three of the most impressive speeches of the entire debate, by Haggart, Mills, and Weldon. Haggart, like Foster under suspicion during the January 'strike,' ridiculed Laurier's inconsistency on the question, but concentrated his fire against McCarthy for forgetting the strong arguments favouring the protection of provincial minorities which had been used by McCarthy himself during the Jesuit estates' debate. Haggart concluded, in declaring his support for the most moderate bill he thought feasible, that the agitation being stirred up was largely 'because a few disappointed parties have not got the influence or precedence in the Conservative Party which they think their abilities entitle them to.'[31]

David Mills's speech was a truly remarkable performance. In a presentation filling sixty-two pages of Hansard, Mills worked out one careful distinction after another establishing the possibility of federal interference in the case more forcefully than anyone on the government side had yet done. At the same time he accused the Conservatives of so mishandling the case that the bill at hand could only be considered a gross mistake. In particular, Mills criticized the entire procedure which had surrounded the remedial order of 1895, and the summoning to Ottawa of the Manitoba government while it was still in session. 'You dealt with them as the Sultan of Turkey might deal with an Armenian,' Mills stated. Minister of Public Works Ouimet was singled out as the chief architect of bullying Manitoba: 'forbearance has been refused to enable the Minister of Public Works to appear as the conqueror of Manitoba before the electors of his own province,' Mills charged. Referring to Conservative efforts, beginning with the Verchères election, to swing the Catholic hierarchy behind them, Mills contended that the government had 'ostentatiously invoked the aid of parties who ought not to have been drawn into a public controversy at all.' Mills was somewhat unrealistic about the willingness to cooperate evidenced by the Manitoba government's replies, but he insisted that the attitude of some of the French members of the government in particular could only be regarded 'as a gauntlet thrown down, not to Manitoba alone, but to the whole Protestant population of the Dominion.' In conclusion, Mills once more struck a balance. He admitted that legislation finally might

30 Canada, House of Commons, *Debates*, 1896, pp.3394–413, 3198–211
31 *Ibid.*, pp.3757–78

have to come, and that it would probably not wreck the country, but he was sure that the Conservative procedure would have precisely that disastrous effect.[32] So well did Mills put the case for the possibility of remedial legislation, that Sir Charles Tupper thanked him profusely and somewhat maliciously pointed out that he had had 'the better opportunity of listening to him because he was not interrupted by deafening cheers from the gentlemen who sit behind him.'[33]

R.C. Weldon's speech was, for the most part, a candid argument against separate schools as such, and an elaboration on the Protestant feelings that would be wounded just as Catholics would have been had the Jesuit Estates' Act been disallowed in 1889. At the same time, Weldon, a New Brunswicker known for his French fluency and sympathies,[34] disclaimed any anti-Catholic feeling in his position. He maintained that if there was genuine desire to restore the Manitoba separate schools, the bill before them was 'absolutely useless ... unworthy ... of able men and of lawyers.' Like the earlier position of Beausoleil on the Liberal side and Sproule on the Conservative, Weldon insisted on loyalty to his party in other matters, and simply regretted that 'the administration of today has taken a course on the school question which I cannot follow.'[35]

Of the speeches on the final day of debate on the second reading, only those of Sir Donald Smith and Flavien Dupont were of major significance. Smith stated publicly what was already being rumoured, that he would vote for the bill only on condition that a delegation would in fact go to Manitoba, and that he hoped as a result 'there will be no remedial bill required from this House.'[36] Dupont, clearly one of the spokesmen of A.R. Angers and the Castor wing of the Conservatives, confirmed the report that he would propose an amendment to the provincial grant arrangement, clause 74 of the bill. Dupont insisted, however, that the second reading should be voted for, and that the imperfections which the Liberals were so loud in condemning could be, if good will were forthcoming, amended in committee.[37] After two and one-half weeks of debate on the second reading, the House finally divided at 6:00 AM March 20. Laurier's amendment was defeated 115 to 91; the second reading of the bill was sustained 112 to 94. Three Ontario Tories, Hughes of North Middlesex, McGillivray of North Ontario, and

32 Ibid., pp.3816–78
33 Ibid., 3878
34 La Presse, April 9, 1896
35 Canada, House of Commons, Debates, 1896, pp.3906–29
36 Ibid., pp.4129–40
37 Ibid., pp.4171–87

Ross of Dundas, cast a negative vote in both cases, thus giving the difference in the tally. Seven Liberals – Beausoleil, Devlin, Vaillancourt, Frémont, Delisle, Charles Angers, and McIsaac – voted against Laurier. Eighteen Conservatives, all from Ontario except Weldon, plus McCarthy and Stubbs, voted with Laurier.[38] Thus, while the government had been sustained on both counts, its majority without the Liberals was down to a mere four. Threatening future Conservative hopes, more public and more unmanageable rifts than any previously encountered had become evident during the debate and vote. Liberal defections from Quebec, while important, had not been as numerous as Conservative supporters had counted on. Of most immediate concern, the government was faced, under pressure from Sir Donald Smith, with a delay of uncertain duration when, as far as the remedial bill was concerned, time was already a matter of life and death.

For the most part, reaction to the debate in the press followed predictable lines. Inevitably, Laurier's hoist motion and his protest against ecclesiastical interference brought out the most emphatic comment. The initial *Globe* editorial, for which Laurier thanked Willison personally, far from espousing a radical 'no interference in any case' stance similar to Charlton's, contented itself with praising Laurier's moderation. Contrasting the Liberal leader's position with that of Tupper, whom it styled as the 'past master in coercion,' the *Globe* pointed to Laurier's support for a 'possible case for interference,' but stressed his insistence on 'inquiry and conciliation.' Avoiding any gloating over Laurier's rejection of ecclesiastical pressure, the editorial called the statement simply 'a courageous position, a wise position,' and quoted the opinion of 'an old parliamentarian' that the speech had been 'unequalled in force, eloquence and effect upon the House.'[39] The moderate Liberal Toronto *Weekly Gazette* also praised Laurier's combination of firmness and restraint. 'It would have been easy,' the *Gazette* stated, 'for Mr. Laurier to cater to those who like to see the Roman Catholic clergy put on the spit.' Instead of that, the paper observed, Laurier 'spoke the mind of Canadian Liberalism,' and eloquently refuted any charge against Quebec of 'illiberality and narrowness.'[40] *L'Electeur* praised in particular Laurier's strategy of calling for the six months' hoist

38 *Ibid.*, pp.4240. L.C. Clark adds the important point that some of the Ontario Conservatives such as Moncrieff and Taylor voted for the second reading only with the proviso of substantial amendments in Committee or in view of Tupper's promise of negotiations (Clark, 'The Conservative Administrations' (thesis), II, p.479).
39 Toronto *Globe*, March 4, 1896
40 March 7, 1896

rather than the expected commission of inquiry. As a result, Pacaud's newspaper pointed out, anti-remedialist Conservatives who might have opposed an inquiry amendment, now would be forced into the open and would have to vote against their party on all counts. As for the radical rejection of the bill implied in the Laurier motion, *L'Electeur* insisted that the absolute inefficacy of the measure deserved such treatment. 'On peut amender une loi, mais on ne peut amender ce qui n'est qu'un simulacre de loi,' the paper stated.[41]

Naturally enough, Conservative newspapers put a quite different interpretation on the exchange between Tupper and Laurier. The Toronto *Mail and Empire* highlighted Tupper's stress on the 'bargain' of confederation as witnessed by the compromises of Galt, Brown, and Mackenzie. Furthermore, the paper insisted, 'the action that is suggested to Parliament is not of a severe or coercive character,' nor did it rule out settlement by the Manitoba authorities themselves. For Laurier, however, the *Mail and Empire* insisted, the bill did not go far enough, if any credence was to be given to his earlier statements. Without even mentioning his challenge to ecclesiastical pressure, the Toronto Conservative organ concluded that 'Mr. Laurier's position is not that of the statesman, but of the lower class of politician, who changes his views to meet altered circumstances.'[42]

In Montreal, *La Minerve* proclaimed that Liberals from Quebec who had been crying about the inefficacy of the bill had been dealt 'un coup de tête de leur chef ... C'est le principe même qui est en jeu et que M. Laurier vient de repousser au nom du parti libéral.' Worst of all, the Bleu newspaper charged, was the unrelieved negative quality of Laurier's position. 'Toute la synthèse politique de M. Laurier est là: nier, reculer, éviter, rompre, ne jamais s'engager,' *La Minerve* concluded. 'Cette préoccupation constante de neutralité l'immobilise dans un continuel piétinement sur place.'[43] The more independent *La Presse* was equally critical. Ridiculing, like *La Minerve*, the lack of substance in Laurier's stand, it called the Liberal leader's practical position 'aussi nuageux qu'un traité de philosophie allemande.' More seriously, *La Presse* charged that Laurier had reduced the debate 'aux proportions des intérêts de son parti et de ses chances de conquérir le pouvoir.'[44]

When the report came of Beausoleil's defection from Liberal-party solidarity, French-Conservative papers were prompt to cheer. *La Minerve* spread the report that Laurier had told Beausoleil that, had he not been

41 March 5, 1896
42 March 4, 1896

43 March 5, 1896
44 March 4, 1896

party leader, he too would have supported the remedial bill. 'C'est comme chef que M. Laurier a capitulé en face de l'ennemi,' *La Minerve* taunted.[45] Once again Tarte came in for a good deal of abuse in the Bleu editorials, and was charged with more malice than was Laurier. *Le Manitoba*'s charge against Tarte as the grey eminence behind Laurier was unsparing. 'C'est Tarte qui l'a poussé dans ce bourbier,' the newspaper charged. 'Cet homme n'a jamais fait autre chose que trahir toutes les causes.'[46] *Le Manitoba* was also widely quoted in the Quebec Conservative press for an article which appeared soon after the presentation of the remedial bill. Taken as the unofficial voice of Archbishop Langevin, the article stated that the Manitoba minority accepted the bill, 'tout en se réservant de faire modifier en comité de la Chambre certains détails qui laissent à désirer.'[47]

Despite the challenge to clerical domination contained in the Laurier speech, it should be noted that not only did the French-Canadian MPs and newspapers who supported him take up a 'more-Catholic-than-the-bill' position, but *L'Electeur* in particular spent a good deal of effort to establish the image of important clerical support. On March 10 *L'Electeur* published a short notice from its Toronto correspondent that Archbishop Walsh had approved Laurier's position. The same dispatch added the startling sugges- tion that, referring to the anti-coercion resolution of the Ontario Legisla- ture of March 4, 'C'est à la demande de la hierarchie que M. Mowat a fait adopter les résolutions que vous connaissez.'[48] *L'Evénement* was quick to deny *L'Electeur*'s claim.[49] On March 11, 12, 13, and 14, however, *L'Electeur* repeated at some length the claim that the Conservative news- paper could not deny the Toronto dispatch with any authority.[50] But on March 14, *L'Evénement* printed a Walsh telegram which was widely quoted in other Bleu newspapers, and which ended *L'Electeur*'s brief campaign in Walsh's direction. 'The Toronto dispatch to *L'Electeur* re- garding my attitude on the Manitoba school question is an audacious falsehood,' the Walsh message stated.[51]

The Toronto Archbishop was not the only important Catholic authority brought forward by the Liberals. A critical pamphlet by Senator L.G. Power of Halifax dated March 3 and entitled *The Remedial Bill from the*

45 March 13, 1896
46 March 12, 1896
47 Quoted in *Le Courrier du Canada*, March 10, 1896
48 March 10, 1896
49 March 11, 1896
50 March 11, 12, 13, 14, 1896
51 *L'Evénement*, March 14, 1896

Point of View of a Catholic Member was quoted by several Liberal speakers during the debate and was cited approvingly by the *Globe*.[52] *L'Electeur* did not hesitate to bring forward Senator Power as an influential and respected Catholic authority. It referred to the pamphlet on numerous occasions, and printed a full French translation of the senator's criticism of the bill.[53] On March 7, *L'Electeur* reported the approval of 'un curé important' for the stand taken by Laurier, and on March 12 printed a letter to Laurier dated March 4 from 'un prêtre distingué de Québec.' Referring to Laurier's speech, the priest congratulated the Liberal leader 'de votre attitude ferme, honnête et loyale,' and agreed with Laurier's condemnation of the bill 'parce que tel qu'il est, il donne du coup la mort aux écoles séparées.' Equally prepared as were the Conservatives to use the narrowly denominational argument, *L'Electeur* did not hesitate to recommend the advantages of 'un chef catholique au lieu d'un chef orangiste,' and charged that both the *Mail and Empire* and Chief Whip Taylor, 'les deux porte-paroles les plus accrédités du gouvernement,' had attacked Laurier precisely because he was a Catholic. 'Tous deux demandent aux conservateurs orangistes,' *L'Electeur* insisted, 'de voter pour la loi – telle qu'elle est sinon que M. Laurier arrivera au pouvoir et accordera une restitution complète à ses frères de l'ouest.'[54]

BISHOPS' REACTION: A PROJECT SCUTTLED

A particularly effective charge, which *L'Electeur* as well as Laurier's French supporters in Parliament were able to make repeatedly, was that the bill did not have anything like official ecclesiastical approval. Conveniently ignoring what its attitude might have been had such approval been forthcoming, *L'Electeur* challenged *Le Courrier du Canada* with the question, 'Où est-elle la direction des évêques?' Pacaud's newspaper pointed out that the Cameron and Labrecque statements had been made well before the law had appeared. As for the Lacombe letter, *L'Electeur* insisted that 'l'épiscopat a déclaré que le Rev. Père n'avait pas reçu autorité de parler en son nom.'[55] Not until Amyot's angry interjection of Langevin's February 22 telegram into Monet's speech on March 12, did a Conservative speaker make an explicit claim for official episcopal support of the bill. Clearly, the fact that the Quebec episcopate did not follow up Langevin's approval of the bill with their own endorsement, as well as the fact that Langevin did

---

52 March 11, 1896
53 March 21, 1896

54 *L'Electeur*, March 7, 12, 18, 1896
55 *Ibid.*, March 11, 1896

not give a more public statement once the bill had been presented for second reading, gave Liberal apologists wide scope for claims and suppositions.

The explanation of this episcopal reticence involved a number of important factors not immediately evident either in the parliamentary debate or in the newspapers, but vital in the increasing tension of church–state involvement. First was the fact that the government needed desperately to avoid the image of church dictation. Moreover, Langevin himself, despite the approval expressed in his February 22 telegram, was again hedging and trying to maintain enough latitude to enable himself to press for further concessions. Although the French members of the cabinet were quoted by Lacombe as giving verbal assurances that amendments in committee would make up deficiencies in the law,[56] Langevin hesitated and dodged when it came to an unreserved public approval of the bill. Typical of the vacillation of the Archbishop's attitude was his letter to Bégin of March 3. It was clear that he wanted the bill to pass even as it stood and was not slow to condemn the Liberal opposition which was gathering. Yet he did not seem able to bring himself firmly to accept a compromise. Moreover, while he showed appreciation of the complexities of the situation, Langevin's manner of approaching the problem only added to the confusion. With a heavy sprinkling of emotional interjections and exclamation marks, Langevin jumped from one subject to another with little logical pattern.[57] So uncertain were the directives coming from St Boniface that Lacombe again felt obliged to bring pressure on Langevin for a renewed approval of the bill. 'Après votre télégramme approbatif, il n'y a plus à réculer,' Lacombe insisted. '… C'est incroyable tout ce que les libéraux inventent de mensonges!'[58] Even when Langevin was brought to issue a second approval on March 14, both in form and content it was far less emphatic than had been his February telegram:

I can approve of this law in as far as it gives us a real control of our schools and an immense relief in our long agony.

If some verbal changes or additions were made according to the suggestions of Mr. John Ewart and to those of Hon. Mr. Bernier and Hon. Mr. LaRivière, especially for the books, the exemptions of taxes, the inspectors and the Government grant, the Remedial Act would be as much as we can expect from the

56 AASB, Lacombe to Langevin, February 28, 1896
57 AAQ, Langevin to Bégin, March 3, 1896
58 AASB, Lacombe to Langevin, March 13, 1896

Government who cannot give us more than what we had before and who must follow the lines of the judgement of Honourable Privy Council of England, and of the 'Remedial Order.'[59]

The St Boniface prelate was not, however, the only source of potential episcopal approval, nor did his indecision pose the only problem. The fact was that unanimity, instead of growing among the Quebec bishops, was steadily declining. The most profound cause of division was a plan that went far beyond mere endorsement of the bill. This was the project of sending a collective episcopal letter to all Catholic MPs, requesting or even attempting to oblige them to vote for the remedial bill. As was often the case, the course pursued by Bishop Laflèche tended to be in turn the cause and the target of decisive action. As early as December 18, 1895, Laflèche had sent to Bégin a sketch of a mandement which would require Catholic voters to exact written promises of support for remedial legislation from candidates on the hustings.[60] His comments on Labrecque's action in Charlevoix indicated that he was solidly in favour of the 'hard line' pursued by the Chicoutimi prelate.[61] The bishop of Trois-Rivières had been close to the centre of decision in sending the fateful letter to Laurier. When Langevin's telegram approving the remedial bill finally came through on February 22, Laflèche's logic led him with little hesitation to the necessity of an even bolder episcopal step. 'Une lettre collective épiscopale bien explicite et immédiate, d'adhésion à cette loi, *et d'obligation de conscience pour les députés catholiques* de l'appuyer de leurs suffrages, au moins des évêques des provinces (écclesiastiques) de Québec, Montréal, et Ottawa est desirée et même attendue avec hâte par tous les amis de cette cause sacrée,' Laflèche stated to Bégin on February 26.[62] Whether Laflèche had reached his conclusion alone or after consultation, rumours of such a collective episcopal demand appeared in the *Ottawa Citizen* on February 20 and were repeated with varying degrees of credence and apprehension by other papers. Date-lined Montreal, 19 February, the *Citizen* report told of great excitement in political circles and saw the projected mandement as a 'natural sequence' of the Paquet article and the episcopal statements made in Charlevoix and Antigonish. An unidentified 'prominent politician' was quoted as saying that 'the Government was expecting to get every

59 AAQ, Langevin to Lacombe, Langevin to Bégin, March 14, 1896
60 *Ibid.*, Laflèche to Bégin, December 18, 1895
61 *Ibid.*, February 6, February 21, 1896
62 *Ibid.*, February 26, 1896

Catholic vote in both houses,' but equally expressed profound worry over possible repercussions. In any case, the *Citizen* concluded, 'the mandement is sure to create a great sensation, as it will be the first direct action of the hierarchy with respect to Dominion legislation.'[63] Not until the February 25 report of the Bégin reassurances to the Liberal delegation did the journalistic rumours predicting a collective letter die down.

Responsibility for handling the rumoured episcopal action, and for effectively putting in motion or scuttling such a project, had to come ultimately from Archbishop Bégin, in his capacity as metropolitan of the primatial see. Although plagued by an illness which confined him to hospital during part of the crisis, when Bégin did speak he gently but effectively blocked the campaign. According to Lacombe's report, and however much the newspapers were stating that the Paquet article reflected Bégin's position, the Metropolitan, even before February 20 made it clear to the missionary that he was opposed to the idea of an immediate mandement. Lacombe himself soon joined the side of caution. Whether in the glare of the reaction over his letter to Laurier, or because of alarm expressed by his contacts among the government strategists, Lacombe conceded to Bégin that a collective order to the members of parliament would probably have the effect 'de surexciter le fanatisme de nos adversaires dans Ontario, sans peut-être exercer l'influence espérée sur les libéraux.'[64] More clearly than ever acting as spokesman for the government, Lacombe on February 28 cautioned Langevin on the danger of a collective letter:

Si vous écrivez une lettre publique, comme vous le conseille Mgr. Laflèche, vous avez besoin d'être bien sûr de toutes vos paroles, qui vont être commentées. Pour moi, je vous conseillerais de ne rien dire pour le moment, vis-à-vis la conscience des voteurs. Malgré ce que prétend l'Evêque des Trois-Rivières, je vous prierais d'attendre pour publier une lettre quelconque. En disant cela, je suis l'interprète de nos amis du Gouvernement, de Bowell, Ouimet, Anger &.[65]

On the following evening, having made the circle from Montreal to Quebec and back to Trois-Rivières, Lacombe reinforced his argument to Langevin. 'Pour le moment,' he insisted, 'vu le désir du Gouvernement et la disposi-

63 February 20, 1896
64 AAQ, Lacombe to Bégin, February 21, 1896. Interestingly, Rumilly, (*Mgr. Laflèche et Son Temps*, p.383) quotes Sentaor Landry as using precisely the same wording as Lacombe in a similar letter to Bégin. Whoever was quoting whom, there was no mistaking the apprehension in government circles.
65 AASB, Lacombe to Langevin, February 28, 1896

tion des esprits, un document quelconque de la part des évêques (quand même on le saurait venir du ciel), ferait un mauvais effet et injurierait grandement notre cause.' Lacombe then added the watchword 'Le silence est d'or,' to which even Laflèche had agreed for the moment.[66]

Restraining Bishop Laflèche, however, was not a simple matter, and the main effort remained with Bégin, even though he was still in hospital. In reply to the older prelate's sketch of a collective letter which seemed to take acceptance for granted, Bégin promptly insisted that, in his opinion, imposing an obligation in conscience on the deputies was going too far.[67] Marois supplemented Bégin's letter with a summary of his superior's arguments against a mandement. Two points in particular were stressed, the impossibility of getting the agreement of all the bishops, and the danger of alienating Protestant Conservative members from Ontario, 'disposés à voter pour la loi rémédiatrice pour des motifs d'intérêt particulier, mais qui ne veulent pas paraître subir la direction ni le joug de la hiérarchie catholique.' As a final point, Marois quoted Bégin to the effect that bishops might contact individual MPs belonging to their own dioceses. However, 'toute intervention plus directe, plus solonnelle et d'un caractère coercitif, mettrait toute la cause de Manitoba en danger, et cela au jugement même des hommes politiques qui s'intéressent à l'adoption de la loi, et compromettrait peut-être notre propre système scolaire.'[68] As a sequel to this letter, Lacombe's hurried visit to Quebec and Trois-Rivières on February 29 at the behest of Bégin and Marois was at least in part to devise a scheme of handling Bishop Laflèche.

In response to this combination of pressures. Laflèche showed himself prepared to change. Apparently before Lacombe arrived on February 29, Laflèche wrote briefly to Bégin that he agreed to the withholding of the collective letter.[69] In a longer letter to Marois, Laflèche went to some length to assure that he did not wish to impose his views on the other bishops, and admitted the force of the arguments received from Quebec. But Laflèche predicted that if justification was being sought for a strong episcopal letter 'M. Laurier nous en fournira sous peu l'occasion.'[70]

If a collective mandement seemed inadvisable, the somewhat less ominous project of private letters to individual deputies was another possibil-

66 *Ibid.*, February 29, 1896
67 AAQ, Bégin to Laflèche, February 27, 1896
68 *Ibid.*, Marois to Laflèche, February 27, 1896
69 *Ibid.*, Laflèche to Bégin, February 29, 1896
70 *Ibid.*, Laflèche to Marois, February 29, 1896

ity. Temporarily at least, this was the alternative espoused by Bégin. Once again, however, the Quebec archbishop did not wish to proceed if any other bishop had serious objections to even this restricted project. On March 2, Marois sent out a draft of a letter which Bégin proposed to send to the deputies from his own diocese and which he offered as a working model to others who might wish to use it. The letter began by insisting on the religious dimension of the case as the sole reason for the letter. 'Je n'ai pas la pensée,' Bégin's letter went on, 'de vouloir gêner en aucune manière la liberté de votre suffrage, que vous devez donner selon la dictée de votre conscience.' Nevertheless, the deputy had a right to know whether his bishop approved the law. Despite admitted imperfections, the answer clearly was in the affirmative, and the conclusion was in the form of a question: 'Est-il nécessaire, après cela, d'ajouter que je compte sur vous, Monsieur le Député, pour favoriser, par tous les moyens à votre disposition, l'adoption de cette loi?'[71] This was close to taking away with the left hand what had been given with the right, yet it clearly stopped short of imposing an open and shut case of conscience.

With the parliamentary debate due to begin immediately, no time was lost in sending replies to Bégin's proposal. Duhamel of Ottawa, Moreau of St Hyacinthe, Gravel of Nicolet, Larocque of Sherbrooke, Lorrain of Pontiac, Labrecque of Chicoutimi, and Vicar General Langis of Rimouski, all approved the draft. Gravel and Labrecque said, however, that they did not favour the paragraph that softened the motion of obligation in conscience. Only Moreau and Langis indicated that they were prepared in fact to send letters to their own deputies.[72] Fabre and Emard posed different problems. Lacombe had already indicated to Langevin that there might be a problem getting even the requested approval of Langevin's February 22 telegram from Montreal and Valleyfield. 'Je crains la manière de voir des évêques Fabre et Emard, surtout ce dernier,' Lacombe wrote. 'Ce serait fatal s'il était connu que même un seul évêque nous serait contraire.'[73] Then, as he hurried to visit Fabre on March 1, Lacombe added, 'Pauvre Evêque de Montréal, s'il fallait que par entêtement, il refusât d'approuver votre télégramme!'[74] Lacombe's pressure produced brief endorsements from Fabre and Emard, but a minimum of enthusiasm. 'Mgr. Langevin et

71 AAQ, Draft letter from Bégin to MPS, March 2, 1896
72 *Ibid.*, Duhamel, Moreau, Gravel, Larocque, Lorrain, Labrecque, and Langis to Bégin, March 3, 4, 5 and 6, 1896. Several English-speaking bishops also replied, expressing approval of the remedial bill, but without agreeing to the project of letters to deputies.
73 AASB, Lacombe to Langevin, February 29, 1896
74 *Ibid.*, March 1, 1896

ceux qui l'entourent,' Fabre replied, 'sont les plus intéressés dans cette affaire. Ils sont sur les lieux; dès lors qu'ils trouvent suffisant, je n'ai aucune objection à le voir devenir loi.'[75] As for the Bégin proposal, Fabre called it 'excellente,' but thought a letter from Langevin to the Catholic members of parliament would be more proper than letters from each individual bishop.[76] Emard had misgivings about the entire plan and felt that even Langevin's approval for the bill would be better expressed through Ewart, lest the church be too inescapably identified with the government bill. Apprehensive about even a private letter sent to a deputy, Emard warned that such a message 'infailliblement deviendra publique.' He did not wish to constrain Bégin's freedom of action, Emard concluded, but he repeated that, however one approached the bill, 'je considérerais comme un très grand péril qu'elle fût votée à la demande expresse, formelle de l'épiscopat de notre province.'[77]

Surprisingly, it was now Bishop Laflèche who joined Emard in advising against Bégin's restricted proposal. 'Les lettres de Mgr. Gravel et du Père Lacombe ont causé une telle explosion de fanatisme que je crois que *le silence est d'or* pour le moment,' Laflèche wrote on March 3. He quoted Lacombe in support of his position, and stated that even Langevin had given the same advice in his last letter.[78] It was indicative of the confusion coming from St Boniface that Langis was quoting Langevin in precisely the opposite sense.[79] In any case, there was evidence of sufficient episcopal dissent for Marois to send out the decision of his archbishop, still in hospital, at least to defer the projected letter.[80] The decision succeeded in completely confusing Bishop Moreau and more particularly Vicar General Langis, who had been on the point of mailing letters to Rimouski deputies when the decision to halt arrived. Langis wired back that he had to write something since both one of the Catholic deputies and the Protestant Liberal, Fauvel, had made requests for a statement.[81] Marois' next telegram indicated that Langis could certainly answer a request.[82] Unfortunately, the Marois-Langis exchange of telegrams somehow became public and appeared, complete with criticisms of clerical pretensions, in the

75 AAM, Fabre to Lacombe, March 2, 1896
76 *Ibid.*, Fabre to Bégin, March 3, 1896
77 AAQ, Emard to Marois, March 3, 1896
78 *Ibid.*, Laflèche to Marois, March 3, 1896
79 *Ibid.*, Langis to Marois, March 6, 1896
80 *Ibid.*, Marois to all Canadian bishops, March 4, 1896
81 *Ibid.*, Langis to Marois, March 6, 1896
82 *Ibid.*, Marois to Langis, March 6, 1896

Montreal *Star*.[83] Thus, although the public flurry was relatively brief, the hierarchy received a taste of the negative effects of a project which they in fact had shelved. Nonetheless, as Emard was quick to point out to Marois, the lesson of needed caution could not be missed.[84]

As far as can be ascertained, very few letters were actually sent. Significantly, one that did go out was from the man whose decision it was to oppose the collective letter and then to drop the project of a series of private letters. The letter in question was Bégin's March 2 message to Laurier himself. Specifically replying to Laurier's own letter of February 24, which had enclosed Senator Scott's objections to the remedial act, Bégin endorsed the statements he had given to the Liberal delegation of February 22. Again the archbishop made no attempt to impose an obligation in conscience, but equally left no doubt about his attitude to the bill. 'Bien qu'elle ne soit pas parfaite,' Bégin wrote, the bill would be 'un grand pas vers une solution juste et équitable,' and 'mon plus grand bonheur, comme mon plus ardent désir, serait de voir tous les députés catholiques s'unir dans ce but patriotique et religieux.' The archbishop's conclusion, written before his decision to drop the project, was that he might send similar statements of his position to the other federal deputies from the archdiocese of Quebec.[85] It is not certain whether Laurier had received Bégin's letter before delivering his March 3 manifesto in the House. In any case, Bégin's moderation would give the Liberal leader further evidence that Lacombe's inflexible position was not quite representative.

Thus a high pitch of ecclesiastical activity ended with little visible result. However much clerical interference was represented by the Lacombe letter, a good deal more might have been, and nearly was, attempted. There was some bowing to government pressure in dropping the project but, on the whole, the episode represented a retreat from Labrecque's earlier 'crossing of the Rubicon' and from the absolute stand taken by Lacombe. Once again, the reaction following the release of the letter to Laurier and the Liberal handling of the case must be seen as a major factor. Lacombe's simplistic approach to Laurier may in fact have had the quite unintended effect of heading off a much more explicit and official pressure. In any case, 'the letter-that-never-was' marked a victory, if not for a clear-sighted moderate ecclesiastical policy, at least for hesitation or confusion sufficient to avert a head-on clash. If the painful consequences of too direct ecclesias-

83 March 9, 1896
84 AAQ, Emard to Marois, March 9, 1896
85 *Ibid.*, Bégin to Laurier, March 2, 1896

tical interference were not yet completely evident, lessons for the future had been learned. From opposite ends of the policy spectrum, both Emard and Marois agreed that the attempt to establish a consensus of opinion through the mails was both ineffective and dangerous.[86] More important, both 'hawks' and 'doves' would come to the mandement conference in May with the issues clearer, the opposition identified, and their own arguments well honed.

SIR DONALD'S WINNIPEG CONFERENCE: DELAY WITHOUT BENEFIT

As the debate on the second reading drew to a close, attention in and out of Parliament turned more and more to the project laid down by Sir Donald Smith as the condition for his support of the remedial bill. This was the proposal of an eleventh-hour conference between the representatives of the two governments involved, during which time action on the remedial bill was to be suspended. As had been the case with Sir Donald's February visit to Winnipeg, Lord and Lady Aberdeen were again actively in support. In retrospect, it is difficult to see the project as anything but abortive, doomed to failure from the beginning. Certainly the lines of both parties to the dispute in Manitoba had hardened to a degree which made a mutually acceptable compromise practically impossible. Langevin's negative reaction to Smith's visit was reaffirmed in his March 3 letter to Bégin in which he called Greenway 'un traitre, moins fanatique que Sifton et Cameron, mais pratiquement tout aussi déterminé à nous sacrifier.' As for the possibility of a conference, presumably at Ottawa, Langevin expostulated that he simply would not go. 'Je ne descendrai ni avec Greenway ni avec un autre,' Langevin stated, 'et personne ne sera autorisé à traiter avec eux – qu'Ottawa fasse son devoir et au plus vite!'[87] A March 6 telegram from Bowell indicated that the government was prepared to ask Smith and Dickey 'to proceed West to try and effect settlement.'[88] On the following day LaRivière reported to Langevin that he and Bernier had seen Tupper in an attempt to dissuade official government sponsorship of the mission. LaRivière gave a capsule summary of what would be the repeated objection of the Catholic minority to the Smith mission. Not only would Greenway offer too little, they contended, but if he offered even a minimum and it had

---

86 AAQ, Emard to Marois, March 9, 1896; AEV, Marois to Emard, March 11, 1896
87 AAQ, Langevin to Bégin, March 3, 1896
88 PAC, Bowell Papers, Bowell to Smith, March 6, 1896

to be turned down, wavering supporters might abandon the government for failing to compromise.[89] The official announcement in Parliament of the Winnipeg Conference came on March 10, and LaRivière took great pains to insist with Langevin that Smith's demand was the only reason why the conference was being held.[90] Two days later, the Provencher deputy reported that Tupper had even tried to start trouble between Smith and Greenway by publishing their exchange of telegrams 'pour se débarasser des ennuis que lui causent Sir Donald et le G.G.'[91] A letter from Caron to Lacombe on the same day, however, indicated that there was no way to avoid the mission in view of Smith's attitude. At the same time, Caron tried to reassure the missionary (and through him Langevin and Bégin) that the procedure would not hold up the remedial bill and that the government had already decided to change the Dominion Lands Act in order to supplement the heavily criticized clause 74 of the bill.[92] Here Caron was either expecting naïveté or grasping at straws, since it was very quickly evident that there would be a substantial delay in the bill, and that the financial provisions would remain very much in doubt.

As the time for the mission drew nearer, there was no indication of a more accommodating attitude on the part of those interested in restoring the Catholic schools. Dansereau told Chapleau that his contacts in Ottawa insisted that 'les nouvelles négociations avec Greenway ne veulent rien dire.'[93] A.R. Angers added his voice to those urging no compromise,[94] and Bégin told Sir Hector Langevin that the proposed conference 'ne me dit rien de bon.' In view of the passions already aroused, Bégin felt, a moderate federal law would be better than 'tous les meilleurs compromis qui livreront, tôt ou tard, la minorité à la merci des persécuteurs.'[95] Archbishop Langevin sent an English note, obviously destined for circulation, to Lacombe on March 14 stating that in view of Greenway's promises during the recent provincial election, it would be impossible for the premier to make enough concessions. As a consequence, Langevin stated, he considered the idea of the proposed conference 'as a great mistake and a great misfortune.'[96] Langevin's Ottawa correspondents continued to

89 AASB, LaRivière to Langevin, March 7, 1896
90 Ibid., March 10, 1896. It was clear from the debate, of course, that many other Conservatives besides Smith could be held in line only by promise of a conference.
91 Ibid., March 12, 1896
92 AASB, Caron to Lacombe, March 12, 1896
93 PAC, Chapleau Correspondence, Dansereau to Chapleau, March 13, 1896
94 AASB, Angers to Langevin, March 13, 1896
95 APQ, Chapais Collection, Bégin to H. Langevin, March 13, 1896
96 AAQ, Langevin to Lacombe, March 14, 1896

strengthen, even to insist on, his rigid attitude. On March 18, Lacombe wrote that he had just seen Bowell, Desjardins, Ouimet, Caron, and Daly and had delivered Langevin's March 14 conditional approval of the bill. Lacombe was sure that Greenway, even if he accepted the conference, would not offer anything approaching the provisions of the remedial bill, and then added a condescending dismissal of the whole project. 'Sir Donald Smith,' Lacombe wrote, 'supporté par Rideau Hall, veut avoir la satisfaction d'être un homme important. Laissons-lui cette consolation ... ne faisons rien pour augmenter les difficultés – pourvu que nous ayons notre Bill, soyons grandement contents.'[97] Lacombe included Desjardins among those who were insisting that Langevin make no concessions. Furthermore, on March 21, when it was announced that the senator would accompany Smith and Dickey to Winnipeg, LaRivière hastened to inform Langevin that Desjardins had not changed his attitude. 'Entre nous,' LaRivière wrote, 'il m'a chargé de dire à votre Grandeur d'être de la plus grande fermeté, quelles que soient les menaces qui soient faites.'[98] Thus at least one member of the delegation was anything but prepared for compromise.

There was a good deal more to the federal government's motivation for the Winnipeg conference than a concession to Smith and the sources of funds which he commanded. As the debate showed, uneasy supporters for the bill from English Canada were ready to take any possible alternative to forcing the bill through. While it was still believed that the proposed conference would be in Ottawa rather than in Winnipeg, a former close friend of Greenway, Dr J.D. Rollins of Exeter, Ontario, sent an anxious confidential letter to the premier. Rollins stated that on March 11 he had been visited by a 'prominent supporter of the present Federal Government right from Ottawa.' The visitor had little doubt that the bill would pass, but was equally emphatic that 'all the politicians and parties are heartily sick of it and never want to try to force the Bill into operation.' There was every danger, the visitor feared, that public commitments and 'the spirit of dignity and formalism that such affairs generally assume,' would spoil any chance of real progress at the meeting. Although Rollins was not sure whether anyone in the cabinet was aware of the scheme, the visitor proposed that the doctor act as an intermediary in an informal meeting in Ottawa before the official encounter. He seemed confident enough that, if the meeting could be arranged, 'he would simply notify the Government that I would be down at Ottawa at the time you came down.'[99] Nothing

97 AASB, Lacombe to Langevin, March 18, 1896
98 Ibid., LaRivière to Langevin, March 21, 1896
99 PAM, Greenway Papers, Rollins to Greenway, March 12, 1896

came of the proposed private conference when the decision was made to go to Winnipeg, but it was a significant comment on the attitude of at least one wing within the federal government toward the Smith mission.

If Langevin's position on the conference was unpromising, there was equal indication that the Manitoba government would be little disposed to make an offer which they thought would be accepted. Federal Liberal strategists had no doubt on the matter and were prepared to applaud. J.D. Edgar's comment on the Manitoba government resolution in late February against the remedial bill was indicative. 'That does not look like compromise, does it?' Edgar wrote Willison. 'Sifton has behaved just as we wished.'[100] When Tupper, under Lord Aberdeen's pressure, invited Laurier to join the federal delegation, the Liberal leader showed his own reluctance to get involved in a potentially compromising and not very hopeful situation by demanding a condition which Tupper felt obliged to refuse – the revelation of all correspondence between the two governments.[101] Certainly there was no indication of compromise on Greenway's part in the exchange of telegrams with Donald Smith in early March. Lieutenant Governor Patterson's message to Bowell on March 10 indicated that the Manitoba premier agreed even to an Ottawa conference, but that 'at the same time, he stated frankly that he did not see what practical results would be attained by the proposed visit.'[102] Charles Boulton, the Manitoba senator who was Greenway's confidant, advised compromise with the Smith delegation if possible, but insisted that Greenway argue from strength, assuring the premier that the remedial bill could be defeated in the Senate if not in the House. 'The Government cannot ... afford to waste much time on parleying,' Boulton wrote. In any case, 'in your Conference I do not think you need fear any future effects from this Bill, so that it should weigh in your consideration of the question.'[103]

100 PAC, Willison Papers, Edgar to Willison, February 26, 1896
101 *L'Electeur*, March 20, 1896. Lady Aberdeen's version of this particular interlude placed the full responsibility for Laurier's exclusion from the commission with the Conservative leaders, stating that 'if anything is to come of this Conference, they wish to get all the glory' (*Journal*, March 21, 1896). While Laurier cannot be blamed for either the political intrigues of the government or for Sifton's tactics, he did nothing to enhance the possibility of settlement.
102 Canada, *Sessional Papers*, 1896, 11, no.39c, Patterson to Bowell, March 10, 1896
103 PAM, Greenway Papers, Boulton to Greenway, March 21, 1896. Even more pointed advice on how to gain political advantage from the conference without risking a settlement was contained in two unsigned memoranda received from Ottawa by Sifton (see Dafoe, *Clifford Sifton in Relation to His Times*, p.90). From Sifton's later correspondence, there are strong indications that the Ottawa strategist was D'Alton McCarthy (see below, pp.230–1).

Thus an elaborate network of bluff was being built up on both sides. Joseph Pope's entry in his diary of March 23 was to the point: 'Dickey, Desjardins and Sir Donald Smith left today for Winnipeg on their mission of conciliation which is altogether likely to be a wild goose chase.'[104] The newspapers, meanwhile, carried on a lively exchange. Not unexpectedly, while the *Globe* applauded the mission despite the irregularities of the action of Smith and the governor general,[105] *L'Electeur* saw hypocrisy on the part of the government. The Quebec Liberal paper had gotten wind of the opposition of Langevin and Lacombe to the mission, and for once agreed with these ecclesiastics. 'La compagnie du Pacifique qui mène l'intrigue,' *L'Electeur* stated, 'va triompher et les intérêts catholiques vont être sacrifiés.'[106] *La Minerve* was notably reserved in its comments. While it praised Smith's good will, the Montreal Bleu organ admitted that there was little chance of Greenway making acceptable concessions.[107] Significantly, *La Presse* followed up its increasingly explicit suspicion of the government with thorough hostility for the Winnipeg manoeuvre. As early as 29 February, *La Presse* had referred to statements made by Ontario Tory MP McNeil which suggested the possibility of obstruction of the remedial bill until the expiry of Parliament.[108] What *La Presse* feared was a Conservative plot with at least the tacit approval of Sir Charles Tupper; the implication was that the Smith mission fitted the same picture. All during the week of the conference, the *La Presse* editorials remained extremely critical, and the newspaper's April 1 answer to *Le Monde*'s reproof summarized its position. The accusation against Smith in particular was that he had imposed 'cette inutile et humiliante conférence, qui nous faisait perdre une semaine dans un temps où les heures sont comptées, et qui mettait en péril l'adoption de la loi.'[109] Reports of the sequence of events of the conference seemed to bear out *La Presse*'s further accusation of both charade and humiliation imposed by the Manitoba government. While the enforced haste of the federal delegation put them in a vulnerable position, the Manitoba tactic, according to *La Presse*, was to quickly terminate the session of the legislature on March 21, to have Greenway leave for his home in Crystal City, and to have Sifton and Cameron meet with the federal commissioners only after a significant delay. The Montreal paper decried

104 *Journal*
105 March 23, 1896
106 March 23, 1896
107 March 27, 1896
108 *La Presse*, February 29, 1896
109 *La Presse*, April 1, 1896

'l'ostentation avec laquelle M. Greenway s'est absenté pour leur faire faire anti-chambre,' and the charge of a deliberate snub was substantiated by the report of the Toronto *Mail and Empire*.[110]

Archbishop Lengevin was contacted by Desjardins through Ewart and by letter, but they avoided a personal meeting lest collusion be charged.[111] Langevin's letter to Bégin on March 28 indicated that he had been informed of the offer the federal commissioners intended to make and contained a copy of his own reply. 'We could not refuse what you would obtain for us from our local rulers' and 'we are quite willing to examine a more definite scheme,' Langevin wrote, but 'how can you ask us, Honourable Gentlemen, to renounce certain fundamental rights and declare that we are satisfied?'[112] Desjardins' reply, again sent before the meeting with Sifton and Cameron, was much less hopeful than had been his original greeting. 'D'après ce que vous me dîtes,' he wrote, 'nous n'aurons guère à prendre d'autre partie après la journée de demain qu'à nous assurer de l'heure du départ du train pour Ottawa.'[113]

Both the newspaper reports and the official documents submitted to the governor general after the conference showed that there was no real chance of an agreement. The *Winnipeg Tribune* was unrelieved in its denunciation of the federal government pretensions and concentrated most of its comment on a main objection brought by the Manitoba representatives, that the remedial bill was not withdrawn but simply delayed during the negotiations.[114] The Manitoba *Free Press*, in a more factual report, indicated on Monday, March 30, that the federal delegates had made little progress. 'The local ministers are in the best of humour,' the *Free Press* reported, 'and from their appearance the discussion has not been unfavourable to the Manitoba Government side.'[115] It should be noted that the proposal of the federal commissioners was, in their own words, 'much less than what we understand to be involved ordinarily by the establishment of separate schools.'[116] On one detail at least, the number of children required before a Catholic teacher could be demanded, the federal pro-

110 *La Presse*, April 1, 1896; Toronto *Mail and Empire*, March 27, 1896
111 AASB, Desjardins to Langevin, March 26, 29, and April 2, 1896, (all these letters nearly illegible)
112 AAO, Langevin to Bégin, March 28, 1896
113 AASB, Desjardins to Langevin, March 29, 1896
114 *Winnipeg Tribune*, March 28 and 30, 1896
115 Manitoba *Free Press*, March 30, 1896
116 Canada, *Sessional Papers*, 1896, 11. no.39c, Document c. Full details of the offers made by each side are contained in the Sessional Papers.

posal was less favourable to the minority than the later Laurier-Greenway agreement would be. Certainly the federal offer could never have received the approval which Desjardins promised he would get from Langevin before any final agreement. On the other hand, the one substantial concession offered by Sifton and Cameron, beyond the unrealistic alternative of complete secularization of the schools, was religious teaching and exercises between 3:30 and 4:00 PM, to be conducted by a Christian clergyman of the district or his delegate.[117] No more pointed summary of the hopelessness of the negotiations could be found than that given by Sifton and Cameron in their final reply on April 1. In the first place, they stated, the point of departure of the federal delegates on the 'legal rights in connection with separate schools' was completely incompatible with 'our declaration of policy preceding our last election.' Secondly, 'any settlement between the Government of the Dominion and that of Manitoba must, by the very terms of your instructions, be subject to the sanction of a third party,' and, whatever approval either group of negotiators might get from their respective governments, 'that approval would be worthless without the sanction of the representatives of the minority.'[118] The calm sense of assurance in the Manitoba replies was in marked contrast to the lack of certainty and consistency in the proposals of the federal delegates.

The documents, however, only reflected the confusion of the federal government procedure throughout the episode. The commission had been sent under duress and without clear definition of its powers. With the appearance almost of an afterthought, an amendment to the order-in-council authorizing the delegation was issued on March 27, granting 'full power to effect an arrangement with the Government of Manitoba on such terms as shall be satisfactory to the said minority.'[119] Indications from the French cabinet ministers when the conference had first been rumoured were that the remedial bill would not be held up at all.[120] When the delegation did get under way, however, the commissioners felt they had been assured that action on the bill would be completely suspended during negotiations. According to their own complaint in their final submission to the Manitoba delegation, the federal representatives were 'as much surprised as yourselves to find that late on the night of the Friday sitting (March 27) the Bill was advanced a stage. We cannot say what considera-

117 *Ibid.*, Document B
118 *Ibid.*, Document D
119 *Ibid.*, Amendment to Order-in-Council, March 27, 1896
120 AASB, Caron to Langevin, March 12, 1896

tion forced the Government to the conclusion that this step was necessary.'[121]

Perhaps most unhappy and uncertain of all was the predicament into which the Smith mission forced Langevin. It was known to Desjardins at least that the St Boniface archbishop saw no future in the conference. Reflecting the outlook of his Ottawa correspondents, Langevin had told Bégin that it was only a sop for Sir Donald Smith; 'mais j'oubliais que ce vieillard a des millions, ou qu'il peut en trouver ... donc cette conférence serait pour le parti un moyen de se débarasser de nous,' he said bitterly.[122] Nonetheless, Langevin was, by the terms of the Commission, obliged to consider their proposals, while at the same time, for reasons of diplomacy, remaining very much in the background. How the feelings of the Manitoba majority had been whipped up was seen in the burning in effigy of the remedial law on the night of the Smith Commission's arrival in Winnipeg.[123] Langevin's mercurial temperament did incline him at least to suggest compromise in his reply to the federal delegates of March 28. 'Je ne veux pas paraître intransigeant,' he wrote to Bégin on the same day.[124] So much was Langevin's impulsiveness a cause of concern among those who believed that the fate, if not of the Manitoba schools, at least of their own political lives, was tied to the remedial bill, that LaRivière fired off a code telegram to the archbishop on March 30. 'You submit too easily,' the telegram ran, 'accept only complete independent schools. Delegation instructed to do nothing unsatisfactory to us.'[125] Despite these occasional inconsistencies, there was little chance that Langevin would in fact concede. Furthermore, however much he had to agree with the policy of such as LaRivière, Caron and Ouimet, Langevins's attitude, like that of *La Presse*, was more and more turning against the government and the policy which had imposed or at least allowed the Smith mission. Both to Fabre and Bégin, Langevin wrote a sorrowing letter which was an interesting commentary on the federal government and on his own action, then and later:

121 Canada, *Sessional Papers*, 1896, 11, no.39c, Document c. The 'stage' referred to was to go into committee of the whole for clause-by-clause discussion of the bill. No serious pressure was exerted by Tupper, however, until the commission returned and full debate resumed on April 6.
122 AAQ, Langevin to Bégin, March 16, 1896
123 *La Presse*, April 1, 1896
124 AAQ, Langevin to Bégin, March 28, 1896
125 AASB, LaRivière to Langevin, March 30, 1896

Evidemment le Gouvernement nous a mal servis; ses retards prolongés et fréquents nous fait [sic] autant de mal que l'opposition des Libéraux – Si, comme il y a lieu de le croire, la conférence ne nous donne point satisfaction et si le 'Remedial Act' ne passe pas à Ottawa, je suis d'avis (je tiens énormément à connaître votre opinion) que nous devons demeurer neutres durant les prochaines élections – Si nous n'avons point de loi, aujourd'hui, c'est la faute des Libéraux qui ont voté contre la loi rémédiatrice – mais c'est aussi celle du Gouvernement – Comment défendre ce dernier?[126]

A further complication with which Langevin had to deal was the continued interest, not to say interference, of the Aberdeens. Characteristically, Lady Aberdeen in particular was not content to relinquish the fate of conciliation to a single effort. The point of contact on this occasion was Archbishop Bégin, to whom Her Ladyship paid a special visit while in Quebec on March 25. She extracted Bégin's promise to write to Langevin 'pour addoucir les rouages et lui faire agréer une entente avec les délégués fédéraux à Winnipeg.' In Lady Aberdeen's view, the remedial bill would be 'd'une exécution difficile, quasi impossible.'[127] Bégin complied, although he added his own opinion that Langevin could concede only details and not the essence of separate schools in the current negotiations.[128] Langevin's reply to Bégin of March 30, sent on to Lady Aberdeen with the writer's consent, stated that 'je ferai l'impossible pour m'entendre avec ces messieurs,' and referred to the reply he had given to the federal commissioners' enquiry. Langevin pointed out, however, that he was not directly represented at the conference, that 'Messieurs les délégués ont offert aux Hon. Sifton et Cameron un arrangement qui est l'extrême limite des concessions,' and that he had little hope that a mutually satisfactory formula would be found. Somewhat turning the tables on Lady Aberdeen, Langevin concluded by expressing the hope that 'les anges de la paix useront de leur influence auprès de l'Hon. Laurier et des députés libéraux qui le suivent afin qu'ils pressent le Gouvernement de prouver son bon vouloir en faisant passer la loi rémédiatrice.'[129] Bégin sent the letter on to Lady Aberdeen, adding his own hope that the remedial law could be passed lest it become at the elections 'un terrible brandon de discorde.'[130] Lady Aber-

126 AAQ, Langevin to Bégin, March 28, 1896
127 Ibid., Lady Aberdeen to Bégin, March 25, 1896
128 PAC, Aberdeen Papers, Bégin to Lady Aberdeen, March 25, 1896
129 AAQ, Langevin to Bégin, March 30, 1896
130 PAC, Aberdeen Papers, Bégin to Lady Aberdeen, April 3, 1896

deen passed the correspondence on to Laurier, who in turn expressed the hope that, 'at a later day, your kind influence may prevail upon them to accept an honourable compromise, which would practically give them all that they want, without any violence to the express will of the majority.'[131] Again it may be wondered whether Laurier would have cheered a successful Winnipeg conference.

In any case, Langevin's sense of betrayal at the hands of the government for having sent the Smith mission was, if anything, deeper at the end than at the beginning. Despite claims that this 'last-ditch' effort proved the government was willing to try every expedient to avoid coercion, it was difficult to refute the charge made by L'Electeur and others that the government could not afford to have the conference succeed, since this would have proven Laurier's 'sunny ways' approach correct.[132] Langevin could only agree with such eastern correspondents as Archbishop Walsh of Toronto that the only hope remaining was that 'the Dominion Government will not hesitate to force through the Remedial Bill, and carry it out to a successful issue.'[133]

Throughout the ten-day delay in dealing with the remedial bill occasioned by the Smith mission, L'Electeur and La Minerve kept up an exchange which could be called a contest to find the greatest traitor to the French and Catholic cause – Laurier or the government. Certainly the cries of 'Bravo!' from such papers as the Winnipeg Tribune made Laurier an easy target for La Minerve; even the now-elderly former priest Chiniquy was featured in a pro-Laurier sermon in a Montreal Protestant church, and was added to La Minerve's litany of Laurier supporters.[134] On the other hand, Ouimet's parliamentary speech of March 24 outlining the offer to be made by the Smith mission, gave L'Electeur and, not far behind, La Presse, an open field for attack.[135] Ouimet's address, which even La-Rivière called 'tout à fait compromettant,'[136] was used repeatedly by

131 Ibid., Laurier to Lady Aberdeen, April 24, 1896
132 L'Electeur, March 30, 1896
133 AASB, Walsh to Langevin, April 1, 1896
134 La Minerve, March 25, 1896. Charles Pascal Chiniquy (1809–99) was a prominent temperance preacher from the diocese of Quebec, who left the Roman Catholic church in the 1850s to become one of the most vehement anti-Catholic crusaders of the late nineteenth century. His appearance, however token in his eighty-seventh year, in the 1896 struggle was a sign of the genuine danger Laurier was running of guilt by unsolicited association.
135 L'Electeur, March 25, 1896
136 AASB, LaRivière to Langevin, March 25, 1896

L'Electeur to illustrate that the Conservatives were playing for political advantage and not settlement throughout the Winnipeg conference. That such political gain may indeed have been achieved with English Protestant voters was illustrated by the reaction of the Toronto *Mail and Empire*, the *Montreal Gazette*, and, significantly, the *Winnipeg Tribune* and the Manitoba *Free Press*. Despite the *Globe*'s contention that government strength had been dissipated by the conference,[137] the *Tribune*'s Ottawa correspondent stated that 'it is generally felt that the Dominion Commissioners have succeeded in greatly strengthening the position of their Government by the moderation of their stand, while the offer of the provincial delegates was somewhat impracticable.'[138] At the very least it could be maintained that every effort short of a federal bill had been tried and, implicitly, might be tried again. On the other hand, if a more acceptable approach had been found for those who were desperately looking for a way to stay with the Conservatives rather than trust a settlement of the school question to Laurier, and in the background, J. Israel Tarte, French Conservative supporters, including Archbishop Langevin, had been driven further into a corner. They might complain bitterly about delay and betrayal on the part of the government, but they had nowhere else to go.

OBSTRUCTION AND WITHDRAWAL OF THE BILL

Betrayal or not, the delay was an inescapable fact. Evidence of the tension involved came with the death on March 30 of one of the most vocal proponents of the remedial bill, Colonel Amyot of Bellechasse. The cause of death was a stroke, brought on, according to LaRivière, by strain and return to an old habit of excess drink.[139] For the shape which the debate in the House meeting as a committee of the whole would assume, as well as for the degree to which federal Liberal policy was at the mercy of Clifford Sifton, no clearer indication could be found than the exchange of letters between Sifton and McCarthy following the departure of the federal com-

137 April 3 and 6, 1896
138 *Winnipeg Tribune*, April 4, 1896. K.M. McLaughlin points out that the lengths to which the Conservative government proved it was prepared to go through the Smith mission was an important factor in the revival of Conservative favour in the *Manitoba Free Press*, and ultimately in the province's swing to the Conservatives in the 1896 federal election (Unpublished manuscript, University of Toronto, 1968, Chapter II, pp.9–14).
139 AASB, LaRivière to Langevin, March 30, 1896. Colonel Amyot had always exhibited strong feelings of French-Canadian nationalism. He had broken with the Conservatives over the Riel affair, but returned to the party in 1892 in protest against Liberal trade policy.

missioners. Stating that he had been 'much assisted' in his tactics by a McCarthy letter which apparently had given assurances that the remedial bill could be stopped, Sifton called the conference 'entirely abortive' and felt that it would not be possible to 'throw the blame upon us.' Sifton assured McCarthy that 'the proceedings will show that the cause of failure of the Conference was not that we were unreasonable, but that the Dominion Government were tied to the Church.' Expressing confidence that additional Ontario Conservatives would now have to oppose the bill, Sifton left little doubt that the provincial Liberal objective at the Winnipeg Conference had been, like the Conservative, political advantage at Ottawa.[140] McCarthy's April 4 reply congratulated the Manitoba attorney general, and assured him that 'you may rely on it that the Bill will not pass.' McCarthy astutely pointed out that Tupper's efforts to blame the failure of the bill exclusively on the Liberals 'with a view of damaging Mr. Laurier and his French followers in the Province of Quebec,' was ignoring the 'enormous English vote which is just as much pleased with the failure of the Government to pass the Bill.' McCarthy added that unless Tupper placated the latter, his tactics would be 'a two-edged sword, the sharpest edge of which will be used to the destruction of his own followers.'[141] Subsequent letters between the two men commented on the success of the obstruction tactics and the usefulness of the Wade pamphlet, but turned more and more to Sifton's ultimately successful plan to have McCarthy run in Brandon and have the Liberal candidate withdraw at the strategic moment.[142] The collusion between Manitoba Liberals and McCarthyites at Ottawa continued to illustrate how party lines faded in the face of an issue as profoundly felt as the school question. In the immediate situation, it showed that French Liberal cries about an ineffective bill were unrealistic if not indeed hypocritical, and that Laurier's ultimate success would have to be built on elements at least as contradictory as those in the Conservative party.

Resumed under pressure on March 31 while the Winnipeg conference was still in progress, the debate in committee on the remedial bill entered the endurance stage on Monday, April 6. Determined to provide a brave if not successful performance, Tupper, with only brief intermissions for dinner, kept the House in session from Monday at 3:00 PM until Saturday midnight, and again from Monday, April 13, until 2:30 AM on Thursday,

---

140 PAC, Sifton Papers, Sifton to McCarthy, April 2, 1896
141 *Ibid.*, McCarthy to Sifton, April 4, 1896
142 *Ibid.*, Sifton to McCarthy, April 11, 1896; McCarthy to Sifton, April 16, 1896

April 16. Sixteen hundred columns of Hansard were added to the mountain already built up.[143] The account of the marathon by Lionel Groulx remains the classic: 'Moins un tournoi d'éloquence qu'une lutte athlétique où la victoire devait appartenir aux plus endurants, les équipes d'orateurs se relayèrent ... comme en deux tranchées d'ennemis, deux équipes de sentinelles et de tirailleurs.'[144]

Numerous reports survive of strange and unruly incidents during the record sitting. *La Presse* had a caustic comment on the prevalence of alcohol. 'Le seul homme qui ait profité de ce désordre,' the paper remarked, 'est le restaurateur de la chambre, qui a dû faire des brillantes affaires, si on en juge par le ton des discours.'[145] By April 15, Joseph Pope, for all his belief in the remedial bill, called the situation resulting from obstruction 'a howling farce, and the sooner Parliament is prorogued the better.'[146] With no more than 15 of the 112 clauses passed, in the early hours of the following morning Tupper finally withdrew the bill to consider supply, claiming, to no one's belief, that he wished to 'leave the question open to resume the Bill the moment supplies are obtained.'[147]

If the Winnipeg conference had been a charade, this 'debate' which followed in Ottawa was worse. Although it was clear that the federal commissioners to Winnipeg had offered a settlement well short of restoration of separate schools, once the debate on the bill was again heated up, this 'vacillation' was ignored as if it had never happened. On the Opposition side Laurier was content to let the initiative pass to the sworn enemies of all remedialism. Relying on the fact that the government was under the enormous tactical handicap of having to keep enough members available to avoid defeat by a snap motion, while the opposition needed only to furnish the lung power of a few men at a time, obstruction was the order of the day. The diary of the principal Liberal organiser of the filibuster, John Charlton, gave a good picture of the battle:

April 7: I spoke twice, as long each time as I could stand upon my feet.
April 8: The members are standing it well: we have four shifts, and each one has to hold the ground eight hours.
April 9: Our men are holding their ground easily.

143 Canada, House of Commons, *Debates*, 1896, pp.4919–6498
144 *L'Enseignement Français au Canada*, II, 112–13
145 April 13, 1896
146 *Journal*, April 15, 1896
147 Canada, House of Commons, *Debates*, 1896, p.6459

April 13: It is our intention to obstruct the Bill to death. It cannot possibly get through now. Our organization is perfect.

April 15: The Government side shows signs of caving in.

April 16: The Government withdrew the Remedial Bill this morning at 2:00 o'clock.[148]

Prominent among the shock troops gloated over by Charlton were the Conservatives who had voted against the second reading. Wallace, O'Brien, and several others took their turn with the McCarthyites and anti-remedialist Liberals, and did not hesitate to get involved in long and sometimes acrimonious wrangles with each other, as long as time was consumed. T.S. Sproule, one of the most emphatic of the Conservative obstructionists, was read out of the party by Tupper.[149] The *Globe* reported a near fist fight in the House between Sproule and Conservative stalwart Ferguson while a Liberal member was speaking.[150] On April 10 a potentially dangerous quarrel erupted over the charge by the Conservative Louis Belley that Laurier had stated during an 1895 visit to Chicoutimi that there were no Orangemen in the Liberal party.[151] Laurier succeeded in averting the charge, and, with his French Liberal followers, was by and large content to maintain a virtuous and safe abstention, to the high disgust of the Quebec Conservative papers, including *La Presse*.[152] *L'Electeur* was quick to accept the charge that McCarthy and Charlton had indeed taken the lead against the bill and to point out that even the Tory *Montreal Gazette* had cleared Laurier of charges of obstruction. *L'Electeur* continued enthusiastically to quote Tardivel's *La Vérité* on charges of government insincerity.[153] Evidently to prevent Tupper from gaining credit for having 'tombé en brave,' a remarkable number of hitherto disparate voices took up the theme of blaming the Conservative leader for the failure of the bill. J.W. Bengough's cartoon in the *Globe* showed Sir Charles as murderer of the bill plotting to fix the blame on Laurier.[154] More remarkable still, Clarke Wallace added his weight to accusations of treachery. Pursued by Edgar on the question of Tupper's sincerity, Wallace stated that he would not venture a positive opinion. Nonetheless, he said, 'the Government

148 John Charlton, *Diary*, April 7–16, 1896
149 Canada, House of Commons, *Debates*, 1896, p.4598
150 April 11, 1896
151 Canada, House of Commons, *Debates*, 1896, pp.5964–71
152 April 6, 1896
153 April 9 and 14, 1896
154 April 16, 1896

could have brought this question before the house at an early date, and having a large majority at their back, they could have passed this measure into law, notwithstanding the protests of those who are opposed to it.'[155]

French Conservative newspapers showed high disdain for the accusations being made against Tupper in particular. Although it continued to criticize the government on many points, *La Presse* quoted with approval *Le Courrier du Canada*'s satire on the case against the Conservative leader. At age 76, *Le Courrier* mimicked the critics, Tupper had risked his own health and had broken with former faithful supporters, 'et de tout cela, c'est une comédie! Au fond du cœur Sir Charles désire que la loi ne passe pas!!'[156]

There was in fact evidence that, at least from the time of the Winnipeg conference, the government was aware that the final spectacular effort to put the bill through would not be successful. As early as April 1, Ouimet's letter to Langevin admitted that there was little hope for the bill during the current session, and was already urging the need for episcopal support during the coming elections in order to increase the number of French Conservative members.[157] John Ewart arrived in Ottawa on Sunday, April 5, and wrote to Langevin that in his opinion the proposed plan of day and night sessions would not work. 'I am afraid that the Liberals see too clearly the advantage which they will have at the elections if the Bill is not passed,' Ewart reported.[158] At the end of the week Ewart's discouragement was even deeper. 'No one now believes that there is any chance of the Bill being passed,' he wrote. Furthermore, 'the general impression is that the Government will almost certainly be beaten at the coming elections. Their mismanagement of everything perhaps justly entitles them to defeat ... the members of the Government are almost helpless as against McCarthy and his friends and stagger along in the most foolish fashion.'[159]

Archbishop Langevin himself, in the wake of his disillusion over the Winnipeg conference, required more than a little convincing to swing back to any confidence in the government. Arriving in Ottawa on April 11, the prelate was finally persuaded to accept the bill without pressing for the Dupont Amendments.[160] Langevin's April 12 letter to Bégin showed that

155 Canada, House of Commons, *Debates*, 1896, p.6208
156 *La Presse*, April 10, 1896
157 AASB, Ouimet to Langevin, April 1, 1896
158 *Ibid.*, Ewart to Langevin, n.d., (probably April 6, 1896)
159 *Ibid.*, Ewart to Langevin, date unclear (probably April 13, 1896)
160 According to Groulx, Abbé L. Colin, superior of Le Grand Séminaire, Montreal, was the one who finally persuaded Langevin to send the belated telegram from Montreal (Groulx,

he had returned to placing all the blame on 'l'alliance monstrueuse des McCarthyites et des Libéraux.'[161] Not until Monday, April 13, however, did Langevin officially send an unconditional acceptance of the remedial bill to Tupper and Bowell:

In the name of the Catholic minority of Manitoba that I represent officially, I ask the house of Commons to pass the whole 'Remedial Act' as it is now amended. It will be satisfactory to the said Catholic minority that will consider it as a substantial, workable & final settlement of the school question according to the constitution.[162]

Langevin's burning of all bridges on the remedial bill was read by Tupper in the House on April 14, but the bridgehead had long since been lost.

Whatever his personal opinion on the chances of success and his motivation for undertaking the spectacular effort, Sir Charles Tupper kept up a brave front concerning the remedial bill until the very end of the marathon session. Not only was he unwavering in the House, but letters to Hugh John Macdonald and other supporters during the debate gave no sign of backing away from the bill as long as the measure was still alive.[163] Later letters indicated more accommodation and compromise,[164] and, as McCarthy pointedly observed to Sifton, Tupper in withdrawing the bill did not commit himself to reintroducing it if the government was returned.[165] Delays, pressure brought by Smith for the Winnipeg conference, and the ultimate failure of the bill, undoubtedly fitted the desires and political fortunes of many Conservatives, including several in the cabinet. On the other hand, however much it may be argued that Tupper's firmness was simply a tactical necessity during the debate, no compelling evidence exists to convict the Conservative leader of the deep duplicity charged by a wide spectrum of critics. One modern biographer concludes that the main goal of Tupper's political activity was to prepare the way for his son, and the means visible to him was the support of the Catholic vote and the hierarchy in particular. The same author's parallel conclusion that Tupper's struggle was 'dictated to a greater degree by political opportunism than by sym-

L'Enseignement Français au Canada, II, p. 115). The Dupont amendments concerned the financial provisions of clause 74.
161 AAQ, Langevin to Bégin, April 12, 1896
162 Canada, House of Commons, *Debates,* 1896, p.6282
163 PAC, Tupper Papers, Tupper to H.J. Macdonald, April 10, 1896; Tupper to C.R. Maclean, April 7, 1896; Tupper to A. Elliot, April 11, 1896
164 *Ibid.*, Tupper to H.J. Macdonald, April 15, 1896
165 PAC, Sifton Papers, McCarthy to Sifton, April 16, 1896

pathy for the plight of a small group of people who had been dispossessed of their rights.' seems to cast the question of motivation in too simplistic terms.[166] The fact that Laurier's position during this particular session and on the entire question of remedialism was, if anything, more equivocal than Tupper's, should not be lost from view. It might be fairer, if less flattering, to both leaders, to say that each was groping, without much light, to make the best of a bad situation over which he had little control. In any case, what was actually true may have been less important than what was thought to be true. Particularly significant was the assessment of blame by the clerically influential La Vérité toward the end of the long debate. Tardivel's newspaper called Laurier 'grandement blamable' for the motion for the six months' hoist. If, however, the government attempted to place all blame for the remedial bill's failure on the opposition, 'nous ne croyons pas que nos populations se laissent aveuglées ainsi.' As for the root of failure within the government, La Vérité felt that it was 'aveuglement chez les uns, duplicité chez les autres.' The newspaper's conclusion was an argument which would be hard for the Conservatives to overcome during the approaching campaign:

Au fond, il importe peu de savoir à quel mobile le gouvernement a obéi. Ce qui est manifeste, c'est que, soit de propos délibéré, soit par imprévoyance, il a rendu impossible l'adoption, pendant le parlement actuel, de la législation solennellement promise. C'est une faute énorme qui ne perd rien de son énormité si elle a été commise par incapacité.

Il n'est pas plus permis aux gouvernements d'être incapables que d'être malhonnêtes.[167]

166 Mackintosh, 'The Career of Sir Charles Tupper in Canada, 1864–1900' (thesis), p.436
167 La Vérité, April 11, 1896. The acknowledged influence of the ultramontane editor was reflected in Langevin's attempt, apparently unsuccessful, to get Bégin to pressure Tardivel to shift his attack: 'Il faut absolument que Tardivel cesse d'accuser le Gouvernement et qu'il jette carrément le blâme sur Laurier' (AAQ, Langevin to Bégin, April 22, 1896).

8

The Tupper cabinet,
the early campaign,
and the bishops' mandement

THE BRIEF TRIUMPH OF LES CASTORS

Little more than a week of the legal life of the seventh Parliament of Canada remained when the remedial bill was withdrawn. With much wrangling over a militia expenditure and the Shortis case, there was barely time to provide for current expenses of government. According to Lady Aberdeen's *Journal*, only pressure from her husband, through his aide Captain Sinclair, persuaded Laurier to let the bare essentials of the estimates go through on the promise of a summoning of Parliament immediately after the election.[1] On the evening of April 23, Parliament was dissolved, June 23 was set as the date for the general election and July 16 for the meeting of the new House. None of this proceeding brought any great surprise, no more than did Bowell's resignation, submitted April 27 without recommendation as to his successor. Despite a brief campaign in favour of Donald Smith, as well as his own and his wife's continued prejudice against the elder Tupper, Lord Aberdeen asked the Nova Scotian to form a government. 'Wonderful to say,' was Lady Aberdeen's sardonic comment, Sir Charles 'undertook the commission to form a ministry.'[2]

More than a little manoeuvering and bargaining preceded Tupper's formation of a cabinet. Two sets of negotiations were especially significant in relation to the school question. The men involved were Hugh John

1 Lady Aberdeen, *Journal*, April 21, 1896
2 *Ibid.*, April 27, 1896

Macdonald of Winnipeg, son of the late prime minister, and Adolphe Chapleau, lieutenant governor of Quebec. Reflecting the importance that he attached to securing Macdonald as his Western anchor, Tupper had approached Hugh John as early as the cabinet crisis in January. Macdonald demurred for reasons of health, personal distaste, and his own inability as a speaker, but focused on the school question as his chief stumbling block. He admitted that the Privy Council decision gave the federal government little alternative to 'remedial legislation of some sort' if Manitoba made no move. Yet he was afraid that he 'would not be willing to go nearly so far as the Dominion government would consider necessary.' During the provincial election campaign which had just been completed, Macdonald said that he had often taken the stand against Sifton. His reaction was that throughout the province 'the feeling amongst Conservatives as well as Reformers is so strong on this subject that if any attempt is made to restore separate schools it will be resisted even to the extent of rebellion.'[3] Further Macdonald letters, after he had been chosen chairman of the Central Manitoba Conservative Association, followed the same theme, with his February 28 note showing evident emotion because of Tupper's dissatisfaction with Hugh John's criticisms of the remedial bill.[4] By April 3, however, Macdonald showed himself much placated by a subsequent letter from Tupper, and was now willing to serve in the prospective cabinet 'if we can hit upon any means by which I can do so without sacrificing my self respect.' The Winnipeg lawyer again admitted the 'duty of the Dominion Govt.' to some kind of remedial legislation, yet did not believe it necessary to re-establish separate schools, 'which I consider a curse to the country.' Macdonald called the current remedial bill 'a most dangerous measure,' but stated that if it could be passed before the election, his personal dilemma would be greatly reduced. On the other hand, if Tupper were forced 'to go to the country on the Remedial Bill itself, I really do not see how I could become your colleague without throwing principle to the winds.' Still, an inviting door was left open. 'You are a much older and abler politician than I am,' Hugh John concluded.[5] Pursuing the same thought on April 7, Macdonald repeated that he could not endorse the provisions of the existing bill, and might have to resign if a further remedial bill were brought before the new

3 PAC, Tupper Papers, H.J. Macdonald to Tupper, January 17, 1896. Macdonald's professed anti-restoration stand which led to his resignation of a federal seat in 1893 must also be remembered. See above, p.39.
4 *Ibid.*, February 28, 1896
5 *Ibid.*, April 3, 1896

House. Nonetheless, 'if it will be enough for me to support the principle of Dominion interference, my services are at your disposal.'[6]

Tupper was not slow to take advantage of the opening. In a letter drafted in high optimism by Joseph Pope,[7] Tupper insisted that Macdonald's views on separate schools should be no obstacle to his entering the cabinet. He recalled that Hugh John's father had gone much further in compromise on the matter of separate schools than anything called for by the remedial bill and stressed the moderation of the position adopted by the Smith commission. Finally, Tupper left the way open for Macdonald to retire after the first session should he feel so obliged.[8] On April 15, with the remedial bill clearly doomed, Tupper was even more explicit in allowing for Macdonald's dissent. He assured Hugh John that admission of the principle of remedial action was sufficient, and stated that a new bill 'will not necessarily follow the same lines as the old one – in fact the question will be open for reconsideration as to the best policy to be pursued to accomplish the object we have in view with the least possible friction.' Tupper expressed confidence that the election could be won, and that they would be able 'to arrive at a satisfactory settlement with Manitoba without the matter coming before Parliament at all.' The prospective prime minister stated that he would hold himself bound 'in the strictest manner by the statement made in my appeal to you on this question,' and anticipated with relish how the *Globe*'s current assurance that Manitoba and the Northwest would go Liberal would be rudely shaken by Hugh John's decision.[9] An April 15 letter from Macdonald, which evidently crossed Tupper's letter of the same date, confirmed the agreement that Hugh John could 'support the Government on their general policy and maintain their action in introducing remedial legislation, and at the same time preserve my right to object to such clauses in the present act as seem to me unworkable and likely to do harm rather than good when the *New Bill* ... comes before Council for discussion.'[10] A letter of the same date from Sir Charles's son in Winnipeg, J. Stewart Tupper, reflected the same spirit which Hugh John had expressed; the younger Tupper was sure that being freed from the provisions of the existing bill would give Macdonald plenty of latitude.[11]

6 *Ibid.*, April 7, 1896
7 *Journal*, April 9, 1896
8 PAC, Tupper Papers, Tupper to Macdonald, April 10, 1896
9 *Ibid.*, April 15, 1896
10 PAC, Tupper Papers, Macdonald to Tupper, April 15, 1896
11 *Ibid.*, J.S. Tupper to Tupper, April 15, 1896

Tupper's success in convincing a key man who was known to be against the remedial bill was not paralleled in his attempts with the vital figure of the opposite persuasion. Ever since Sir Charles had returned from England in late 1895, it had been rumoured, even taken for granted, that any Tupper team which might be formed would include Adolphe Chapleau.[12] Although not enjoying the unreserved approval of all Roman Catholic authorities – 'ce n'est pas lui qui le [le parti] consolidera au point de vue doctrinal,' Langevin had written in February[13] – the lieutenant governor of Quebec was regarded as the one man who could rally the shaken forces of the Bleu contingent. Chapleau was on a visit to Atlantic City, New Jersey, when the crucial decision had to be made. According to a letter to his friend Dansereau in Montreal, Chapleau received Tupper's invitation on April 14 and sent his refusal, reinforced by a note to Lord Aberdeen, on April 18.[14] A second appeal from Tupper met with an even firmer rejection on April 29.[15] To Dansereau, Chapleau spelled out several solid and disturbing arguments for his refusal to join what he called 'la lutte du désespoir':

J'ai écrit cette nuit à Tupper, en réponse à une lettre de lui, du 14 courant, lui disant: mes déceptions de 1887 et de 1891, mon engagement écrit à Mgr. Taché, à la demande et avec l'approbation subséquente de Sir John A. Macdonald en 1891; les paroles de Thompson quand je le pressais de prendre action sur la question Manitoba Schools: 'If, between now and the next general elections, we cannot settle that question and render justice, we deserve to lose the seats we occupy around this table;' les défiances de l'électorat de Québec à l'endroit des promesses les plus accentuées du ministère; enfin les trahisons qui s'ourdissaient en ce moment, dans le sein même du cabinet (j'en ai la preuve); et j'ai conclu en disant que je ne pouvais lui donner de réponse, ni même des espérances.

Further significant points mentioned by Chapleau were the government's increasing dependence on railway money and the explicitly non-partisan stand taken by Bishop Emard in a recent pastoral letter; even the confidently predicted support of the church seemed to be fading away. 'Je n'ai ni le goût, ni la confiance nécessaire pour aller me jeter dans cette

12 See, for example, AASB, Bernier to Boucher de la Bruère, April 22, 1896
13 Groulx, 'Correspondance Langevin-Audet,' p.276; Langevin to Audet, February 14, 1896. Among other points, the fact that Chapleau's wife was Protestant had always stood against him in more 'orthodox' circles.
14 ACSM, Dansereau Collection, Chapleau to Dansereau, April 18, 1896 (excerpts from this collection kindly made available by Laurier LaPierre)
15 PAC, Tupper Papers, Chapleau to Tupper, April 29, 1896

galère,' Chapleau added on April 22. 'Si la mesure avait passé, je me serais cru engagé en honneur d'aller la soutenir devant l'électorat pour lui assurer une efficacité qui lui manquait ... Comme sont les choses, ma lettre à Mgr. Taché m'obligerait plutôt d'aller dénoncer le parti qui s'est laissé acculer et blaguer ainsi!' The degree of soul-searching which was involved in his refusal, however, was shown in the conclusion to Chapleau's letter: 'Je puis me faire illusion. Je suis si dégouté de la politique depuis 1891! Qu'en dis-tu franchement? ... Dois-je faire le sacrifice?' he asked Dansereau.[16] In the end, even Archbishop Langevin's last-minute appeal to Chapleau to add his strength to the forces needed to restore the Manitoba schools met with a respectful but firm refusal.[17]

Chapleau later admitted that he had indeed promised Tupper to join a projected cabinet, and that Tupper 'in the heat of temper aroused by this disappointment accused me of having deceived him.' But the passing of a remedial bill had been the condition of that promise, and this had not been fulfilled.[18] Was the failure of the remedial bill the real reason for Chapleau's refusal? The lieutenant governor's old hostility to the Castors must equally be remembered;[19] perhaps it was even more a case of fearing that he would not be able to control the Castor element in the Quebec delegation, or simply, in the later words of the *Ottawa Free Press*, that he was 'too wily an old fox to risk himself in the Tupper gang.'[20] Tupper believed that it was Tarte who persuaded Chapleau not to join the cabinet, perhaps by holding out the reward of a second term as lieutenant governor of Quebec should Laurier come to power.[21] It should also be remembered that Chapleau's

16 Dansereau Collection, Chapleau to Dansereau, April 18, 1896, April 22, 1896
17 AASB, Chapleau to Langevin, April 30, 1896. Bishop Laflèche's similar letter, which, in Chapleau's words, 'm'honore autant qu'elle m'a profondément touché,' did not reach the lieutenant governor until his return to Montreal when the crisis was over (AETR, Chapleau to Laflèche, May 6, 1896). Langevin asked Bégin as well to write to Chapleau; there is no record of whether or not Bégin complied with the request (AAQ, Langevin to Bégin, April 22, 1896).
18 PAC, Bowell Papers, Chapleau to Bowell, May 9, 1896. This was Chapleau's letter of tribute to Bowell on his retirement, and did not spare criticism of lingering treachery in the new government. 'The dark conspiracy which prevented you from passing that measure was alone sufficient to prevent me from joining the conspirators, even if my health had allowed me to enter the field,' Chapleau stated. The crisis with the lieutenant governor did not prevent Tupper from adding Chapleau's name to the list of those recommended for Queen's Honours.
19 Neatby and Saywell, 'Chapleau and the Conservative Party in Quebec,' p.21. See below, p.242, n22.
20 June 18, 1896
21 *Recollections of Sixty Years in Canada*, p.163

health was far from robust at this time. Yet it is difficult to conclude other than that Chapleau's main reason for not joining the cabinet was his suspicion, if not of Sir Charles personally, at least of the sincerity of the government as a whole on the school question.[22]

Failure to obtain Chapleau seems to have changed Tupper's approach, perhaps in exasperation, to the Quebec wing of his cabinet. There was no way to avoid the argument presented by Desjardins that speed as well as strength was vital in selecting the new team; 'every day of suspense is adding to our difficulties in Quebec,' the senator insisted.[23] While the newspapers carried on a spirited guessing game about the composition of the cabinet, the pendulum in Quebec swung back sharply to A.R. Angers. Although perhaps overly generous in estimating the degree of his own influence, Archbishop Langevin wrote to Bégin shortly after his last-minute telegram to Chapleau: 'Il est à peu près certain que Chapleau n'entrera dans le cabinet; j'ai cru devoir recommander à Sir Charles (qui a demandé mon avis) d'appeler Angers et de lui laisser choisir ses collègues – il m'a promis de la faire.'[24] Angers's message to Tupper on April 29 confirmed the impression that the Quebec field had been substantially given over to himself.[25] At first it had seemed likely that either Pelletier or Thomas Chapais would be included, but on April 30 the following wire to Ottawa drew the definitive lines: 'Mr. Taillon, Premier of Quebec, accepts. Messrs. Ives, Ross, Desjardins and myself complete the ticket. Going up with Taillon during the night.'[26]

Although the French Canadians had been granted a fourth member in

22 The argument presented by Clark, 'The Conservative Administrations' (thesis) pp.491–3, 540–5, which would substantially downgrade both the significance and the motives of Chapleau's refusal, overlooks the importance attached to the lieutenant governor's accession to the cabinet by Archbishop Langevin, Bishop Laflèche, and Father Lacombe, to say nothing of Tupper himself. Chapleau's recalcitrance may indeed have been ultimately inspired by disappointed ambition; such a conclusion, however, must discount heavily Chapleau's own statements during the episode. Clark's dismissal of the 'Castor' factor gives no notice to the elusive but important role of J.P. Tardivel and La Vérité. In any case, an unfavourable interpretation of Chapleau's motives does not negate the point that the Angers' faction, whether called 'Castor,' 'ultramontane,' or some variation thereof, was given great and, in the eyes of many, ruinous sway within the Quebec wing of the party during the campaign (See La Presse, June 24, 1896; PAC, Caron Papers, Routhier to Caron, May 1, 1896; AASB, Routhier to Langevin, June 28, 1896).
23 ACSM, Desjardins Collection, Desjardins to Tupper, April 29, 1896
24 AAQ, Langevin to Bégin, April 27, 1896
25 PAC, Tupper Papers, Angers to Tupper, April 29, 1896
26 Ibid., April 30, 1896. A good summary of the careers of the four French-Canadian members may be found in Neatby, Laurier and a Liberal Quebec, pp.75–7

the new cabinet, it was difficult to avoid the conclusion drawn by
L'Electeur that the Quebec wing represented anything but Tupper's first
choices. Charging that they were in fact closer to third and fourth rate in
Tupper's estimation, the Liberal newspaper dismissed them as 'un ministère de bouchestrous.'[27] The fact that three of the new men were senators,
and the fourth, Taillon, premier of Quebec with a rapidly decreasing
popularity, symbolized and heightened the forlorn political situation already faced by Tupper in French Canada. Chapleau's refusal to come in
had not only given Angers a free hand; it had removed any real political
power from the French wing in the cabinet. In fact, as Dansereau sardonic-
ally pointed out, the arrangement could be called 'le ticket anglais ... des
mangeurs de prêtres qui impose trois castors.'[28] However much their
influence had declined, Caron and Ouimet had represented the Bleu persuasion in the inner circles of government; Caron's loss in particular,
according to Cartwright's later estimate, was a serious blow.[29] The power
vacuum elevated the ultramontanes to a leadership backed by neither
popular support nor local party organization. Ironically, considering
Dansereau's remark, in place of normal political support the Conservatives
had to fall back on the church as the only solid base in sight.

Angers suffered from more than the disability of having occasioned the
winter cabinet crisis. There were those who had not forgotten or forgiven
his dismissal of Mercier when Angers had been lieutenant governor of
Quebec. And there was some irony in the fact that Tupper gave the
portfolios with the greatest scope for patronage, those of postmaster general and public works, to the two men least likely to exploit their political
possibilities, Taillon and Desjardins. The fact was that the strength expected by Tupper from the new Quebec team lay clearly in a direction other
than the pork barrel.

Even in advance of the election, however, there were grave doubts
about putting political eggs in an ecclesiastical basket. L.P. Pelletier and
Bishop Laflèche might exult over the cabinet composition as proof of
Tupper's sincerity on remedialism – 'la meilleure garantie que Sir Charles
pourrait donner de sa volonté à rendre justice,' Laflèche told Duhamel[30] –
but others were not so sure. Abbé Proulx wondered about the ability of the

27 *L'Electeur*, May 2, 5, 1896
28 PAC, Chapleau Papers, Dansereau to Chapleau, n.d., but certainly between April 24 and
   28. Within less than a week, Dansereau could have said 'quatre Castors.'
29 *Reminiscences*, p.354
30 AAO, Laflèche to Duhamel, April 28, 1896

new Quebec wing, however clerically approved, to convince the electorate. Pointing out that all the former Ontario ministers were back and had been joined by the known opponent of remedialism, Hugh John Macdonald, Proulx outlined the dilemma faced by the Quebec voter in a letter to his friend Abbé Payette. 'Personne ne doutera de la bonne volonté des nouveaux ministres,' Proulx wrote, 'ni de l'énergie de leur chef; mais on dira: "Angers a résigné, deux autres sont restés dans le cabinet, ni l'une ni l'autre chose n'a fait aboutir la loi rémédiatrice." ... l'histoire pourrait bien se répéter.'[31] More profound was the lament sent by Monsignor J.O. Routhier, vicar general of Ottawa and Bleu sympathizer, to his friend Adolphe Caron. Singling out the pervasive influence of Tardivel, Routhier wrote what might be called the funeral oration of 'l'école de Cartier' in the Conservative Party:

Je ne puis vous laisser partir sans vous dire que je regrette profondément votre départ. Je regrette la formation canadienne du ministère, car elle est pour moi le triomphe d'Angers. Je ne sais ce que l'on peut gagner à faire triompher l'homme de la Vérité. Enfin on a voulu Angers – que la Providence veille et nous épargne ses châtiments. Je savais déjà qu'Angers ne voulait pas être ministre avec Mm. Caron et Ouimet. C'était bien naturel que l'inspirateur de la Vérité ait de pareilles idées. J'espère que le ministère saura vous recompenser et qu'il vous donnera une position que l'on regardera comme une récompense de vos mérites passés.[32]

As had been the case since the crisis of the previous summer, the school question during the cabinet reformation episode impelled both wings of the Quebec Conservative party, Bleu and Castor, to be more unbending than ever. Once Chapleau had made his decision, Tupper's strategy seems to have been to concede to the most uncompromising remedialist elements in Quebec, while attempting to insulate them from the rest of the country. He could still hope that French Canada would be safe with church backing, and could concentrate his efforts in English Canada, with as little attention as possible given to the chieftains left in charge in Quebec.

TUPPER AND THE ANTI-REMEDIALISTS

The dilemma faced by Sir Charles in filling his cabinet was witnessed by the glaring contradictions of the requirements for the new team outlined by

31 ASST, Proulx Papers, Proulx to Payette, May 4, 1896
32 PAC, Caron Papers, Routhier to Caron, May 1, 1896

Quebec and Ontario newspapers. The ministerial papers in both provinces, such as *La Minerve* and the *Mail and Empire*, maintained an understandable reticence both before and after the new cabinet was announced on May 1. *La Minerve* was sorry to see Caron and Ouimet left out, but loyally admitted that 'les exigences de la situation ont déterminé un résultat différent ... Sir Charles Tupper ne pouvait faire un changement plus acceptable.'[33] The *Mail and Empire* expressed surprise that Chapleau had not returned; but it praised the new group of Quebec ministers, especially Taillon, on its record of honesty in provincial politics.[34] The Toronto paper made no mention at all of the attitude of the new Quebec members to the school question. *L'Electeur* took delight in featuring Tupper's difficulties first with Chapleau and then with the Angers wing. Pacaud's newspaper managed, however, to be persistently inaccurate in its predictions and observations during this episode, including a May 2 charge that the selection of Taillon was a direct Chapleau plot to rid Quebec of its ultramontane premier.[35]

Both the Toronto *Globe* and the independent Conservative *La Presse* were more to the point. From opposite points of view, they brought into harsh light the fact that, whatever he did in Quebec, Tupper would have to be at least as accommodating to the anti-remedialist feeling in Ontario. The day the remedial bill was withdrawn and the election date announced, the *Globe* pointedly explained not only why no new Ontario lieutenant had emerged for Tupper, but why there had not yet been a single nomination of a candidate, Conservative or Liberal, in any of the four Toronto ridings. 'What is everyone waiting for?' the *Globe* asked. 'That is easy of explanation. The Conservative Party is waiting for some Moses to tell it in which direction Canaan lies, and the Liberals are waiting courteously until Moses is discovered ... There is one central fact that stands out prominently ... no man can be elected in Toronto who is not pledged to the teeth against the coercionist policy of the government.'[36] When the name of the chief justice of Ontario, William Meredith, was strongly rumoured as a possible replacement for Bowell, the daily *Globe* ridiculed the prospect of such a backer of the 'Protestant horse' supporting a remedialist policy,[37] while the weekly *Globe* expressed the hope that the chief justice would not allow himself such a 'lamentable departure from the path of honour and political rectitude.'[38] At the same time, the daily *Globe* was insisting that the

33 May 2, 1896
34 May 2, 1896
35 *L'Electeur*, May 2, 1896

36 April 16, 1896
37 *Ibid.*, April 22, 1896
38 April 22, 1896

government should not be allowed to get away with what seemed to be its current design, to treat the remedial question 'as the prime political issue in Quebec and as removed from the field of politics in Ontario.'[39] When the composition of the new cabinet had been announced, the *Globe* felt that its suspicions had been confirmed. 'The surrender to Mr. Angers indicates that the Government intend to give the co-ercionists full swing ... from Montreal to Gaspé,' the newspaper stated, 'but outside of Quebec the Government candidates evince not the slightest intention to 'fight like lions,' as *L'Evénement* says, for that policy.' David Tisdale's accession to replace Bowell, while not as inflammatory as Meredith's would have been, brought little strength, and simple meant, in the *Globe*'s view, that 'the Bolters have had a free hand. They have got rid of Sir Mackenzie Bowell and of three of the ministers who stood by him in the crisis – Daly, Ouimet and Caron.'[40] *La Presse*, on the other hand, while it had been extremely concerned over the Meredith rumours – 'se confier de nouveau à ces fanatiques c'est se jeter dans le feu dans l'espoir de guérir une brûlure'[41] – appeared quite satisfied with the final result. The fourth French-Canadian portfolio was seen as 'une concession importante,' and the new ministry was called the strongest possible under the circumstances. *La Presse* rejected the suggestion of an eclipse of the school of Cartier, and a week later insisted that the Liberals had been taken aback by the strength of the new cabinet, and by its favourable acceptance in all sectors of the country. Replying in particular to the Montreal *Witness* which had shouted 'ultramontane' at the French wing of the new ministry, *La Presse* insisted that 'le principal grief que l'on reproche au premier ministre, c'est d'avoir appeler dans son conseil des hommes qui ont la réputation d'être bien vus du clergé catholique.'[42]

However, none of the Conservative apologists could hide the near contradictions which remained. Those who had been loyal to Bowell were indeed out or kept in minor offices, and all seven bolters of January except the strongest remedialist, C.H. Tupper, were back.[43] The prime minister's approach to Britton B. Osler, QC, of Toronto, to take the post of minister of

---

39 April 21, 1896   40 *Ibid.*, May 2, 1896
41 *La Presse*, April 27, 1896
42 *La Presse*, May 1, 2, 4, 9, 1896
43 It must be observed that C.H. Tupper took the non-cabinet role of solicitor general to avoid charges of a 'family compact,' and that the Bowell men who remained, Costigan, Ferguson, and Frank Smith, hardly merited advancement on ability. Costigan, however, did request promotion to the postmaster generalship, and was not accommodated (PAC, Costigan Papers, Costigan to Tupper, April 26, 1896).

justice apparently had hedged a good deal on remedialism.[44] Tupper's May 19 letter to Osler's brother, Edmund, on the latter's candidacy in West Toronto, clearly compromised further than he had done even with Hugh John Macdonald:

I think they should be quite satisfied with your pledge to vote against remedial legislation which is certainly all they have a right to demand. Any person who wishes to go further than that is simply playing the McCarthyite game to destroy the Government and bring Laurier into power. I quite agree with you in the hope that this vexed question should be disposed of by the local government; and after we have obtained a good majority, as I have no doubt we shall, I think there is every reason to suppose that the Manitoba Legislature will pass the necessary legislation to remove the question from the domain of Dominion politics.[45]

It is true that Tupper continued to impress on both protesting and encouraging Conservative supporters that the issue was 'not one of the creation of separate schools, but of maintaining the law and constitution of the country.'[46] Moreover, Tupper's electoral manifesto published before he departed for Winnipeg to open the campaign, was firm enough on the principle of remedialism to prompt a protest from the *Week* magazine against the prime minister's 'determination to go on.'[47] Once the campaign got underway, however, a great deal more duplicity of interpretation became evident. Not only did those such as Osler and Commons' Speaker Peter White reflect a phalanx of Conservative candidates in Ontario who came out squarely against remedialism in any form, but Tupper's opening of his campaign in Winnipeg with Hugh John Macdonald, left more than a little scope for doubt on the government's ultimate intentions. At Selkirk in a preliminary meeting, Tupper was quoted as saying that he 'did not believe that the necessity for federal legislation would ever arise.'[48] The *Mail and Empire*'s report from Winnipeg on Tupper's arrival told of a 'magnificent ovation ... the death knell of Mr. Martin ... the school question was a dead issue tonight. It was forgotten, as it will be forgotten on polling day ...

44 For this contention, see Willison, *Reminiscences*, pp.251ff. The charge that Tupper actually offered to withdraw all promise of a Remedial Bill was hotly disputed by C.H. Tupper and restated with equal firmness by Willison in 1919. See *The Canadian Magazine*, March, 1919, and the Toronto *Globe*, April 23, 24, 1919.
45 PAC, Tupper Papers, Tupper to E.B. Osler, May 19, 1896
46 *Ibid.*, Tupper to Rev. J. Coffey, New York, April 25, 1896
47 (Toronto), May 8, 1896
48 *Manitoba Free Press*, May 8, 1896

Whatever Conservatives might have been dissatisfied with Sir Charles Tupper's course on remedial legislation have wheeled into line.'[49] The resolutions of the Winnipeg Conservative convention of the following day concentrated on economic development and did not even mention the question of remedialism. In his speech of May 8, Hugh John Macdonald insisted that the provincial government should settle the question, and stressed that Greenway would certainly concede more to Laurier than to Tupper. Macdonald stated that, if elected, he would 'endeavour to give the smallest amount of relief necessary to meet the demands of justice.'[50] Tupper left his remarks on the school question very much to the end of his speech which followed Hugh John's. He said that Macdonald's words made it almost unnecessary for anything to be added. Nonetheless, Tupper went through the 'bargain' idea of confederation again, stressing the compromises made by Brown, Mackenzie, and Galt toward separate schools. The *Mail and Empire* report briefly mentioned Tupper's 'dwelling on the constitutional aspects of the case' and on the heavy rainstorm which 'drowned his voice.'[51] John Costigan's later reflections on the campaign mentioned Tupper's Winnipeg utterances as evidence of his bad faith on remedial legislation.[52] The reports of Vicar General Allard and Senator Bernier, however, were much more complimentary. Allard wrote Langevin that he and Bernier had attended the Winnipeg rally, and that Tupper's statements 'ne laissent rien à désirer, à mon humble avis.'[53] Bernier was not as satisfied with Hugh John Macdonald's statement, but added that it was, after all, Tupper who counted.[54] Like the *Mail and Empire*, both the *Winnipeg Tribune* and *Manitoba Free Press* put quite a different interpretation on the net significance of the Tupper-Macdonald rally, but *Le Manitoba* and *La Presse* were, with Bernier and Allard, satisfied with the official stand taken on remedialism.[55]

These French commentators on Tupper's campaign opening chose to overlook the fact that the prime minister's statement was sufficiently vague

---

49 May 8, 1896
50 *Ibid.*, May 9, 1896. The *Free Press* version of this phrase was 'some remedy ... as mild as it possibly can be to meet the requirements of the case' (*Manitoba Free Press*, May 9, 1896).
51 May 9, 1896; again the *Free Press* report gave greater emphasis to Tupper's insistence on some redress for the Catholics, if necessary through federal intervention, but generally subordinated the school question to Tupper's stress on economic development (*Manitoba Free Press*, May 9, 1896).
52 PAC, Costigan Papers, Costigan to ?, n.d.
53 AASB, Allard to Langevin, May 11, 1896
54 *Ibid.*, Bernier to Langevin, n.d.
55 *La Presse*, May 9, 1896 and *Le Manitoba*, quoted by *La Presse*, May 26, 1896

to allow each side of the remedialist controversy to take a favourable interpretation. Furthermore, they ignored an aspect of the Winnipeg speech which became an effective plea in Manitoba, but a highly vulnerable one in Quebec. It had already been widely reported that Laurier's campaign opening in Quebec had insisted that he was prepared to pass a stronger remedial bill than Tupper's.[56] Tupper asked if anyone could logically justify himself 'if he oppressed a feeble minority and that for the purpose of bringing into power a Roman Catholic French Premier, who declares he will do more.' Should voters abandon Tupper, he asked, for a man who was so unprincipled as to have opposed a moderate bill only to propose an extreme one?[57] Nonetheless, Tupper had raised the question of Laurier's race and religion, and the Liberal leader at Ste Cunegonde on May 11 accused the prime minister of appealing to 'the fanaticism of electors.'[58] The political gravity of Tupper's mistake in raising the issue became particularly evident when Laurier was able to turn the charge against the prime minister before English-speaking audiences. 'When Sir Charles Tupper dares to say that I should not be intrusted with power because I am French and a Catholic,' Laurier declared at Westmount, 'I hurl back the words in his face, as his greatest condemnation. It is not to my countrymen of French origin that I appeal, but it is to my fellow countrymen of British origin, because you belong to the race that has always been the champion of liberty.'[59]

LAURIER'S EARLY GAINS: MOWAT AND ST ROCH

Whatever the duplicity of the Tupper campaign, Laurier and the Liberal side could hardly be credited with greater rectitude or unequivocal expression. On the one hand, the campaign of Liberal candidates such as John

---

56 The *Manitoba Free Press* continued to give much emphasis to this report, thus attempting to negate the idea in Manitoba Protestant minds that they would be safer with Laurier than with Tupper. On May 16 the *Free Press* printed a full translation of *L'Electeur*'s version of Laurier's St Roch address. See below, p.254.

57 *Manitoba Free Press*, May 9, 1896

58 Toronto *Globe*, May 12, 1896

59 *Ottawa Free Press*, May 19, 1896. Paralleling the prominence given by the *Manitoba Free Press* to Laurier's St Roch address, *L'Electeur* featured Tupper's Winnipeg address again and again to convince Quebec voters that their compatriots were not safe with Tupper (*L'Electeur*, May 13, 14, 15, 16 and 18, 1896). *La Presse*, on the other hand, felt that Tupper's explanation of his Winnipeg statement, especially that given in the face of Liberal hecklers in Montreal, was quite acceptable from the French viewpoint (*La Presse*, May 16, 1896).

Charlton matched McCarthy and the anti-remedialist Conservatives in vehemence. Charlton's diary recorded deals and attempted deals, involving remedialism and other factors, with both Conservatives and Patrons.[60] Through Sifton, collusion continued between McCarthy and the Manitoba Liberals.[61] On the other hand, at the very time McCarthy was taking over the initiative in obstructing the remedial bill, Laurier let it be known that he was actively seeking the support of Sir Oliver Mowat and, if possible, his agreement to enter a prospective cabinet.[62] At first, as Laurier told his young Gatineau lieutenant, Henri Bourassa, there was grave doubt that the Ontario leader would come in because of age and ill health. Nonetheless, Laurier stated, 'j'ai la promesse de son concours actif pour la règlement de la question des écoles, dans le cas où nous serions appelés à la régler.'[63] Soon, however, a new intermediary was brought into the picture. This was none other than the man who was at once Archbishop Langevin's right hand man in legal matters and Mowat's nephew, John Ewart. Ewart's preliminary report to Laurier from Toronto was not very hopeful. The conditions which Ewart suggested as necessary to sway Sir Oliver included the rather drastic one of 'the offer of the Premiership' and 'the inclusion of such of his present colleagues as he might think it advisable to carry with him.'[64] Laurier's April 20 reply was equally drastic, if perhaps a little questionable as to its ultimate sincerity. 'The interest which I take in the Manitoba school question,' he wrote Ewart, 'and my desire to see it settled in a way that will give satisfaction to the minority, are so great that it would be a pleasure for me to make any sacrifice, in order to induce Sir Oliver to enter federal politics. 1) the question of Premiership can be easily settled. I would most gladly make way for Sir Oliver.' Laurier mentioned financial arrangements for a life annuity for Mowat which could be made through George Cox and S.H. Janes of Toronto. The one objection which Laurier found in Ewart's suggestions concerned the inclusion of Mowat's

60 *Diary*, April 28, May 4, 5, 15, June 3, 8, 9, 1896
61 PAC, Sifton Papers, McCarthy to Sifton, April 29, May 7 and 9, 1896. It is significant to note that McCarthy believed Tupper's Winnipeg speech was a serious threat both to himself and to the Liberals. 'He is making a bid to purchase Manitoba as he bought Nova Scotia some time ago at the public expense, and it is quite evident that we will have all we can do to hold our own in the Prairie Provinces,' McCarthy told Sifton (McCarthy to Sifton, May 9, 1896).
62 *La Presse*, April 6, 1896
63 PAC, Bourassa Papers, Laurier to Bourassa, April 18, 1896
64 PAC, Laurier Papers, Ewart to Laurier, April 17, 1896

colleagues.[65] Ewart's reply, this time from Winnipeg, was quite optimistic, stressing that Laurier's 'self-sacrifice w. refer. to the P. ship will do much to move Sir O.M. to meet your views.' In a final note, Ewart added that he had learned that Hugh John Macdonald would run in Winnipeg opposing Martin. Showing to which side he was now definitely leaning, Ewart added that he was 'afraid' that Martin would win, since 'Martin will be much more trouble to you than Mcd.'[66]

Laurier's powers of persuasion were successful, and on May 4 the announcement was made of Sir Oliver's agreement to join the federal Liberals.[67] It would be difficult to over-emphasize the importance to the Liberal cause of the acquisition of Mowat. Both the Ontario and Quebec Liberal newspapers repeatedly featured full-page portraits of Laurier and Mowat, or the two together. The Ontario Liberal defender of separate-school rights was a great comfort to many Catholic Liberal waverers in the English-speaking provinces. John Costigan, who was later to accuse the Conservatives of treachery on the school question, saw such a serious threat in Mowat's move that he felt obliged to present a long and careful anti-Mowat brief to Archbishop Walsh. While admitting the Ontario premier's service to Catholic schools in Ontario, Costigan insisted that Mowat's joining Laurier did not change Liberal anti-remedialism. He hoped, without making a specific request of Walsh, that Mowat would not be allowed to pre-empt the Ontario Catholic vote for the Liberals.[68] Approaching the same phenomenon from precisely the opposite direction, D'Alton McCarthy urged audiences to vote McCarthyite, since he felt that Mowat's accession almost guaranteed Laurier's getting a majority and restoring French and Catholic schools to Manitoba.[69] It is interesting to note, however, that Mowat, whether out of greater wisdom or less devotion than his counterpart Taillon of Quebec, did not resign the Ontario premiership until after the election, and did not contest a Commons seat.

Even John Charlton recorded his pleasure at Mowat's decision, although for reasons obviously far different from the Roman Catholic.[70]

65 Ibid., Laurier to Ewart, April 20, 1896. Laurier's offer to step down was, in view of Mowat's health and his own activity, quite clearly 'pro forma.' But it underlined the importance attached to getting Mowat to enter the campaign.
66 Ibid., Ewart to Laurier, April 22, 1896
67 L'Electeur, May 5, 1896; Toronto Globe, May 5, 1896
68 PAC, Costigan Papers, Costigan to Walsh, May 11, 1896
69 Toronto Globe, Toronto Star, May 5, 1896
70 Diary, May 9, 1896

Paralleled after the general election by the agreements of Fielding of Nova Scotia and Blair of New Brunswick to join the Liberal team, provincial rightists could hardly have been given a more reassuring symbol. Furthermore, manufacturing and financial interests would have much less reason to fear a radical change in economic policy with Mowat to balance Cartwright in Ontario.[71]

It was in Quebec, however, that Mowat proved of greatest strength to the Liberal cause. Laurier mentioned him constantly in connection with promises to settle the school question.[72] L'Electeur held Mowat up almost to the exclusion of all others as the sure proof that the cause of the Catholic minority and the Manitoba schools would be in safe hands with the Liberals.[73] A huge cartoon in L'Electeur's May 8 edition showed Laurier and Mowat trampling underfoot dwarf-like figures of the Conservative cabinet; the caption read 'Les pygmées [les ministres] se sauvent devant les géants.' The same issue reprinted a report of La Patrie telling of the reply of a rural curé in the diocese of Montreal to several worried farmers who wished to vote Liberal and had come to consult him. 'Votez selon les dictées de votre conscience, et vous ne voterez jamais mal,' the curé was quoted as saying. He added, and the paper emphasized: 'Vous ne trahirez ni votre race ni votre foi en votant pour des hommes comme Laurier et Mowat.'[74]

Probably Laurier's most important meeting preceding the announcement of Mowat's decision was that held at Sohmer Park in Montreal on Friday, April 24, the day after the dissolution of Parliament. Laurier's speech balanced fairly equally the familiar charges of failures of the Conservative government toward the Manitoba minority with promises of investigation and conciliation, the latter somewhat for the benefit of co-speakers L.H. Davies, of Prince Edward Island, and Richard Harcourt, representing the Ontario government. La Presse found Laurier's statements still quite unsatisfactory and fervently wished that the Liberal leader

---

71 Mowat's words on this subject to Laurier were terse but eloquent: '... Many Conservative and other manufacturers ... are disposed, perhaps anxious, to vote with us this time ...
They are content with what I said on the subject in my published letter to you, and if they had something to the same effect from you it would remove all doubt and hesitation' (PAC, Laurier Papers, Mowat to Laurier, May 22, 1896). Tarte provided similar assurances for protectionists in Quebec (Rumilly, Histoire, VIII, pp.56–7).
72 L'Electeur, May 7, 8, 1896
73 Ibid., May 5, 6, 1896
74 Ibid., May 8, 1896

'nous présentera bientôt un vrai programme du gouvernement.'[75] Much more positive statements began coming when Laurier's campaign officially got underway with a rally of great enthusiasm in Quebec City on May 6. Even before leaving the train station, the Liberal mayor of the city, S.N. Parent, sounded the keynote for the image to be promoted of the Liberals and their leader in Quebec. According to *L'Electeur*, Parent accused the Conservatives of attempting to use the church as a windbreak in Quebec, 'pendant que l'autre fraction, dans les provinces protestantes, fulmine contre les évêques et la religion catholique, et proclame partout que jamais il ne sera question d'une pareille loi à Ottawa tant que les conservateurs seront au pouvoir.' Parent claimed Liberal unity in face of these divisions, and concluded that the Liberal party was 'uni sur les questions de tarif comme sur toutes les autres, unanime à dire que pleine et entière justice doit être rendue à la minorité catholique de Manitoba.' The parade that followed through the streets to the Academy of Music was described by *L'Electeur* as 'le plus imposant qui se soit vu à Québec.'[76] *La Presse* was almost as glowing as *L'Electeur* in its description of the welcome accorded Laurier and in its approval of Laurier's statement on the school question. Laurier paid a good deal of attention to the presence of G.W. Ross, the Ontario minister of education, and again pointed to the significance of Mowat's agreement to join a potential Liberal cabinet. 'Le premier homme,' Laurier proclaimed, 'qui entrera dans l'administration Libérale, dans le gouvernement Laurier, sera Sir Oliver Mowat. Lorsque je vois un homme comme M. Mowat, qui a donné vingt-trois ans de ses travaux à la province d'Ontario, entrer dans un gouvernement dont je serai le chef, pour régler cette grande question des écoles, je sens qu'il rendra au peuple un service qui ne saurait qu'être apprécié à une trop grande valeur.' Laurier's conclusion on his Manitoba policy was that 'justice sera rendue à la minorité du Manitoba, sans préjudice à la majorité.'[77]

It was on the following day, however, at La Salle Jacques Cartier in the St Roch district of his own riding of Quebec East, that Laurier received his most tumultuous reception and made his most emphatic statement on the school question. 'On se demande s'il y a encore des conservateurs à Québec,' declared *L'Electeur* in its report. Henri Joly de Lotbinière was the principal speaker to precede Laurier and proclaimed that the Manitoba

75 *La Presse*, April 25, 1896
76 May 7, 1896
77 *La Presse*, May 7, 1896

minority had the right to demand not 'une demie justice comme l'on a prétendu vouloir lui donner, mais une justice complète, pleine et entière.' Joly concluded that, as a Protestant, he fervently hoped 'que la minorité de Manitoba soit traité avec la liberalité avec laquelle, nous avons été traités parmi vous.'[78]

Laurier's response to Joly's gallantry was to insist that if ever the rights and privileges of the Protestant minority in Quebec were attacked, he and the voters from his own district would be the first to defend them. Then the Liberal leader moved to the real, not hypothetical case:

Si le peuple du Canada me porte au pouvoir comme j'en ai la conviction, je réglerai cette question à la satisfaction de toutes les parties intéressées. J'aurai avec moi dans mon gouvernement Sir Oliver Mowat qui a toujours été dans Ontario, au péril de sa propre popularité le champion de la minorité catholique et des écoles séparées. Je le mettrai à la tête d'une commission où tous les intérêts en jeu seront représentés, et, je vous affirme que je réussirai à satisfaire ceux qui souffrent dans le moment. Est-ce que le seul nom vénéré de M. Mowat n'est pas une garantie du succès de ce projet?

Et puis, en fin de compte, si la concilation ne réussit point, j'aurai à exercer ce recours constitutionnel que fournit la loi, recours que j'exercerai complet et entier.[79]

Later commentaries on the campaign cast some doubt on the authenticity of this final sentence in Laurier's St Roch statement,[80] but the Liberal leader's own comment on the matter to Willison did not deny the words, protesting only that they were being quoted out of context by the Tory press.[81] At all events, it was clear even in the early campaign that, in sharp contrast to the picture the Conservatives were able to present of the English wing of the cabinet, the Liberals in Quebec presented Mowat as a

---

78 *L'Electeur*, May 8, 1896
79 *Ibid.*, May 8, 1896
80 Groulx's doubts on the passage are serious: 'Promesse claire, décisive, si elle avait quelque chance d'authenticité. Par malheur, ainsi veut la tradition, la finale de l'orateur ne serait pas de lui; elle serait l'œuvre d'un ami politique qui, estimant trop réticentes les promesses de son chef, y aurait ajouté cette valable ponctuation' (Groulx, *L'Enseignement Français au Canada*, II, p.119). Groulx, however, gives no authority for 'la tradition' except Mowat's 1897 statement that Laurier had always held for almost any negotiated compromise as preferable to federal legislation. The St Roch promise was clearly and repeatedly accepted as authentic by Quebec Liberals during the campaign.
81 PAC, Willison Papers, Laurier to Willison, May 16, 1896

champion of separate schools. Mowat's accession seems to have mellowed even J.P. Tardivel and *La Vérité* toward Laurier. On May 2 the ultramontane paper had severely criticized Laurier because of Joseph Martin's support, but on May 8, *L'Electeur* reported a very friendly encounter between Laurier and Tardivel. In any case, at no time did *La Vérité* relax its suspicion of treachery among the Conservatives.

PREPARING THE MANDEMENT

Without doubt, the feature of the election campaign of 1896 which drew the greatest attention, then and later, was the episcopal mandement published in all the dioceses of Quebec on May 17. The period preceding the drafting of the mandement on May 6 witnessed a burst of ecclesiastical activity unmatched in volume and anxiety throughout the whole episode of the school question. Several factors were clearly at work. First of all, from the beginning of discussion on a possible mandement, the division of the bishops into two camps of strongly differing outlooks was unmistakeable. With the background of tension over the proposed letter at the time of the remedial bill debate in March, both those who favoured strong and unequivocal episcopal action and those who cautioned moderation had worked out further arguments and been subjected to new influences. Not surprisingly, central among the new pressures favouring a strong ecclesiastical thrust was that applied by Conservative politicians. Whereas in March they had been apprehensive about the danger of an episcopal letter to the deputies, in April political lives as well as minority rights were hanging in the balance. Archbishop Langevin was the primary target of the Conservative campaign to have the bishops bring direct pressure on the voters. From his temporary neutrality and even bitterness against the government during the Smith mission, Langevin had been brought to the point of sending the telegram read by Tupper in Parliament on 14 April and, once the remedial bill was forced into retirement, to a far harder line explicitly favouring the Conservatives. Ouimet began the process as early as April 1 by insisting that the real weakness of the campaign for the remedial bill was a basic one of numbers – 'la conséquence du petit nombre de députés conservateurs français en chambre.' Thus, Ouimet concluded, 'le règlement de la question dépend entièrement de l'attitude et du vote des catholiques ... espécialement dans Québec.'[82] On April 13 (although on that very day it still required pressure to get Langevin to send his telegram of unreserved

82 AASB, Ouimet to Langevin, April 1, 1896

approval to Tupper), L.P. Pelletier, provincial secretary of the Quebec government, did not hesitate to ask for Langevin's direct influence at crucial electoral points:

Le danger du moment est que le peuple fasse fausse route aux prochaines élections. Pour conjurer ce danger, n'est-il pas urgent qu'à l'exemple du passé, dans cet imbroglio qui intéresse à un si haut point la religion et la nationalité même, le clergé dirige le peuple? A tout événement, dans les comtés maintenant unis de Laprairie et Napierville, il est certainement important que les Pasteurs dirigent. Je suis bien heureux que vous allez de ce coté.[83]

Bishop Laflèche added his voice pressing Langevin to request an explicit episcopal statement to the electorate. 'Il faut donc,' Laflèche wrote Langevin, 'prendre nos mesures pour défendre cette cause sacrée et nationale devant l'électorat de la puissance comme nous l'avons fait devant le gouvernement fédéral.'[84]

One of the most important influences encouraging the bishops to issue a mandement was a letter from Rome received by Bishop Labrecque. Quickly circulated to the other Quebec bishops, the letter contained replies in classic Roman Curia style to three questions submitted by the Chicoutimi prelate after the Charlevoix by-election. The first reply indicated that a Catholic deputy could not with a clear conscience vote against a law accepted by the bishops for the restoration of Catholic school rights ('tuta conscientia votum suum dare contra legem ab Episcopis acceptatam'). The second reply stated that such explicit rebellion would constitute a serious sin, and the third repeated the same injunction against a voter who would with full knowledge ('scienter') vote for such a deputy. A short commentary at the end of the questions, however, suggested that private exhortations might be more effective and more prudent than statements from the pulpit.[85] Labrecque saw these replies as full approval of his action in the Charlevoix election; on April 13 Bégin interpreted them in a similar severe manner to Langevin.[86] As further letters from Rome pointed out, however, the replies in this letter tended to be read as answering more than the questions had asked, as well as overshadowing the cautions in the commentary.[87] It should be noted, too, that Labrecque's phrasing of the

83 *Ibid.*, Pelletier to Langevin, April 13, 1896
84 AETR, Laflèche to Langevin, April 14, 1896
85 AAQ, Ledochowski to Labrecque, March 13, 1896
86 AASB, Bégin to Langevin, March 13, 1896
87 See below, pp.270–1.

questions inaccurately implied an official and explicit acceptance of the actual remedial bill by all the bishops.

The current of episcopal thought was far from moving in one direction only. Following the negative position he had taken on the question of a letter to the members of parliament, Bishop Emard continued throughout March and April to express grave misgivings about the remedial bill and anything resembling joint episcopal approval for it. The Valleyfield bishop let several of his colleagues know that he was preparing a pastoral letter on elections for his own people.[88] Entitled 'Le Devoir Electoral,' it began with a strong condemnation of electoral corruption by money, liquor, or any other means. Its culmination was a clear statement of unwillingness to dictate the vote or to have candidates make political capital of episcopal, or at least of Emard's, statements:

Désirant observer dans le cours de la présente Lettre une neutralité complète, et remettant chacun de vous aux dictées de sa conscience, nous déclarons ne vouloir, ni par voie de conseils, comme notre qualité civile nous y autorise, ni par voie de direction épiscopale, influencer votre vote en faveur d'aucun parti ou d'aucun homme. Nous nous élevons à la région supérieure des principes généraux, vous abandonnant le soin de les appliquer à votre meilleur escient dans toutes les élections à venir, comme de bons citoyens et de bons chrétiens.

Donc, une fois pour toutes, nous répudions, dès maintenant, toute interprétation que l'on prétendait faire de nos paroles en faveur ou à l'encontre d'un parti ou d'un candidat quel qu'il puisse être. Nous espérons d'ailleurs employer un langage assez clair pour qu'aucune ambiguité ne soit possible, et que nos avis soient acceptés de tous avec empressement, et suivis avec la même docilité dans le cours de la lutte, et la distribution finale des suffrages.

Le vote, N.T.C.F., est loin d'être une chose quelconque ou banale. C'est un acte officiel et raisonné par lequel un citoyen, ayant à cet effet les qualités légales voulues, désigne un de ses concitoyens et le choisit pour gérer les intérêts généraux de la nation.[89]

So impressive was Emard's statement that Laurier hastened to insist with Pacaud that the letter be published in L'Electeur 'sans commentaire aucun, et simplement dire que tu attires l'attention de tes lecteurs sur cette lettre dont l'importance ne devra échapper à personne.'[90] It was clear from

---

88 AAQ, Emard to Bégin, March 9, 1896
89 AEV, 'Le Devoir Electoral,' April 12, 1896
90 PAC, Pacaud Papers, Laurier to Pacaud, April 13, 1896

their correspondence that Fabre had approved Emard's letter before publication, although the Montreal archbishop preferred silence to a statement in either direction. Fabre's attitude, like Emard's, continued to be shaped by his grave misgivings about the long-range effects of the remedial bill. Writing to Bishop Moreau in reply to the latter's suggestion of an official episcopal statement to support the government during the final struggle for the bill, Fabre showed the kind of dissent which would gravely weaken Conservative electoral campaign claims about clerical unanimity:

Quant à Manitoba, je ne crois pas qu'il soit prudent de faire une démarche commune vis-à-vis les membres du ministère. Ce bill accepté par Mgr. Langevin serait un désastre s'il nous était appliqué. Ne faisons rien qui puisse nous compromettre dans ce sens. Je regrette beaucoup que Mgr. de St. Boniface ait pris sur lui de dire que nous l'approuvions tous. Puisque le Bill lui convenait, nous n'avions pas d'objections, voilà tout. La démarche que suggère Votre Grandeur dirait beacoup plus, et je ne serais pas seul à refuser de signer.[91]

It was not that Fabre and Emard were being left free of pressure from politicians. Abbé Dauth, the editor of *La Semaine Religieuse* of Montreal, wrote Emard to inform him that A.R. Angers had just visited the archbishop's palace in Montreal. The ultramontane leader had insisted that if the bishops did issue a public statement, it should be 'une direction de nature à ne laisser aucun équivoque dans l'esprit des électeurs.' In Angers' view, a document which would require only a general desire to work for justice for the Manitoba minority would be inadequate if not harmful; not only the goal but the means to achieve the goal had to be clearly indicated. This meant as a prime requirement, Angers had said, that the bishops had to approve 'd'une façon bien claire la loi rémédiatrice telle que présentée à la dernière session.' Hinting at Emard's own pastoral letter, Dauth repeated Angers' insistence that any episcopal statement should be 'très catégorique et très tranché, car, en restant en delà de la position déjà prise par quelques-uns, elle ne ferait qu'affaiblir la situation présente du gouvernement.' So much did Angers fear an equivocal official statement, Dauth concluded, that he actually preferred the idea of 'une direction privé et confidentielle donnée par chaque ordinaire aux curés de son diocèse et communiquée par ceux-ci aux paroissiens sur la bonne volonté desquels ils pourront compter.'[92] That Emard was not particularly impressed by these and the arguments of other Conservative politicians was shown in his

91 AAM, Fabre to Moreau, April 2, 1896
92 AEV, Dauth to Emard, n.d. (late April, 1896)

correspondence with Archbishop Fabre. 'Je suis intimement persuadé,' Emard wrote, 'qu'il vaut mieux tâcher d'obtenir que les élections se faisent avec le plus de calme possible, puis ensuite réitérer auprès du nouveau parlement quelle que soit sa composition, les pétitions déjà présentées.'[93]

As had been the case in the matter of the abortive letter of March, the burden of decision or at least of the bringing together of opinion on a pre-election mandement fell to Archbishop Bégin. Four questions had to be solved and solved quickly. First and most obvious was whether a mandement should be issued at all. Second, what kind of mandement should it be? What precisely should it require of Catholic voters? Third, and very closely connected to the problem of advisability, when should it be issued? Finally, how should such a mandement be prepared in the short time available? Only the last of these questions could be answered easily; in the light of the March confusion, Bégin quickly got agreement that a meeting of all the bishops, at least of Quebec, perhaps even of the entire country, had to be the forum of final decision. The other questions were not so simply answered; fortunately Bégin possessed the talent required to make their solution at least possible. Ideologically, the Quebec archbishop leaned toward the right and duty of making a strong statement; temperamentally, he was clearly inclined toward the side of caution. In the test of practice, Bégin maintained a remarkable openness toward each point of view and was the key figure in achieving a concerted if compromise action.[94]

From Montreal on Monday April 20, Langevin submitted the draft of a prospective mandement to Bégin, indicating that he believed Fabre approved at least the principle of a collective statement. The crucial clause in Langevin's draft, strongly weighted towards the Conservative bill already presented, would demand that Catholic deputies promise to vote for 'une loi fédérale rémédiatrice donnant satisfaction à la minorité, et approuvée par le réprésentant official de cette minorité,' It implied further that electors would require candidates to extract a promise from their leaders that such a bill would be introduced.[95] From Kingston on April 22, Langevin indicated that Archbishop Cleary had told him of a prospective meeting of the Ontario bishops on the election question. Cleary also spoke of a private directive to be given to his own priests, which would favour the Conservatives but would forbid any statement from the pulpit.[96] Returning to Ottawa via Toronto on April 25, Langevin reported an encouraging visit with

93 AAM, Emard to Fabre, April 17, 1896
94 See above, p.49.
95 AAQ, Langevin to Bégin, April 20, 1896
96 Ibid., April 22, 1896

Archbishop Walsh. The Toronto prelate had approved the idea of a mandement, but felt that it would be dangerous for the Ontario bishops to sign it.[97] Back in Montreal on April 27, Langevin wrote that he had once more encountered opposition with Fabre, where he thought there had been approval a week earlier. 'Désastre!' cried Langevin, adding that he thought he would go to Valleyfield in order to prevent Emard from becoming adamant against a collective letter.[98]

There was good reason for Langevin to be concerned. Not only had Emard's neutral pastoral appeared, but Fabre told the Valleyfield bishop that he had been misled by Langevin's initial hints about a letter. 'Le projet de mandement ne me va pas,' Fabre wrote on April 22. 'Quand Mgr. Langevin m'a dit dimanche dernier qu'il m'enverrait des notes je ne soupçonnais pas qu'il s'agissait d'un mandement collectif.'[99] Emard's own reaction to the draft mandement was both more detailed and more vehement. In a long April 23 letter to Bégin, Emard spelled out his reasons why he could not sign at least Langevin's version. The doctrinal part, Emard pointed out, had been recently covered in the joint pastoral on education. The historical survey was vulnerable to attack; the Conservative remedial bill was too categorically approved. The core of Emard's protest, however, was an eloquent exposition of the seemingly unexamined dangers, risked without sufficient reason, of a document of such partisan implications as that outlined by Langevin:

Il est uniquement propre à jeter, une fois de plus, le discrédit sur la personne des évêques, dont la parole, malheureusement réputée partisane, sera discutée, servant d'appui pour les uns et de prétexte aux insultes des autres. Il n'y a moyen de faire croire qu'un tel document serait indépendant des partis; et je ne puis faire acte de foi dans aucun d'eux. Il faut nous ménager une position ténable et honorable, pour le cas très possible, ou nous devrons nous présenter, comme pétitionnaires, devant un gouvernement composé des adversaires d'aujourd'hui. Les parlements changeront; notre droit, même dans l'honorabilité des revendications, doit demeurer intact et indéfini, jusqu'à victoire complète. Je ne suis pas convaincu, comme évêque, que la passation d'une loi rémédiatrice par le Parlement d'Ottawa, soit le moyen unique, sur et prompt de rendre justice à la minorité Manitobaine; avec une majorité de 40, le parlement actuel n'a pas pu réussir. S'il avait réussi, il restait à appliquer la loi au milieu des difficultés encore plus grandes, sous un gouvernement hostile; et si elle

97 *Ibid.*, April 25, 1896
98 *Ibid.*, April 27, 1896
99 AEV, Fabre to Emard, April 22, 1896

était mise en pratique, on gardait les moyens de la rendre passablement illusoire ... Dès lors, faut-il par un langage absolu, fermer toute issue à d'autres modes de règlement possibles, peut-être même plus faciles dans des circonstances données? Le mandement projeté rencontrera une opposition formelle chez un grand nombre, non seulement de protestants, mais même de catholiques, qui n'y verront qu'une tyrannie électorale; il est connu que des politiciens travaillent à obtenir ce document. Est-il de bonne conduite administrative de mettre les fidèles dans le cas certain de nous désobéir, de désobéir à l'Eglise sans l'espoir fondé d'un bien général plus considérable que le mal? Car, et ceci est sérieux, supposons que le mandement produise tout son effet chez les catholiques, croyez-vous qu'il empêchera l'élection de L.L.G.P. et M.? Non; or il ne reste que trois ou quatre candidats qui hésiteront à faire une promesse qu'ils trouveront bien dure et bien compromettante pour la dignité d'un député. Tout le mandement collectif qui met en jeu, d'un manière presque décisive, l'autorité et le prestige temporel des évêques, n'aurait d'application que pour trois ou quatre. C'est trop peu, en prévision des conséquences trop graves.[100]

There was no mistaking the antipathy of the two points of view and the intensity of the problem of conscience which was being brought close to the surface. Beyond Emard's careful protest, Bégin had before him the deeply troubled letter of Dr C. Rinfret, his own diocesan and Liberal MP for Lotbinière. Rinfret was protesting the election-slanted manner in which LaRivière was using a Langevin telegram of mid-March to prove that all the bishops were solidly behind the Conservatives and the remedial bill. Against this the sins of the Conservatives and the weaknesses of the bill were recounted by Rinfret like a litany. 'Nous ne sommes pas infaillibles,' Rinfret wrote to Bégin, 'nous avons pu nous tromper quand nous avons voté contre la seconde lecture du Bill réparateur; en le faisant cependant nous avons agi d'après les dictées de notre conscience.' Then came Rinfret's key question: was Langevin's statement, 'Aucun évêque ne diffère avec moi,' to be taken literally? Did all the bishops agree fully with him? 'Je serai absolument affligé de cette appréciation,' Rinfret concluded.[101]

Bégin's answer was a gentle insistence that, in his estimation, all the bishops indeed wished the remedial bill to pass, 'tout en l'améliorant dans la mesure du possible.' He reminded Rinfret that the bishops were not as

---

100 AAQ, Emard to Bégin, April 23, 1896. The Liberals referred to by initial only were probably Laurier, Langelier, Geoffrion, Pouliot or Préfontaine, and Monet.
101 AAQ, Rinfret to Bégin, April 18, 1896

outside the current of events as some Liberals would have it, and said that he was sadly convinced that it was the Liberals more than the Conservatives who were sacrificing religion and race to party interests. Bégin's conclusion left room for conscientious opposition but equally left no doubt on his own position: 'Je respecte vos intentions et j'aime à croire qu'elles sont excellentes; que puis-je en dire autant de votre vote!'[102] Rinfret's next letter actually asked for an episcopal statement on similar laws in the future, at least sufficient to reduce confusion.[103]

Dealing with a single MP's dilemma did not solve the group episcopal problem, although it may have heightened Bégin's sensitivity to the dangers involved. The Quebec archbishop, through Marois, sent a copy of Emard's objections to the other bishops. How deeply Bégin had been impressed by the hazards outlined by Emard and perhaps by Rinfret was shown in a note he sent to Langevin on the same day as the Emard document. Bégin admitted that Emard was right in stressing extreme caution and advised Langevin to visit Emard with the idea that the Valleyfield bishop might be willing to sign a more neutral document. Bégin stated that he himself would prepare an alternate draft, and indicated that he was still open on the advisability of both the fact and the nature of the mandement. 'Si l'on me convaincu que le silence est préférable,' Bégin stated, 'je ne veux pas mettre le feu aux poudres, je ne dirai rien – chose extrêmement facile – mais je ne suis pas encore convaincu que ce silence serait d'or actuellement.'[104] It should be noted that, along with Emard's manifesto, Marois sent comments aimed at meeting the Valleyfield bishop's objections, and revealed polite but not always minor differences with his own archbishop, with the vicar general emphatically favouring the harder line.[105]

Among the bishops, the most adamant and detailed opposition to Emard's position came from Labrecque of Chicoutimi. Writing first to Bégin in comment on the latter's draft mandement and Emard's April 12 pastoral, Labrecque based his arguments strongly on the letter received from Rome. The Chicoutimi bishop held that 'il y aurait plus d'imprudence à se taire qu'à parler dans les circonstances actuelles.' Furthermore, in Labrecque's view, if there was to be a document, it would have to be much

102 PAC, Laurier Papers, Bégin to Rinfret, April 29, 1896
103 Ibid., Rinfret to Bégin, May 1, 1896
104 AASB, Bégin to Langevin, April 25, 1896
105 For example, AAO, Marois to Duhamel, April 30, 1896; AESH, Marois to Moreau, May 1, 1896

more specific than Emard's letter had been, or it might do more harm than good:

Se contenter de dire des généralités, comme l'a fait Mgr. Emard dans son mandement, à mon avis, c'est parler pour parler. Surtout, laisser entendre, ou même dire ouvertement comme il l'a fait, qu'on s'en remet à la conscience des députés et des électeurs c'est abdiquer son rôle de sentinelle de l'Eglise, de guide des consciences, c'est déserter le champ de bataille juste au moment de la mêlée. A mon avis, *en conscience, nous devons parler, et parlet net, parce que nos ennemis parlent, et parlent net.*

Labrecque concluded with the somewhat anguished statement that at the bishops' meeting some way would have to be devised to take the policy lead away from Fabre and Emard.[106] After receiving Emard's long manifesto of objections from Marois, Labrecque repeated and elaborated on the sentiments he had expounded to Bégin. Despite the heightening emotion, however, Labrecque revealed that the problem of over-identification with the Conservatives had been raised by Emard in a way which could not be escaped. Clearly showing that a tender spot had been touched, Labrecque reacted against one of Emard's most specific objections. 'Espère-t-on empêcher l'élection de Laurier, Langelier, etc.?' Labrecque asked. 'Mais en vérité est-ce là la question? Qui parle d'empêcher l'élection d'un tel? Ce que les évêques peuvent et doivent faire c'est d'obliger les députés à se déclarer favorable à une législation réparatrice, mais non à se déclarer pour tel parti ou tel autre.'[107] In many ways, this question and accusation of party identification became the turning point of the episcopal debate. Certainly the men who opposed Emard's objections did not see themselves as party men, while they were sure that Emard himself was leaning in that direction. Yet they could not, in fact, avoid the image if not the substance of partisanship; once again the concept of party government was probably little understood.

The reactions of Bishop Laflèche were much like those of Labrecque, although they proceeded with greater calm and logic. To Duhamel of Ottawa on April 28, Laflèche expressed the view that Emard's objections were not unlike those which would be posed by the Ontario bishops, but was reasonably confident that Emard could be persuaded. Replying to Marois in comment on the Emard manifesto, Laflèche showed that there

106 AAQ, Labrecque to Bégin, April 29, 1896
107 *Ibid.*, Labrecque to Marois, May 1, 1896

was no doubt in his mind that the aim of the mandement ought to be to give some recompense and recognition to the efforts of the party of Tupper and Bowell, 'deux hommes d'état vraiment de ce non, protestants et même l'un orangiste, mais honnêtes dans leur conviction et soutenus en grande partie par une majorité de protestants également honnêtes.' By the same token, Laflèche insisted, the letter ought to condemn the Liberals and particularly the Catholics who had voted against the remedial bill – 'des hommes qui se disent catholiques et cela au nombre de vingt-neuf – et qui sont conduits par un chef qui s'est vanté d'entrer en guerre contre l'épiscopat.' Thus, Laflèche concluded, a collective letter should be pressed for, or, failing that, at least a letter from Archbishop Langevin signed by as many bishops as possible. Whatever else happened, Laflèche promised that he could not and would not keep silent, 'de manière ne pas mériter du Souverain Juge qui m'appellera bientôt à son tribunal suprême le reproche de chien muet incapable d'aboyer aux approches du loup.'[108] Less flambuoyant but clearly supporting a collective letter were the replies of Moreau and Descelles of St Hyacinthe, Blais of Rimouski, and LaRocque of Sherbrooke.[109] Duhamel of Ottawa also favoured a mandement, although he insisted that it would have to be 'une lettre ... rédigée avec un soin extrême,' and felt that the whole episode might well result in the sending of a permanent apostolic delegate to Canada.[110]

THE MONTREAL MEETING

The clash of opinion over both the fact and character of the mandement heightened the importance of the third question, that of timing. Here again there was no unanimity, but on the point at least of drafting the document, the party favouring more radical and immediate action won out. Bégin, as late as April 29, spelled out a carefully reasoned letter to Langevin urging postponement of the definitive meeting on the mandement until May 19, when the majority of bishops had already agreed to attend a ceremony of dedication of a new pipe organ at Ste Anne de Beaupré. Bégin showed great anxiety to avoid the excitement and comment that a special bishops' meeting would cause, in particular the possible charge that one objective of this meeting would be to give a kind of 'imprimatur' to Tupper's new

108 AAQ, Laflèche to Marois, May 1, 1896
109 *Ibid.*, Moreau to Marois, May 2, 1896; Blais to Marois, May 2, 1896; LaRocque to Marois, May 2, 1896
110 *Ibid.*, Duhamel to Marois, May 2, 1896

cabinet. Most of all, Bégin felt, the bishops had to be given time to study the various drafts of a mandement. He insisted that Langevin face with realism the opposition which would come from Emard and Fabre, and recommended that Emard be visited at sufficient length to assure that 'un fiasco complet' would not be the result of the plenary session. In a trenchant Latin postscript, Bégin summarized the danger which had to be feared: 'Si unus episcoporum dissentit, omnia cessant. Tunc adversarii hunc episcopum cantabunt usque ad sidera et ceteros omnes despiciant.'[111] Bégin's arguments, however, did not carry the day. It was on this point of timing that the differences between Bégin and Marois came most into view. Clearly without consulting his superior, Marois also wrote to Langevin on April 29, urging that if a letter was to be published, it should be early enough to precede the major campaign tours and before the lines had become hard and fast. Publishing it on May 19 would, in Marois' opinion, be too late.[112]

Although it had been Bégin who had acted as co-ordinator of opinion and action up to this point, it was Langevin as the most directly concerned who made the final decision on the time and place for the bishops' meeting. On May 1, Canon Archambault of Montreal sent the following invitation to all the archbishops and bishops of Quebec, as well as to Archbishop Walsh: 'Sa grandeur Mgr. L'Archevêque de St. Boniface désire rencontrer, à Montréal, NN. SS. les archevêques et les évêques de la province de Québec, au sujet de la question des écoles du Manitoba.'[113] The hurry and confusion which remained till the hour of sending the letter was shown by the date fixed for the meeting, 'le six' being written in over 'le huit' in the draft kept in the Montreal chancery. Langevin's choice of Montreal as the locale may have been designed partly for convenience and partly to involve Archbishop Fabre as host of the meeting. When Bégin learned of Langevin's decision, he quickly sent back his assent, adding that he would have been willing to go to British Columbia if it were helpful to arrive at the right solution.[114]

Bégin's work as mediator and his concern with reducing differences to proportions which could be resolved at a single meeting seemed to have paid dividends. Although he had only a day earlier sent a telegram telling

111 AASB, Bégin to Langevin, April 29, 1896 (If one Bishop dissents, everything will come to a halt. Then our adversaries will praise that bishop to the stars and despise all the others.)

112 AASB, Marois to Langevin, April 29, 1896

113 AAM, Archambault to Quebec bishops and to Walsh, May 1, 1896

114 AASB, Bégin to Langevin, May 3, 1896. It should be noted too, that Langevin at forty-one years, was considered somewhat a protégé of the sixty-nine-year-old Fabre; Fabre had been his consecrator in 1895.

Emard that he could not come to Valleyfield,[115] Langevin was sufficiently impressed by Bégin's urgent message to change plans. On May 2 Langevin's short note to the Quebec archbishop related that Emard had been visited, had warmly supported the idea of the Montreal meeting, and had been 'fort impressionné' by Bégin's alternative draft.[116] Bégin's own letter to Emard prepared the ground for a working consensus by admitting the importance of the latter's objections, while at the same time quoting a second letter from Cardinal Ledochowski which supported the idea of a collective appeal for justice. Bégin tackled the 'party identification' problem by insisting, probably with the Rinfret letters in mind, that 'ici les deux partis s'attendent à ce que l'épiscopat donnera une direction aux fidèles.' Bégin was sure that the bishops could in fact speak 'sans faire ce qu'on appelle de la politique, sans nous lier le moindrement à un parti,' and that a collective document could be produced, 'non pas quelconque, mais bien fait, inattaquable à tout égard.'[117]

The excitement and anticipation caused by rumours of a special plenary episcopal meeting was reflected in the columns of the French language newspapers. La Patrie of May 4 gave as a source of its information Curé Taillon of St Michel de Laprairie, brother of the new cabinet minister. This rumour of an immediate session, La Patrie reported, had been sidestepped without being denied by Archbishop Fabre.[118] L'Evénement of May 5 stated that a mandement would soon be forthcoming from a meeting of all the bishops, and left no doubt on the pro-Conservative character of the document which it expected and demanded. 'Il importe que ... l'épiscopat canadien indique à l'électorat la route à suivre,' L'Evénement proclaimed. The one tragedy to be guarded against at all costs would be 'si notre peuple ratifie par son verdict l'alliance que vient de faire M. Laurier avec les sectaires d'Ontario.'[119] L'Electeur reported the arrival of Bégin and other bishops in Montreal and scoffed at the presumption of L'Evénement that the episcopate would explicitly endorse one political party. Exhibiting, like La Patrie, no evident apprehension about the outcome of the meeting, L'Electeur once again leaned heavily on the importance of Mowat's agreement to join Laurier's team. 'Comment les Bleus pourraient-ils obtenir un mandement défavorable à un ministère dont Sir Oliver Mowat ferait partie?' L'Electeur demanded. 'L'épiscopat d'Ontario ne serait pas lent à

115 AEV, Langevin to Emard, May 1, 1896
116 AAQ, Langevin to Bégin, May 2, 1896
117 AEV, Bégin to Emard, May 1, 1896
118 La Patrie, May 4, 1896
119 L'Evénement, May 5, 1896

en lancer un encore plus énergique en faveur de son ami et protecteur.'[120] Although there seemed to be no major news leaks immediately after the Montreal meeting, *La Presse* on May 8 significantly joined Liberal journals in assuring its readers that the bishops' statement would not tie itself to one political party. They might indeed give 'reconnaissance à ceux qui ont mis le plus d'empressement à seconder leurs efforts,' *La Presse* stated, but 'les deux partis, dans notre province, étant composés de catholiques également soumis aux enseignements de l'Eglise, ce serait faire injure à NN. ss. les Evêques, que de leur supposer l'intention d'en ostraciser l'un au profit de l'autre.'[121]

No official minutes of the bishops' meeting were preserved, but consent, grudging or otherwise, to the final product, was clearly a prime concern. In order to get the absent Bishop Labrecque's signature, as well as to assure that the letter would reach remote parishes and thus be published simultaneously throughout the province, the decision was taken to defer publication until Sunday, May 17.[122] To avoid conflicting interpretations, curés were strictly directed to read the mandement without commentary.

Two early sections of the document finally agreed upon should be particularly noted:

En vous parlant ainsi, N.T.C.F., notre intention n'est pas de nous inféoder à aucun des partis qui se combattent dans l'arène politique; au contraire, nous tenons à réserver notre liberté. Mais la question des écoles du Manitoba étant avant tout une question religieuse ... nous croirions trahir la cause sacrée dont nous sommes et devons être les défenseurs, si nous n'usions de notre autorité pour en assurer le succès.

Following this statement, with perhaps an oblique reference to Laurier, the mandement went on:

Remarquez bien, N.T.C.F., qu'il n'est pas permis à un catholique, quel qu'il soit, journaliste, électeur, candidat, député, d'avoir deux lignes de conduite au point de

120 May 6, 1896
121 *La Presse*, May 8, 1896
122 Labrecque, according to Bégin, was absent on pastoral visitation and did not receive his invitation in time to attend the Montreal meeting. It should be noted that, possibly out of deference to the Ontario bishops who felt they could not sign the mandement, and thus to avoid the charge that the document divided Catholics along French-English lines, Langevin himself abstained from signing the mandement, leaving it as the voice of the Quebec bishops alone.

vue religieux: l'une pour la vie privée, l'autre pour la vie publique et de fouler aux pieds, dans l'exercice de ses devoirs sociaux, les obligations que lui impose son titre de fils soumis de l'Eglise.

The concluding section of the mandement became one of the most quoted paragraphs in Canadian history:

C'est pourquoi, N.T.C.F., tous les catholiques ne devront accorder leur suffrage qu'aux candidats qui s'engagement formellement et solennellement à voter, au Parlement, en faveur d'une législation rendant à la minorité catholique du Manitoba les droits scolaires qui lui sont reconnus par l'honorable Conseil Privé d'Angleterre. Ce grave devoir s'impose à tout bon catholique, et vous ne seriez justifiables ni devant vos guides spirituels ni devant Dieu lui-même de forfaire à cette obligation.[123]

Several reports following the Montreal meeting revealed the intensity of feeling and the seriousness of the clash of opinion which preceded agreement on the final version. A letter to Marois from Bégin on the night of May 6 reported that there had been three long sessions, that his own rather than Langevin's draft had by and large been adopted, and that even here many 'retranchements' reflecting the Fabre-Emard position had been accepted. The result, in Bégin's opinion, was 'encore un beau document, très calme, digne, serein, innattaquable, se tenant dans les sphères les plus éléves.'[124] Commenting to Langevin a few days later, however, Bégin reflected somewhat ruefully on the difficulty of producing a collective document. He admitted that 'nous avons été à un cheveu d'un désastre véritable, car ne faire aucun document ou en publier un qui n'eût pas reçu l'adhésion de tous nos collègues, c'était nous suicider moralement aux yeux du public.'[125] Evidence that the mandement might have gone further than even the Langevin version suggested, was found in a letter from Bishop Cameron asking for a declaration from the St Boniface prelate for use in the elections in the Antigonish diocese. Cameron wanted the letter to restate that the remedial bill had been necessary and satisfactory, and 'that therefore you beseech us and every loyal upholder of the constitution, whether Catholic or Protestant, to poll our votes, as in duty bound, for the Conservative candidates and thus enable the government to pass the Remedial Act in

123 *Mandements ... Publiés dans le Diocèse de Montréal depuis son Erection*, XII, pp.196–205
124 AAQ, Bégin to Marois, May 6, 1896
125 AASB, Bégin to Langevin, May 12, 1896

spite of obstruction.'[126] A later message reacting to the text of the mandement which Langevin sent along with a special letter addressed to the
French Canadians of Cape Breton made it clear that Cameron found the
Quebec document too weak. He regretted that the bishops in concert 'did
not act on your suggestion by insisting upon the leaders of both parties
committing themselves to remedial legislation, or upon every candidate's
pledging himself solidly to oppose any government that would not introduce such a measure and stand or fall by its fate.' As for impartiality
between the parties, Cameron's blunt comment was that it was 'little short
of judicial blindness to treat him [Laurier] otherwise than as an enemy of
the only practical remedy available under the circumstances.'[127]

REPROOFS AFTER MONTREAL, ROME'S RESERVATIONS

An indication of the courage required of Emard to maintain his stand
throughout the bishops' meeting came in a letter of reproof from the elderly
Bishop Moreau on May 9. 'A coup sûr,' the St Hyacinthe prelate told
Emard, 'aux yeux de tous les évêques présents, vous vous êtes rangés au
nombre de ces évêques libéraux qui sacrifient les droits et les libertés de
l'Eglise pour plaire à un gouvernement ou à un parti.'[128] Moreau insisted in
this and subsequent letters that his motive was that of fraternal charity and
a sense of obligation to point out danger where he honestly thought it
existed.[129] Emard, perhaps over-reacting under the strain, protested in
consternation and sorrow to Moreau himself and to the three archbishops,
Fabre, Duhamel, and Bégin.[130] The three metropolitan prelates reassured
Emard of the propriety of his action at Montreal[131] and, as usual, Bégin
managed to convey the greatest sense of balance and diplomacy. 'Bien que
je me sois prononcé dans un sens différent de votre,' Bégin wrote, 'je me
plais à reconnaître cependant que vous nous avez été fort utile en nous
signalant des écueils que nous n'aurions peut-être pas aussi soigneusement
évités. C'est du choc des opinions que jaillit la lumière.'[132]
　　Under the stimulus of Moreau's criticism, Emard hastened to send a

126 *Ibid.*, Cameron to Langevin, May 5, 1896
127 *Ibid.*, May 18, 1896
128 AEV, Moreau to Emard, May 9, 1896. Next to the forty-one year old Langevin, Emard at
　　forty-three was the youngest of the bishops at the meeting.
129 *Ibid.*, May 16, 1896
130 AAQ, Emard to Bégin, May 10, 1896; AEV, Emard to Fabre, Emard to Duhamel, May 10,
　　1896
131 AEV, Fabre to Emard, May 12, 1896; Duhamel to Emard, May 13, 1896
132 AEV, Bégin to Emard, May 13, 1896

detailed report of the episcopal meeting and of its result to Cardinal Ledochowski in Rome. Emard's letter was paralleled by a strikingly similar one from Archbishop Fabre reporting as chairman of the meeting. Both accounts were detailed and articulate, Emard's concentrating on a defence of his own approach, with an eye perhaps to a possible complaint from one or more of the other bishops. Emard stated that both he and Fabre would have preferred no mandement at all, but that 'enfin mes objections ont cédé devant une rédaction qui élimine aussi complètement que possible les dangers que je croyais inhérents sans compensation suffisante, au mouvement tel que d'abord projeté.'[133] Fabre's letter elaborated on the absence of specific preference for one party against the other in the mandement. 'Nous avons jugé très opportun,' Fabre wrote, '... de ne faire aucun éloge et de ne jeter aucun blâme ... Nous nous sommes donc abstenu de tout ce qui aurait pu paraître de la partisannerie et nous n'avons pas voulu nous prononcer sur la manière précise dont le gouvernement fédéral doit accomplir son devoir et arriver à une solution satisfaisante.' Without mentioning names, Fabre expressed a continuing doubt concerning the commitment of the existing government to protection for the Manitoba Catholics, as well as the desirability of avoiding an impossible position should the Liberals gain power. Fabre left little doubt that the wishes of many Conservative politicians had been disappointed. The mandement, he said, 'ne répond peut-être pas aux espérances de certains hommes politiques qui auraient aimé faire de l'intervention des évêques un instrument de popularité et un moyen puissant de servir leurs intérêts.' Against this, Fabre concluded with a hint of satisfaction, the collective letter seemed to have the merit 'd'être conforme aux enseignements de notre Saint Père le Pape Léon XIII, et même d'être plus efficacement utile par là à la cause des écoles.'[134]

What perhaps should be noted most of all is the fact that it was to this long and careful letter from Fabre stressing moderation that Cardinal Ledochowski addressed a letter of mild reproof after the election, criticizing the specific demands required of voters and candidates in the mandement:

Probo summopere et consilium edendi Pastoralem Epistolam, ejusque tenorem a personalibus considerationibus politicisque recriminationibus alienum. Maluissem etiam ut ea pars reticeretur, quae respicit peculiarem pactionem a candidatis ineundam cum catholicis electoribus, uti conditionem ad habendum votum. Inde

133 AEV, Emard to Ledochowski, May 11, 1896
134 AAM, Fabre to Ledochowski, May 8, 1896

enim mali homines aut leves occasionem fortasse habere possent adversandi Ecclesiam. Qua in re illud etiam animadverto quod non facile de peccato gravi coargui debent, qui favorabiles quidem restitutionem iuris violati catholicorum Manitobensium, de opportuniori modo ambigant. Etenim responsio hac super in re Episcopo Chicoutimiensi data, respicit casum absolute in se inspectum qui tamen multipliciter variari in concreto potest ex additis circumstantiis.[135]

The remainder of the letter urged continued efforts on behalf of the Manitoba minority, but the rebuke, particularly to what many bishops had considered a too-mild injunction, could not be taken easily. Many of the representations to the Vatican even before the Laurier-Greenway agreement were prompted by the sting of the 'Maluissem' letter, and by its implicit greater reproof of the subsequent Laflèche 'extension' of the mandement. A similar but briefer letter of restrained criticism was sent to Bégin from Rome, dated before the election had taken place.[136] In any case, the point of an over-zealous reading of the replies to Labrecque could not be avoided, and the suggestion remained of what might have been Rome's reaction had the harder line desired by Langevin, Laflèche, and Cameron been adopted.

One further incident heightened tension and illustrated diversity of episcopal position in the period between the drafting and the publication of the mandement. A quite substantial clash took place between Archbishops Fabre and Langevin over a series of sermons which the latter undertook in the district immediately south of Montreal, Laprairie-Napierville. The situation was complicated by the fact the federal riding in the area was represented by one of Laurier's more abrasively Rouge supporters, Dominique Monet, that St Isidore de Laprairie was Langevin's home parish, and by the personal friendship between Fabre and Langevin. Even before the bishops' Montreal meeting, Langevin had delivered several

135 'I heartily approve both the wisdom of issuing a pastoral letter, and the tenor of the statement, free as it is from personal considerations and political recriminations. I would also have preferred that that part be removed which has to do with the specific pact to be entered into by candidates with Catholic voters as a condition of obtaining the vote. For from this, evil or frivolous men may find occasion to oppose the Church. In this matter I also note that they ought not easily to be burdened with grave sin who, although favouring the restoration of the injured right of Manitoba Catholics, differ as to the more opportune means. Moreover, the reply given earlier to the Bishop of Chicoutimi looks at the case considered in the abstract, which however can be varied in many ways by added circumstances in the concrete' (AAM, Ledochowski to Fabre, July 8, 1896).
136 AAQ, Ledochowski to Bégin, June 16, 1896

sermons, notably one at Joliette on May 5, which had gone to some lengths to renew unreserved approval of the Conservative remedial bill and those who had promoted it in Parliament.[137] On May 13, the Montreal newspapers, French and English, gave prominent space to the report of an emotion-laden Langevin address at St Isidore on the evening of May 11. The St Boniface prelate had not only returned to the theme of the remedial bill, but had made some very pointed references about 'les dispositions des chefs.' According to the report of *La Presse*, the Liberal candidate Monet went to the Montreal chancery to protest. Fabre was absent, but Canon Archambault apparently gave a sympathetic hearing to Monet, who concentrated his attack not so much on Langevin as on 'les abus que font certains cabaleurs' working for Pelletier, the Conservative candidate.[138] *La Patrie* was not so gentle. 'Mgr. Langevin est plus en campagne électorale que ne l'est M. Pelletier dans le comté de Laprairie,' the Rouge newspaper charged. 'Ses sermons ont l'air plus inspirés par Tupper que par le Saint-Esprit.' Calm reaction was recommended, however. 'L'attitude imposante de neutralité et de dignité que prend l'épiscopat dans la présente lutte forcera fatalement Mgr. Langevin à retourner à Winnipeg ou à ne plus faire de politique,' *La Patrie* concluded.[139] In a similar vein, the *Montreal Herald*, quoted later by the *Globe*, roundly criticized Langevin. 'The youthful prelate,' stated the *Herald*, 'is working the cause of the church in the Province of Quebec an incalculable injury ... doing what must be gravely condemned by the older heads in the council of Bishops at which he has sat during the past week.'[140]

That Langevin in fact wished his words to influence the vote was clearly shown in a note sent to Bégin on the night of the sermon. 'On dit que ce sermon a modifié les idées de plusieurs qui vont voter pour le candidat conservateur,' Langevin wrote.[141] When the news of Langevin's activity reached Fabre, he was both displeased and baffled. 'Mgr. Langevin me désole,' Fabre told Emard. 'Il fait un campagne électorale qui va provoquer des mouvements facheux ... Quel absence de gouvernail! C'est pitié.'[142] Emard replied expressing similar disapproval,[143] but it was Fabre who was faced with action. In a letter of quiet but unmistakeable reproof sent on May 12, Fabre asked the younger prelate to desist:

137 *La Presse*, May 6, 1896
138 *Ibid.*, May 13, 1896
139 May 13, 1896
140 *Montreal Herald*, May 13, 1896; Toronto *Globe*, May 14, 1896
141 AAQ, Langevin to Bégin, May 11, 1896
142 AEV, Fabre to Emard, May 12, 1896
143 AAM, Emard to Fabre, May 14, 1896

Dans notre dernière réunion, nous étions convenus d'avertir nos prêtres qu'ils auraient à lire notre mandement sans le commenter. Une des raisons que nous avions pour agir ainsi était la diversité d'interpretation qu'il y avait à craindre.

J'avais dit que le sermon de Joliette ne me convenait pas. Je pensais qu'il serait le dernier. St. Isidore a eu le sien, depuis, et les journaux annoncent d'autres. Je me vois dans le dure nécessité de vous demander de cesser de traiter ce sujet en chaire.

La manière d'exposer le sujet ne me plait pas, les plaintes arrivent, je me verrais dans la nécessité de parler et ce serait fâcheux. Il vaut mieux que le mandement seul soit l'expression officielle de notre direction.

Je compte sur votre vertu pour sacrifier ce qui vous semble utile, pour ne pas mettre le trouble dans un diocèse étranger.[144]

Langevin's reply of May 14 was one of submission and of acceptance of the verdict. Like Emard confronted by Moreau, however, the depth of Langevin's feeling of injury, particularly against Canon Archambault, was revealed in a letter to Bégin, going so far as to suggest yet another statement of protest to the Holy See.[145] Nonetheless, to the evident disappointment of Conservative organizers, Langevin complied faithfully with Fabre's directive. In its report of two Langevin sermons in Montreal on May 13 and 14, *La Presse* stated that the St Boniface prelate 'n'a pas prononcé une seule parole sur la difficulté scolaire.'[146]

In summary on the background and preparation of the mandement, the impression of a genuine compromise stands out. Emard had been a persuasive leader for reserve and caution, with Fabre not far behind. The other bishops, moreover, in spite of strongly held views witnessed by Moreau's reaction, had shown themselves far from immovable. However much concession was involved on the part of Fabre and Emard to agree to any collective statement, the transition from Langevin's original draft to the final text of the mandement was quite striking. The importance of the agreement to publish without commentary had been underlined, and the general impression of a document which could be interpreted in a nonpartisan manner had been established. At the same time, there was no mistaking that a major ecclesiastical foray into the political process of Canada had been launched.

144 *Ibid.*, Fabre to Langevin, May 12, 1896
145 AAQ, Langevin to Bégin, May 17, 1896
146 *La Presse*, May 15, 1896

9

The June election: clerical activity, campaign highlights, and an analysis

As early as February 1894, J.I. Tarte had told Wilfrid Laurier that the key to his gaining and holding power in Canada would be to establish a solid political base of 50 seats in Quebec.[1] The election of June 23, 1896, came uncannily close to fulfilling Tarte's precise requirement. Quebec gave 49 of its 65 seats to Laurier, a gain for the Liberals of 14 more Quebec members than they had at dissolution, and of 12 more than they had in 1891. In Canada as a whole the 1896 result was: Liberals, 118; Conservatives, 88; others, 7.[2] Interest in the 1896 vote has rightly focused on this crucial Quebec swing of political strength from the Conservative to the Liberal side, but the element in the contest that has remained unexamined, despite its notoriety, is the impact of clerical influence. The precise extent and result of such interference is difficult to establish. For purposes of analysis, at least three questions must be distinguished. What amount and what kind of clerical activity took place? How was that clerical action used or countered by politicians, campaign managers, and newspapers? How did the electorate view and react to the statements and actions of the clergy? These questions will be considered first in a review of the release of the general episcopal mandement, the spectacular sermon of Bishop Laflèche, and the subsequent activity of other bishops and clergy. Next will come a brief review of the closing weeks of each party's campaign. Finally, the questions will be approached through a partial analysis of election results in selected ridings in the province of Quebec.

1 PAC, Laurier Papers, Tarte to Laurier, February 5, 1894
2 See Appendix 2.

RECEPTION OF THE MANDEMENT

The bishops' letter was read from the pulpit on Sunday, May 17, and the immediate reaction was one of remarkable calm and equanimity. Beyond the fact that *L'Electeur* scooped the curés and the other newspapers by publishing the text a day early[3] there was little initial sensation in the French-language newspapers. Although *L'Evénement* continued to group the Liberals with the McCarthyites and saw the mandement as 'une approbation éclatante de la politique d'intervention à laquelle s'est lié le parti conservateur,'[4] *La Presse* praised the high tone and impartiality of the document. *La Presse* emphasized the right of the bishops to require candidates to support a remedial law, but 'nous n'y voyons rien qui puisse porter ombrage aux libéraux et les empêcher d'y souscrire avec empressement.'[5] Like the Toronto *Mail and Empire*,[6] The Conservative *Montreal Gazette* tried to keep from arousing unnecessary excitement. It called the mandement a 'very mild sort of a document,' giving 'sound advice,' and leaving 'the Roman Catholic people's choice free between the candidates of the two parties.'[7] On the Liberal side, however, immediate reaction ranged from relief to jubilation. *L'Electeur* spoke of the 'sentiment général de satisfaction qu'éprouve la population catholique.' The result of the document would be, in *L'Electeur*'s words, 'un respect plus grand, une affection plus vive, une considération plus élevée pour la hiérarchie qui nous commande tous, conservateurs comme libéraux dans le domaine spirituel.'[8] Even *La Patrie* ventured on a rare excursion into filial devotion for the church. 'Le document lancé hier est assez éloquent par lui-même que nous serons assez délicat pour ne pas le commenter,' *La Patrie* stated. The Montreal Rouge newspaper was grateful that the bishops 'se sont maintenus sur des hauteurs de la neutralité,' and indulged in righteous indignation at the reaction of disappointed Conservatives. 'Il est vraiment scandaleux,' *La Patrie* wrote, 'd'entendre les conservateurs de certains ministériels hier aux portes des églises. "C'est tout ce qu'ont pu avoir Taillon et Angers," disaient-ils, "c'est ça le mandement; il est en faveur des libéraux; nous sommes flambés etc."'[9] The Toronto *Globe*, on the other hand, could hardly avoid some criticism. The Liberal newspaper spoke of 'a feeling of regret ... among Liberal minded men ... that the bishops of Quebec have seen fit to invade the political field with their

3 May 16, 1896
4 May 18, 1896
5 May 18, 1896
6 May 18, 1896

7 *Montreal Gazette*, May 18, 1896
8 May 18, 1896
9 May 18, 1896

spiritual weapons.' The *Globe* stressed the loss of Protestant sympathy for the Manitoba minority which the mandement would bring, and insisted that, however much one might regret it, 'the Manitoba school question cannot be got rid of by refusing to think about it ... the Bishops have made the issue.'[10] Quoting the *Globe* extensively, the *Winnipeg Tribune* was less restrained. 'Are the Canadian people to hand over the country to the hierarchy?' the Manitoba Liberal organ demanded.[11]

Laurier was cautiously satisfied with his first impressions of the impact of the bishops' letter. Following an optimistic statement made to Willison on the day preceding the publication that 'things are moving very well in this province,'[12] the Liberal leader reported a fairly neutral reaction on the mandement to Mowat. 'I am glad that you do not think that the mandement has seriously altered the situation in Quebec,' Mowat replied on May 22. 'It has not affected the situation so much here as I apprehended when I wrote.'[13] Tarte reflected much the same attitude when he told Willison that 'the famous mandement ... is not as wicked as it might have been although it is doubtless directed against us.' Tarte expressed mild concern about the 'reflection on the independence of the electors of my province,' but was quite sure that the Liberals in Quebec would be 'able to face the mandement without much loss.'[14] Among clerics of Liberal leanings, there was more than a little relief at the moderation of the statement. 'Je n'en avais presque pas dormi de plaisir le première nuit après sa réception,' Abbé Proulx told Abbé Payette.[15]

In Payette's diocese, however, the mandement was not allowed a peaceful entry on the scene. Not surprisingly, and in spite of the 'no commentary' injunction issued to all curés along with the mandement, Bishop Laflèche moved to fulfil the strong promise he had made to Langevin before the Montreal conference. At High Mass on May 17 in the cathedral of Trois-Rivières, the seventy-eight-year-old prelate appeared in the pulpit with the mandement in one hand and a copy of Hansard in the other. He denounced the stand enunciated by Laurier in his March 3 speech in Parliament as 'le libéralisme condamné par l'église,' and insisted that Catholics, under pain of grave sin, could not vote for Laurier or his followers until they had publicly disavowed this position and unless they promised to vote for 'une loi réparatrice acceptée par les éveques.' In assessing the impact of this spectacular 'obiter dicta' to the general epis-

10 May 18, 1896   11 May 21, 1896
12 PAC, Willison Papers, Laurier to Willison, May 16, 1896
13 PAC, Laurier Papers, Mowat to Laurier, May 22, 1896
14 PAC, Willison Papers, Tarte to Willison, May 17, 1896
15 ASST, Proulx Papers, Proulx to Payette, May 22, 1896

copal letter, it should be noted that Laflèche's sermon did not receive widespread publicity until a significant moderate reaction to the collective statement had been experienced. Secondly, although *L'Electeur*'s subsequent vehemence against Laflèche evoked a good deal of sympathy for the elderly prelate from other bishops, such did not necessarily imply imitation. Moreover, while propagandists in both parties quoted the Laflèche manifesto widely, its extremity allowed Liberal publicists to assume the role of champions of the official mandement of the bishops. Finally, according to editor Pacaud, Laflèche and his quoters had polarized the clergy in Laurier's favour far more than prudence would allow them to proclaim.[16]

The Laflèche sermon and *L'Electeur*'s over-reaction demonstrated the degree to which the school question tended to disrupt the normal flow of political forces. Regardless of the point of departure, any survey of the campaign constantly encounters the complication introduced by the religio-racial-constitutional issue of remedialism and by the church-state tension at many levels. Laflèche had proceeded through an emphatic 'fait accompli' to answer the apparently unasked question whether a bishop in his own diocese could disregard the 'no commentary' rule imposed on the curés. Fabre's argument, when he restrained Langevin, that conflicting interpretations had to be avoided, logically extended to Quebec bishops; Laflèche evidently thought otherwise and opened the door for others to follow his example. The elderly bishop's bold action faced others with the choice of repudiation, silence, sympathy, or imitation. Thus the question remained: how much clerical interference following the Laflèche pattern and going beyond the mandement would be attempted?

CHARGES OF 'INFLUENCE INDUE'

Evidence on the precise degree of such clerical activity is, to say the least, garbled. Most of the secondary accounts seem to have relied on strongly partisan sources. Survey writers from Willison through Skelton, Lower, McInnis, Wade, and Schull have accepted the Laflèche mentality and statement as typical and universal among the Quebec clergy.[17] Two of the

---

16 AAQ, Pacaud to Laflamme, n.d. There may have been some suggestion here of a swing to Laurier by the lower clergy in opposition to the higher, but very little was made of this point by either Liberals or Conservatives during the campaign. For further details of the Laflèche episode, see Crunican, 'Bishop Laflèche and the Mandement of 1896,' pp.52–61

17 The accounts of Saywell in his introduction to *The Canadian Journal of Lady Aberdeen, 1893–98* and of Clark in *The Manitoba School Question*, 1968, strongly suggest the need for revision of the traditional interpretation.

favourite French sources for more recent works have been R. Rumilly and
L.O. David. Rumilly records a fairly large group of newspaper excerpts,
but generally selects the most extreme statements from each paper.[18]
David's work, especially *Le Clergé, Sa Mission, Son Oeuvre*, was much
closer to campaign literature than to a sober record of the 1896 campaign.
'Le clergé n'a rien vu, rien entendu, excepté ce qui lui permettait d'écraser
le parti libéral,' David wrote, and included 'la plupart des prêtres' in his
indictment.[19] The transition to the description of Laurier being 'denounced
from every pulpit' was an easy one.[20] A further embarrassment in many
existing accounts, deserving mention only because of a curious reliance
persistently accorded, is the repetition of hallowed but unsubstantiated
anecdotes. Most popular among these are Rumilly's tale of two farmers at
the Bonsecours market in Montreal, and Renaud Lavergne's account of a
Bégin campaign against Laurier in Mégantic county in late May. Both
stories remain as monuments to the ease with which vague rumour hardened into solemn truth, and each is contradicted by known facts and
documents.[21]

Probably the most careful attempt to draw up a survey of the number and
degree of clerical excesses during the election was that compiled by Abbé
J.B. Proulx on behalf of Laurier and his supporters for presentation to the
Vatican authorities in late 1896 and early 1897. Entitled *Documents pour
servir à l'intelligence de la question des écoles du Manitoba*, Proulx's work
paralleled a document sent to Rome under the title of *An Appeal of Catholic
Liberal Members of Parliament and Senators*.[22] The latter statement,
however, like L.O. David's booklet, *Le Clergé*, suffered from indiscrimi-
nate accusation and included several major errors of fact. Probably written
with a knowledge of the mildly reproving letters from the Holy See to the
bishops, the *Appeal* made no mention of the position, so hotly maintained
during the election, that Liberals as well as Conservatives subscribed to the
mandement. Conveniently ignoring Sir John Thompson, the document
devoted a rather lengthy passage to the importance of Canada having a
Catholic prime minister for the first time. The *Appeal* accused 'plusieurs
évêques et un grand nombre de prêtres' with active Conservative cam-

18 *Mgr. Laflèche et son temps*, pp.400–17
19 *Le Clergé Canadien, Sa Mission, Son Oeuvre*, p.74
20 Lower, *Colony to Nation*, p.396
21 Rumilly, *Mgr. Laflèche et Son Temps*, p.415; Lavergne, 'Mémoires' (manuscrit
   dactylographié), p.129. See below, pp.283–5.
22 PAC, Laurier Papers, November 1896. Tarte later brought the attention of the House of
   Commons to this *Appeal* (Canada, House of Commons, *Debates*, 1897, March 30, p.190).

paigning, not mentioning Emard or anyone else of more moderate persuasion.[23] Proulx's *Documents pour servir* was likewise a lawyer's brief presenting cases to substantiate a point. Unlike the *Appeal*, however, it was restrained in tone and careful in its distinctions on the degree of 'influence indue' charged against individual clerics. After a general review of the history of the school question, Proulx presented the general episcopal mandement, and insisted that 'les libéraux en général ... ont reçu cette lettre pastorale avec le plus grand respect.'[24] Proulx's comments appearing as footnotes to the mandement and subsequent documents, made a key point of the distinction between '*une* législation' which the mandement had called for and the Liberals promised to support, and '*la* loi,' meaning the Dickey remedial bill, which the Conservatives kept claiming had been specified by the bishops.

Predictably, Laflèche's anti-Laurier sermon occupied a prominent place in Proulx's charges. Insisting, as Liberal speakers did throughout the campaign, that Laflèche had taken Laurier's celebrated parliamentary statement completely out of context, Proulx complained of the triumphal use made of the bishop's words by Conservative organizers and candidates. Worst of all, Proulx's commentary claimed, was the chain reaction of approval and imitation which the Laflèche sermon had set off among 'quelques évêques' and 'un nombre de prêtres.'[25] The indictment then proceeded to specific instances of charges against individual bishops and priests. Among the bishops other than Laflèche, those most directly accused were Labrecque, Blais, and Cameron. Labrecque's June 11 letter to Laflèche, calling the latter's sermon 'si juste, si plein de doctrine et si nécessaire,' was taken as full agreement with the elderly bishop.[26] There was, however, no suggestion that Labrecque had proceeded to imitate Laflèche's sermon.

The citations against Blais were more numerous and elaborate. Although once again there was no claim that the Rimouski bishop had given a Laflèche-style sermon, Blais' legalistic defence of Laflèche's right to speak as he did in his own diocese evoked Proulx's criticism.[27] The focus of

23 *Ibid.*, p.7639

24 Proulx, *Documents pour servir à l'intelligence de la question des écoles du Manitoba*, p.38. Laurier later felt obliged to deny that Proulx had been sent on any kind of official mission, but it is clear that Proulx was one of the influences prompting the 1897 peace-making visit of Mgr Merry del Val (Canada, House of Commons, *Debates*, September 17, 1899, p.1371).

25 *Ibid.*, p.54   26 *Ibid.*, p.106

27 *Ibid.*, p.108

complaint, however, was an interview which Blais gave on May 28 at Saint Hubert to the Conservative candidate for Temiscouata, P.E. Grandbois, and to his supporters. According to the account of the meeting given by C.E. Pouliot, the Liberal candidate, and by Blais himself in reply to Pouliot, the bishop did not forbid voting for Liberal candidates, but leaned strongly toward the Conservatives in his remarks. The most controversial statement made by Blais at Saint Hubert and in a letter to an unnamed curé (which, according to Proulx, 'circule dans les presbytères du diocèse ... pendant les dix derniers jours de la campagne') was a description of the Conservatives as having 'déjà travaillé et combattu sous la bannière des évêques.'[28] Pouliot and his Liberal counterpart in Rimouski riding, Dr J.B.R. Fiset, both had given written statements to Blais of their unconditional acceptance of the mandement, and both understood that the bishop had accepted their declarations. As a consequence, both sent elaborate protests to Blais over the Saint Hubert incident. The bishop's treatment of these two candidates who had repeatedly protested their loyalty to the church and the mandement appeared in Proulx's document as, at the very least, double-dealing.[29] In Pouliot's separate protest to the Vatican, moreover, charges more specific than those by any other candidate were made against a group of six curés in Temiscouata riding. It should be noted, however, that even here the charge of a Liberal vote being branded as sinful, was pointed out as an extremity – 'même quelques-uns ont ajouté que c'était péché de voter pour moi dans les circonstances,' Pouliot stated.[30] Furthermore, although several statements in the bishop's subsequent correspondence confirmed his strong endorsement of the Conservatives, Blais in his letters never simply equated a Liberal vote with disobedience to himself or to the bishops generally. Finally, and what may have been politically most important for Pouliot, it was known that the curé of his home parish, Fraserville, also named Blais, was at least neutral and was one of the clerics being regarded as pro-Liberal.[31]

Bishop Cameron's stark pro-Conservative stand in Antigonish was briefly mentioned and held up for reproof in Proulx's indictment.[32] Two other prelates, Gravel and Bégin, were cited in the documentation. In the

28 *Ibid.*, p.117
29 *Ibid.*, p.116
30 PAC, Lapointe Papers, Correspondance et Memoranda, 1935–1941, Pouliot to the 'Congregatio Pro Propaganda Fide,' n.d.
31 *L'Electeur*, May 25, 1896. Fraserville became Rivière-du-Loup in 1919
32 Proulx, *Documents pour servir à l'intelligence de la question des écoles du Manitoba*, p.115. See below, pp.307–9.

case of Bishop Gravel, the statement reproduced was that prelate's June 21 pastoral letter which specifically referred to the conduct of J.H. Leduc, Liberal incumbent and again candidate for Nicolet Riding. Gravel quoted from a statement he had given Leduc after the latter had made the declaration required by the mandement. The bishop's directive, although it specifically exempted those voting Liberal from the possible charge of grave sin, leaned, in Proulx's words, 'tout à fait dans le sens conservateur.' According to Gravel's letter, the reason for making a statement criticizing the Liberal position was that, after Leduc's declaration accepting the mandement had been received, 'j'ai été informé qu'on faisait circuler la rumeur que j'étais rallié au programme libéral.' Gravel added that he had first made these clarifications about Leduc to the parishioners of Saint Celestin.[33] Perhaps coincidentally, the curé of Saint Celestin, Monsignor Marquis, was a Laurier supporter and had written the Liberal leader that he would give at least unobtrusive support to Leduc, 'au risque de donner à certains gens des crises de nerfs.'[34]

The situation involving Archbishop Bégin was more complicated and, because of the fifteen federal seats included in his diocese, more significant. Proulx's charge against Bégin, like that in many subsequent accounts, focused on a much-publicized letter sent from Vicar General Marois to Curé J.E. Rouleau of Saint Ubalde in Portneuf riding on 4 June:

En réponse à votre lettre demandant s'il y a péché mortel pour quiconque ne suivra pas la direction donnée par les Evêques dans leur mandement collectif, touchant le réglement de la question manitobaine, lorsque son attention aura été attirée sur le fait que cette direction oblige en conscience, je suis chargé par Monseigneur l'administrateur de vous dire qu'il y a faute grave – péché mortel – de ne point suivre la direction des premiers pasteurs, et que les paroles que vous citez de la page 7 du mandement signifient exactement que ce sera une faute grave et mortelle d'agir ainsi, c'est-à-dire de ne pas obéir aux Evêques. Si quelqu'un vous dit: en dépit de vos raisonnements, j'ai plus de confiance en M. Laurier et je vote pour son candidat, cet électeur à moins d'avoir perdu le sens commun, sera coupable de faute grave et mortelle.[35]

Proulx's footnotes to the Marois statement were careful to point out the distinction between the first sentence of the letter, which quoted Bégin, and

33 *Ibid.*, p.128
34 PAC, Laurier Papers, Marquis to Laurier, n.d.
35 Proulx, *Documents pour servir*, pp.123–4

the second, which did not. Concerning the conclusion that a vote by a reasonable person for a Laurier candidate had to be considered a grave sin, Proulx was convinced that this was Marois' personal 'obiter dicta.' 'Nous doutons fort,' Proulx wrote, 'qu'il se soit inspiré de la prudence de son archevêque en formulant la déduction que renferme la deuxième phrase; car Monseigneur Bégin ne nous a pas accoutumés à le voir se compromettre ainsi à propositions évidemment discutables et carrées.' Proulx stated that the main complaint against Bégin was that the Marois letter had not been explicitly repudiated by the archbishop, and that this had prompted several curés who might otherwise have abstained, to come out against Laurier.[36] In point of fact, Bégin was absent from Quebec City on his pastoral and confirmation tour from late May until at least June 15, and it is not clear when he received the report of the Marois letter. On June 12, however, a second message was sent to another curé of Portneuf County, again by Marois in Bégin's name. 'Vu les déclarations à moi faites par M. Joly,' the statement read, 'on devra s'abstenir de dire aux gens que c'est un péché mortel de voter pour lui,' Reflecting an appreciation of the tendency of each party to play up any episcopal statement as full-blown approval, the message concluded: 'Cela ne veut pas dire que les curés doivent engager leurs paroissiens à lui donner leurs suffrages.' Just as the letter to Rouleau found its way into Conservative publications, the June 12 letter quickly appeared in *L'Electeur*.[37]

Proulx's conclusion that Bégin refused to go beyond the general mandement was supported by several independent pieces of evidence. The archbishop's letters to Rinfret, Pouliot, and especially to Henri Joly de Lotbinière reaffirmed his personal conviction of the need for a remedial law, but in no sense condemned either the Liberal candidates or Laurier. On June 9, Bégin told Joly that, as bishop, his duty was not to approve or reject political candidates, but to insist on the religious duty of voters to follow the mandement. 'En adhérant formellement et solonellement à ce document,' Bégin wrote, 'vous ne pouvez être ostracisé par les électeurs catholiques ou être réputé indigne de leurs suffrages.'[38] Bégin's thought was more clearly revealed in his fairly extensive correspondence with Archbishop Langevin during the campaign. While Langevin was still in Quebec province, and before the appearance of the mandement, Bégin had

36 *Ibid.*, p.124
37 June 15, 1896
38 AAQ, Bégin to Joly, June 9, 1896; also *L'Electeur*, June 15, 1896. *L'Electeur*, however, failed to carry a second Bégin letter to Joly, dated June 15, which was much more specific in demanding support for a remedial law (AAQ, Bégin to Joly, June 15, 1896).

a wry comment on the sudden devotion of politicians. 'Je suis assiégé d'hommes politiques ces jours-ci,' Bégin told Langevin. 'Leur dévotion et leur dévouement à l'épiscopat s'accroissent avec les approches du danger.'[39] No specific names were mentioned, but it seems that people from both parties were bending a little too low for Bégin's taste. On his way to the West after officiating at the marriage of the daughter of Sir Hector Langevin, the St Boniface archbishop wrote Bégin from Ottawa that he had left Quebec City 'avec la tristesse au cœur.' What was bothering Langevin 'n'est pas le ton modéré du magnifique mandement collectif ... mais c'est l'apathie de certains prêtres et la mauvaise esprit de quelques autres.' Clearly showing his own partisan position, Langevin lamented the attitude of the people of Saint Roch, and simply rejected Laurier since the Liberal leader 'ne fait que des promesses ou déclarations vagues et qui ne l'engagent à rien; s'il arrive, nos écoles sont perdues.' Leaving no doubt about his approval of Laflèche, Langevin stated that 'le sermon de Mgr. Laflèche démasquant et dénonçant Laurier, le Hansard d'une main, et la lettre collective de l'autre, a fait sensation et a dû ouvrir les yeux à plusieurs.' Langevin concluded his quite despondent letter with the suggestion that he might send an open letter to Laurier in an attempt to get the Liberal leader to make a more precise promise of remedial legislation.[40]

Bégin's reply to Langevin, written on June 2 from Saint Anselme, Dorchester county, stated that the western bishop's letter had just caught up with him on his pastoral tour. Bégin's opinion was that an open letter to Laurier would not bring a more specific pledge than before, and would only result in Langevin's being called more than ever the dupe of a party which the Liberals said had deceived him and Bishop Taché for six years. Without mentioning Laflèche, Bégin insisted that the best policy was to show no opposition to any candidate pledging his support for remedial legislation, irrespective of party. Only such a stand, Bégin stated, would restrain independent Conservatives like Tardivel, 'qui sont certainement très dévoués à la cause de vos écoles catholiques et qui vous trouvent bleu, trop bleu, c'est à dire trop confiant dans le gouvernement conservateur; ils craignent que vous n'éprouviez encore des déceptions.' Then came a perceptive analysis about what the election would bring:

Pour apprécier justement la position que prennent nos catholiques en très grand nombre, il faut bien se mettre dans l'esprit qu'ils sont profondément convaincus

39 AASB, Bégin to Langevin, May 12, 1896
40 AAQ, Langevin to Bégin, May 27, 1896

que M. Laurier seul fera rendre justice aux Catholiques du Manitoba, et que les Conservateurs ne vous feront qu'une demi-mesure ou même rien du tout. Je ne dis pas que leur opinion et leur confiance sont justifiables, mais je dis que leur vote libéral ne peut pas être interprété comme un acte d'hostilité à l'épiscopat et aux écoles séparées. Ainsi s'explique le vote que les gens de St. Roch donneront à M. Laurier; ces gens-là pour la plupart, croiront faire acte de religion en refusant de donner leur suffrage à un candidat conservateur. Vous trouvez cela étrange, et pourtant c'est l'exacte vérité.

Bégin next reminded Langevin of the importance of the tariff and other economic questions, a point which many of the bishops too easily forgot. Commenting on Langevin's fear that a large number of priests in the Quebec diocese were actively favouring Laurier, Bégin stated that this was simply unfounded. In any case, he was sure that not ten out of the total of five hundred in the diocese had said a word of open criticism against the bishops' general mandement. The great majority had kept out of any direct action beyond reading the mandement as directed, Bégin said; 'nos prêtres en général,' he stated, 'tiennent à être en bons termes avec tout leur monde et à ne pas faire de politique.' Finally, regarding Angers's reported complaint to Marois that certain bishops had given letters of support to Liberal candidates, Bégin said that he did not know what others had done, but that personally he had simply refrained from reproof of anyone if pledges were given as directed.[41]

It must at least be concluded that the all-embracing significance attached to the Marois letter to Rouleau has not been warranted. Furthermore, it hardly needs stressing that Lavergne's colourful anecdote about a fiery Bégin crusade against Laurier in Mégantic just before the Quebec prelate's letter to Langevin is more than suspect.[42] Considering the use made of Laflèche's statements by the Conservative press and organizers, any similar utterance by Bégin would certainly have been trumpeted without hesitation. Not a single such report was made during the campaign.

SIGNIFICANT ABSTENTIONS

The conduct of the bishops not mentioned in Proulx's indictment was also significant. Most important of these was Archbishop Fabre. With eighteen

41 AASB, Bégin to Langevin, June 2, 1896
42 Schull, *Laurier*, p.319, and Frère Antoine (Maurice Carrier), 'Laurier, citoyen d'Arthabaska' (thesis), both use this unreliable story to add colour to their accounts.

ridings within his direct jurisdiction – more than any other bishop – his statements and actions were watched very closely. Already ill with jaundice, which would take his life before the year was out, Fabre's activities during the campaign seem to have been limited to checking those who went too far in either direction. Archbishop Langevin had been restrained in mid-May in his home riding of Laprairie-Napierville; at the end of the month and in early June, it was Curé Bédard of St Constant in the same riding accused of being actively pro-Laurier, who was gently but firmly reproved. The Conservative candidate, Conrad Pelletier, had complained about Bédard's activities to Langevin, saying that the curé and his assistant were stating openly that Fabre disagreed with Langevin over the remedial law. 'N'y a-t-il pas moyen de faire cesser M. le curé Bédard?' Pelletier demanded. 'Il fait un cabal ouvert chez lui.'[43] On June 8, Langevin wrote an emotional letter of protest to Fabre, implying that the latter had given in to pressure from D. Monet, the Liberal candidate, when he had restrained Langevin in May. Despite repeated expressions of respect for Fabre, the St Boniface archbishop stated that he had in fact written to Rome defending his own action. As for the reports about Bédard's activities, Langevin bewailed that 'tout cela me fait mal au cœur. Sans me plaindre, j'oserais espérer qu'un simple curé n'aura pas le liberté de contrebalancer mon action dans mon propre comté.'[44] Fabre's reply, written from Chambly, denied first of all Langevin's suggestion about Monet's influence. Concerning Bédard's sermons, extracts of which had been received from Pelletier, Fabre's judgment was that 'les extraits ... prouvent qu'il s'embrouille dans les faits, mais ne me semble pas bien dangereux.' It does not seem that Fabre went beyond an injunction which he sent to Bédard on May 30: 'Je vous défends de faire des commentaires.'[45]

Somewhat ironically, it was the Laprairie-Napierville riding and Monet's difficulties with the clergy which La Patrie singled out after the election as a special victory over 'l'influence indue.' La Patrie charged that all but one curé (presumably Bédard) in the two counties had been active against Monet.[46] It is not impossible that the youthful and irrepressible Liberal candidate provoked an escalation of criticism during the campaign; his telegram to Laflèche in the first flush of victory was the most notable and, as far as can be ascertained, the only case of overt 'rubbing it in'

43 AASB, Pelletier to Langevin, June 2, 1896
44 AAM, Langevin to Fabre, June 8, 1896
45 *Ibid.*, Fabre to Langevin, June 12, 1896; Fabre to Bédard, May 30, 1896
46 June 26, 1896

against the hierarchy after the election.[47] In any case, Archbishop Fabre's name remained conspicuously absent from the charges. Later comments on Fabre's criticism of the subsequent Laurier-Greenway agreement used the Montreal prelate's impartiality during the election campaign as a point of emphasis; 'His Grace ... never gave any indication of the tendency of his political choice. He allowed his flock to decide for themselves whether Sir Charles Tupper or Wilfrid Laurier was the right man to place in power.'[48]

Even Liberal partisan news comment grouped LaRocque of Sherbrooke and Lorrain of Pontiac with Emard in the matter of neutrality during the campaign. As for Moreau of St Hyacinthe and Duhamel of Ottawa, on several occasions clear sympathy for the Conservative cause was expressed in their correspondence. Each wrote to Laflèche expressing sympathy bordering on support after the attacks of L'Electeur.[49] Yet there was little indication during or after the campaign that either went beyond the mandement in any public statement.

Contemporary and subsequent partisan accounts on both sides tended to highlight the instances of open clerical interference favouring the Conservatives. Cases of overt pro-Liberal clerics were, probably with justification, looked upon as exceptions. They were sufficiently numerous, however, to be complained about not only by Langevin but by several other pro-Conservative clerics as well as by Conservative candidates. Besides Bédard of St Constant, Marquis of St Celestin, and Blais of Fraserville, Canon Archambault of the Montreal Chancery, Abbé Proulx of St Lin (Assomption Riding) Abbé Dugas of Ste Anne des Plaines and Mgr Guay of Lévis were 'mentioned in dispatches' as actively pro-Liberal.[50] Others, such as Curé Gingras of Château Richer and Georges Dugas, the former Manitoba missionary, were cited as being violently critical of Conservative 'betrayals,' following the lead of Tardivel and La Vérité.[51]

The incidence of clerical abstention and neutrality is most difficult of all to establish, except negatively, if only because intervention was so much more newsworthy. However, several instances of refusal to bow to pressure to align specifically with the Conservative position were recorded by

47 AETR, Monet to Laflèche, June 23, 1896; it was later reported that Laurier reproved his youthful supporter for this gesture of defiance (AASB, Béliveau to Langevin, August 3, 1896).
48 Daily Nor'Wester, November 28, 1896
49 AETR, Moreau to Laflèche, June 10, 1896; Duhamel to Laflèche, June 9, 1896
50 AASB, Abbé Hermas Langevin to Langevin, June 12, 1896; L'Electeur, June 15, 1896
51 Ibid., Bégin to Langevin, June 2, 1896

L'Electeur and *La Presse*. Perhaps most notable was the case of Monsignor Laflamme, superior of the Quebec Seminary. After more than a little Conservative publicity had been given to the inscription for the first time of the seminary priests on the voters' lists – 'on en concluait un soulèvement en masse du clergé de Québec durant la campagne électorale,' *La Presse* reported – Laflamme requested that the priests' names be withdrawn from the lists 'pour enlever tout prétexte de croire que les prêtres de notre maison tiennent à se mêler de politique.'[52] On June 4, *L'Electeur*, insisting that it was not thereby claiming pro-Liberal activity, praised the neutrality of the clergy of Montmorency riding. The Liberal newspaper mentioned three specific curés, McCrea of St Joachim, Blais of St Laurent, and Leclerc of St François de l'Ile d'Orléans, who had explicitly resisted Conservative pressure to go beyond the requirements of the mandement. Finally, *L'Electeur* concluded, 'Les Réverends Pères Rédemptoristes de Ste. Anne [de Beaupré] gardent également la plus stricte neutralité et donne le bel example de la déférence la plus digne aux injonctions de l'épiscopat.'[53] As for the clergy in the Valleyfield diocese, Bishop Emard in his post-election report to Rome was satisfied that they had followed the injunction to neutrality between political parties which had accompanied the mandement.[54] In summary, from the evidence in ecclesiastical sources alone, it must be concluded that the traditional picture of a unanimous anti-Liberal clerical crusade in Quebec in 1896, represents a major, if attractive, misreading of the event.

CLERICAL ACTIVITY AND RESULTS OUTSIDE QUEBEC

The performance of the Roman Catholic bishops and clergy outside Quebec was also watched with great care. The suggestion that the English-speaking bishops, especially those in Ontario, would sign the mandement was effectively dropped after Langevin's visit to Archbishop Walsh during the last week of April. It was clear, however, that the motive for this reticence was, in most cases, one of prudence with regard to their own local situation, rather than one of disagreement with the principle or

52 April 29, 1896
53 *L'Electeur*, June 4, 1896. Ironically, Montmorency was one of only two ridings in the entire Quebec City district to return a Conservative.
54 AEV, Emard to Ledochowski, July 6, 1896. It should be noted that on Sunday, June 14, Emard published a brief pastoral letter which simply gave renewed emphasis to the general mandement scheduled to be read a second time on June 21. In view of the Laflèche affair, however, this move was regarded in some quarters as pro-Liberal.

content of the mandement. *L'Electeur* made the statement that Walsh was against the mandement and had refused to sign it; evidently hoping that its readers would forget Bishop Cameron at least, the newspaper added a similar remark about the Maritime bishops.[55] Hurried messages from both Marois and Bégin urged Langevin to obtain a statement from Walsh contradicting *L'Electeur*'s claim.[56] Langevin's reply was that he had in fact contacted Walsh and the remaining Ontario bishops to request at least private statements of support for the mandement.[57] Walsh's letter to Langevin of May 19 contradicted *L'Electeur*'s story, and indicated that personally, he too could only see the Conservatives as able to give justice. The Toronto archbishop felt that it was impossible to contradict every misrepresentation by a newspaper, but at the same time revealed a quite definite pro-Conservative reading of the mandement. 'Why,' Walsh exclaimed, 'the *Electeur* in one of its last issues laboured to prove to its readers that the principles enumerated in the mandement fully justify the Catholics in voting for the Liberal candidate!' Walsh pointed out that the Ontario bishops had refrained from a public statement as a matter of prudence, but agreed that 'the situation in Lower Canada is quite different.' The Ontario decision, therefore, should not be taken as a criticism of what the Quebec bishops had done. 'I would not dream of obtruding my views and opinions on the venerable and learned Lower Canadian bishops,' Walsh stated. 'To do so would appear to me to be both presumptuous and impertinent.'[58] Archbishop Cleary was, if anything, more sympathetic to Langevin in his letter of May 21. Cleary stated that he had considered having the Kingston clergy read the mandement from their pulpits, 'but, since the other bishops of Ontario think that action on our part would effect little or no good, and would result probably in frustrating our purpose and turning away many now indifferent, I prefer to preserve a prudent silence before the public, as the "tutior pars."' Somewhat wryly, Cleary added that his own views were not unknown already.[59] Brief approvals of the mandement were sent by Bishops O'Connor of Peterborough on May 21 and Macdonald of

55 May 15, 1896
56 AASB, Marois to Langevin, May 15, 1896; Bégin to Langevin, May 16, 1896
57 AAQ, Langevin to Bégin, May 17, 1896
58 AASB, Walsh to Langevin, May 19, 1896. In his treatment of this episode, Paul Stevens notes that Walsh declined to sign the mandement, but does not give sufficient weight to the personal encouragement Walsh gave Langevin, nor to Walsh's rejection of Liberal attempts to enlist his name. Stevens, 'Laurier and the Liberal Party in Ontario' (thesis), pp.144–5
59 AASB, Cleary to Langevin, May 21, 1896

Alexandria on May 26, each indicating, however, that no public statement would be made.[60]

One further incident involving *L'Electeur* again brought Archbishop Walsh into the picture. This was a sermon preached by a Father Minehan of Toronto, sharply criticizing Bishop Laflèche's extension of the mandement and his condemnation of Laurier. According to *L'Electeur*, the Minehan sermon had been preached in the Toronto Cathedral in Walsh's presence, and thus it implied his approval.[61] T.C. Casgrain, the Conservative candidate for Montmorency, quickly got word to Walsh that his name was once more being paraded as a champion by the Quebec Liberals. According to *La Minerve*, Walsh wired Casgrain a denial of *L'Electeur*'s version of the Minehan affair. 'Father Minehan is pastor of a small suburban church,' Walsh stated, 'and his utterances were made without my knowledge and have received my condemnation.'[62] That the question of support for one party or the other was left open for Toronto and Ontario Catholics, however, was shown by the attitude of the widely respected *Catholic Register* of Toronto. The *Register* calmly but firmly disagreed with Laflèche's interpretation of Laurier's parliamentary declaration, and called the Trois-Rivières bishop's sermon 'beyond the limits of an authentic interpretation of their joint declaration' and 'only the individual opinion of Mgr. Laflèche.'[63]

Post-election comments about Catholic clerical activity in Ontario reflected a mixed picture. David Mills, feeling badly thanked for the case he had made in Parliament in favour of Manitoba Catholic claims, attributed his defeat in Bothwell to a 'beautiful combination of the parish priests and the P.P.A.'s.'[64] Some pro-Conservative action by priests was charged in

60 *Ibid.*, O'Connor to Langevin, May 21, 1896; Macdonald to Langevin, May 26, 1896
61 May 28, 1896
62 *La Minerve*, June 1, 1896. A post-election letter from Minehan to Laurier suggested that, despite Walsh's reproof of his statements, 'the Archbishop of this diocese was not very sorry they were said ... They showed that the Catholic Church in Canada was not tied to the Tory Party' (PAC, Laurier Papers, Minehan to Laurier, July 6, 1896). Re Walsh, see below p.290.
63 Quoted in *L'Electeur*, May 29, 1896
64 PAC, Laurier Papers, Mills to Laurier, June 25, 1896. The incidence and effect of Protestant activists in even more difficult to establish than the Roman Catholic. The resolutions of the Methodist and Presbyterian assemblies, and, more violently, the manifesto issued to Canadian Orange Lodges, took adamant stands against the official policy of the government. At the same time, several Liberal partisans reported either pro-McCarthy or anti-Laurier sermons by Protestant ministers in their ridings. See, for example, E. Stewart to Laurier, June 25, 1896; Dean Egan (Barrie) to Laurier, July 4, 1896.

Bishop Macdonald's diocese of Alexandria.[65] On the other hand, W.H. Barry, enthusiastic Liberal lawyer from Ottawa, reported significant clerical favour for Laurier, and added the interesting note that 'the Sisters of Loretto Abbey at Toronto have been your staunch friends during the campaign ... written across my current number of "Leaflets from Loretto" are the words "Hurray for Laurier!" '[66] The defeated Liberal candidate for Dundas, Adam Johnston, placed the greatest blame for his defeat on the influence of canal officials on the workers. On the Catholic factor, Johnston remarked that 'the Catholic Liberals voted for me to a man as they had previously done. The Rev. Father Twomey supported me heartily though he judged it best not to vote himself.'[67] Frank Anglin, continuing to be one of Laurier's chief contacts in the Toronto area, had words of praise for both Bishop Lorrain, whose diocese included Renfrew and Pembroke, and for Archbishop Walsh. Anglin spoke of Walsh's resistance to 'a very strenuous endeavour made by less discreet ecclesiastics to induce our archbishop to come out openly in favour of the government.' Anglin claimed to have persuaded Walsh in at least one constituency 'to intervene on behalf of the Liberal candidate,' and added that only Emerson Coatsworth, the single government nominee in the Toronto area who was not radically anti-remedialist, had received any word of approbation from the archbishop.[68]

In the Maritimes, clerical action can best be viewed in a survey of the effect of the school question on the campaign of the two major parties. On April 25, Sir Charles Tupper wrote to two Cape Breton parish priests requesting their support in the forthcoming election.[69] Also by letter, Sir Hibbert Tupper approached Archbishop O'Brien of Halifax, who was in Rome until mid-June. O'Brien replied that he would 'endeavour to help what I believe to be the right cause.'[70] O'Brien's 'help' came in the form of a public letter to the Catholic voters of Halifax, published in the leading Nova Scotian Roman Catholic newspaper, the Antigonish *Casket*, on May 21. After stressing the necessity of abiding by the constitution, the O'Brien letter struck out strongly against the idea of an inquiry as a 'hollow pretense.'[71] In Antigonish, there was little chance of mistaking the attitude

65 PAC, Laurier Papers, J.L. Wilson to Laurier, June 25, 1896
66 *Ibid.*, Barry to Laurier, June 30, 1896
67 *Ibid.*, Johnston to Laurier, July 17, 1896
68 *Ibid.*, Anglin to Laurier, June 25, 1896. It is significant, of course, that Coatsworth was opposed and defeated in Toronto East not by a Liberal but by an anti-remedialist Independent Conservative.
69 PAC, Tupper Papers, Tupper to McNeil, Tupper to McPherson, April 25, 1896
70 PAC, C.H. Tupper Papers, O'Brien to C.H. Tupper, April 30, 1896
71 Antigonish *Casket*, May 21, 1896

of Bishop Cameron. Cameron had already let it be known that he considered the Quebec Bishops' mandement too weak.[72] In the spirit of his
'hell-inspired hypocrites' letter of the Cape Breton by-election in February, the elderly prelate issued an equally anti-Liberal directive at the end
of the general campaign. Addressed on June 20 to the Catholics of Antigonish County, Cameron's letter stated that he had studied carefully the
positions of the government and the opposition on the school question and
bluntly proclaimed that 'it is the plain conscientious duty of every Catholic
elector to vote for the Conservative candidate; and this declaration no
Catholic in this diocese, be he priest or layman, has a right to dispute.'[73]
Understandably enough, the Cameron letter was cited by Proulx as the
most flagrant case of ecclesiastical alignment with one political party
during the campaign.[74] At the same time, the fact that it was issued so late
in the campaign, combined with the pro-minority attitude of the Liberal
candidate, McIsaac, reduced its impact. It was significant that the two
leading newspapers of the province, the Conservative Halifax *Herald* and
the Liberal Halifax *Morning Chronicle*, deliberately played down the issue
of the school question during the campaign.[75] As reflected by these journals, neither party avoided the school problem, but both strove to reduce
the danger of an appeal to religious prejudice. Led by such prominent
supporters of the remedial bill as the prime minister himself, his son Sir
Charles Hibbert, and the man who introduced the remedial bill, Minister of
Justice A.R. Dickey, Conservative candidates stood by the official party
policy to 'uphold the constitution.'[76]

On the Liberal side, Laurier's call for an inquiry in Manitoba was the
main theme pursued on the school question. Probably the most significant
role in the campaign was that played by W.S. Fielding, premier of Nova
Scotia. Not a candidate himself, yet tentatively though unofficially in line
for an important cabinet post, Fielding lent support to Liberal candidates
all across the province, while Sir Charles Tupper was for the most part
resting in preparation for the exhausting tour still to come in Ontario.[77]

---

72 AASB, Cameron to Langevin, May 18, 1896
73 PAC, Laurier Papers, v. II, no.4359, June 20, 1896
74 Proulx, *Documents pour servir à l'intelligence de la question des Ecoles du Manitoba*,
   p.115
75 See McLaughlin, 'The Canadian General Election of 1896 in Nova Scotia' (thesis),
   pp.118–21
76 *Ibid*., p.191
77 *Ibid*., p.127. This picture of Tupper's relative inactivity revises the impression of a busy
   tour given in Mackintosh, 'The Career of Sir Charles Tupper in Canada, 1864–1900'
   (thesis), p.454.

With impeccable credentials in the field of provincial rights, Fielding was a natural promoter of Laurier's 'sunny ways.' At the same time, with Senator L.G. Power and Benjamin Russell in Halifax and Colin McIsaac in Antigonish prominent in the Liberal team, there was little suggestion that the Manitoba minority's pleas for justice would be ignored. Letters to Laurier both during and after the election spoke of the impact of clerical activity against Liberal candidates, but Senator Power's comment on the election in Halifax of one Protestant Conservative (Borden) and one Protestant Liberal (Russell) over two Catholics, Kenney and Keefe, stressed that neither victory nor defeat was particularly connected with religion or the school question. McIsaac's victory in Antigonish, however, was, in Power's opinion, a 'death blow to Bishop Cameron's influence.'[78] In the defeat of A.R. Dickey in Cumberland, it may be concluded that, despite Baptist and Methodist opposition to the justice minister on remedialism, it was 'impossible to assign any single factor as the predominant issue.'[79] Once again, the most important single fact in the five-seat gain which the Liberals achieved in Nova Scotia seems to have been the success of Fielding and his colleagues in shifting the focus of the campaign to the new Liberal trade platform.[80]

From Prince Edward Island, where the Conservatives gained one seat and the Liberals lost two (with one seat disappearing in redistribution), there were scattered reports of clerical pro-Conservative activity.[81] But as in Nova Scotia it seemed that the main focus of attention was kept on the trade question. In New Brunswick, with two fewer seats because of redistribution, the Conservatives dropped from thirteen to nine members and the Liberals rose from three to five.[82] On the issue of the school question, there was at least no outright rejection of remedialism. The strongest pro-remedialist, John Costigan, after obtaining a letter of support from Archbishop Langevin, was returned with a solid majority in the expanded riding of Victoria.[83] At the same time, R.C. Weldon, the one vocal anti-remedialist among the Conservatives, lost his seat to W.J. Lewis, an Independent Liberal. Finance Minister Foster, although accused in Quebec by *L'Electeur* and *La Presse* of ignoring the school question,

78 PAC, Laurier Papers, Power to Laurier, June 25, 1896
79 McLaughlin, 'The Canadian General Election of 1896 in Nova Scotia' (thesis), p.180
80 *Ibid.*, p.192–3
81 See for example PAC, Laurier Papers, S. Perry to Laurier, July 11, 1896
82 See Appendix 2.
83 AASB, Costigan to Langevin, May 27, 1896; PAC, Costigan Papers, Langevin to Costigan, June 4, 1896; *The Canadian Parliamentary Guide, 1897*, p.203

clearly did not repudiate the official government policy or the remedialist position he had taken in the March debate and had no trouble retaining his massive majority in York.[84]

Manitoba provided the counterpart to Quebec in producing a startling result in the election. Presumed to be solidly against the federal government, because of the January provincial election, the 'threatened' province, gaining two seats in redistribution, returned four Conservatives, two Liberals (one of these by the margin of one vote) and D'Alton McCarthy in Brandon, who ran as an independent.[85] Several factors have been suggested to explain the outcome. The patron candidates clearly hurt the Liberals more than the Conservatives, perhaps changing the result in Marquette and Macdonald ridings.[86] More significant, however, was the Conservatives' handling of the school question and its juxtaposition with the issue of expansion and development. Only one of the four successful Conservative candidates, Roche in Marquette, took an adamant anti-remedialist stand.[87] LaRivière, the candidate with the widest margin of victory, scored heavily with the votes of his co-religionists in Provencher. N. Boyd in Macdonald riding and Hugh John Macdonald in Winnipeg both spoke in favour of moderate redress of minority grievances, urging, however, that this should and could be done at the local level.[88] Macdonald, after several accusations of equivocation on his version of the government's school policy, was prompted by a near-ultimatum from Archbishop Langevin to make his strongest statement in the direction of possible remedial legislation. Macdonald first rejected the suggestion that a speech he had given in Edmonton had endorsed Laurier's inquiry plan. 'If a dozen commissions of inquiry were appointed,' Macdonald wrote to Langevin, 'they could find nothing but what we know already.' He continued to favour settlement on the local level if possible, but 'if ... the provincial Gov't. turn a deaf ear in the future as they have done in the past to the request that they should right the wrong done, then I am in favour of remedial legislation, which will have become an undoubted duty.' Stretching the truth more than a little in describing the conditions under which he had agreed to enter Tupper's cabinet in the spring, Macdonald stated that 'had I not been in perfect accord with his views on this important question,

84 *La Presse*, May 27, 29, 30, 1896; *The Canadian Parliamentary Guide, 1897*, p.204
85 See Appendix 2.
86 Cooke, 'The Federal Election of 1896 in Manitoba' (thesis), p.205
87 *Ibid.*, p.206
88 *Ibid.*

I would not have accepted office in his cabinet.'[89] It was clear that what Macdonald, with the support of the *Manitoba Free Press*, successfully managed to do during the campaign was to play down the school question and stress economic development. The *Winnipeg Tribune* kept up its emphasis on the school question. The *Free Press*, avowedly independent but favouring the Conservatives, insisted that 'if wise, we shall drop it and the men who cling to it.'[90] Insisting that in any case the school question was safer with Tupper than with the untried French Canadian Laurier, the *Free Press* successfully emphasized the concrete promises made by Tupper for Northwest development and the building of the Hudson's Bay Railway. Replying to Joseph Martin's appeal to Winnipeg voters not to lose the sympathy of Ontario stirred up during the preceding years, the *Free Press* revealed an authentic Western restiveness against Eastern domination of all kinds. Referring to 'Ontario's sympathy,' the paper stated that 'it is a pity we ever have it, and the sooner it is lost the better. The school question would have been settled years ago if the Ontario politicians had kept their noses out of it ... They care little whether we have a school system of any sort.'[91] On the whole, the Conservative tactic of 'Manitoban opportunism' beginning with the Smith commission, turned out to be remarkably adept.[92]

As for Archbishop Langevin, he continued to be highly agitated, but in fact refrained from any sensational action. There was no doubt that Langevin subscribed to the Laflèche mentality favouring positive action wherever deemed necessary. Several priests in both Manitoba and the territories spoke of and were reported to have taken an explicitly pro-Conservative stand during the campaign.[93] In a letter to Duhamel, however, Langevin stated that there was such unanimity among Catholics, French and other, on the issue of remedialism, that he did not believe it necessary to risk the danger of a public episcopal statement. Ironically, it would seem that his warning to Hugh John Macdonald was the closest Langevin came to an official proclamation. That the archbishop was highly pleased with the results in Manitoba was more than evident.[94]

If the government was successful in retaining its standing in Manitoba, the Territories and British Columbia swung sharply to the Liberals, with the Conservatives retaining only three of the ten seats they had held.

89 AASB, H.J. Macdonald to Langevin, June 16, 1896
90 April 24, 1896
91 *Ibid.*, June 12, 1896
92 K.M. McLaughlin, unpublished manuscript, University of Toronto, 1968, Chapter II, p.35
93 AASB, G. Michel to Langevin, June 8, 1896; Père Leduc to Langevin, June 10, 1896
94 AAO, Langevin to Duhamel, June 8, 1896; AAM, Langevin to Fabre, June 24, 1896

Scattered reports showed some but not exclusive concentration on the school question in both areas. Judging from E.G. Prior's earlier pronouncements on remedialism, the two Conservative candidates who managed to retain their seats in British Columbia at least moderately supported the official government policy on the school issue.[95]

ONTARIO AND QUEBEC CONTRADICTIONS, LAURIER'S ADVANTAGE

In Ontario and Quebec, the dimensions of the later campaign of the two political parties were not greatly changed from the lines established at the beginning of the struggle. On the Conservative side, serious situations concerning the choice of candidates arose in both the central provinces. Clearly reflecting uneasiness, twelve sitting Conservatives from Quebec failed to contest their seats. Taillon resigned from the premiership of Quebec and Desjardins and Angers from the Senate to contest crucial and difficult ridings. Opposing Liberal stalwart Geoffrion in the combined riding of Chambly-Verchères, Taillon revealed to Langevin a frame of mind which was hardly that of a confident champion expecting to lead a people to victory.

J'ai hâte de constater jusqu'à quel point les catholiques du Bas Canada vont se laisser guider par l'esprit de parti. Je me défie d'eux, et c'est pour cela que j'ai consenti à m'engager dans la lutte. Si le peuple ne fait pas son devoir, on devra du moins reconnaître que les classes dirigeantes ont compris la situation.[96]

The situation involving Sir Adolphe Caron was equally unpromising for the Conservatives. Still smarting over his exclusion from Tupper's cabinet, Caron received the Conservative nomination for Dorchester County, south of Quebec City. According to a letter from his Castor rival, Angers, to Prime Minister Tupper, Caron from this vantage point was 'doing all he can to hurt us under the appearance of walking in the ranks.'[97] L'Electeur insisted that Caron's retirement from the Dorchester candidacy had been a manipulation on the part of the Angers faction.[98] Ironically, Caron man-

---

95 Prior, like Foster, Haggart, and Montague, was accused in Quebec of ignoring if not betraying the school question. See La Presse, May 27, 1896.
96 AASB, Taillon to Langevin, May 28, 1896
97 PAC, Tupper Papers, Angers to Tupper, May 13, 1896
98 June 8, 1896

aged to find an opening in the safe seat of Trois-Rivières–St Maurice; his replacement in Dorchester also won over the incumbent Independent Liberal, Dr Vaillancourt, while the three Castor cabinet ministers seeking seats were all defeated.

The most profound problem of the Conservatives, however, was that the Ontario and Quebec branches of the Tory team were irreconcilably embarrassed by each other. In the eyes of Quebec the image of a 'tolerant Ontario Toryism' simply ceased to exist.[99] In its place, there was evident a widespread sentiment against remedialism in any form among sitting members, new candidates and party faithful alike. Certainly nothing hurt the Conservatives in Quebec more than the number of Tory candidates in Ontario who were adamant and vocal opponents of separate schools under any circumstances. Among the Ontario Conservative leaders, both Haggart and Montague were suspected by L'Electeur and La Presse of having scuttled the remedial bill.[100] The extremity of schism within the official Conservative party was symbolized by Clarke Wallace's address to the electors of West York. So roughshod was Wallace's treatment of the Quebec bishops and Sir Charles Tupper alike that La Presse felt compelled to praise Dalton McCarthy in comparison with the Orange Master. McCarthy might be anti-Catholic and anti-French, La Presse admitted, but was at least 'un esprit cultivé et un avocat de premier ordre,' while Wallace could only be described as 'un rustre à peine dégrossi: il a obtenu des succès de hustings et s'est cru homme d'état.'[101] The Mail and Empire tried to steer a middle course between the official party stand and the anti-remedialist Conservatives all around Toronto, but the Hamilton Spectator reflected enthusiasm over the Conservative selection of outright 'antis' in that city. The Reverend R.G. Boville, a Baptist minister and one of the Conservative nominees for Hamilton, insisted that 'the thing for Hamilton to do was what Toronto had done – send men pledged to oppose remedial legislation. If this was done remedial legislation would never be heard of again, and the N.P. would be as safe as it ever had been.'[102] L'Electeur listed forty-three anti-remedialist Conservative candidates for Ontario; even the faithful La Minerve after June 8 began to list the anti-remedialists in the Independent

---

99 Clark, 'The Conservative Party in the 1890's,' p.73. In this article and in the elaboration of the theme in his thesis, Clark perhaps to exclusively concentrates on this radical shift in Ontario Toryism, but at the same time documents it beyond question.

100 L'Electeur, June 12, 1896; La Presse, May 27, 29, 30, 1896

101 May 7, 1896

102 Hamilton Spectator, May 22, 1896

column, showing only forty-nine official Conservative candidates for the ninety-two Ontario ridings.[103]

So widespread was the Tory phenomenon of breaking rank on the school question that the opposition *Globe* felt obliged to insist that the list was exaggerated, and that in any case official party policy was more important than individual promises which could not be kept.[104] Lacking alternatives, Tupper had little choice but to make the best of this internal revolt. He continued, as he had with E.B. Osler, to weave his official net loosely enough to attempt to contain the dissidents. At the same time, it is worth remembering that, if the phenomenon of Ontario anti-remedialism caused grave suspicion in Quebec, the performance of Bishop Laflèche and the Conservative chorus which formed behind him, was no less an embarrassment in Ontario and elsewhere. As Bowell wrote to Tupper from the blessed exile of London, England, Laflèche's tirade was at best 'exceedingly ill timed.'[105]

As for Tupper himself, he swung through the crucial Ontario campaign with an energy that belied his seventy-five years. In a two-week tour from June 10 until election day, Tupper made thirty-one major speeches throughout the province. Beginning at Oshawa and Bowmanville, the prime minister attempted to spike Liberal attacks which were repeatedly using his Winnipeg speech by accusing them of being the ones who were making the school question an issue of race and religion, instead of adherence to the constitution.[106] He renewed the same charges at a huge gathering at London late on June 11, and referred to his making way for Edward Kenney in Canada's first cabinet as proof of his lack of prejudice against Catholics. Nonetheless, as he had in the much quoted Winnipeg address, Tupper proposed for his listeners a choice between himself as dedicated to justice, though already proven to be restrained, and Laurier as untried, two-faced and suspect because he was a 'French Roman Catholic ... who says they [Conservatives] do not go far enough.'[107]

103 *L'Electeur,* May 23, 1896; *La Minerve*, June 8, 17, 1896
104 May 19, 1896
105 PAC, Tupper Papers, Bowell to Tupper, May 26, 1896
106 Toronto *Daily Mail and Empire*, June 11, 20, 1896
107 *Ibid.*, June 13, 1896. Whether because of Liberal 'infiltration' of his audience, as Peter Waite suggests (*Canada 1874–1896*, p.272), or simply because the credibility gap was growing, Tupper's 'constitutional defence' position got little hearing as the campaign neared conclusion. See Toronto *Daily Mail and Empire*, June 20, 1896. The manner in which issues other than the school question were featured in the campaign is also summarized in Waite *Canada*, 1874–1896, pp.242–7.

Unfortunately for Tupper, aspects both dangerous and ludicrous crept into the campaign because of the clerical dimension which his colleagues were attempting to use to the fullest in Quebec. Fairly early in the campaign, Senator Philippe Landry, one of the star Conservative participants in the 'assemblées contradictoires,' attempted to get Liberal candidates and Laurier in particular to sign a declaration which would involve practical retraction of the whole opposition to the remedial bill presented in March.[108] By the second week of June, Landry was reported to have declared that Tupper would accept any resolution of the Canadian Roman-Catholic hierarchy as settlement of the school question. Having received an excited telegram from his son J. Stewart in Winnipeg that Landry's declaration was causing a good deal of trouble,[109] Tupper wired from Petrolia, Ontario, on June 12 that he had 'never before heard of Senator Landry's statement, and report carries absurdity on its face.'[110] Sir Charles likewise found himself obliged to deny the report that he had received Archbishop Langevin's blessing before leaving Winnipeg, and, on his knees, had kissed the bishop's ring.[111] On the other side of the coin, Tupper at the end of the campaign had to deny emphatically the Liberal report which was being spread in Quebec that he had promised to call off remedial legislation in return for Ontario Orange support. Writing to Angers on June 21, Tupper called the report a 'monstrous lie,' saying that he had 'everywhere in Ontario spoken as I spoke in Quebec,' and hoping that no one would be 'misled by the schemes and inventions of the enemy.'[112]

Perhaps the most eloquent witness to the radical nature of the dilemma posed for the Conservatives by remedialism could be found in the contradictory ways in which Tory candidates and newspapers in Quebec and Ontario attacked Laurier. In Quebec, they continued to quote the Laflèche condemnation; La Minerve in particular repeated the refrain that a man could be judged by the company he kept and by those whose praise he received. Laurier was thus grouped with McCarthy, Wallace, Martin, Chiniquy, and the Montreal Witness, with the added charge of traitor for good measure.[113] Mowat received equally rough treatment. La Minerve, echoing Conservative speakers, called Mowat's defence of separate

---

108 La Minerve, May 27, 1896
109 PAC, Tupper Papers, J.S. Tupper to Tupper, June 11, 1896
110 L'Electeur, June 15, 1896
111 Winnipeg Tribune, May 28, 1896; PAC, Tupper Papers, Tupper to J.S. Tupper, May 29, 1896
112 PAC, Tupper Papers, Tupper to Angers, Tupper to Desjardins, June 21, 1896
113 La Minerve, June 9, 1896

schools in Ontario sheer opportunism, and pointed to the March resolution in the Ontario Legislature against remedialism as final proof.[114]

In Ontario and Manitoba, there were repeated Conservative attempts to prove that Laurier in every way was as coercionist as Tupper, and potentially more so. Just as *La Minerve* scorned any thought of Laurier as French and Catholic champion, the Toronto *Mail and Empire* rejected the suggestion that the Liberal leader could in any sense be accepted as an anti-clerical champion. 'Those of us who read the Ontario papers only,' the *Mail and Empire* observed, 'will possibly imagine that Mr. Laurier is engaged in a hand to hand conflict in Quebec on behalf of liberty and against the bishops and priests. There could not be a greater mistake.' The purpose of the misrepresentation, the Toronto paper stated, was to awaken 'Protestant sympathy for the victim.' Insisting that Laurier was in fact 'an advocate of ecclesiastical interference in politics,' the *Mail and Empire* concluded that the Liberal leader was 'anti-bishop and anti-coercion in Ontario in order to deceive Protestants, and pro-bishop and pro-coercion in Quebec in order to deceive Roman Catholics.'[115]

However, much the *Mail and Empire* charge against Laurier was a caricature, it pointed up the dilemma which the Liberal leader shared with Sir Charles Tupper. The platform on the school question which worked in Quebec simply could not be used in Ontario. In the English province, as shown by the seeming ease with which Tupper kept coming back to the point, Laurier's Frenchness and Catholicism was always an unknown factor, an area of potential vulnerability. As already suggested, Tupper's use of the issue proved something of a two-edged sword, with Laurier repeatedly quoting the prime minister's Winnipeg speech in an appeal to British fair play. Two words, however, would seem to be particularly applicable to Laurier's handling of the school question in Ontario: de-emphasis and vagueness. Laurier was in Ontario from June 3 through 13, making perhaps half as many stops as did Tupper. When the schools were mentioned, Laurier concentrated on government mishandling and threats to the peace of the country rather than the details of his own proposals. Returning Conservative charges in similar coin, the Liberal leader vilified the 'double-faced' policy which allowed Hugh John Macdonald in Manitoba to promise no federal interference, while Tupper and his lieutenants in Quebec were promising a new remedial bill. More explicitly than in the past when dealing with the school issue, Laurier at Massey Hall on June 12

114 May 26, June 5, 1896
115 June 4, 1896

stressed that 'the principle of provincial rights is the basis of Confederation.' As for section 93, it was 'not in accord with that principle,' but, 'since it is there, it should be met in a statesmanlike manner.' On what this would mean in practice, Laurier was no more specific than to promise to 'investigate the subject and do right according to the evidence produced.' Clearly, Laurier's stand was based not on an overriding conviction about provincial rights, but on the political realities of the situation. He avoided any extended references to difficulties with the clergy in Quebec, although promising not to bow to dictation, and ably shifted attention back to a trade platform which promised adjustments without radical upheaval.[116]

One item that distracted and delighted Liberal appetites was the charge of huge rail subsidies granted by the government since dissolution. The *Globe* ran an open letter to Lord Aberdeen charging that over $12 million had been granted by order-in-council, and that the benefitting rail companies were being properly grateful to the Conservative campaign fund.[117] Investigation showed that Tupper's denial of the charges were founded in fact, but his reputation for well-timed favours did not help his position. In any case the accusation was precisely the sort of issue that the Liberals could use to nullify the danger which the school question posed for Laurier, especially with Patrons, PPAS and anti-remedialist Conservatives flooding the field. As in Tupper's case, what Laurier said provided little guarantee, especially in Ontario, of what his campaign managers and candidates would say. But it was by and large 'unnecessary for them to voice the anti-Catholic sentiments which the anti-remedialist Conservatives indulged in so freely.'[118] On several occasions the *Globe* kept the Catholic vote in mind by reminding readers of Conservative militancy against separate schools in Ontario. Finally, there were so many easy Conservative targets visible on the school question, ranging from Clarke Wallace to Bishop Laflèche, that Liberals found it fairly easy to gloss over contradictions within their own party.

It was fortunate for Laurier that such a blurring over was possible. With the exception of the *L'Electeur*-Laflèche clash, the dominant theme of Quebec Liberals during the campaign was that Conservative ineffectiveness if not betrayal would be replaced by Liberal effectiveness, friendly if possible, coercive if necessary. As for the promises specified by the bishops' mandement, Liberal election pamphlets and later surveys, Liberal and Conservative, of the campaign, stressed the degree to which

116 Toronto *Globe*, June 13, 1896
117 *Ibid.*, June 9, 1896
118 Clark, 'The Conservative Administrations,' p.520

Liberal candidates had complied with the requirement.[119] Laurier and perhaps two other Liberal contestants avoided any written statement. All, however, gave verbal promises to support remedial legislation if conciliation failed, and many paid little attention to the idea of a preliminary inquiry. It does not seem that Laurier repeated the veiled threat of the St Roch address, at least during the final week of the campaign after returning from Ontario on June 14. *L'Electeur*, however, and according to its columns, most French Liberal candidates, had no hesitation in keeping the much-quoted final sentence of the St Roch statement before the voters' eyes, using large print, front-page features, and dramatic comparisons with Tupper's Winnipeg statements.[120] Just as Conservative treatment of Laurier was a good barometer of their approach, so Liberal treatment of Tupper was eloquent testimony of the message they wanted the electors to hear. With such chapter titles as 'L'Orangisme Envahissant' and 'Les Minorités Sacrifiées au Fanatisme,' a favourite Liberal election pamphlet called Tupper's efforts on behalf of the Manitoba Catholics too little, too late, and insincere. 'Laurier seule est en mesure de donner une solution satisfaisante,' the pamphlet concluded.[121]

The case of François Langelier in Quebec Centre illustrated how a prominent and outspoken Liberal was able at least to neutralize the mandement as a potential threat by giving a written declaration of support for remedialism. Apparently Monsignor Laflamme had been asked by Bégin to contact Langelier; a June 2 note from Laflamme to the archbishop revealed worry about the delay and the rumoured vagueness of the statement from Langelier. Laflamme's June 5 letter, however, enclosed Langelier's written declaration and voiced the seminary rector's relief and satisfaction. 'Je crois qu'elle est parfaitement satisfaisante à tous les points de vue,' Laflamme wrote. 'Je vous avoue que j'en ai été très heureux.'[122]

QUEBEC JOURNALISTS AND THE CHURCH:
LIBERALS AVOID DANGER

As already suggested in the review of ecclesiastical sources, the primary attention of the French-language newspapers, Liberal and Conservative,

119 See, for example, the Liberal election pamphlet, *La Question des Ecoles du Manitoba*, p.110; the Conservative brochure, *La Difficulté Scolaire Manitobaine*, p.41.
120 *L'Electeur*, May 16, 18, 21, 1896; also May 23, June 8, 10, 13, 1896. *La Presse*, as well as the more partisan Conservative papers, reminded readers that Laurier had not repeated the St Roch declaration (*La Presse*, June 15, 1896).
121 *La Question des Ecoles du Manitoba*, p.110.
122 AAQ, Laflamme to Bégin, June 2, 5, 1896

was focused on the mandement and on clerical activity during the campaign. True to custom, the journalists with few exceptions became more violently partisan as the contest neared its conclusion. As sources of information, therefore, they provide a good deal of colour, along with something less than a sure guide to an unbiased picture. As the 'assemblées contradictoires' became more heated, the 'faithful' Conservative papers, especially *La Minerve, L'Evénement*, and *Le Courrier du Canada*, grew more explicit in their adoption of the full Laflèche doctrine. Charging that the Liberals were claiming that the mandement had been drawn up in their favour, *La Minerve* did not hesitate to quote Laflèche as the best interpreter of the bishops' general statement, and to emphasize the claim in block letters: 'Ce vieil et saint évêque ajoute même *qu'il est défendu à un catholique de voter pour un candidat qui supporte monsieur Laurier.'*[123] *La Presse* followed a more checkered course: the Montreal daily sternly warned the Conservative party that it might throw its full support to Laurier if Tupper's Ontario colleagues continued to differ with their leader on remedial policy.[124] After the controversy over the anti-Laflèche articles in *L'Electeur*, however, *La Presse* swung back to criticizing the Liberals for forming an ultra-Protestant alliance which would 'prèche une guerre sainte et soulève les masses contre le clergé catholique.'[125] Taunting *L'Electeur* about the latter's readiness to meet every episcopal statement with the authority of an ever-available theologian, 'aussi distingué qu'anonyme,'[126] *La Presse*, despite reassertion of its independence, returned to the Conservative camp at the end of the campaign. On June 19 it quoted Cartier against the idea of a French-Canadian prime minister and on June 22, the day before the election, *La Presse* lined up episcopal statements that were explicitly pro-Conservative, including a translation of Bishop Cameron's straight party plea.[127] At no time, however, did the *La Presse* editorials imitate *La Minerve* in denouncing the prospect of Catholics voting for Liberal candidates. On voting day, in fact, *La Presse* insisted that it was concluding its campaign 'sans amertume contre qui que ce soit,' and even insisted that 'si les discussions dans la presse française ont été aussi vive qu'autrefois, le ton général a été beaucoup plus digne, plus courtois et plus relevé.'[128] This reflection may have been somewhat optimistic in view of the sharpness of the verbal battles which followed *L'Electeur*'s joust with Bishop Laflèche. Yet *La Presse*, Canada's largest

123 June 18, 1896
124 May 27, 29, 30, 1896
125 *Ibid.*, June 15, 1896

126 *Ibid.*, June 15, 1896
127 *Ibid.*, June 19, 22, 1896
128 June 23, 1896

newspaper in number of subscribers, had manifestly not given the hard-line interpretation of the episcopal position pursued by such as *La Minerve*, and had played an important role in publicizing the anti-remedialism of a large bloc of Ontario Conservatives. *La Vérité*, for all its criticism of Liberal dalliance with McCarthy and company, continued to be almost as suspicious of the Conservatives. With less than two weeks remaining in the campaign, Tardivel's paper reproved the Liberal doctrine of 'laissez donc faire les évêques,' but at the same time reminded the Conservatives that their campaign was coming dangerously close to identifying religion with party survival, and was thus directly in conflict with the teaching of Leo XIII.[129]

On the Liberal side, the newspapers varied from one another only in the degree to which they canonized Laurier. *Le Reveil* and *La Patrie* with their strong anti-clerical tone were mildly disavowed by such as *L'Electeur*, *Le Soir*, and *Le Cultivateur*. It should be noted, however, that not until the day following the election did even *La Patrie* describe the electoral struggle in Quebec as a straight contest between Liberal and ecclesiastics: 'le clergé a essuyé hier une plus écrasante défaite que le parti conservateur lui-même dans la province de Québec,' Beaugrand's newspaper proclaimed in the afterglow of victory.[130] Two days earlier, *La Patrie*'s version of a clerical phalanx had not been nearly so absolute. Quoting an interview with Cardinal Gibbons of Baltimore in which the American prelate had praised Laurier, *La Patrie* insisted that the opinion of such a 'personnage illustre et éclairé comme le Cardinal Gibbons vaut cent fois mieux pour la conscience d'un honnête homme que les sermons politiques de quelques curés sans instruction et aveuglés par l'esprit de parti.'[131]

As Tarte's biographer points out, at no time during the campaign did Tarte's newspaper, *Le Cultivateur*, mount a program of high-pitched protest, at least not against the bishops. Even in the flurry of excitement surrounding the Laflèche sermon, *Le Cultivateur* was remarkably restrained.[132] As for *L'Electeur*, once the disavowal of the anti-Laflèche articles had been made, it largely restricted its criticisms to the use the Conservatives were making on the hustings of the statements of Laflèche and other ecclesiastics. Adopting anything but a consistent anti-clerical stance, *L'Electeur* on Saturday, June 20, urged its readers to listen care-

129 *La Vérité*, quoted in *L'Electeur*, June 11, 1896
130 June 24, 1896
131 *Ibid.*, June 22, 1896
132 LaPierre, 'Politics, Race and Religion in French Canada,' (thesis), p.302

fully to the general mandement scheduled to be read a second time the next day:

Electeurs catholiques, prenez comme guide le mandement collectif de NN. SS. Les Evêques qui vous sera lu une seconde fois demain.

Il n'y a que le Pape qui pourrait vous justifier de ne pas en suivre les Ordonnances ...

Si l'Episcopat eût eu l'intention de s'inféoder au parti bleu, comme les bleus le prétendent, est-ce que l'épiscopat ne l'aurait pas dit au moment où il était à tracer le devoir des catholiques?

On nous dit que Mgr. Laflèche va plus loin que le mandement collectif. Mais si les vues de Sa Grandeur des Trois Rivières ont été rejetées par les autres évêques, pourquoi, vous simple électeur catholique, seriez-vous tenu de vous y soumettre?

N'est-ce pas au contraire votre devoir de suivre la majorité des évêques?[133]

In the same issue, a Montreal correspondent signing himself 'Un Catholique Effrayé' expressed concern about the effect which the clergy of Quebec, Trois-Rivières, Rimouski, and Chicoutimi might have in condemning French Canada 'à l'infériorité et l'impuissance dans la confédération.' The correspondent was sure that the general mandement would be the guiding light in the Montreal diocese.[134] Changing his pseudonym to 'Un Catholique Rassuré' the day after the election, the correspondent wanted *L'Electeur* to thank 'les membres du clergé qui ne sont pas tombés dans le piège qu'on leur tendait et ont fait de nobles efforts pour empêcher leurs collègues.'[135] On June 26 the same writer stated that there had been more clerical interference than expected in the Montreal area, but insisted that the names of Bishops LaRocque of Sherbrooke and Lorrain of Pontiac should be added to the acknowledgment given to Bishop Emard, 'qui a empêché le mandement collectif d'être semblable au sermon de Monseigneur Laflèche.'[136] *L'Electeur*'s subsequent reflection on the campaign, entitled 'Faisons la Paix,' recommended recourse to Rome against extremists among the clergy and against politicians who had attempted to use clerical influence. Its main thought, however, paralleling that in *Le Soir*, was a tribute to the bulk of the clergy who had remained calm:

C'est, en effet, une grave erreur que de s'imaginer que le clergé était contre nous

133 *L'Electeur*, June 20, 1896
134 *Ibid.*, June 20, 1896

135 *Ibid.*, June 24, 1896
136 *L'Electeur*, June 26, 1896

aux dernières élections. Nous savons personellement que des centaines de prêtres étaient sympathiques à notre cause. Comme ces prêtres observaient une neutralité sage et digne, leur conduite a passé inapperçue et le public n'a entendu que les cris de leurs confrères fanatisés par de vulgaires agioteurs.

Il y a plus. Tous les curés qui ont commis ces incartades si malheureuses l'ont fait en désobéissance à la voix de l'épiscopat. En effet, la direction donnée par Nos Seigneurs les évêques par leur mandement collectif ne pouvait être plus sage et plus digne.

Aussi avons-nous le droit de compter sur l'épiscopat pour aider à faire censurer les quelques prêtres qui se sont oubliés jusqu'au point de venir dire aux fidèles confiés à leur garde que c'était un péché mortel que voter pour un candidat de M. Laurier.[137]

From the leading Liberal newspapers, therefore, as from the tone and emphasis of the Liberal candidates, it must be concluded that Laurier's forces in Quebec in no sense tried to present themselves as fighting a classic Rouge battle with the church. Clearly, many clerical and Conservative party statements branded a Liberal vote as outright disobedience to the authority of the church; 'Choose the bishops or Barabbas Laurier' may indeed have been a fair summary of what the extreme element, clerical and political, was saying.[138] There was, however, not a single reported instance of a Liberal statement which might be paraphrased: 'Reject the bishops and vote for Laurier.' Always the refrain was, even in the columns of La Patrie and Le Reveil, 'Those who claim that voting Liberal means disobeying the Church are mistaken (or malicious)'; 'the majority of bishops is more important than Laflèche,' etc. Only after the contest was past did the extreme interpretation begin to appear in Quebec Liberal writing, and then largely in the radical publications. The hard-line Conservative journals, granted the dead-end street they had constructed for themselves and, in their view, for ecclesiastical authority, had little choice but to see a defeat for the church in the defeat of the Conservatives.[139] The moderate papers, however, had not burned so many bridges; they could, as did L'Electeur, Le Soir, and La Presse, insist that neither ecclesiastical authority nor redress for Manitoba Catholics had been rejected. In a similar manner, ecclesiastics, however much the element of face-saving was pres-

137 Ibid., June 29, 1896; see also L'Electeur's quotation of Desjardins to the same effect on June 27, and Le Soir, June 24, 1896.
138 Skelton, The Life and Letters of Sir Wilfrid Laurier, I, p.485.
139 See for example La Minerve, June 26, 1896

ent, for the most part saw a successful Liberal interpretation of the mandement rather than disobedience on the part of the electorate.[140] Even those who belonged to the Laflèche school of open warfare confirmed this view, giving post-election recriminations against the 'weakness' of the mandement and of the general ecclesiastical stand. 'Le mandement était si peu clair,' Abbé Hermas Langevin wrote his brother the archbishop, 'que les libéraux l'ont interprété dans leur sens, y ont applaudi, et ont fait croire au peuple ce qu'ils ont voulu. Comme toutes les demi-mesures, cela a fait un tort immense à la bonne cause.'[141]

Opinion outside Quebec easily gravitated toward the more sensational interpretation of a full-scale Liberal victory over church domination. While the Toronto *Mail and Empire* was moderate, quoting Tupper's opinion that 'the great majority of the French Canadian voters respected the mandement and voted according to its tenor,'[142] the *Globe*, naturally elated, saw at least a triumph over extreme clericalism.[143] Newspapers in England featured the theme of French Canada's throwing off the clerical yoke; the London *Times* applauded a much delayed loss by the Roman Church of its 'ancient power over the laity.'[144] American papers that commented drew a similar picture. The result made it plain, the Boston *Journal* stated, that 'the French Canadian Catholic voter is capable of listening in silence to the political commands of his church, and then going to the polls and disregarding them.'[145]

A VOTING SURVEY

A survey of voting results in a representative group of ridings across the province of Quebec supports the view that a 'triumph of race over religion' was not the dominant theme in the election. It should be noted first of all that the number of ridings located in dioceses where the bishop was accused of branding a Liberal vote as a sin totalled nine out of sixty-five.[146]

140 See AAQ, Moreau to Bégin, June 24, 1896; AAM, Langevin to Fabre, June 24, 1896; AASB, Bégin to Langevin, July 7, 1896. Canon Bruchési of Montreal, the future archbishop, was a good deal less optimistic in his immediate reaction, referring to the Quebec outcome as 'une humiliante défaite' (AAQ, Bruchési to Bégin, June 24, 1896).
141 AASB, Hermas Langevin to Archbishop Langevin, June 29, 1896
142 June 25, 1896
143 June 27, 1896
144 June 24, 1896; also London *Daily News* and London *Chronicle*, June 24, 1896
145 June 25, 1896
146 See Appendix 3.

Most evidently calling for scrutiny was the area under the jurisdiction of Bishop Laflèche. Enclosing three ridings, Champlain, Maskinongé, and the newly combined constituency, Trois-Rivières–St Maurice, the diocese of Trois-Rivières was, with Nicolet (before 1885 part of Trois-Rivières) the only area which showed a net gain for the Conservatives over the vote of 1891. This gain, a very slim one, would seem to indicate that the election's most explicit pro-Conservative clerical pronouncement did have some effect. At the same time, there was some evidence, that, even in Trois-Rivières, sufficient interpretations and subtle distinctions had been made to assure that a Liberal vote was not necessarily seen as disobedience to the church. Tardivel was quoted on June 20 as recommending support for Fiset, a Liberal, against the Conservative Caron. Fiset's own report to Laurier after defeat did not mention Laflèche among the factors which he believed had beaten him; instead he blamed Caron's use of 'la corruption, l'argent et le whisky.'[147] Bishop Laflèche's own city showed a moderate net gain for the Liberals.[148]

In Témiscouata riding in Bishop Blais's diocese, a more detailed scrutiny of the clerical factor was possible, since Pouliot, the victorious Liberal candidate, singled out six curés in an official complaint to Rome. The over-all victory, referred to by La Presse as one of the Liberals' most impressive over old traditions and by L'Electeur as 'une des plus belle victoires de tout le Dominion,'[149] saw a Liberal net gain of approximately 20 per cent over 1891, 765 in a total vote of 3775. In 1891, out of thirty-five polling subdivisions, seventeen went to each party, with one tied. In 1896, only eight went to the Conservatives, twenty-six to the Liberals, with one tied. Of the nine subdivisions going over to the Liberals, two, St Georges de Cacouna and Ste Rose du Dégelée, showed a vote switch of nearly 35 per cent. The eight subdivisions retained by the Conservatives all gave a reduced margin, and no parish or town switched from Liberal to Conservative. In the parishes where Pouliot specifically complained of 'influence indue,' a lesser gain was registered by the Liberals (36 out of a total vote of 795 – 4.5 per cent) than in the remainder of the riding. In contrast, the most significant gain made by Pouliot was in Fraserville (254 in a total vote of 627 –approximately 40 per cent) where the curé was reportedly in his favour. It should be noted that Fraserville was Pouliot's home, and that it still gave a Conservative majority. On the whole, it would seem that the pro-

147 PAC, Laurier Papers, Fiset to Laurier, June 25, 1896
148 See Appendix 5B.
149 La Presse, June 24, 1896; L'Electeur, June 27, 1896

Conservative curés helped to hold the line, although not spectacularly, against the Liberals.[150] In any case, the Liberals made net gains in all four ridings in Rimouski diocese.

In Chicoutimi diocese, subsequent reports revealed Bishop Labrecque's emotion against those Liberals who had criticized the clergy during the campaign. The impeccable performance of Paul Savard and Charles Angers, however, made it impossible simply to identify Liberal and rebel in the Charlevoix and Chicoutimi et Saguenay ridings. Savard, who was sometimes listed as an independent Conservative and sometimes as a Liberal, registered large gains throughout his riding of Chicoutimi et Saguenay. His most notable increases came in the parishes around the perimeter of Lac St Jean, such as Roberval and St Prime, and in the quite isolated village of St Fulgence on the north shore of the Saguenay, where *L'Electeur* had reported pro-Conservative efforts by the curé.[151] Charles Angers's majority in Charlevoix was slightly down from his by-election victory in January; in any case, in both ridings of the diocese, Liberals seem to have acted in a restrained but effective manner to circumvent whatever clerical effort was brought against them.

In Bishop Emard's diocese of Valleyfield, all five ridings showed net gains for the Liberals over the 1891 result, with the largest increase (602 – approximately 24 per cent) coming in Chateauguay. The Liberals gained Soulanges riding from the Conservatives, but Bergeron retained Beauharnois against J.I. Tarte. Tarte managed a net gain of 255 in the riding, but, notwithstanding rumblings over the Shortis case, intense local loyalties which resented the intrusion of an outsider, especially one as 'nouveau venu' to the Liberals as Tarte, apparently saved Beauharnois for the government.[152] Taking Valleyfield diocese as a whole, and keeping in mind the significant English vote in the area, it may be concluded that the absence of clerical activity did not produce a notable variation of voting pattern from either Rimouski or Chicoutimi.

Elsewhere throughout the province, a fairly constant pattern of electoral swing to the Liberals was evident. As was the case in Valleyfield, gains were registered in areas with a substantial English vote in about the same proportion as in the all-French or nearly all-French ridings.[153] On the

150 See Appendix 5C.
151 See Appendix 5D.
152 See Appendix 5E.
153 See Appendix 3 and Appendix 4; distinction based on ridings which, according to 1891 census, were likely to have an English vote of 10 per cent or higher.

whole, the shift in popular vote was not as dramatic as the decisive Liberal gain in seats. In 1891, the Conservatives got 50.8 per cent, the Liberals 47.5 per cent, and others 1.7 per cent, of the popular vote. In 1896, the division was: Liberals, 53.5 per cent, Conservatives, 45.8 per cent, others, .7 per cent, giving the Liberals a gain of 6 per cent and the Conservatives a loss of 5 per cent.[154] In the fifty-one seats out of sixty-five where gains were 'measurable' (excluding re-distributed ridings of Montreal and seats retained by the party formerly holding the seat by acclamation) the Liberals registered net gains in thirty-five, the Conservatives in sixteen.[155]

Twelve ridings were involved in redistribution. In 'contracted' areas, largely rural, eight former seats, divided 5-3 at dissolution in favour of the Liberals, were combined into four seats which went 3-1 for the Liberals. In 'expanded' areas, Montreal, which had gone 3-0 Conservative in 1891 and was 2-1 Conservative at dissolution, was expanded to six ridings (including Maisonneuve) which divided 4-2 in favour of the Liberals in 1896. Ottawa County, Liberal at dissolution, was divided into Wright and Labelle ridings, both of which went Liberal. In all of the redistricted areas, therefore, a division of 7-5 favouring the Liberals at dissolution became 9-3 for the Liberals after the election.[156]

Again excluding the redistributed areas, sixteen seats 'switched' from Conservative to Liberal, four from Liberal to Conservative. Interestingly, one of these Conservative gains, Jacques Cartier, as well as Montreal Ste Anne in the redistricted area (largely Montreal Centre) were the two seats which had been such crucial Liberal victories in the by-elections of December 1895.[157] Even taking into account these Montreal 'reversals,' the urban areas of Montreal and Quebec showed solid Liberal gains in both French and English districts.[158] As for the remaining Conservative gains, Nicolet would seem to have been largely a case of independent votes of 1891 going Conservative in 1896.[159] In Dorchester, the incumbent member, Dr Vaillancourt, lost his seat to J.B. Morin, who replaced Sir Adolphe Caron as Conservative candidate. Vaillancourt, who had listed himself as 'Nationalist' in 1891 but was regarded as a Liberal, may have suffered from his insistence on again running as an independent. As for Stanstead, the remarkable Conservative gain there seems to have been a case of the

154 Beck, 'The Democratic Process at Work in Canadian General Elections,' p.9.
155 See Appendix 3.
156 See Appendix 3.
157 See Appendix 4.
158 See Appendix 5A.
159 See Appendix 5F.

personal popularity of their candidate, A.H. Moore, who had served several terms as mayor of Magog.[160]

SOME CONCLUSIONS

In summary, except perhaps in Trois-Rivières, the pattern of vote swing to the Liberals across the province does not seem to have been very predictable by whether the clergy were active, or accused of being active, for the Conservatives. Rimouski, where 'influence' was charged, and Valleyfield, where it was not, showed comparable Liberal gains; Nicolet, where some pro-Conservative clerical effort was in evidence, returned Conservative increases, as did certain 'exempt' Montreal and Sherbrooke ridings. If therefore the ecclesiastical thrust on the Conservative side was occasionally significant, it was only so, as Laurier himself had estimated after Laflèche's sermon, in a limited area. In a matter where even a few instances constituted a serious situation, there is no doubt that, in certain parishes, the election was held 'à coups de péchés mortels.'[161] By and large, however, the Liberals were successful in convincing enough voters that the gap between what the bishops were demanding and what the Liberals were promising, was not as wide as Bishop Laflèche, some of the curés and Conservative campaigners had painted it. Laflèche had opened the door for a simplistic interpretation by some clerics and politicians during the campaign and not a few historians after it. The actual case revealed more subtlety and energy on the part of Liberal organizers, more understanding and variety on the part of ecclesiastics, and more sophistication and flexibility on the part of the French-Canadian electorate than has generally been accepted.

If the Quebec election result in 1896 cannot be explained as a choice of race over religion, the factor of race in the choice loses none of its importance. For all the evidence of English as well as French backing of Laurier in Quebec, it was clearly French-Canadian enthusiasm for their compatriot which produced the decisiveness of the political anchor dreamed of by Tarte. If there was one point above all others for which Tarte deserved full credit as strategist, it was his insistence that any harsh light which might fall

160 See Appendix 3 and *The Canadian Parliamentary Guide, 1897*, p.170. The tentative and clearly selective analyses of voting patterns in the present study, point up the need for more thorough and wide-ranging investigations testing various factors in this and other Canadian elections.

161 AEV, Abbé h. Têtu, Laval University, to Emard, April 17, 1897

on Laurier because of clerical opposition, could best be met by the still stronger light of French and even Catholic hero. The image created was indeed much more in the Cartier than in the Mercier tradition, a champion with others, not despite them, but a French and Catholic champion nonetheless – and perhaps the last one. As Cartwright later pointed out, Tarte was 'most emphatically of the opinion that Sir Wilfrid's best chance lay in convincing his people that if they turned him down at this juncture, Quebec need never hope to see a French Premier in the Dominion.'[162]

Tarte's role as organizer was not limited to the promotion of an image. Every close observer of the inner workings of the Quebec scene of 1896 has noted the importance of the journalist-politician's energy in reorganizing and revitalizing the Liberal party at the constituency level. It was here, too, that the parallel Conservative effort suffered most by comparison. As *La Presse* put it, 'les ministres ... n'étaient en rapport avec aucun des chefs de comptés.'[163] It was at this level that the collapse of party morale because of the 'Castor-Bleu' quarrel was most damaging. With the magnetic appeal of Laurier to oppose, the Conservatives could offer no figure remotely comparable to hold party loyalty in line. The supposed anchor man on the Quebec Conservative team, A.R. Angers, had, partly through his prolonged 'strike' from the cabinet, lost most of the appeal he once had. Even Angers's own district of Quebec City was, in *La Presse*'s words, 'en révolte ouverte contre son représentant dans le Cabinet.'[164] A more scathing and perhaps more perceptive analysis, stressing the clerical and journalistic dimension of the 'Castor' disruption within the Conservative party, was given by Monsignor J.O. Routhier of Ottawa in a post-election letter to Archbishop Langevin. Routhier lamented the result of the election and the danger to religious discipline which might result from recriminations, deserved or otherwise. Even more, however, Routhier feared that 'le clergé ne comprendra qu'à demi la leçon, et se remettra à la remorque de *La Vérité*, qui est pour lui toute la Loi et les Prophètes ... Tardivel continue son œuvre de division.' However much Angers had sacrificed to do battle in the election, Routhier was sure that his influence, and, behind him, the 'éminence grise' of Monsignor Marois, had been nothing but destructive since 1895:

Le résultat politique je l'avais prévu et je m'y attendais. Déjà je m'étais étonné de

162 Cartwright, *Reminiscences*, p.346
163 June 24, 1896
164 *Ibid.*, June 24, 1896

voir Mgr. Marois essayer à diriger le parti conservateur, en ne prenant ses renseignements que chez les Landry, les Belleau, Tardivel, Charlebois, etc ... et cherchant à précipiter les évêques dans le gouffre où devaient tomber des hommes qui méritaient d'être écrasés. Déjà ils avaient commencé à briser le parti conservateur – les élections de Montréal l'avaient promi. Quand on fit l'impossible pour amener Pelletier à la place d'Angers, Mgr. Marois et ses aviseurs s'opposèrent et demandèrent à garder vide la place d'Angers, que pour les évêques, que pour le parti, que pour la cause, il ne devait pas occuper ... Mais c'est fait. Angers a perdu le parti conservateur, et les évêques avec lui.[165]

It should be added that the Quebec provincial Conservatives had little strength to contribute to the federal cause. Beset by troubles which included a reaction in favour of Mercier after his death late in 1894 and the strict economy which the Taillon and Flynn governments were obliged to maintain, the provincial party was fighting a rearguard action which would culminate in a 57-17 loss to the Liberals on May 11, 1897. Above all, they had no one, any more than did the Federal Conservatives, to match Laurier's personal magnetism. Never was Chapleau's absence more keenly felt; never was it proven more clearly that clerical action, weak or strong, was 'a poor substitute for political leadership.'[166] As was the case with the Liberals, evasion and equivocation on the school question was inevitable, perhaps laudable. For the Conservatives, however, the outcome was by and large the collapse of the party in Quebec. Not a single Macdonald minister remained to fight for the Bleu formula of pragmatic compromise; the devoted, limited men who entered the battle were all beaten.[167]

165 AASB, Routhier to Langevin, June 28, 1896
166 Saywell, Introduction, *The Canadian Journal of Lady Aberdeen, 1893-98*, p. lxxv
167 Once again, as suggested above (p.29), it should be noted that the 1896 Quebec shift to the Liberals culminated a trend which began with the reaction to the Riel execution in 1885. The voting pattern was as follows:

	Conservatives		Liberals		Others	
	Seats	Percentage of Vote	Seats	Percentage of Vote	Seats	Percentage of Vote
1882	51	52.3	13	42.2	1	5.5
1887	33	49.6	32	48.9	—	1.5
1891	28	50.8	37	47.5	—	1.7
1896	16	45.8	49	53.5	—	.07

(See Beck, 'The Democratic Process at Work in Canadian General Elections,' p.9.)

In Ontario, the Liberals captured forty-three seats, eleven more than they held at dissolution, but one less than they had won in 1891. With increased support from business and finance, the Liberals gained one seat in Toronto and two in Hamilton. At the same time, although the three Patrons and three McCarthyites elected could generally be counted upon for support, the presence of these two factions in the election probably hurt the Liberals more than the Conservatives. Despite Mowat's prestige and his impact in Quebec, he was seventy-six and had been unable to campaign strenuously. Other Ontario leaders, Cartwright and Charlton, were also aging, and Mills had been defeated; new blood was obviously needed.[168] From a Liberal point of view, it was indeed true, as Charlton told Willison, that 'Quebec had shamed Ontario.'[169] The result, combined with the Manitoba reversal, simply highlighted the significance of the Quebec swing to Laurier.

On the question of remedialism, one further point was evident throughout the campaign in all sections of the country. As in the debate on the remedial bill, the Liberals had the benefit of being on the negative side. While exhibiting as wide a range of opinion on the Manitoba problem as did the Conservatives, the Liberals enjoyed the incalculable advantage of one of the oldest rules in politics: attack requires less unity than defence. A factor that increases in significance as emotions become more important than cool reasoning. Laurier was to suffer heavily from this hard rule in 1911; in 1896 it was all to his benefit. However much it might be stated by such as Hugh John Macdonald that a new bill was not inevitable, the Conservatives had presented a measure of black-and-white dimensions, and seventeen of their number had voted against it. For the radical anti-remedialists in their ranks, this meant that there was no way of stating their position without revealing great rents in the fabric of party unity. Nor could these rifts be kept secret or disguised from other parts of the country; the choice was too open and shut to hope for blessed ambiguity. Conservative anti-remedialism won battles in Ontario and Manitoba, but it helped lose the war in Quebec.

168 For a fuller account of the Ontario result, see Stevens, 'Laurier and the Liberal Party in Ontario' (thesis), p.148–52. Interestingly, Willison's later reflection was that 'the revolt among Orangemen gave many constituencies to the Liberal party' Reminiscences, p.251. Similarly, L.C. Clark, in contrast to Stevens, holds that the 'Independent' vote helped the Liberals rather than the Conservatives (Clark, 'The Conservative Administrations,' (thesis), pp.532–4).
169 PAC, Willison Papers, Charlton to Willison, June 26, 1896

The Liberals on the other hand never quite had to define what policy would be followed if power actually came their way. They did not have to exhibit an alternative which was so definite and detailed that it could not contain at the same time such diverse spirits as Joseph Martin and Henri Bourassa. In Ontario and Manitoba, following the Toronto *Globe* and the *Winnipeg Tribune*, Liberals could shout at the Conservative remedial bill violated provincial rights, rode roughshod over the repeated vote of the Manitoba majority, and insulted the good faith of the Manitoba government by refusing an investigation. In Quebec, with *L'Electeur* and *Le Cultivateur*, they could cry that the bill was inefficacious, that it was the culmination of six years of Conservative betrayal of French Catholics in Manitoba, and at the same time that the only way to initiate any sane policy would be by an investigation satisfactory to all. In either case, the only positive action which had to be promised was inquiry. In English Canada the impression was given that the result of investigation would be to leave Manitoba alone, with perhaps some minor concessions granted. In Quebec, the conclusion was very easily drawn that inquiry would be the prelude either to large concessions by the Manitoba government or to a federal law, which, by some unstated but certain alchemy, would be effective where the Conservative bill was not. Quebec had not yet had to face in the cold light of practical action that the Liberals too would have to compromise; they had not yet experienced the realities which 'sunny ways' might bring.

In so far as the 1896 vote could be called a referendum on remedialism, neither the 'pros' nor the 'antis' would hold a sure majority in the new House. It was clear, however, that Ontario's rejection of the policy was at least as strong as Quebec's endorsement of it. Not only most Ontario Liberals, but fifteen Conservatives who had voted against the remedial bill plus several new anti-remedialist Conservative members, as well as the McCarthyites and Patrons, were pledged to oppose any renewal of a coercive measure. There was no mistaking the depth of feeling which a man such as Wallace had been able to generate; from a modest majority in West York in 1891, Wallace in 1896 more than tripled the combined vote of two opponents.[170] On the still explosive remedial question, the division of the new House would be rather Ontario and some of the West against Quebec and some of the Maritimes, than it would be Liberals versus Conservatives. No matter what policy the new leader chose, it would have to be pursued with great dexterity.

170 *The Canadian Parliamentary Guide*, 1897, p.204

Whether the cause or the occasion of Conservative defeat, the school question was the focus around which the electoral battle of 1896 had been fought. At the end, the key point was that, particularly by neutralizing the potential 'religious' threat in Quebec, Laurier had devised a successful 'Canadian' political formula, whereas the Conservatives had failed. As ever, much would be forgiven and forgivable to the man who held a fresh lease on power.

Epilogue

With the election concluded, the settlement of the school question as a federal-provincial issue, although by no means an easy process, was at least possible.[1] The danger that the case would once again become a major point of contention in the federal arena simply did not materialize. Laurier's much-trumpeted idea of 'une enquete' headed by Mowat quietly vanished.

1 The wide-ranging political and constitutional significance of Laurier's victory is somewhat beyond the scope of this study. The main points may be summarized as follows: politically, 1896 formed the most important single watershed in Canada's first century of existence. The shift of much of the moderate 'école de Cartier' to the Liberals produced the familiar twentieth-century pattern that the 'normal' Canadian political result based on the Quebec bloc falls on the Liberal rather than on the Conservative side. In this political shift, as in the cultural clash, the election involving the school question represented only the continuation of the movement begun with the Riel affair, the Jesuit estates' crisis, and the Mercier phenomenon. However much the school issue was one which Laurier circumvented rather than used, the net result, cemented by the glory and prestige of 'un des nôtres' as prime minister, was that the Quebec centre of gravity of Canadian political ballast swung to the party bearing the once anathematized name of Liberal.

The end of the Macdonald era and the beginning of the Laurier era meant more than the defeat of the Conservatives. The presence on the Laurier team of Mowat, Fielding, Blair, and later Sifton, signalled that a new phase had been reached in Canadian constitutional history. Reinforced by other Privy Council decisions directly involving the federal-provincial relationship, the episode of the school question both reflected and speeded up the growth of provincial self-assertion. That three of the stalwarts of the Interprovincial Conference of 1887 would now conduct public business from Ottawa meant that not a little of their contention against the Macdonald vision of the overriding role of the federal government had been accepted. Sifton's accession represented a major acknowledgment of the possibility of a provincial stand, whether right or wrong, quite substantially dictating

At the same time, the presence of a Liberal government in Ottawa, the swing to the Conservatives in the Manitoba federal voting, and, not least, the prize of the ministry of the interior at least unofficially held out to Sifton, or perhaps Greenway, all pointed toward the likelihood of an agreement. Laurier's keeping R.W. Scott in the cabinet, despite known opposition among Ontario Liberals, even among Irish Catholics whom he was supposed to represent, was an important step toward capturing the favour of the Ontario hierarchy.[2] The involvement of Judge A.B. Routhier in the negotiations with Manitoba was a further bonus in the ecclesiastical direction, although Tarte's prominence came close to negating it.[3] As for the Laurier-Greenway settlement reached in November 1896, in certain

an important federal policy of both national parties. It may be that this did not mean the absolute weakening of the central government; it is at least arguable that it simply meant greater maturity of both the parts and the whole of the nation. On the other hand, if the Macdonald view of the federal-provincial balance had been refocused, the substance of the Conservative chief's National Policy, including a viable appeal to manufacturing and finance, had been effectively assimilated by the Liberals; in this context, Laurier's giving the finance portfolio to Fielding rather than to Cartwright was important both as symbol and as strategy. In terms of political style, the narrowness of the Clear Grittism and Rougeism which had plagued the Mackenzie administration and the subsequent attempts to dislodge Macdonald had by and large been put to rest.

Somewhat as a corollary to the shift in the federal-provincial relationship, the struggle and the outcome of the school question represented a blow struck by the newly emerging West against the metropolitan East. Even though an Eastern fire-eater had been involved in the initiation of the controversy, the manner in which the Manitoba government used and developed the issue had strong overtones of a developing area rejecting the restrictions imposed by the older section, whether French or English. Paradoxically, the successful appeal made by Tupper and the *Manitoba Free Press* to return attention to the question of economic expansion and development of the West indicated that the school question had been fairly well exhausted of its potential as a symbol of protest.

2 See Stevens, 'Laurier and the Liberal Party in Ontario' (thesis), pp.156–7. Senator Richard Scott, Lieutenant Governor Fitzpatrick of Ontario, and J.S. Ewart, in their letters of congratulations to Laurier, all were strongly of the opinion that Manitoba's vote in the face of Greenway's appeal for a Liberal sweep in the federal ballot made it easier for Laurier to demand concessions and for Greenway to grant them (PAC, Laurier Papers, Scott to Laurier, June 24, 1896; Fitzpatrick to Laurier, June 27, 1896; Ewart to Laurier, June 27, 1896). Interestingly, Greenway's old friend, Dr J.A. Rollins of Exeter, drew precisely the opposite conclusion that Manitoba was relying on Greenway's promise of no compromise and that any move to grant concessions would 'ruin you politically' (PAM, Greenway Papers, Rollins to Greenway, July 5, 1896).

3 LaPierre, 'Politics, Race and Religion in French Canada' (thesis), p.314. *Ibid.*, pp.310–21, Stevens, 'Laurier and the Liberal Party in Ontario' (thesis), pp.153–91, and Neatby, *Laurier and a Liberal Quebec*, pp.82–99, have analysed the Manitoba school settlement and the Laurier–Greenway agreement in some detail.

aspects it was more advantageous to the Catholics and especially to the French than had been the offer of the Smith Commission in the spring.[4] At the same time, a system of separate schools was not established. That ground was yielded on each side in reaching the final federal-provincial agreement was made clear in the Laurier-Sifton correspondence in August and September; Sifton wanted fewer and Laurier wanted more generous privileges granted to the minority than were actually made in the final settlement.[5]

The story of the ecclesiastical response to the Laurier-Greenway agreement and the subsequent conflict which led to the mission of Merry del Val and the *Affari Vos* letter of Leo XIII represents a further chapter in Canada's church-state history. That the settlement was achieved without Archbishop Langevin's consent and did not approach the minimum he believed to be called for by the second decision of the Privy Council was more than evident. At the same time, it should be noted that some of the vehemence of the Liberal-versus-hierarchy struggle which has been traditionally attributed to the pre-election period in 1896 has probably been read back into that period from the clash which followed the Laurier-Greenway agreement. This would seem to be particularly true of the response of Archbishop Bégin, whose name headed the list of five bishops (the others were Laflèche, Labrecque, Blais, and Gravel) who signed the pastoral letter of November 22, 1896, condemning the Laurier-Greenway agreement and Pacaud's newspaper, *L'Electeur*.[6]

Only in a limited sense did the Manitoba school struggle and settlement represent a victory over the principle of denominational schools. However adamant against the concept majority opinion in Manitoba remained, Catholic schools did not cease to exist in the province. Particularly in urban

---

4 See Skelton, *The Life and Letters of Sir Wilfrid Laurier*, II, pp.13–21. Three major points were contained in the settlement. A half-hour of denominational religious teaching by Christian clergy was authorized for the end of the school day when requested by parents of ten children in rural areas or of twenty-five in urban. Secondly, when requested by parents of twenty-five children in rural districts or forty in urban schools, at least one certified Roman Catholic teacher was to be employed; a reciprocal concession was given for areas with a Protestant minority. Third, provision was made for bilingual teaching where ten or more pupils in any school spoke French or any other non-English language. Without a designation of specific numbers, it was agreed that there would be some Catholic representation among administrative personnel, such as inspectors, examining boards, and the advisory council. Finally, it was agreed that there would be an attempt to decide on mutually acceptable textbooks. (Canada, *Sessional Papers*, 1897, no.35.)
5 PAC, Laurier Papers, Sifton to Laurier, August 28, September 5, 1896
6 See Rumilly, *Histoire*, VIII, pp.140ff

areas with their populations of mixed religions, parochial schools simply continued under greater handicaps and with greater potential for periodic abrasion on all sides.[7] That the entire incident heightened Catholic-Protestant tensions throughout Canada to a dangerous degree goes without saying.

With all the 'might-have-beens' of history, the intriguing question, 'Would remedial legislation have worked?' remains unanswerable. It may nonetheless throw light on some aspects of the struggle, even on the sincerity or perspicacity of the main figures. On the one hand, it can be said that everyone involved realized that remedial action and its consequences did not give assurance of a final solution; on the other, most admitted that such legislation could be made to bring some relief. Differences centred on the degree of probable change and the possibility of adverse results outweighing gains even for the minority. As the struggle progressed, repeated claims were made on both sides of the argument; later reminiscences remained equally divided in judgment. John Willison, for example, was sincerely convinced that confederation might have disintegrated had the law gone through;[8] Archbishop Langevin claimed to have Sifton's word that Manitoba would not resist a federal remedial law, once it was passed.[9] With American civil-rights legislation as a useful if not exact parallel, it is clear that local determination could frustrate federal legislation for an almost indefinite period. Further questions, equally unanswerable, present themselves: presuming provincial resistance to a federal law, what would happen next? what would the Catholic minority have done if faced with new assaults? what about subsequent federal response – and would it have been the same federal government had the law gone through?

In retrospect, it is easy enough to construct a convincing argument against nearly every main figure at some point during the struggle; it is at the same time quite difficult to make a case for any individual, civil or clerical, having followed the most praiseworthy course at every turn. One reason at least is obvious. Beyond the normal complication of 'the art of the possible,' the church-state dimension continually added its peculiar confusion. It may well have been, as seemed particularly clear in the case of Lacombe, that ecclesiastics were naïve about the implications of party

7 See Ready, 'The Political Implications of the Manitoba School Question' (thesis); Morton, 'Manitoba Schools and Canadian Nationality'; and Cook, 'Church, Schools and Politics in Manitoba.'
8 Toronto *Globe*, April 2, 1896
9 AAQ, Langevin to Bégin, January 2, 1896

politics. Clerics were getting into the inner forum of the machinery of civil power and had to know and abide by the rules of the game being entered. It should not be forgotten, however, that they were in the fray for different and, from their point of view, compelling reasons. With all allowances made for individual cases of simple power-seeking, churchmen were concerned with the Manitoba school question because it was a religious issue, politicians because it was a political issue. While the religious issue could perhaps be resolved by a law, the political issue could be affected but not resolved. The political goal was to gain or retain the confidence of the electorate, and the school question was only one of many factors at any given time. For the politician, moreover, the issue was a continuing one. He had to look beyond a single law to long-range personal, party, and national results; whereas the cleric could, once his specific political battle had been won or lost, move back into his normal field of work with the sigh of relief expressed by Père Lacombe.

This again poses the thorny question of legitimate and viable tactics for the church in such a politico-religious crisis. In the best of all possible worlds, it might be possible to produce an ecclesiastical manifesto which would be, or at least would seem to be, pure and direct from Mount Olympus. Given regional differences, fallible judgments, personal jealousies, and known party sympathies, such could never be the case. As Bishop Emard starkly put it to his fellow bishops when the 1896 mandement was being prepared, 'Il est connu que des politiciens travaillent à obtenir ce document.'[10] At the same time, could the church have remained totally silent on the issue without being open to the charge of abdication? It must not be forgotten that there was a good deal of unhappy coincidence in the timing of the school question on the national level. Much of the overtness and heavy-handedness of clerical efforts stemmed from the weakness encountered in the political arena. It was not the bishops' fault that, when they felt obliged to take their strongest stand directly touching the workings of the national government, the confident and flexible grasp on the reins of power, which was most needed from the politicians on whom they hoped to rely, was simply non-existent. To a marked degree, the case exhibited the classic, cruel dilemma of clergy and laity torn between the conflicting demands and loyalties of church and state.

Yet the point perhaps most easily overlooked in this study of church-state interplay was the degree to which politicians took the initiative to involve clerics. And, however opportunistic or even cynical this pressure

10 AAQ, Emard to Bégin, April 23, 1896

may have been in certain cases, expediency was not the whole story. It must be suggested that the anguish of the problem, at least in part, stemmed from the temper of the socio-religious atmosphere of late-nineteenth-century French Canada. If there was political impotence, did not the shadow of a particular kind of episcopal power contribute to that weakness? The ultramontane or semi-ultramontane mind, clerical or lay, expected that church pressure in politics should and would be exercised. Here the complication of the cultural factor was of particular significance. For the mentality inspired by Bishops Bourget and Laflèche, the dominance of the church culturally as well as religiously, was elevated to such a degree that Colonel Audet could tell the future Archbishop Langevin, as if echoing what seemed to him a matter of common consent, 'Le clergé canadien est la seule organisation qui parmi nous puisse agir sur la masse du peuple d'une manière solide, permanente.'[11] Adding a particular theological reinforcement, the simplistic interpretation by such as Bishop Laflèche of the clear design of divine providence in the history of the French-Canadian people led him to assign to himself and to the church an automatic leading role in the struggle for 'survivance.' The clerically dominated religious and social atmosphere of Quebec of the late nineteenth century may have been an important reason why the battle was fought on the school rather than on the language issue. That same atmosphere, however, contained the seeds of later acrimony both in religion and in culture.

Another major point raised at the outset of the study and a constant factor throughout the sequence comes into focus. However much the school battle was fought along Catholic-Protestant lines, the loss of the battle over Manitoba schools meant the loss of another French bulwark outside Quebec. It may in fact be true that the net outcome would not have been greatly different if the external structure of the outpost had never been attacked or had in the end been restored. The relative decline of the French in Manitoba preceded the school crisis, and, faced with the choice, most emigrating French Canadians chose the truly colonial situation of New England over the potentially equal-partner situation of the Canadian West. It may be argued that their choice of the United States was another victory of economics and geography over history. But the French decline in the West was not simply something that English Canadians caused to happen to French Canadians. It was also something that French Canadians, by doing something else, allowed to happen to themselves. Nonetheless, the determination of the Manitoba majority, and of the government which in

11 AASB, Audet to Langevin, September 13, 1893

turn stirred it up and reflected it, deeply convulsed the Canadian 'cultural entente.'

At the very least it may be said that the manner and tone of the Manitoba stance and its Ontario reverberations did something to Canada which with great anguish is being re-examined and readjusted only now, three-quarters of a century later. Despite Willison's praise of the official Manitoba statements for their 'clearness, directness, simplicity and dignity,'[12] it must be added that they also excelled in unfortunate, if blissful, short-sightedness.[13] The refrain, gaining volume in post-centennial Quebec, that members of French enclaves in the remainder of Canada have little to hope for from the kind of federal system that has evolved since 1867, repeatedly looks to the Manitoba school case as an object lesson. Section 93 of the BNA Act and section 22 of the Manitoba Act were proven to be dead letters as safeguards of minority rights against local majority rule. Subsequent rude shocks, notably in Ontario and once again in Manitoba in the era of World War I, bore a similar though somewhat less explicit message. The profound, if late-blooming, separatist stance in Quebec is hardly a startling corollary of the attrition of French privileges in English-speaking provinces.

At the opposite extreme, whether acting for cultural or religious reasons, Laflèche and his imitators were the unwitting teachers of a hard and not easily accepted lesson to the Roman Catholic church, particularly in French Canada. With all the reservations made in the traditional picture of a frontal clash between Laurier and the Quebec clergy in the 1896 election, the episode remained Canadian history's most extensive and concerted effort on the part of church authorities to influence the national political process. Bishop Laflèche's determined non-recognition of the implication of Canadian religious pluralism, and the danger of over-identification with one political party, were contained only with difficulty. Like the Protestant extremists, Laflèche and other staunch clericalists pushed more moderate, if less forceful men, into positions which they did not set out to take and which they did not want to follow to their logical conclusions.

12 Willison, *Sir Wilfrid Laurier and the Liberal Party*, II, p.212
13 L.C. Clark points out the coincidence of the ardent British imperialism of many of those who promoted and backed the attack on French and Catholic privileges (*The Manitoba School Question*, p.5). Without denying the complexities of the imperialist persuasion, it may be suggested that the Jameson Raid and the McCarthy excursion to Portage la Prairie were not as far apart as a half-globe of distance would indicate. The best study on imperialism is Carl Berger, *The Sense of Power*.

But there were signs of a new era. Bishop Emard, for one, represented the change in ecclesiastical approach from the time of Pius ix to that of Leo xiii. After Laflèche's death in 1898, the tone and style of the Quebec church tended to be set by Bégin, who reverted to the Taschereau principle of avoiding unnecessary clashes, and by Paul Bruchési, who succeeded Fabre at Montreal and became a close friend of Laurier despite their initial animosity. There was some revival of the ultramontane thrust among the clerics who supported Henri Bourassa, as well as in the surviving Conservative party and its Union Nationale successor, but the 'Castor-Rouge' tension continued to prevent the coalescence of all ultramontanes into a single political camp. The most important single factor in establishing a new church-state equilibrium was Laurier himself. His practice of Catholicism was never unruffled, yet among Laurier's major contributions to Canada must be counted his success in divorcing a substantial number of his compatriots from the narrow grouping of race, religion, and politics inspired by the tradition of Bishops Bourget and Laflèche. In a parallel, although less direct, manner, Laurier taught the same lesson to English Canada.

With all its difficulties, civil and religious, the episode of the Manitoba school question brought many basic Canadian questions into clearer outline. If scars there were, was Canada not the wiser for it? If section 93 did prove ineffective as a positive protection for minorities, did it not at least retain some negative value as a deterrent? Were not other majorities somewhat less likely to repeat attempts to flaunt it, lest worse divisions follow? Conversely, if guarantees to minorities actually were to become pretexts for enduring anachronisms, was it not likely that solutions would be worked out with some diplomacy at the local level? Finally, may not the church have learned something?

It may be concluded that several extreme options within the Canadian spectrum were blunted in a necessary, though painful, manner. Although there were many lessons still to be learned, neither such a direct assault on the clear intent of the original frame of the constitution in the matter of minority rights, nor the degree of direct interference in elections desired and attempted by some clerics, again took place. In the crisis of the 1890s, opportunists were not lacking to seek political capital out of the irreconcilable stands of the champions of obduracy. Perhaps one measure of the stature of the men, political and ecclesiastical, who struggled through the middle, if not always sunny way, was the resiliency and relative stability which they managed to salvage for Canada from one of its most enduring and dangerous convulsions.

Appendices

1a/The British North America Act, section 93

In and for the Province the Legislature may exclusively make laws in relation to education, subject and according to the following provisions:

1 Nothing in any such law shall prejudicially affect any right or privilege with respect to denominational schools which any class of persons have by law in the Province at the Union.

2 All powers, privileges and duties at the Union, by law conferred and imposed in Upper Canada on the separate schools and school trustees of the Queen's Roman Catholic subjects, shall be and the same are hereby extended to the dissentient schools of the Queen's Protestant and Roman Catholic subjects in Quebec.

3 Where in any Province a system of separate or dissentient schools exists by law at the Union, or is thereafter established by the Legislature of the Province, an appeal shall lie to the Governor-General in Council from any act or decision of any Provincial authority affecting any right or privilege of the Protestant or Roman Catholic minority of the Queen's subjects in relation to education.

4 In case any such Provincial law as from time to time seems to the Governor-General in Council requisite for the due execution of the provisions of this section is not made, or in case any decision of the Governor-General in Council, on any appeal under this section, is not duly executed by the proper Provincial authority in that behalf, then, and in every such case, and as far only as the circumstances of each case required, the

Parliament of Canada may make remedial laws for the due execution of the provisions of this section, and of any decision of the Governor-General in Council under this section.

1b / The Manitoba Act, section 22

In and for the Province the said Legislature may exclusively make laws in relation to education, subject and according to the following provisions:
1 Nothing in any such law shall prejudicially affect any right or privilege with respect to denominational schools which any class of persons have by law or practice in the Province at the Union.
2 An appeal shall lie to the Governor-General in Council from any Act or decision of the Legislature of the Province, or of any Provincial authority, affecting any right or privilege of the Protestant or Roman Catholic minority of the Queen's subjects in relation to education.
3 In case any such Provincial law as from time to time seems to the Governor-General in Council requisite for the due execution of the provisions of this section is not made, or in case any decision of the Governor-General in Council on any appeal under this section is not duly executed by the proper Provincial authority in that behalf then, and in every such case, and as far only as the circumstances of each case may require, the Parliament of Canada may make remedial laws for the due execution of the provisions of this section, and of any decision of the Governor-General in Council under this section.

2 / Party Standings by Province, 1891 and 1896*

Totals: 1891, 215 seats; 1896, 213 seats, fixed by Redistribution Bill of 1892 following Census of 1891

PROVINCES	1891 Cons.	1891 Lib.	1896 Cons.	1896 Lib.	1896 Ind.	
ONTARIO (standing at 1896 dissolution: C, 57; L, 33; I, 2)	48	44	43	43	6	(3 McCarthyite, 3 Patron)

*Source: J.M. Beck, 'Democratic Process in Canadian General Elections,' in J.C. Courtney, ed, (Toronto 1967), *Voting in Canada*.

PROVINCES	1891 Cons.	1891 Lib.	1896 Cons.	1896 Lib.	1896 Ind.
QUEBEC (standing at 1896 dissolution: L. 35; C. 30.)	28	37	16	49	
NOVA SCOTIA (lost one seat in redistribution)	16	5	10	10	
NEW BRUNSWICK (lost two seats in redistribution)	13	3	9	5	
PEI (lost one seat in redistribution)	2	4	3	2	
MANITOBA (gained two seats in redistribution)	4	1	4	2	1
BRITISH COLUMBIA	6	0	2	4	
TERRITORIES	4	0	1	3	
TOTALS	121	94	88	118	7

3 / Quebec Electoral Results by Constituency, 1896*

Appendix 3 indicates: 1/ the net gain in the popular vote by the winning party over the previous vote (in 1891 or a subsequent by-election); 2/ the diocese in which the riding was located (a very few crossed diocesan lines); 3/ the racial composition of the riding (those ridings called French-English have a 10 per cent or higher English-speaking population, estimated from the 1891 census); and 4/ redistribution where applicable.

Appendix 3 begins overleaf.

*Canada, *Sessional Papers*, 1891, no.27a, 1897, no.20; *The Canadian Parliamentary Guide*, 1891, 1897.

French or French-English	Constituency and candidates (diocese)		Vote
F-E	ARGENTEUIL (Montreal)		
	Dr Thomas Christie	L	1125
	Harry Abbott	C	1050
	Majority		75
	Votes polled		2175
	Eligible voters		3139
	Net gain	C	128
	(Dr Thomas Christie, 203)*		
F	BAGOT (Nicolet)		
	F. Dupont	C	Accl.
	Eligible voters		3873
	(F. Dupont, 23)*		
F	BEAUCE (Québec)		
	Jos. Godbout	L	3003
	Geo. Cloutier	C	2576
	Majority		427
	Votes polled		5579
	Eligible voters		8092
	Net gain	L	6
	(Dr Jos. Godbout, 421)*		
F	BEAUHARNOIS (Valleyfield)		
	J.G.H. Bergeron	C	1582
	J.I. Tarte	L	1534
	Majority		48
	Votes polled		3116
	Eligible voters		4135
	Net gain	L	251
	(J.G.H. Bergeron, 303)*		
F	BELLECHASSE (Quebec)		
	O.E. Talbot	L	1537
	J.E. Roy	C	1227
	Majority		310
	Votes polled		2764
	Eligible voters		3603
	Net gain	L	416
	(G. Amyot, C, 106)*		
F	BERTHIER (Montreal)		
	C. Beausoleil	L	Accl.
	Eligible voters		4142
	(C. Beausoleil, Lib. Ind., 157)*		
F-E	BONAVENTURE (Rimouski)		
	W.L. Fauvel	L	1644
	Geo. P. Roy	C	1331
	Majority		313
	Votes polled		2975
	Eligible voters		4365
	Net gain	L	243
	(W.L. Fauvel, 70)*		
F-E	BROME (Sherbrooke)		
	Sydney A. Fisher	L	1677
	George P. Foster	C	1344
	Majority		333
	Votes polled		3021
	Eligible voters		3841
	Net gain	L	336
	(Dyer, C, 3)*		
F-E	CHAMBLY-VERCHERES (Montreal)		
	C.A. Geoffrion	L	2511
	Hon. L.O. Taillon	C	2117
	Majority		394
	Votes polled		4628
	Eligible voters		6266
	Net gain	L	143
	[two ridings in 1891: R. Préfontaine (Chambly), 87; C.A. Geoffrion (Verchères), 164]		
F	CHAMPLAIN (Trois-Rivières)		
	F.A. Marcotte	C	2411
	P. Trudel	L	2035
	Majority		376
	Votes polled		4446
	Eligible voters		5982
	Net gain	C	299
	(Carignan, C, 77)*		

* Incumbent at dissolution with majority.
L = Liberal
C = Conservative

French or French-English	Constituency and candidates (diocese)		Vote	French or French-English	Constituency and candidates (diocese)		Vote
F	CHARLEVOIX (Chicoutimi)			F	DEUX MONTAGNES (Montreal)		
	L.C.A. Angers	L	1403		J.A.C. Ethier	L	1227
	S. Cimon	C	1313		Joseph Girouard	C	1210
	Majority		90		Majority		17
	Votes polled		2716		Votes polled		2437
	Eligible voters		3978		Eligible voters		3288
	Net gain	C	61		Net gain	L	405
	(L.C.A. Angers, 151)*				(Joseph Girouard, 338)*		
F-E	CHATEAUGUAY (Valleyfield)						
	J. P. Brown	L	1594	F	DORCHESTER (Québec)		
	C. Lecavalier	C	894		J.B. Morin	C	1480
	Majority		700		C.E. Vaillancourt	L	1150
	Votes polled		2488		Majority		330
	Eligible voters		3906		Votes polled		2630
	Net gain	L	602		Eligible voters		4110
	(J.P. Brown, 98)*				Net gain	C	330+
					(Dr Vaillancourt, accl.)*		
F-E	CHICOUTIMI ET SAGUENAY						
	(Chicoutimi)			F	DRUMMOND-ARTHABASKA		
	(took in new areas of Sept-Iles and				(Nicolet)		
	Anticosti)				Joseph Lavergne	L	1593
	P.V. Savard	L	3059		E. Désy	C	1128
	L. de G. Belley	C	1973		Majority		465
	Majority		1086		Votes polled		2721
	Votes polled		5032		Eligible voters		9781
	Eligible voters		8879		Net gain	C	497
	Net gain	L	1114		(J.A. Lavergne, 962)*		
	(L. de G. Belley, 28)*						
F-E	COMPTON (Sherbrooke)			F-E	GASPE (Rimouski)		
	R.H. Pope	C	1948		R. Lemieux	L	1658
	F.F. Willard	L	1475		Thomas Ennis	C	1616
	Majority		473		Majority		42
	Votes polled		3423		Votes polled		3274
	Eligible voters		6111		Eligible voters		4573
	Net gain	L	593		Net gain	L	42+
	(Rufus Pope, 1066)*				(Joncas, C, accl.)*		

* Incumbent at dissolution with majority.
  L = Liberal
  C = Conservative

French or French-English	Constituency and candidates (diocese)		Vote	French or French-English	Constituency and candidates (diocese)		Vote
F-E	HOCHELAGA (Montreal)			F	KAMOURASKA (Quebec)		
	A.C. Madore	L	2127		H.G. Carroll	L	1414
	Dr. S. Lachapelle	C	1621		Linière Taschereau	C	1403
	Majority		506		Majority		11
	Votes polled		3748		Votes polled		2814
	Eligible voters		11243		Eligible voters		3879
	Net gain	L	506+		Net gain	C	84
	(Dr S. Lachapelle, accl.)*				(H.G. Carroll, 95)*		
				F	LABELLE (Ottawa)		
F-E	HUNTINGDON (Valleyfield)				(new seat, part of former Ottawa County, see Wright riding)		
	Julius Scriver	L	1546		Jos. H.N. Bourassa	L	2175
	W.H. White	C	827		S.R. Poulin	C	1706
	Majority		719		Majority		469
	Votes polled		2373		Votes polled		3881
	Eligible voters		3956		Eligible voters		5612
	Net gain	L	436		Net gain	L	
	(Julius Scriver, 283)*						
				F	LAPRAIRIE-NAPIERVILLE (Montreal, St Hyacinthe)		
F-E	JACQUES-CARTIER (Montreal)				D. Monet	L	1734
	F.D. Monk	C	2329		L.C. Pelletier	C	1458
	Arthur Boyer	L	2216		Majority		276
	Majority		113		Votes polled		3192
	Votes polled		4545		Eligible voters		4164
	Eligible voters		6764		Net gain	L	312
	Net gain	C	687		[Two ridings in 1891: L. Pelletier (Laprairie), 54; D. Monet (Napierville), 18]		
	(Charbonneau, L, 574)*						
F	JOLIETTE (Montreal)			F	L'ASSOMPTION (Montreal)		
	Charles Bazinet	L	1769		Joseph Gauthier	L	1335
	Dr V.P. Lavallée	C	1453		H. Jeannotte	C	1216
	Majority		316		Majority		119
	Votes polled		3222		Votes polled		2551
	Eligible voters		4424		Eligible voters		3358
	Net gain	L	376		Net gain	L	119+
	(Lippe, C, 60)*				(H. Jeannotte, accl.)*		

* Incumbent at dissolution with majority.
L = Liberal
C = Conservative

French or French-English	Constituency and candidates (diocese)		Vote	French or French-English	Constituency and candidates (diocese)		Vote
F	LAVAL (Montreal)			F	MAISONNEUVE (Montreal)		
	Thomas Fortin	L	1541		(new seat, from Montreal)		
	F.J. Bisaillon	C	1449		R. Préfontaine	L	3912
	Majority		92		Geo. E. Baril	C	2342
	Votes polled		2990		Majority		1570
	Eligible voters		3948		Votes polled		6254
	Net gain	L	626		Eligible voters		10,770
	(Ouimet, C, 534)*						
				F	MASKINONGE (Trois-Rivières)		
F	LEVIS (Quebec)				J.H. Legris	L	1384
	Dr P.M. Guay	L	2271		C.J. Coulombe	C	1094
	Joseph E. Gelley	C	1963		Majority		290
	Majority		308		Votes polled		2478
	Votes polled		4234		Eligible voters		5072
	Eligible voters		5372		Net gain	L	182
	Net gain	L	27		(J.H. Legris, 108)*		
	(Dr P.M. Guay, 281)*						
				F	MEGANTIC (Quebec)		
					Geo. Turcot	L	2073
F	L'ISLET (Quebec)				L.J. Fréchette	C	1410
	A.M. Déchène	L	1038		Majority		654
	Adolphe Dionne	C	1032		Votes polled		3483
	Majority		6		Eligible voters		5072
	Votes polled		2070		Net gain	L	765
	Eligible voters		2999		(L.J. Fréchette, 111)*		
	Net gain	C	30				
	(Tarte, L, 36)*						
				F-E	MISSISQUOI (St Hyacinthe)		
					D.B. Meigs	L	1687
F	LOTBINIERE (Quebec)				G.F. Slack	C	1471
	Dr Rinfret	L	1620		Majority		216
	Dr J.A.P. Lord	C	1214		Votes polled		3158
	Majority		406		Eligible voters		5189
	Votes polled		2834		Net gain	L	375
	Eligible voters		4183		(Baker, C, 159)*		
	(Dr Rinfret, accl.)*						

* Incumbent at dissolution with majority.
  L = Liberal
  C = Conservative

French or French-English	Constituency and candidates (diocese)		Vote	French or French-English	Constituency and candidates (diocese)		Vote
F	MONTCALM (Montreal)			F-E	MONTREAL, ST ANTOINE (Montreal)		
	L.E. Dugas	C	1202		Dr Roddick	C	3077
	L.V. Labelle	Lib. 1.	907		Robt. McKay	L	2904
	Majority		295		Majority		173
	Votes polled		2109		Votes polled		5981
	Eligible voters		3470		Eligible voters		9346
	Net gain	C	138		(from Montreal West / D. Smith, C, 3708)*		
	(L.E. Dugas, 157)*						
F	MONTMAGNY (Quebec)			F	MONTREAL, STE MARIE (Montreal)		
	P.A. Choquette	L	1143		H. Dupré	L	3341
	A.J. Bender	C	901		A.T. Lépine	C	1978
	Majority		242		Majority		1363
	Votes polled		2044		Votes polled		5319
	Eligible voters		2899		Eligible voters		10,011
	Net gain	C	191		(from Montreal East / A.T. Lépine, 805)*		
	(P.A. Choquette, 433)*						
				F-E	MONTREAL, ST LAURENT (Montreal) (new seat from Montreal Centre and West)		
F	MONTMORENCY (Quebec)						
	Hon. T.C. Casgrain	C	1096		E.G. Penny	L	3632
	Chas. Langelier	L	1046		R. Wilson Smith	C	2915
	Majority		50		Majority		717
	Votes polled		2142		Votes polled		6547
	Eligible voters		2499		Eligible voters		11,047
	(Turcotte, C, accl.)*						
F-E	MONTREAL, STE ANNE (Montreal)			F	MONTREAL, ST JACQUES (Montreal) (new seat from Montreal Centre and East)		
	M.J.F. Quinn	C	3104				
	Jas. McShane	L	2919		O. Desmarais	L	3423
	Majority		119		L.A. Lavallée	C	2054
	Votes polled		6023		Majority		1369
	Eligible voters		9040		Votes polled		5477
	(from Montreal Centre / James McShane, 336)*				Eligible voters		8776

* Incumbent at dissolution with majority.
  L = Liberal
  C = Conservative

French or French-English	Constituency and candidates (diocese)		Vote	French or French-English	Constituency and candidates (diocese)		Vote
F	NICOLET (Nicolet)			F-E	QUEBEC OUEST (Quebec)		
	F. Boisvert	C	2377		R.R. Dobell	L	1057
	J.H. Leduc	L	2239		Thos. McGreevy	C	826
	Majority		138		Majority		231
	Votes polled		4616		Votes polled		1883
	Eligible voters		6443		Eligible voters		2562
	Net gain	C	139		Net gain	L	246
	(J.H. Leduc, 1)*				(Thos. McGreevy, 15)*		
F-E	PONTIAC (Pontiac)			F	QUEBEC CENTRE (Quebec)		
	W.J. Poupore	C	1980		Hon. F. Langelier	L	1469
	Dr T.C. Gaboury	L	1341		Hon. A.R. Angers	C	1150
	Majority		639		Majority		319
	Votes polled		3321		Votes polled		2619
	Eligible voters		5520		Eligible voters		3217
	Net gain	L	102		Net gain	L	241
	(Bryson, C, 741)*				(F. Langelier, 78)*		
F	PORTNEUF (Quebec)			F	QUEBEC COMTE (Quebec)		
	Sir H. Joly de Lotbinière	L	2086		Chas. Fitzpatrick	L	1982
	L.H. Stafford	C	2050		J.J.T. Frémont Lib. I.		1058
	Majority		36		Majority		924
	Votes polled		4136		Votes polled		3040
	Eligible voters		5338		(J.J.T. Frémont, L, 340)*		
	Net gain	C	114				
	(Delisle, L, 150)*						
				F	RICHELIEU (St Hyacinthe)		
F	QUEBEC EST (Quebec)				A.A. Bruneau	L	1609
	Hon. W. Laurier	L	3202		Hon. Alp. Desjardins	C	1475
	C. Leclerc	C	1011		Majority		134
	Majority		2191		Votes polled		3084
	Votes polled		4213		Eligible voters		4717
	Eligible voters		7346		Net gain	L	62
	(W. Laurier, accl.)*				(A.A. Bruneau, 72)*		

* Incumbent at dissolution with majority.
  L = Liberal
  C = Conservative

French or French-English	Constituency and candidates (diocese)		Vote	French or French-English	Constituency and candidates (diocese)		Vote
F-E	RICHMOND ET WOLFE (Sherbrooke)			F-E	SHERBROOKE (Sherbrooke)		
	M.P. Stenson	L	2782		Hon. W.B. Ives	C	1478
	C.C. Cleveland	C	2544		Hon. Henry Aylmer	L	1221
	Majority		238		Majority		257
	Votes polled		5326		Votes polled		2699
	Eligible voters		7723		Eligible voters		4481
	Net gain	L	519		Net gain	C	216
	(C.C. Cleveland, 281)*				(Hon. W.B. Ives, 41)*		
F	RIMOUSKI (Rimouski)						
	J.B.R. Fiset	L	2443	F	SOULANGES (Valleyfield)		
	Louis Taché	C	2177		Dr. A. Bourbonnais	L	1054
	Majority		266		Elz. Lanthier	C	861
	Votes polled		4620		Majority		193
	Eligible voters		6059		Votes polled		1915
	Net gain	L	528		Eligible voters		2436
	(A. Caron, C, 262)*				Net gain	L	232
					(Mousseau, C, 39)*		
F	ROUVILLE (St Hyacinthe)						
	L.P. Brodeur	L	1840				
	J.A. Fournier	C	870				
	Majority		970	F-E	STANSTEAD (Sherbrooke)		
	Votes polled		2710		A.H. Moore	C	2018
	Eligible voters		4439		T.B. Rider	L	1583
	Net gain	L	901		Majority		435
	(L.P. Brodeur, 69)*				Votes polled		3601
					Eligible voters		5621
					Net gain	C	537
F-E	SHEFFORD (Sherbrooke)				(T.B. Rider, 102)*		
	C.H. Parmelee	L	2191				
	P.J.S. Pelletier	C	1726				
	Majority		465				
	Votes polled		3917				
	Eligible voters		6227	F	ST HYACINTHE (St Hyacinthe)		
	Net gain	L	288		M.E. Bernier	L	Accl.
	(J. Sanborn, L, 177)*				(M.E. Bernier, 506)*		

* Incumbent at dissolution with majority.
  L = Liberal
  C = Conservative

French or French-English	Constituency and candidates (diocese)		Vote	French or French-English	Constituency and candidates (diocese)		Vote
F	ST JEAN ET IBERVILLE (St Hyacinthe)			F-E	VAUDREUIL (Valleyfield)		
	F. Béchard	L	1849		H.S. Harwood	L	1296
	P.H. Roy	C	1342		Alderic Séguin	C	801
	Majority		507		Majority		495
	Votes polled		3191		Votes polled		2097
	Eligible voters		5834		Eligible voters		3006
	Net gain	C	195		Net gain	L	304
	[two ridings in 1891: F. Béchard (Iberville), 484; F. Bourassa L (St Jean), 218]				(H.S. Harwood, 191)*		
F	TEMISCOUATA (Rimouski)			F-E	WRIGHT (Ottawa)		
	C.E. Pouliot	L	2171		C.R. Devlin	L	2975
	Dr P.E. Grandbois	C	1604		J.M. McDougall	C	2593
	Majority		567		Majority		382
	Votes polled		3775		Votes polled		5568
	Eligible voters		5345		Eligible voters		8615
	Net gain	L	765		Net gain	L	282
	(Dr P.E. Grandbois, 198)*				[New seat, part of former Ottawa County, see Labelle riding, C.R. Devlin (Ottawa County), 569]		
F	TERREBONNE (Montreal)						
	L.A. Chauvin	C	1862				
	P.F.E. Petit	L	1734	F	YAMASKA (Nicolet)		
	Majority		128		Dr R.M.S. Mignault	L	1342
	Votes polled		3596		F. Vanasse	C	1324
	Eligible voters		5260		Majority		18
	(Leclerc, C, accl.)*				Votes polled		2666
F	TROIS-RIVIERES–SAINT MAURICE (Trois-Rivières)				Eligible voters		3631
	Sir A.P. Caron	C	1691		Net gain	C	152
	Dr L.P. Fiset	L	1422		(Dr R.M.S. Mignault, 170)*		
	Majority		269				
	Votes polled		3113				
	Eligible voters		4361				
	Net gain	L	76				
	[two ridings in 1891: Desaulniers (St Maurice) C, 145; Langevin (Trois-Rivières) C, 200]						

* Incumbent at dissolution with majority.
L = Liberal
C = Conservative

4 / 'Switching' Ridings in Quebec with Net Gains (Excluding redistributed areas)

LIBERAL GAINS	French or French-English	Net gain over 1891	CONSERVATIVE GAINS	French or French English	Net gain over 1892
Bellechasse	(F)	416	Dorchester	(F)	330
Brome	(F-E)	336	Jacques-Cartier	(F-E)	687
Chicoutimi et					(over 1895)
Saguenay	(F-E)	1114			
Deux Montagnes	(F)	352	Nicolet	(F)	139
Gaspé	(F-E)	42	Stanstead	(F-E)	537
		(over accl.)			
Hochelaga	(F-E)	506	4 gains, 2 with significant English vote		
		(over accl.)			
Joliette	(F)	376			
L'Assomption	(F)	119			
		(over accl.)			
Laval	(F)	626			
Mégantic	(F)	765			
Missisquoi	(F-E)	375			
Québec Ouest	(F-E)	246			
Richmond-Wolfe	(F-E)	519			
Rimouski	(F)	528			
Soulanges	(F)	232			
Temiscouata	(F)	765			

16 gains, 7 with significant English vote, 3 in
Eastern Townships

5 / Analysis of Selected Quebec Ridings: Vote Comparison, 1891 and 1896

A / MONTREAL AND QUEBEC CITY RIDINGS

MONTREAL
1891:   Three ridings only; all won by Conservatives
   Montreal East
   Montreal West
   Montreal Centre
   Total population: 140,747
   Eligible voters: 38,913
   Total voting: 22,007
   Conservative majority: 5,745
(included huge 3,706 majority for Sir Donald Smith in Montreal West and 214 for Curran in
Montreal Centre; McShane won Curran's seat in 1895 by-election by 336 majority)

Suburban:
  Jacques Cartier and Hochelaga: both Conservative in 1891. Jacques Cartier won by Charbonneau, Liberal, in December 1895 by-election by 574 majority.

1896: Five ridings
  Ste Anne (Centre) and St Antoine (West) won by Conservatives slimly
  Ste Marie (East), St Laurent (Centre), and St Jacques (East), heavily Liberal
  Total population: 182,695
  Eligible voters: 48,254
  Total voting: 29,544
  Liberal majority: 3,128
  Net Liberal gain in Montreal city alone 8,873
  Suburban: (Maisonneuve riding added in redistribution)
  Jacques Cartier won by Monk, C. (113)
  Hochelaga won by Madore, L. (506)
  Maisonneuve won by Préfontaine, L. (1,570)

QUEBEC CITY
1891: Quebec Ouest: Conservative majority: 53 (1895 by-election, Conservative majority –
      15)
  Quebec Centre: Liberal majority: 78
  Quebec Est: Laurier acclaimed
1896: Quebec Ouest:

R.R. Dobell	L	1057
Thos. McGreevy	C	826
Majority		231
Votes polled		1883
Net gain (over 1895)	L	246
Quebec Centre:		
Hon. F. Langelier	L	1469
Hon. A.R. Angers	C	1150
Majority		319
Votes polled		2619
Net gain	L	241
Quebec Est:		
Hon. W. Laurier	L	3202
C. Leclerc	C	1011
Majority		2191
Votes polled		4213

Total Quebec City Liberal majority in 1896: 2,741; Liberal net gain 487+

B / RIDINGS IN BISHOP LAFLECHE'S DIOCESE

CHAMPLAIN

1891			1896		
Carignan	C	1976	F.A. Marcotte	C	2411
Ferdinand Trudel	L	1899	P. Trudel	L	2035
Majority		77	Majority		376
Votes polled		3875	Votes polled		4446
			Net gain	C	299

Sharp contrasts evident from one parish to another, but no great changes from 1891 to 1896 elections.

Strong pro-Conservatives remained constant:

CAP DE LA MADELEINE

1891			1896		
Carignan	C	198	Marcotte	C	222
F. Trudel	L	23	P. Trudel	L	21
Majority		175	Majority		201
Votes polled		221	Votes polled		243

Strong pro-Liberals equally consistent:

ST STANISLAS

1891			1896		
F. Trudel	L	420	P. Trudel	L	320
Carignan	C	28	Marcotte	C	59
Majority		392	Majority		261
Votes polled		448	Votes polled		379

Fairly consistent gains for Conservatives in other parishes:

Largest gain: ST TITE

1891			1896		
F. Trudel	L	189	Marcotte	C	238
Carignan	C	172	P. Trudel	L	151
Majority		17	Majority		87
Votes polled		361	Votes polled		389
			Net gain	C	104

More typical: NOTRE DAME DU MONT CARMEL

1891			1896		
F. Trudel	L	154	P. Trudel	L	133
Carignan	C	109	Marcotte	C	117
Majority		45	Majority		16
Votes polled		263	Votes polled		250
			Net gain	C	29

TROIS-RIVIERES ET ST MAURICE

1891: Two separate ridings	1896: Single Riding		
St Maurice won by F.L. Desaulniers (c) 894–749 (majority 145)	Sir A.P. Caron	c	1691
	Dr L.P. Fiset	L	1422
Trois-Rivières won by Sir Hector Lange-	Majority		269
vin (c) 682–482 (majority 200)	Votes polled		3113
	Net gain	L	76

Vote in Trois-Rivières City: won by Caron 674–549, but a net gain of 75 for the Liberals over 1891

MASKINONGE

1891	1896		
Legris, (L.) won by 108 majority.	J.H. Legris	L	1384
	C.J. Coulombe	c	1094
	Majority		290
	Votes polled		2478
	Net gain	L	182

Vote change in total diocese
  Champlain: Conservatives gained 299
  Trois-Rivières et St Maurice: Liberals gained 76
  Maskinongé: Liberals gained 182
  Conservative net gain: 41

C / BISHOP BLAIS'S DIOCESE

TEMISCOUATA

1891			1896		
			Pouliot	L	2171
Grandbois	c	1813	Grandbois	c	1604
Deschenes	L	1615	Majority		576
Majority		198	Votes polled		3775
Votes polled		3428	Net gain	L	765

Switching Subdivisions:
  St Georges de Cacouna: Ste Rose du Dégelée:
  1891: 114–82 Conservative   1891: 70–33 Conservative
  1896: 113–80 Liberal   1896: 63–57 Liberal
  Liberal net gain: 65   Liberal net gain: 43

Parishes where Pouliot specifically complained of curé's 'influence indue':
Trois-Pistoles: St Arsène:
1891: 191–101 for Deschenes   1891: 95–66 for Grandbois
1896: 207–130 for Pouliot   1896: 91–79 for Grandbois
Conservative net gain: 13   Liberal net gain: 17

St Modeste:
1891:   58–50 for Grandbois
1896:   57–57
Liberal net gain: 8

St Clement:
1891:   72–32 for Deschenes
1896:   91–31 for Pouliot
Liberal net gain: 20

Notre Dames des Sept Douleurs:
1891:   33–9 for Grandbois
1896:   37–17 for Grandbois
Liberal net gain: 4
St Hubert:
not listed.

Total Liberal net gain in 'complaint' areas: 36
Fraserville:
1891:   522–185 for Grandbois
1896:   355–275 for Grandbois
Liberal net gain: 254

D / BISHOP LABRECQUE'S DIOCESE

CHICOUTIMI ET SAGUENAY RIDING

1891

P.V. Savard	L	1927
Sir A.P. Caron	C	1807
Majority		123
Votes polled		3721

(Savard subsequently unseated by 28 votes by Belley after election challenged)

1896 (new areas of Sept–Iles to Anticosti added)

P.V. Savard	L	3059
L. de G. Belley	C	1973
Majority		1086
Votes polled		5032
Liberal net gain		1114

Most impressive Liberal gains:
  Roberval   1891:   98–78 for Caron
              1896:   175–83 for Savard
  St Prime   1891:   94–48 for Savard
              1896:   138–41 for Savard

St Fulgence   1891:   61–48 for Savard
              1896:   69–39 for Savard

E / RIDINGS IN BISHOP EMARD'S DIOCESE

VALLEYFIELD

Beauharnois

1891
  Bergeron (C) won with majority of 303.

1896
  Bergeron won over Tarte with majority of 48. (Liberal net gain: 255)

Huntingdon

1891
    Scriver (L) won with majority of 283.

1896
    Scriver defeated W.J. White by a majority of 719. (Liberal net gain: 436)

Chateauguay

1891
    J.P. Brown (L) won with majority of 98.

1896
    Brown defeated C. Lecavalier by 700. (Liberal net gain: 602)

Soulanges

1891
    Mousseau, (C) won with majority of 39.

1896
    Bourbonnais (L) defeated E. Lanthier (C) by 193. (Liberal net gain: 232)

Vaudreuil

1891
    H.S. Harwood (L) won by 191.

1896
    Harwood defeated Séguin (C) by 495. (Liberal net gain: 404)

Total Liberal net gain: 1929

F / BISHOP GRAVEL'S DIOCESE

NICOLET RIDING

1891

J.H. Leduc	L	1502
Prince	C	1501
Houde	I	313
Majority		1
Votes polled		3316

(Leduc got his largest margin in St Pierre les Becquets and Beçancour)

1896

F. Boisvert	C	2377
J.H. Leduc	L	2239
Majority		138
Votes polled		4616

(Boisvert gained where Houde had taken votes in 1891)

Nicolet town and parish

1891

Prince	C	382
Leduc	L	130
Houde	I	44
Majority		252
Votes polled		556

1896

Boisvert	C	429
Leduc	L	132
Majority		297
Votes polled		561

(Nicolet town remained almost exactly as in 1891, with independent votes seemingly going Conservative.)

St Célestin
1891
   Leduc 92; Prince 79; Houde 47

1896
   Leduc 115; Boisvert 145 (46 more voters on list)

Ste Angèle de Laval
1891
   Leduc 57; Prince 42; Houde 21

1896
   Leduc 81; Boisvert 83 (44 more on lists)

Bibliography

The papers of the major public figures involved in the school controversy are held in the Public Archives of Canada and other archives and libraries across Canada. As indicated in the notes, these collections were used extensively in this study. Much of the new material used came from the following ecclesiastical archives: the diocesan archives of Kingston, Montreal, Ottawa, Quebec, St Boniface, Toronto, St Hyacinthe, Trois-Rivières, and Valleyfield, les archives du séminaire de Ste-Thérèse, du séminaire de Trois-Rivières, du Collège Ste-Marie, Montréal, du Scholasticat St-Joseph, Ottawa, de la Société Historique du Saguenay, Chicoutimi. Many newspapers were consulted, some in full-folio collections, others through scrapbooks of newspaper clippings kept in the Public Archives of Canada and of Manitoba. There is a voluminous range of government records on the school question, covering both legislatures and the courts.

The following bibliography represents both a list of works consulted in the preparation of this study and a guide to wider reading in many areas involving late nineteenth-century Canada. It is prefaced by a bibliographic note summarizing recent specialized works dealing with the school question.

The origin and development of the crisis in Manitoba has been investigated in detail by R.E. Clague, 'The Political Aspects of the Manitoba School Question, 1890–96,' MA thesis, University of Manitoba, 1939. The complications of the court proceedings have been carefully reviewed by

W.T. Shaw in his study of J.S. Ewart, 'The Role of John S. Ewart in the Manitoba School Question,' MA thesis, University of Manitoba, 1959. Some aspects of the case's impact on the career of Wilfrid Laurier have been treated in turn by H.B. Neatby, *Laurier and a Liberal Quebec: A Study in Political Management* (Toronto 1973); and by P.D. Stevens, 'Laurier and the Liberal Party in Ontario, 1887–1911,' PH D thesis, University of Toronto, 1967. Effects of the school question in other careers have been dealt with by J.P. Heisler, 'Sir John Thompson, 1844–1894,' PH D thesis, University of Toronto, 1955; A.W. Mackintosh, 'The Career of Sir Charles Tupper in Canada, 1864–1900,' PH D thesis, University of Toronto, 1959; L.L. LaPierre, 'Politics, Race and Religion in French Canada: Joseph Israel Tarte,' PH D thesis, University of Toronto, 1962; and K.M. McLaughlin, 'The Canadian General Election of 1896 in Nova Scotia,' MA thesis, Dalhousie University, 1967. Many aspects of the issue's impact on the federal level, particularly the schism caused in the Conservative party in Ontario, have been dealt with in L.C. Clark's thesis on the post-Macdonald years, 'A History of the Conservative Administrations, 1891–96,' PH D thesis, University of Toronto, 1968. The same author's *The Manitoba School Question: Majority Rule or Minority Rights?* (Toronto 1968) provides a good selection of documents along with perceptive comments. John Saywell and Ramsay Cook, both of whom were involved in the direction of the thesis stage of the present study, have made important contributions to an understanding of the French-Canadian complexities of late-nineteenth-century Canada [J.T. Saywell, ed. *The Canadian Journal of Lady Aberdeen, 1893–98*, 'Introduction.' (Toronto 1960); with H.B. Neatby, 'Chapleau and the Conservative Party in Quebec,' *Canadian Historical Review,* XXXVII (March 1956), 1–22; Ramsay Cook, *Canada and the French-Canadian Question (Toronto 1966)*]. Among general histories, the works of Mason Wade [*The French Canadians*, 2 vols. 2nd ed. (Toronto 1968)] and Robert Rumilly [*Histoire de la province de Québec*, tomes VI, VII, VIII (Montreal, n.d.), *Monseigneur Laflèche et son temps* (Montreal 1938)] provide a wealth of narrative detail on the context of the school question's impact in Quebec. The most recent, and most balanced, general account of the Manitoba controversy is that found in P.B. Waite, *Canada 1874–1896: Arduous Destiny* (Toronto 1971), 245ff. Subsequent developments of the school situation in Manitoba itself are treated in W.B. Ready, 'The Political Implications of the Manitoba School Question, 1896–1916,' MA thesis, University of Manitoba, 1948; W.L. Morton, 'Manitoba Schools and Canadian Nationality, 1890–1923,' in Craig Brown, ed., *Minorities, Schools and Politics*. (Toronto 1969), 10–18, and Ramsay Cook, 'Church, Schools and Politics in Manitoba, 1903–1912,' in the same volume, 19–41. The instances of Protestant 'churchly' pressure during the Manitoba crisis are only briefly touched in the present study, and suggest an important subject for further investigation. The various works of W.L. Morton, J.S. Moir, J.W. Grant, and L.C. Clark form a valuable point of departure in this area.

PRIMARY SOURCES

Printed Document Collections and Ecclesiastical Records

Brophy, Gerald F. *The Manitoba School Case, 1894*. London 1895
Canada Ecclésiastique, Le. Montreal 1886–96
Decelles, A.D., ed. *Discours de Sir Wilfrid Laurier, 1889–1911*. Montreal 1920
Hodgins, W.E. *Correspondence Reports of the Ministers of Justice and Orders-in-Council upon the Subject of Dominion and Provincial Legislature, 1867–1895*. Ottawa 1896
Kennedy, W.P.M. *Statutes, Treaties and Documents of the Canadian Constitution 1743–1929*. Toronto 1930
MacGregor, M.S. *Some letters from Archbishop Taché on the Manitoba School Question*. Toronto 1967
Mandements, Lettres Pastorales, Circulaires et Autres Documents Publiés dans le Diocèse de Montréal Depuis son Erection. Vol. 12. Montreal 1907
Mandements, Lettres Pastorales et Circulaires Des Evêques de Québec. 6 vols. Quebec 1887–90
Marshall, H., ed. 'The Organization and Administration of Public Schools in Canada.' *Dominion Bureau of Statistics, Reference Paper no. 31*. Ottawa 1952
Oliver, E.H., ed. *The Canadian North-West: Its Early Development and Legislative Records*, Vol. II, Publications of Canadian Archives no. 9. Government Printing Bureau 1914
Pacaud, L., ed. *Sir Wilfrid Laurier: Lettres à mon Père et à ma mère, 1867–1919*. Arthabaska 1935
Pope, Sir Joseph. *Correspondence of Sir John Macdonald: Selections from*

the Correspondence of the Right Honourable Sir John Alexander Macdonald, G.C.B., First Prime Minister of Canada. Toronto 1921

Proulx, J.B. *Documents pour servir à l'intelligence de la question des Ecoles du Manitoba, Avec Quelques Notes Explicatives*. Rome 1896

Contemporary Accounts and Memoirs

Aberdeen, Lady. *The Canadian Journal of Lady Aberdeen*. J.T. Saywell, ed. Toronto 1960

Benoit, Dom P. *L'Anglomanie Au Canada, Resumé Historique de la Question des Ecoles du Manitoba*. Trois-Rivières 1899

Bryce, Reverend George. *Manitoba, Its Infancy, Growth and Present Condition*. Winnipeg 1882

Cartwright, The Rt. Hon. Sir R.J. *Reminiscences*. Toronto 1912

Chapais, Thomas. *Mélanges de Polémiques*. Quebec n.d.

Charlton, J. *Diary* (University of Toronto Library)

David, L.O. *Mes Contemporains*. Montreal 1894

Ewart, J.S. *The Manitoba School Question*. Toronto 1894

Hill, Robert B. *Manitoba, History of Its Early Settlement, Development and Resources*. Toronto 1890

Kribs, L.P. *The Manitoba School Question Considered Historically, Legally and Controversially*. Toronto 1895

Langelier, Charles. *Souvenirs Politiques, 1890 à 1896*. 2 vols. Quebec 1912

Morgan, J., ed. *The Canadian Men and Women of the Time*. Toronto 1898

Morton, W.L., ed. *Alexander Begg's Red River Journal and Other Papers Relative to the Red River Resistance of 1869–1870*, The Champlain Society. Toronto 1956

Normandin, Pierre G., ed. *The Canadian Parliamentary Guide, 1891, 1897*. Ottawa 1891, 97

Pope, J. *Journal* (PAC)

Pope, J. *Memoirs of Sir John Macdonald*. 2 vols. Ottawa 1894

Pope, M., ed. *Public Servant: The Memoirs of Sir Joseph Pope*. Toronto 1960

Proulx, J.B. *Dans La Ville Eternelle: Journal de Voyage*. Montreal 1897

Ross, G.W. *Getting into Parliament and After*. Toronto 1913

Savaeté, A. *Voix Canadiennes, Vers L'Abîme*. 12 vols. Paris n.d.

Taché, Most Reverend A. *Denominational or Free Christian Schools in Manitoba*. Winnipeg 1877

– *Ecoles Séparées, Une Partie des Négociations à Ottawa in 1870*. St Boniface 1890

– *Une Page de l'Histoire des Ecoles du Manitoba*. St Boniface 1893
Tupper, Sir Charles. *Recollections of Sixty Years in Canada*. London 1914
Wade, F.C. *The Manitoba School Question*. Winnipeg 1895
Wallace, W.S. *The Memoirs of the Rt. Hon. Sir George Foster*. Toronto 1933
Willison, J.S. *Reminiscences, Political and Personal*. Toronto 1919

Pamphlets and Contemporary Articles

Bethune, A.F. *Is Manitoba Right? A Question of Ethics, Politics, Facts and Law. A Complete Historical and Controversial Review of the Manitoba School Question*. Winnipeg 1896
Bernard, P. *Un Manifeste Libéral*. Quebec 1896
Bryce, Reverend George. *Canadian Pamphlets, 1871–1913*
– 'The Manitoba School Question.' *The Canadian Magazine* (September 1893), 511–16
Caven, W. 'The Equal Rights Movement.' *University Quarterly Review* (June 1890), 139–45
David, L.O. *Le Clergé Canadien, Sa Mission, Son Œuvre*. Montreal 1896
Ewart, J.S. *An Open Letter to the Hon. Thos. Greenway on the School Question in Manitoba*. Winnipeg 1892
– *Lecture on the Manitoba School Question in the Congregational Church*. Winnipeg 1895
– *The Manitoba School Question: A Reply to Mr. Wade*. Winnipeg 1895
Fisher, James. 'The School Question in Manitoba: Letter from James Fisher to the Electors of Russell, September, 1890.' Winnipeg n.d.
'Justitia.' *La Campagne Politico-Religieuse de 1896–97*. Quebec 1897
King, Reverend J.M. *Education, Not Secular nor Sectarian, but Religious*. Winnipeg 1889
Lapatrie, C. *La Campagne Politico-Religieuse de 1896–1897*. n.p./n.d.
– *Le Libéralisme Catholique et les Elections de 23 juin, 1896*. Quebec 1896
Laurier, W. *Manifeste de Laurier, Reciprocité*. Ottawa 1891
Leduc, H. *Hostility Unmasked: School Ordinance of 1892 of the North-West Territories and Its Disastrous Results*. Montreal 1896
Machray, Robert. *Some Remarks on Primary Education by the Bishop of Rupert's Land*. 1889
McCarthy, Dalton. 'Great Speech, December 12, 1889.' Ottawa 1889
– 'The Manitoba Public School Law.' *The Canadian Magazine* (March 1893), 3–8

Power, L.G. *The Remedial Bill–From the Point of View of a Catholic Member*. Ottawa 1896

Sellar, Robert. *Letters Relative to the Rights and Present Position of the Quebec Minority*

Taché, Most Reverend A. 'A Reply to Mr. Tarte.' Open Letter in *Manitoba Free Press*, July 25, 1893

– *Les écoles dites écoles publiques de Manitoba sont des écoles protestantes*. St Boniface 1893

– *Memoire de Mgr. Taché sur la Question des Ecoles en Réponse au Rapport du Comité de l'honorable Conseil Privé du Canada*. Montreal 1894

– *Pastoral Letter on the New School Laws of Manitoba*. 1890

– *Two Letters on the School Question*. 1889

Taillon, L.O. *The Manitoba School Case (1890)*. Ottawa 1895

Watt, D.H. *Poems on the Manitoba School Question*. Toronto 1895

SECONDARY SOURCES

Books

Beaulieu, A. and J. Hamelin. *Les Journaux du Québec de 1764 à 1964*. Québec 1965

Begg, Alexander. *A History of the North-West*. 3 vols. Toronto, 1893–5

Benoit, Dom P. *Vie de Monseigneur Taché*. 2 vols. Montreal 1904

Berger, Carl. *The Sense of Power: Studies in the Ideas of Canadian Imperialism 1867–1914*. Toronto 1970

Biggar, C.R.W. *Sir Oliver Mowat, A Biographical Sketch*. 2 vols. Toronto 1905

Brown, R.C. *Canada's National Policy, 1883–1900*. Princeton 1964

Brown, R.C. ed., *Minorities, Schools, and Politics*. Toronto 1969

Bryce, Reverend George. *A History of Manitoba*. Toronto 1906

Carrigan, D.O. *Canadian Party Platforms, 1867–1968*. Toronto 1968

Charlesworth, Hector. *The Canadian Scene, Sketches: Political and Historical*. Toronto 1927

Clark, L.C. *The Manitoba School Question: Majority Rule or Minority Rights?* Toronto 1968

Colquhoun, A.H.U. *Press, Politics and People – The Life and Letters of Sir John Willison, Journalist and Correspondent of the Times*. Toronto 1935

Cook, G.R. *Canada and the French-Canadian Question*. Toronto 1966

– *French Canadian Nationalism*. Toronto 1970

- *The Maple Leaf Forever: Essays in Canadian Nationalism.* Toronto 1971
- *The Politics of John W. Dafoe and the Free Press.* Toronto 1963
Creighton, D.G. *John A. Macdonald, The Old Chieftain.* Toronto 1955
Dafoe, J.W. *Clifford Sifton in Relation to His Times.* Toronto 1931
- *Laurier: A Study in Canadian Politics.* Toronto 1922
Dalton, Roy C. *The Jesuits' Estates Question, 1760–1888: A Study of the Background for the Agitation of 1889.* Toronto 1969
David, L.O. *Laurier et Son Temps.* Montreal 1905
- *Laurier: Sa Vie, Ses Œuvres.* Beauceville 1919
Désilets, Andrée. *Hector-Louis Langevin: un père de la conféderation canadienne, 1826–1906.* Quebec 1969
Firestone, O.J. *Canada's Economic Development 1867–1953.* London 1958
Foley, J.G. *Resumé of General Elections, 1896–1911.* Ottawa 1915
Fremont, Donatien. *Mgr. Taché et la Naissance du Manitoba.* Winnipeg 1930
French, Goldwin. *Parsons and Politics.* Toronto 1962
Grant, J.W., ed. *The Churches and the Canadian Experience.* Toronto 1963
Groulx, Abbé L. *L'Enseignement Français Au Canada.* 2 vols. Montreal 1931–3
Guide to Canadian Ministries since Confederation. Ottawa 1957
Harkin, W.A., ed. *The Political Reminisciences of the Rt. Hon. Sir Charles Tupper, Bart.* London 1914
Harkness, Ross. *J.C. Atkinson of the Star.* Toronto 1963
Higham, John. *Strangers in the Land: Patterns of American Nativism 1860–1925.* New Brunswick, New Jersey 1955
Hodgins, B., and P. Page, eds. *Canadian History since Confederation.* Georgetown 1972
Hopkins, J. Castell. *Life and Work of the Rt. Hon. Sir John Thompson, Prime Minister of Canada.* Brantford 1895
Howard, J.K. *Strange Empire: A Narrative of the Northwest.* New York 1952
Hughes, Katherine. *Father Lacombe, The Black-Robe Voyageur.* Toronto 1911
Jonquet, E., o.m.i. *Mgr. Grandin, Oblat de Marie Immaculée.* Montreal 1903
Lamb, R., c.s.b. *Thunder in the North.* New York 1957
Langlois, G. *Histoire de La Population Canadienne-Française.* Montreal 1934

Leblanc, P. and A. Edinborough, eds. *One Church, Two Nations?* Don Mills 1968

Le Jeune, L., O.M.I. *Dictionnaire Général du Canada.* 2 vols. Ottawa 1931

Lingard, C.C. *Territorial Government in Canada: The Autonomy Question in the Old North-West Territories.* Toronto 1946

Longley, Hon. J.W. *Sir Charles Tupper.* Vol. VIII, Part II of *The Makers of Canada.* Toronto 1927

Lupul, M.R. *The Roman Catholic Church and the North-West School Question: A Study in Church-State Relations in Western Canada, 1875–1905.* Toronto 1974

Macbeth, R.G. *The Romance of Western Canada.* Toronto 1918

Machray, R. *The Life of Robert Machray, Archbishop of Rupert's Land and Primate of All Canada. Prelate of the Order of St. Michael.* Toronto 1909

McNaughton, K.F.C. *The Development of the Theory and Practice of Education in New Brunswick, 1784–1900.* Fredericton 1947

McWilliams, M. *Manitoba Milestones.* Toronto 1928

Miller, J. *National Government and Education in Federated Democracies, Dominion of Canada.* Philadelphia 1940

Moir, J.S. *Church and State in Canada, 1627–1867.* Toronto 1967

Moore, H. *The Clash: A Study in Nationalities.* Toronto 1918

Moreau, H. *Sir Wilfrid Laurier.* Paris 1902

Morice, Reverend A.G., O.M.I. *Fifty Years in Western Canada.* Toronto 1930

– *History of the Catholic Church in Western Canada.* 2 vols. Toronto 1910

– *Vie de Mgr. Langevin.* St Boniface 1919

Morrison, J.C. *Oliver Mowat and the Development of Provincial Rights in Ontario, 1867–1896.* Toronto 1962

Morton, A.S. *A History of the Canadian West to 1870–71.* London 1939, 2nd. ed. Toronto 1973

Morton, W.L. *Manitoba: A History.* Toronto 1957

– *The Progressive Party in Canada.* Toronto 1950

– *The Shield of Achilles/Le Bouclier d'Achille.* Toronto 1968

Neatby, H.B. *Laurier and a Liberal Quebec: A Study in Political Management.* Toronto 1973

Peel, B.B. *A Bibliography of the Prairie Provinces.* Toronto 1956

Phelan, J. *The Bold Heart: The Story of Father Lacombe.* Toronto 1956

Phillips. E. *The Development of Education in Canada.* Toronto 1957

Preston, W.T.R. *The Life and Times of Lord Strathcona.* Toronto 1914

– *My Generation of Politics and Politicians.* Toronto 1927

Primeau, L. *Mgr. Adélard Langevin, O.M.I.* Montreal 1942
Ross, H.R. *Thirty-Five Years in the Limelight – Sir Rodmond Roblin and His Times.* Winnipeg 1936
Rumilly, R. *Henri Bourassa.* Montreal 1953
– *Histoire de la Province de Québec.* 35 vols. Montreal 1940–65
– *Mgr. Laflèche et Son Temps.* Montreal 1938
– *Sir Wilfrid Laurier.* Paris 1931
Sait, E.C. *Clerical Control in Quebec.* Toronto 1911
Saunders, E.M., ed. *The Life and Letters of the Rt. Hon. Sir Charles Tupper, Bart., K.C.M.G.* 2 vols. Toronto 1916
Savard, Pierre. *Jules-Paul Tardivel, La France et les Etats-Unis, 1851–1905.* Quebec 1967
Saywell, J.T. *The Office of Lieutenant-Governor.* Toronto 1957
Scarrow, H.A. *Canada Votes.* New Orleans 1961
Schmeiser, D.A. *Civil Liberties in Canada.* Oxford 1964
Schofield, F.H. *The Story of Manitoba.* 4 vols. Winnipeg 1913
Schull, Joseph. *Laurier: The First Canadian.* Toronto 1965
Sellar, R. *The Tragedy of Quebec.* Toronto 1910
Siegfried, A. *The Race Question in Canada.* London 1907
Sissons, C.B. *Bilingual Schools in Canada.* Toronto 1917
– *Church and State in Canadian Education.* Toronto 1959
Skelton, O.D. *The Life and Letters of Sir Wilfrid Laurier.* 2 vols. Toronto 1921
Stanley, G.F.G. *The Birth of Western Canada.* 2nd. ed. Toronto 1960
Stubbs, R. *Lawyers and Laymen of Western Canada.* Toronto 1939
Tétu, H. *Histoire des Journaux de Québec.* Quebec 1889
Thomas, L.H. *The Struggle for Responsible Government in the North-West Territories, 1870–1897.* Toronto 1956
Todd, A., ed. *Parliamentary Government in the British Colonies.* 2nd ed. London 1894
Underhill, F.H. *The Image of Confederation.* Toronto 1964
Wade, M. *The French Canadians.* 2 vols. 2nd ed. Toronto 1968
Waite, P.B. *Canada 1874–1896: Arduous Destiny.* Toronto 1971
Walker, F.A. *Catholic Education and Politics in Ontario.* Toronto 1964
Wallace, W.S. *The Dictionary of Canadian Biography.* Toronto 1926
Weir, G.M. *The Separate School Question in Canada.* Toronto 1934
Willison, J.S. *Sir Wilfrid Laurier.* 2 vols. Toronto 1926
– *Sir Wilfrid Laurier and the Liberal Party.* 2 vols. Toronto 1903
Willson, B. *The Life of Lord Strathcona and Mount Royal.* London 1915

Articles

Banks, M.A. 'The Change in the Liberal Party Leadership, 1887.' *Canadian Historical Review*, XXXVIII (June 1957), 109–28
– 'Edward Blake's Relations with Canada during His Irish Career, 1892–1907.' *Canadian Historical Review*, XXXVI (March 1954), 22–43
Bernard, P. 'Memoire sur la question des écoles du Manitoba: l'origine de la question.' *Revue d'histoire de l'amérique française*, VI (décembre 1952), 440–2
Bruchesi, Jean. 'Sir W. Laurier et Mgr. Bruchesi.' *Royal Society of Canada*, Third Series, XL, Sec. I, (1946)
Clark, L.C. 'The Conservative Party in the 1890's.' Canadian Historical Association, *Report* (1961), 58–74
Clark, L.C. and W.L. Morton. 'David Mills and the Remedial Bill of 1896, A Dialogue.' *Journal of Canadian Studies*, I (1966)
Clippingdale, R.T. 'J.S. Willison and Canadian Nationalism.' Canadian Historical Association, *Historical Papers/Communications Historiques* (1969), 74–93
Cole, D.L. 'J.S. Ewart and Canadian Nationalism.' Canadian Historical Association, *Historical Papers/Communications Historiques* (1969), 62–73
Cook, G.R. 'Church, Schools and Politics in Manitoba, 1903–1912.' *Canadian Historical Review*, XXXIX, I (March 1958)
Crunican, P.E. 'Bishop Laflèche and the Mandement of 1896.' Canadian Historical Association, *Historical Papers/Communications Historiques* (1969), 52–61
– 'Father Lacombe's Strange Mission. The Lacombe-Langevin Correspondence on the Manitoba School Question, 1895–96.' Canadian Catholic Historical Association, *Report* (1959), 57–72
Curran, J.J. 'Reminiscences of Sir John Thompson.' *Canadian Magazine*, XXVI (January 1906)
D'Eschembault, Reverend A. 'Histoire du Groupe Français au Manitoba.' *Les Cloches de St. Boniface* (April, May, June, July, August, 1938)
Dupont, Pierre. 'La Question Scolaire Manitobaine: en marge d'une correspondance.' *L'Action Française*, VIII, no. 5 (December 1922), 368–79; no. I (January 1923), 33–41; X, no. 3 (September 1923), 168–177
Fraser, B.J. 'The Political Career of Sir Hector Louis Langevin.' *Canadian Historical Review*, XLII (June 1961), 93–132
Girard, Mathieu. 'La Pensée Politique de Jules-Paul Tardivel.' *Revue*

d'Histoire de l'Amérique Française, 21, no. 3 (December 1967), 397–428

Gouin, J. 'Histoire d'une amitié: Correspondance intime entre Chapleau et DeCelles.' *Revue d'Histoire de l'Amérique Française*, XVIII, no. 3 (December 1964), 363–86; XVIII, no. 4 (March 1965), 541–65

Groulx, L., ed. 'Correspondance Langevin-Audet.' *Revue d'Histoire de l'Amérique Française*, I (1947), 271–77

– 'Mgr. Adélard Langevin d'après une Partie de sa Correspondance.' *Revue d'Histoire de l'Amérique Française*, I (1947), 569–94

Hare, John. 'Nationalism in French Canada and Tardivel's Novel, "Pour la Patrie." ' *Culture*, XXII (1961), 403–12

Heintzman, R. 'The Spirit of Confederation: Professor Creighton, Biculturalism and the Use of History.' *Canadian Historical Review*, (September 1971), 245–75

Kerr, J.B. 'Sir Oliver Mowat and the Campaign of 1894.' *Ontario History* (March 1963), 1–13

Landon, F. 'When Laurier Met Ontario.' *Transactions of the Royal Society of Canada*, Third Series, XXXV (May 1941), 1–14

Lang, S.E. 'History of Education in Manitoba.' *Canada and Its Provinces*, XX (Toronto 1914), 416–26

LaPierre, L.L. 'Joseph Israel Tarte and the McGreevy-Langevin Scandal.' Canadian Historical Association, *Report* (1961)

La Terreur, M. 'Correspondance Laurier–Mme. Joseph Lavergne, 1891–1893.' Canadian Historical Association, *Report* (1964), 37–51

Lederle, J.W. 'The Liberal Convention of 1893.' *Canadian Journal of Economics and Political Science* (1950), 16ff

MacKirdy, K. 'The Loyalty Issue in 1891.' *Ontario History*, LV (September 1963), 143–54

Martin, C. 'The First "New Province" of the Dominion.' *Canadian Historical Review*, I (December 1920), 354–78

– 'The Political History of Manitoba 1870–1912.' *Canada and Its Provinces*, XIX (Toronto 1917), 97–147

Morton, W.L. 'Confederation 1870–1896: The End of the Macdonaldian Constitution and the Return to Duality.' *Journal of Canadian Studies*, I, no. 1 (May 1966), 11–24

– 'Manitoba Schools and Canadian Nationality 1890–1923.' Canadian Historical Association, *Report* (1951), 1–9

– 'The Conservative Principle in Confederation.' *Queens Quarterly*, LXXI, no. 4 (Winter 1965), 528–47

Neatby, H.B., and J.T. Saywell. 'Chapleau and the Conservative Party in Quebec.' *Canadian Historical Review*, XXXVII (March 1956), 1–22

Rumilly, R. 'Monseigneur Laflèche et les Ultramontains.' *Revue d'Histoire de l'Amérique Française*, XVI, no. 1 (June 1962), 95–101

Savard, Pierre. 'Jules-Paul Tardivel, un ultramontain devant les problèmes et les hommes de son temps.' Canadian Historical Association, *Report* (1963), 125–140

– 'Le Cercle Catholique de Québec 1876–1897.' *Culture*, XXVIII (1967), 3–17, 120–136

– 'Note sur l'étude de l'ultramontanisme au Canada français.' La Société Canadienne d'Histoire de l'Eglise Catholique, *Sessions d'Etude* (1966), 13–15

Saywell, J.T. 'Introduction.' *The Canadian Journal of Lady Aberdeen* (Toronto 1960)

– 'The Crown and the Politicians: The Canadian Succession Question 1891–1896.' *Canadian Historical Review*, XXXVII, no. 4 (December 1956)

Scott, S.M. 'Foster on the Thompson-Bowell Succession.' *Canadian Historical Review*, XLVIII (September 1967), 273–6

Silver, A.I. 'French Canada and the Prairie Frontier.' *Canadian Historical Review*, L (March 1969), 11–36

Smiley, D.V. 'The Two Themes of Canadian Federalism' *Canadian Journal of Economics and Political Science* (February 1965), 80–97

Stamp, R.M. 'J.D. Edgar and the Liberal Party: 1867–1896.' *The Canadian Historical Review*, XLV (June 1964), 93–115

Stanley, G.F.G. 'French and English in Western Canada.' *Canadian Dualism: Studies of French-English Relations*, ed. M. Wade (Toronto 1960), 311–50

Underhill, F.H. 'Edward Blake, the Liberal Party and Unrestricted Reciprocity.' Canadian Historical Association, *Report* (1939), 133–41

– 'Laurier and Blake, 1882–1891.' *Canadian Historical Review* (December 1939), 392–408

– 'Laurier and Blake, 1891–1892.' *Canadian Historical Review* (June 1943), 135–55

Watt, J.T. 'Anti-Catholic Nativism in Canada; The Protestant Protective Association.' *The Canadian Historical Review*, LXVIII (March 1967), 45–58

– 'The Protestant Protective Association: An Example of Religious Extremism in Ontario in the 1890's.' in B. Hodgins and R. Page, eds. *Canadian History Since Confederation* (Georgetown 1972), 244–60

Willison, J.S. 'Journalism and Public Life in Canada.' *Canadian Magazine* (October 1905), 554–8

Theses

Banks, M.A. 'Toronto Opinion of French Canada during the Laurier
  Regime, 1896–1911.' MA thesis, University of Toronto, 1950
Carrier, Frère Antoine, s.c. 'Laurier, citoyen d'Arthabaska.' MA thesis,
  University of Ottawa, 1961
Buell, J.P. 'The Political Career of N. Clarke Wallace, 1872–1896.' MA
  thesis, University of Toronto, 1961
Clague, R.E. 'The Political Aspects of the Manitoba School Question
  1890–96.' MA thesis, University of Manitoba, 1939
Clark, L.C. 'A History of the Conservative Administrations, 1891–96.'
  PH D thesis, University of Toronto, 1968
Cooke, Ellen Gillies. 'The Federal Election of 1896 in Manitoba.' MA
  thesis, University of Manitoba, 1943
Cooper, J.I. 'French Canadian Conservatism in Principle and Practice,
  1873–1891.' PH D thesis, McGill University, 1938
Crunican, P.E. 'The Manitoba School Question and Canadian Federal
  Politics, 1890–1896.' PH D thesis, University of Toronto, 1968
Eayrs, L.E. 'The Election of 1896 in Western Ontario.' MA thesis, Univer-
  sity of Western Ontario, 1951
Graham, W.R. 'Sir Richard Cartwright and the Liberal Party.' PH D thesis,
  University of Toronto, 1950
Greening, W.E. 'The Globe and Canadian Politics, 1890–1902.' MA thesis,
  University of Toronto, 1939
Heisler, J.P. 'Sir John Thompson 1844–1894.' PH D thesis, University of
  Toronto, 1955
Holmes, V.L. 'Factors Affecting Politics in Manitoba: A Study of the
  Provincial Elections 1870–1899.' MA thesis, University of Manitoba,
  1936
Jackson, E. 'The Organization of the Liberal Party 1867–1896.' MA thesis,
  University of Toronto, 1962
Jackson, J.A. 'The Disallowance of Manitoba Railway Legislation in the
  1880's: Railway Policy as a factor in the Relations of Manitoba with the
  Dominion.' MA thesis, University of Manitoba, 1945
LaPierre, L.L. 'Politics, Race and Religion in French Canada: Joseph
  Israel Tarte.' PH D thesis, University of Toronto, 1962
Mackintosh, A.W. 'The Career of Sir Charles Tupper in Canada,
  1864–1900.' PH D thesis, University of Toronto, 1959
McLaughlin, K.M. 'The Canadian General Election of 1896 in Nova
  Scotia.' MA thesis, Dalhousie University, 1967

McLeod, J.T. 'The Political Thought of Sir Wilfrid Laurier: A Study in Canadian Party Leadership.' PH D thesis, University of Toronto, 1965

McNaught, K.W. 'The Globe and Canadian Liberalism, 1880–90.' MA thesis, University of Toronto, 1946

Miller, J.R. 'The Impact of the Jesuits Estates Act on Canadian Politics, 1888–91.' PH D thesis, University of Toronto, 1972

Newfield, G.M. 'The Development of Manitoba Schools Prior to 1870.' MA thesis, University of Manitoba, 1937

Noble, E.J. 'D'Alton McCarthy and the Election of 1896.' MA thesis, University of Guelph, 1969

O'Sullivan, J.F. 'D'Alton McCarthy and the Conservative Party.' MA thesis, University of Toronto, 1949

Ready, W.B. 'The Political Implications of the Manitoba School Question, 1896–1916.' MA thesis, University of Manitoba, 1948

Regenstreif, S.P. 'The Liberal Party of Canada: A Political Analysis.' PH D thesis, Cornell University, 1963

Schmeiser, James A. 'Development of the Separate School Legislation in the North-West Territories from 1867 to 1892.' MA thesis, University of Ottawa, 1964

Shaw, W.T. 'The Role of John S. Ewart in the Manitoba School Question.' MA thesis, University of Manitoba, 1959

Sims, E.F. 'A History of Public Education in Manitoba, 1870–1890.' MA thesis, University of Manitoba, 1944

Smith, P. 'Henri Bourassa and Sir Wilfrid Laurier.' MA thesis, University of Toronto, 1948

Stamp, R.M. 'The Political Career of James David Edgar.' MA thesis, University of Toronto, 1962

Stevens, P.D. 'Laurier and the Liberal Party in Ontario, 1887–1911.' PH D thesis, University of Toronto, 1967

Index

Aberdeen, Governor-General Lord 45, 45n; influence on C.H. Tupper 54; invites Greenway to Ottawa 87; failure of Ottawa meeting 93; January 1896 speech from throne 145; and January 1896 cabinet crisis 146–8, 147n, 155, 155n, 156; opposition to Tupper senior 147, 155n; rejects extension of Parliament 167; opposes coercion 178; and Smith visit to Winnipeg 182–3; supports Smith March mission 220; calls Tupper 237

Aberdeen, Lady 44n; on Bowell indecision 45, 117; criticism of Langevin 88n; reaction to July 1895 crisis 106n, 108; and January 1896 cabinet crisis 146–7, 147n, 148–9; opposition to Tupper senior 147, 155n; reaction to Cameron statement 168n; urges moderation with Langevin 179; with Lacombe 180; asks Walsh to intercede 180; urges Smith visit to Winnipeg 182–3; supports Smith March mission 220, 228–9; on Tupper's accession 237

Abbott, Sir John J.C. 133

Affari Vos 318

Allard, Rev. J. 5, 19n, 248

American Protective Association 63, 63n

Amyot, Colonel Guillaume 204, 206, 212, 230, 230n

Angers, Auguste Réal 15n, 16; dismissal of Mercier 33n; financial support of Privy Council appeal 42n; argues for immediate election 47; 1895 Laflèche reaction 48; defended by Bowell 84–5; resigns July 1895 104, 105–6, 109; third-party threats 115–6; criticism of conservatives 133, 136, 139–40; criticized by Audet 144, 153; urges Langevin firmness 221; picks Castor colleagues 242–4; urges hard-line mandement 258; resigns Senate seat 295; charges Caron